Penumbra

Anamnesis

Anamnesis means remembrance or reminiscence, the collection and re-collection of what has been lost, forgotten, or effaced. It is therefore a matter of the very old, of what has made us who we are. But *anamnesis* is also a work that transforms its subject, always producing something new. To recollect the old, to produce the new: that is the task of *Anamnesis*.

a re.press series

Penumbra

Sigi Jöttkandt and Joan Copjec, editors

re.press Melbourne 2013

re.press

PO Box 40, Prahran, 3181, Melbourne, Australia
http://www.re-press.org

National Library of Australia Cataloguing-in-Publication Data

Title:	Penumbra / Sigi Jöttkandt and Joan Copjec (eds.).
ISBN:	9780987268242 (paperback)
	9780987268259 (eBook : PDF)
Series:	Anamnesis.
Notes:	Includes bibliographical references.
Subjects:	Psychoanalysis.
Other Authors/Contributors:	
	Jöttkandt, Sigi, editor.
	Copjec, Joan, editor.
Dewey Number:	150.195

Contents

for Sam

Preface

The Original Instrument

Joan Copjec

The "first" issue of *Umbr(a)* was prefaced by a brief, manifesto-like editorial in which we cited Freud's sarcastic dismissal of Jung's "modification" of psychoanalysis: "He has changed the hilt, and he has put a new blade into it; yet because the same name is engraved on it we are expected to regard the instrument as the original one."[1] This pointed witticism (which cut to the quick; upon reading it, Jung immediately resigned from the Psychoanalytic Association and abandoned his association with Freud and psychoanalysis altogether) was itself a citation from Georg Christoph Lichtenberg's *Sudelbücher* [waste books], a collection of aphoristic observations and reflections that randomly but regularly flitted through the mind of the German scientist.[2] In *Jokes and Their Relation to the Unconscious*, Freud had already salvaged from this *Sudelbücher* numerous witticisms, including the handleless, bladeless Lichtenberg knife, for serious study and had thus rendered that nonsensical, self-annihilating instrument suitable for the critical Q.E.D. position it would occupy at the close of "On the History of the Psycho-Analytic Movement."[3]

This is the way of psychoanalysis: always seizing upon "the bait of [nonsense] to catch a carp of truth," always rummaging through everyone's trash (dreams, jokes, slips of the tongue, the complaints of hysterics and ranting of madmen) to discover a "royal road" to some new-where. Descartes spoke for many serious thinkers when he championed "clear and distinct ideas"; Freud was virtually alone in occupying himself seriously with thought's rubbish. His "Copernican Revolution" entailed not only, as is usually claimed, a de-centering of man from his conscious self, but also a de-centering of our understanding of what really mattered most to man. It is necessary to pay attention to *both* if one wants to hold onto the radicality and singularity of the psychoanalytic intervention. Stripping the human subject of his ballast in animal lust, that is, in instinct which—while working behind his back—acts on his behalf by propelling him toward self-preservation *and* of the beacon of lofty ideals of the Good and True, Freud positioned the subject in a groundless middle ground, a between that wasted the extremes. Man, he insisted, is ruled by a principle of pleasure, a principle he neither celebrated nor condemned but elaborated unblinkingly. Pleasure had been given significant roles to play in the past, but never an independent logic of its own. Raised by Freud into a principle, pleasure dethroned even death, which was forced to renounce its title as "absolute master," and reality, which was demoted to a principle for the prolongation of pleasure. The more Freud studied this principle, the less simple pleasure became. For it was beset by a constitutive excess that rendered it as abhorrent as it was desirable; thus pleasure kept piling up paradoxes, cropping up in the most unlikely places, and diverting Freud's attention toward the ordinary overlooked, the everyday discarded, the obscene of what had until then been thought to be proper objects of thought. In the end, Freud seemed to many to talk too much about this specific nonsense—sexual pleasure—and to find it everywhere; he produced sex in and of itself as promiscuous, wanton.

For this reason he feared he might offend the sensibilities of polite society and the scientific community and thus weaken the chances that his new science would win their respect. He soon learned, however, that the real threat lay not in the likely rejection but in the facile acceptance of psychoanalysis. Against this background, it is instructive to read Freud's "On the History of the Psycho-Analytic Movement" side by side with Foucault's *The History of Sexuality*, vol. 1. The latter could be said to be doing some of Freud's work for him, to demonstrate how the rapid dispersion of psychoanalysis led to a betrayal and distortion of its concepts, were it not for the fact that Foucault does not recognize the betrayal. That Victorian society was not reticent about sex, but talked about it endlessly, as Foucault clearly establishes, does not mean that sex became suddenly ubiquitous— or, again, promiscuous—in Freud's sense. For, all the talk of sex, the endless discoursing about it, was a way of putting it in its assigned place; the result was a narrowing and localization of sex to certain limited practices and to a matter of individual mental and physical hygiene. From Freud's perspective all this sexual chatter was just so much damage control, a frenzied attempt to bury the discovery of the constitutive excess of sexual pleasure, its domain-less nature and hence its refusal of localization.

Freud's "History" approached the betrayal-via-sanitization of psychoanalytic concepts not as it manifested itself among the high priests of Victorian society, who encouraged the confession of sex in minutely clinical terms (measured, categorized doses), but among his own priestly colleagues who—although they *were* reticent about pronouncing the words *sex* and *pleasure*, which they preferred to translate into other terms—were guilty of the same sort of crime evidenced in Foucault's history. Freud picked out for particular censure two colleagues, Adler and Jung, whom he labeled the "neo-Zürich" secessionists and charged them with having carefully selected "a few cultural overtones from the symphony of life and [...] fail[ing] to hear the mighty and primordial melody of the instincts."[4] These colleagues were in his opinion major perpetrators of the cultural plot to concoct for psychoanalysis a "family romance" in which all its major ideas of "lowly"—that is to say, sexual—origin were assigned a "higher," more elevated pedigree.

Freud focused his attack on Adler's popular notion of "masculine protest"—that is, the idea the both sexes recoiled from the feminine position, renouncing the passivity it demanded—in order to expose it as the sorry distortion it was. Hopelessly confusing the "biological, social, and psychological meanings of 'masculine' and feminine,'" the idea of masculine protest reposed on the absurd claim that "a child, whether male or female, [c]ould found the plan of its life on an original depreciation of the female sex and take the wish to be a real man as its 'guiding line'"; and this despite overwhelming evidence to the contrary, to wit: "children have, to begin with, no idea of the *significance* of the distinction between the sexes [...] the *social* underestimation of women is completely foreign to them."[5] This sharp reprimand will strike many of us who were too quick to understand Freud's contention that the little girl, upon noticing "the penis of a brother or playmate, strikingly visible and of large proportions, at once recognize[s] it as the superior counterpart of their own small and inconspicuous organ" as itself such a conflation.[6] Without having to accept the notion of penis envy, we can still appreciate Freud's crucial point: the various social significances assigned to sex do not precede—nor construct—sexual difference, but are, rather, attempts to efface or manage a more disturbing, primordial difference, a kind of torsion in the sexual field, that precedes social and cultural meaning. We can also begin to see how the notion of "masculine protest" came to function as the fulcrum from which the principle of pleasure was dislodged from psychic life, how it led to the complete "ejection of sexuality from its place in mental life." The displacement of the principle of pleasure, in favor of a principle of power, dispensed precisely with the *conflictual* nature of pleasure (which is constitutively afflicted with its own excess, its own beyond). The notion of "masculine protest" installed at the center of the psyche a principle of power that took into account "only those instinctual impulses which [were] agreeable to the [individual] and [were] encouraged by it...all that [was] *opposed* to the [individual]...[lay] beyond [its] horizon."[7] Eschewing the antagonistic principles of sex and pleasure as trifles and reaching for a "grander" and more "virile" principle, Adler robbed himself of psychoanalysis's considerable resources. Nothing was left for him after this initial move but to adopt an old stand-by for thinking the contestations of power; Adler accepted an abstract notion of opposition, which set the individual against all that opposed it. This divided the field without disturbing it, without providing any real conditions that might require the positive exertion of power.

Jung fell prey to the same charges of family romancing. His manner of side-stepping the disfiguring force of sex and pleasure was to deny the conflictual nature of drive; he opted instead for a monistic, de-sexualized conception, one that transformed the archaic, inhuman, insistent pressure that characterized Freud's notion into an infinitely flexible form of "interest." If wherever Freud said *sex*, Adler said *power*, wherever Freud said *libido*, Jung substituted abstract ideas that remained "mystifying and incomprehensible to wise men and fools alike."[8] Mystical ideas that, once again, divided the world in an eternal struggle between opposing terms, but left each, individually, intact.

By now we are ready to synthesize and elevate Freud's various criticisms of the neo-Zürich school into a principle: wherever two terms are found locked together in opposition, one can be sure that a third, exorbitant term is being actively obfuscated. This third term is for psychoanalysis *pleasure*, understood in the paradoxical, disruptive way Freud elaborated it. Lacan later rechristened it *jouissance* (or "enjoying substance") in order to draw out some of the consequences of that elaboration as much as to prevent its being overlooked. Taken alone, the discovery of the unconscious risks being mistaken for the setting up of yet another opposition—conscious versus unconscious—in which the latter, newly privileged, term operates a re-centering of the world, this time beyond consciousness. Only when it is conceptually seized together with the pleasure principle can the unconscious escape this fate. Taken as part of a double discovery, the unconscious becomes visible no longer as a second but now as a third term, a term that performs a decentering of every center. First on the scene, the third permanently routs the second, disbands the duel of abstract opposition. Henceforth, the second will never arrive in a lonely last instance as a bare outside. The middle-ground created by the "thirdness" of psychoanalysis has not ceased being misunderstood in the century since Freud first railed against the foolishness of his colleagues, nor has its consequences for the conception of every battleground, every power struggle, community, and love affair been drawn out.

The Lichtenberg knife aspired to be a kind of Occam's razor, to shave from psychoanalysis the very excess that constituted it, to excise the shadow, the (*a*), which—attaching itself to every (would-be, self-identical) one—seemed to court ridicule and lack necessity. Taking that excess for our title, we announced our intention to participate in the labor, begun by Lacan, of excavating and refining Freud's original instrument. We have done this by focusing, in turns, on concepts specific to psychoanalysis and by trying to bring psychoanalysis to bear on questions generally considered to be outside its purview. Through numerous translations, we have sought to bring important texts to the attention of English speakers and through urgent invitations, we have sought to induce thinkers from adjacent fields to contribute to the psychoanalytic adventure. We have tried throughout to emulate the firm stance taken by Freud in his "History" and warmly thank all who generously and enthusiastically joined us in this.

Notes

1. There is in fact no "first" issue of *Umbr(a)*; there is instead a repetition.
2. For the account of Jung's reaction, see Ronald Hayman, *A Life of Jung* (New York: W.W. Norton, 2001), 191.
3. Sigmund Freud, "On the History of the Psycho-Analytic Movement," *The Standard Edition of the Complete Psychological Works of Sigmund Freud*, trans. James Strachey, et. al. (London: The Hogarth Press, 1953-1974), 14: 66.
4. Ibid., 62.
5. Ibid., 55.
6. Freud, "Some Psychical Consequences of the Anatomical Distinction between the Sexes," *SE*, 19: 252.
7. Freud, "On the History," 55.
8. Ibid., 62,

Introduction

Counter-Memories of the Present

Sigi Jöttkandt

Nachträglichkeit. This is Freud's term to describe how an event may acquire meaning only retroactively, in some cases, many years after the experience took place. To gain a belated or "deferred" understanding of an event, this is in fact the precise wager that psychoanalysis makes. Freud puts it unequivocally in his essay, "Sexuality in the Aetiology of the Neuroses": it is only because "the manifestations of the psychoneuroses arise from the deferred action of unconscious psychical traces, [that] they are accessible to psychotherapy."[1] From this view, any recall of previous events is, in a sense, a future and, potentially, a *counter*-memory of something that has yet to (fully) happen. The present inserts us between two temporalities, in the interim between an event that never was and its future or deferred instantiation. We inhabit the now in the uncanny condition of the future anterior, as subjects of an event that will only ever have been.

Freud's decisive step, then, was to conceive memory not as a recording device but as a power of figuration or inscription. To re-cast the words of Gilles Deleuze slightly, memory produces "a history from nature and transforms history into nature in a world that no longer has its center."[2] Moreover, this decentering of the subject from the world engages another logic as well, in the shape of a crisis of interpretation. Memory becomes a battle-ground for contested pasts and different subjective configurations. Every past event, along with its belated understanding, comprises a site of multiple possible readings, each one capable of transforming our horizon of understanding and eliciting in its turn another potential shock of understanding. For, as Freud observes, belated recognition may at times effect what he calls a "second seduction." There may be a shock that comes from seeing an event or a memory from the perspective of *Nachträglichkeit.*

The essays collected here represent one approach through the precipitate of signifiers that, as special topics, began assembling beneath the journal *Umbr(a)*'s masthead from the moment it declared its commitment to what is 'in' psychoanalysis more than simply the terms and vocabulary of psychoanalytic thought. In our difficult task of selecting among these diverse texts, we have given precedence to contributions that are more than the sum of their individual parts, that is, texts that seem to exemplarily intervene in or stage encounters with the key debates of their time. Moreover, given the increasing difficulty of obtaining many of the journal's back issues—the early ones now circulate only as comically over-priced collectors' items on Amazon—we have principally sought contributions that have not subsequently been republished elsewhere. What emerges in this volume, with the sort of "second seduction" that comes from a *Nachträglich* rereading of *Umbr(a)*'s archive, is the extent to which a fidelity to the work of thinking has maintained its hold over the collective's critical desire from the journal's earliest inception. This volume is a testament to the constancy of those energies as performed by the changing *Umbr(a)* editorial collective at the Center for Psychoanalysis and Culture at the University at Buffalo over many years, and to the inspired intellectual leadership of Joan Copjec, the Center's director.

We open with Sam Gillespie's essay, "Hegel Unsutured: An Addendum to Badiou," his contribution to the inaugural Alain Badiou issue (1996) which contained the first English translations of Badiou's work. Gillespie's essay comprises an in-depth reflection on the nature of the philosophical subject as it has been taken up by psychoanalysis. Although its ostensible topic is Hegel, Gillespie's text is more properly the earliest attempt in English to think rigorously through the differences between Badiou's and Lacan's approaches to the subject. Foreshadowing the concerns of his subsequent work in *The Mathematics of Novelty (2008)*, in this piece Gillespie shows how the key difference revolves around each thinker's conceptions of the One. Gillespie argues that while both Lacan and Badiou jointly share a Cartesian conception of the subject, in Badiou's ecumenical philosophy any finite point can potentially express a subject (for Badiou, the One is what the infinite "passes through"). For Lacan, on the other hand, any One that is produced under the aegis of repetition always maintains a link to the Other insofar as this One remains buttressed by the singularity of *jouissance.*

In emphasising *jouissance* in this way, the predominant focus of the journal had been set. Mobilized by the work of Copjec and Slavoj Žižek, whose meteoric appearance on the academic scene in the 1990s opened the door to Lacan for a new generation of English readers, *Umbr(a)* was soon to become one of the chief voices of the emerging generation of American "New Lacanians." This is a perspective on Lacanian theory that insists on the relevance of psychoanalysis for thinking through the impasses of contemporary political and cultural critique, and it is one that continues to be voiced throughout the rest of the essays collected here, beginning with Charles Shepherdson's essay from the 1997 issue of the journal, "The Elements of the Drive." Addressing the ongoing debate between biological determinism and cultural construction, Shepherdson offers a pointed critique of both positions. His careful revisiting of Freud's and Lacan's accounts of the genesis of the drive highlights the way this extra-representational element can only be signaled in the symbolic as a "malfunctioning" of the Other. The drive, that is, presents neither as simply a biological nor a social effect but as what violates any easy distinction between nature and culture. As such, *der Trieb* emerges as a paradoxically determining non-determinative that requires a fundamental rethinking of our definitions of both nature and culture.

Focusing on the critical role of names in the subject's formation of identity, Russell Grigg's essay, "On the the Proper Name as the Signifier in its Pure State," signals one possible pathway that this reconceptualization of nature and culture might take. In this brief but incisive account of Lacan's thinking on this topic in the '60s, Grigg leads the reader through a number of different conceptions of the proper name as they appear in Lacan's still unpublished *Seminar IX, Identification* (1961-1962). Grigg examines the development of Lacan's concept of the unary trait as something that leaves a mark on the subject, particularly noting the persistent way this mark or "letter" gets carried into symbolic representation. To the extent that the name is the embodiment of the letter in the symbolic, the proper name floods the signifier with the "abundance of sense" that Lacan calls *jouissance.* In answer to the question posed at the beginning of his essay of whether or not the proper name contains sense, Grigg affirms that it must do so, but we cannot understand "sense" here in any conventional meaning of the term.

From linguistic sense, we move on to another of sense's aspects, this time as the key architectonic of the aesthetic realm. Alenka Zupančič's essay, "The Splendor of Creation: Kant, Nietzsche, Lacan" reads as part of the wider interest in questions of beauty and aesthetics that emerged with Dennis Porter's 1992 English translation of *Seminar VII, The Ethics of Psychoanalysis (1959-1960).* In her reading of Lacan's remarkable commentary on Antigone's blinding beauty, Zupančič asks us to reconsider the traditional role of art in the psychoanalytic narrative as a compensatory mechanism. She accordingly rethinks art in terms of a fundamental creativity that ultimately forces a recast of our habitual understanding of the subject-object relation. As Zupančič puts it, "the arch-gesture of art is precisely that of creating an 'excluded interior,' of producing the very void around which it spreads its 'net.'"

When Slavoj Žižek maintains in his essay, "Lacan between Cultural Studies and Cognitivism," that there is a form of knowledge that "touches the real," it is to cut through what he perceives as the chief impasse in late twentieth-century contemporary thought. The notorious "Science Wars"—inaugurated by Alan Sokal's 1996 hoax article in *Social Text* and followed up by his and Jean Bricmont's *Impostures intellectuelles*[3]—appeared to lead to a theoretical dead-end. Žižek's contribution pits these two dominant knowledge practices (or, as he calls them, "theoretical state apparatuses") against each other: historicism's claim that knowledge can only reflect the ideological presuppositions of its given moment versus cognitivism's attempt to re-establish the "'professional,' rational, empirical problem-solving" business-as-usual functioning of academic knowledge. In a move whose familiarity now should not blind us to its continuing theoretical effectiveness, Žižek proposes that we should see this deadlock as its own solution. He asks provocatively, "what if there is no 'universe' in the sense of an ontologically fully-constituted cosmos?" Rather than a fully-constituted, positive "chain of being," Žižek understands reality as ontologically incomplete, and it is this gap at the heart of reality, he contends, that "accounts for the mysterious 'fact' of transcendental freedom."

A concept proposed by the 19th century French author, Villiers de l'Isle-Adam, provides the occasion for further reflections on the paradoxes of this "mysterious 'fact' of freedom." In "The Enjoying Machine," Dolar revives Villiers' notion of the "claque," a fantastical "machine for producing glory" in order to illustrate how subjectivity always implies an alienating otherness. Villiers' conception of a machine hidden in the "orifices of the statues" that would clap, react, hoot, recite, lament and cry for encores in the Parisian theater points to the way that it is not we who enjoy, but rather some*thing* that enjoys in our place. The subject, as subject of desire, is necessarily an interactive subject, yet our enjoying substance is something else, neither an activity nor a passivity, but a drive. While desire first emerges as grounded "only in the contingency of fantasy," once this fantasy is shattered, the only thing that remains is the by-product of the fantasy. If analysis is up to its task, then, it should "dismantle" this mechanism in order to make something else emerge, namely, a new kind of desire from the drive or, in other words, the desire of the analyst.

This focus on the goal of analysis is carried over into Colette Soler's "The Aim of the Analytic Act." Here the Parisian analyst and analysand of Lacan's clarifies the difference between Freud's and Lacan's conceptions of what constitutes the end of analysis. Soler compiles a lucid account of the varying emphases in both thinkers' definitions of the aim of analysis, noting an important shift in Lacan's thinking between 1968 and 1975: where previously Lacan held that the aim of analysis was to produce an "incurable" subject, by the mid-70's we are famously enjoined to "enjoy" our symptom. But given that the symptom represents a constraint for the subject—it is, in many cases, the very reason an analysand enters analysis in the first place—why would Lacan propose it as an analytic goal? Soler explains that the symptom carries the trace of the "contingency of a fateful encounter" with *jouissance* and it is in the opacity of this *jouissance* that the subject must come to recognize itself.

Lacan's changing conception of the relation between the symbolic and real is also the concern of Jelica Šumič's essay, "On the Path of the Semblant." Šumič suggests that Lacan's last period marks a momentous shift in his teaching, which is characterised by a heightened emphasis on the real. Šumič traces this turn back as early as Lacan's *Seminar VII, The Ethics of Psychoanalysis (1959-1960),* in which the concept of the semblant first appears as a "vanishing mediator" that helps us to understand how "fictions" from the symbolic are directed towards the real of the body. As Šumič observes, the semblant marks the beginning of an important turn away from truth and towards the real in Lacan's work. However, it is not until *Seminar XVII, The Other Side of Psychoanalysis (1969-70)* and Lacan's elaboration of the four discourses that the full import of the semblant—as well as the possibility there might exist "a discourse that would not be a semblance" (*Seminar XVIII*)—becomes clear. As Šumič puts it, "the semblant is a symbolic construct which, by quilting, makes us believe that it is the other of the symbolic, namely, the real." Its function, she explains, "is solely to cover up, by its very presence, the empty place of a term which is constitutively lacking." Designed to "mask the nothing," semblants are the "envelopes" of nothing that conceal the fact that behind the semblant there is nothing but the void.

Another name for this void is the Lacanian real. In her essay, "Pierre Loves Horanges: Lévinas-Sartre-Nancy: An Approach to the Fantastic in Philosophy," Catherine Malabou extends her interrogation of what she calls "plasticity" to a discussion of the fantastic in contemporary philosophy. For Malabou, the fantastic is a means of imagining something that is utterly unimaginable, namely, the difference dividing the ontic from the ontological. The fantastic imagination proves capable of delivering in a single image or schema the "very consistency of difference" itself, which takes form in Emmanuel Levinas', Jean-Paul Sartre's and Jean-Luc Nancy's diverse readings of Heidegger as an "objectivity," a "materiality," or "a-reality" emerging from within being's own internal excess. Difference is real, Malabou concludes, insofar as existence must be thought as the reality of ontological difference.

The question of identity and difference is then reopened in Tim Dean's essay, "Sameness without Identity." Like Malabou, Dean turns our attention to the way thought and thinking have as their precondition the rupturing of identity insofar as "there can be no thinking, no movement of consciousness that is not divided by the unconscious." Dean focuses his discussion around the phenomenon of the male "clone." As he explains, this was a look adopted in the 1970s by some American gay men, which is characterized by the embrace of traditional signifiers of masculinity. In Dean's thoughtful reading, the gay clone is found to represent something "more than a stubborn refusal to move beyond the securities of the imaginary into the grown-up world of difference." Rather it offers a productive means for thinking through the ancient but thorny question of identity and difference in "non-imaginary terms." To do so, Dean draws on Leo Bersani's consideration of homosexuality as a dissolution of the habitual conceptual boundaries of self and others, seeing in the gay clone a model of "inaccurate replication" that forces a new understanding of relational being "beyond our comparatively familiar imaginary and symbolic coordinates." The figure Dean proposes for this rethinking is analogy, which serves as the rhetorical underpinnings for a likeness or "non-imaginary form of recognition that would not be susceptible to the vicissitudes of *mis*recognition."

Two different but complementary approaches to the question of the Law are found in Steven Miller's "Lacan at the Limits of Legal Theory: Law, Desire and Sovereign Violence" and Dominiek Hoens' "When Love is the Law: On *The Ravishing of Lol V. Stein*." Miller enquires into the foundation of the Law and its constitutive violence. He shows how the Law in Lacan is self-grounding, a "miracle" which is unsupported by anything other than itself except for a sovereign violence that comes into play "where the law can no longer account for its own existence." Miller locates this sovereign violence in the death penalty which, unlike the divine violence of the rabbinical tradition explored by Levinas, emerges not from the God that gives law but "from a different god," namely, the sovereign power of death itself once it is freed from reference to any determinate authority. For Dominiek Hoens, on the other hand, it is not real but symbolic death in the form of subjective destitution that is at issue in the foundation of the Law. Hoens plots Duras's story along the pathways of thinking found in the sophism analyzed in Lacan's "Logical Time and the Assertion of Anticipated Certainty." The value of this comparison for Hoens lies in the way Duras helps us to see the process of subject formation in Lacan as an event of love in Alain Badiou's sense. Like the prisoners in "Logical Time," subject formation is shown to engage in a three-step process, ending in a moment of concluding that is based on an anticipated rather than actual certainty. To become a subject of desire, Hoens explains, involves an act of identification with a signifier that only *after the event* will have become a founding law. For Hoens, then—as for Miller above—love becomes Law at the moment when a "miracle" occurs, when Lol "embraces finitude by subjectifying [...] infinity." The lesson Lol teaches us, that is, is the possibility of remaining faithful to one's primordial object position—a position of waste and destitution—even as one switches places in love's miracle to become a subject of desire.

We encounter the vicissitudes of the Law again in Petar Ramadanovic's "Antigone's Kind: The Way of Blood in Psychoanalysis," in which the theorist of memory and forgetting sheds light on a buried "logic of blood" at the heart of the identification with the Name-of-the-Father. Approaching Sophocles backwards, Ramadanovic reads against the critical grain of commentaries on *Antigone* that emphasize Polynices' symbolic value to Antigone. In Ramadanovic's reading, it is rather a real tie, the unalterable logic of blood, that underpins her act of burial, the result of which is to make her a "true member of the accursed family of Oedipus." For Ramadanovic, this act ultimately allows Antigone to define for herself what family is, as Oedipus did originally—and as Freud and Lacan subsequently have, to the extent that they conceive of the body of psychoanalytic knowledge as a science, that is, as possessing a *genos*.

From Law to a place where there purports to be no law (and indeed no place, as it is classically understood), this is the topic of Juliet Flower MacCannell's cogitations on the unconscious in "Nowhere Else: On Utopia." This essay's inspiration is MacCannell's perceived need for "alternative futures," ones proposed by art rather than putative assertions of the "end of history" and their corresponding superegoic injunctions. For MacCannell, the archetypal site of such injunctions is found in contemporary suburbia, "that special non-place where incest and murder are no longer punishable transgressions, and where the drives that fuel them need no longer be repressed or even symbolically sacrificed." To help us imagine another place—"neither as a 'nowhere-and-everywhere' nor as a 'never and forever' but simply as *elsewhere*"—MacCannell looks to literature, specifically to James Joyce as he is read by Lacan. MacCannell suggests that, to the extent that Joyce managed to create "unimaginable signifiers," his work offers a means for transmitting an experience of *jouissance* through the medium of language. In Joyce's *sinthome*, Lacan's term for the flooding of language with *jouissance*, MacCannell finds an alternative path for art, one that, like topology and the other forms of integrally transmissible inscription that Lacan utilizes in his later seminars, encompasses the serpentine S-effect of the Other's gaze.

"An image capable of capturing the reflection of what has no image." This phrase is from Joan Copjec's essay, "The Censorship of Interiority," an interrogation of affect in the work of Iranian filmmaker Abbas Kiarostami. Kiarostami's *The Wind Will Carry Us* provides Copjec with the occasion for a complex meditation on the role of anxiety in modernity's break with the past. Copjec begins from the position that shame and guilt, rather than different cultural manifestations, represent different modes by which the subject distances itself from its own fundamental "foreignness" to itself. For as Copjec points out, rather than rendering the modern subject endlessly malleable, the famous break with the past that characterizes modernity produces an attachment to something that tugs the subject away from the deterritorializing impulses of global capitalism and towards what Lacan calls a "prehistoric Other." In Copjec's hands, anxiety—this experience of being attached to a pertinacious nothing that one cannot shed—becomes the Ur-affect that lurks behind both shame and guilt. These two affects accordingly map the extent of the subject's longiquity from its interior foreignness, the subject's "intimate distance" from something that, in offering nothing to remember, is therefore impossible to forget.

The dialectic of proximation and distancing is also invoked in my essay on the importance of the fantasies in effectuating the radical break represented by love which Lacan calls a "change in discourse." In "Signifier and

Letter in Kierkegaard and Lacan," the fantasies are understood as modes of writing in Lacan's sense of the word, namely, a formalization in a medium that "goes beyond speech." Here Kierkegaard's "The First Love" in *Either/Or* anticipates Lacan's insistence that writing will prove the path to love by giving us access to an All that is not part of the desiring chain. However, this All or supplemenary One is found to be structurally dependent upon the failure of the hysteric and obsessional subjects to reach their first love.

Closing the volume is "(Marxian-Psychoanalytic) Biopolitics and Bioracism," by A. Kiarina Kordela. For Kordela, the chief innovation of late global capitalism lies in the way commodity fetishism cultivates the illusion of immortality. In her essay, Kordela argues that this illusion has in the meantime become the object of a properly biopolitical administration, which threatens to deliver us over to a racism by which a "biorace of immortals" wages wars of varying names upon a moving target of bio-mortals. We should resist this war on death itself, she urges.

Umbr(a) was founded by Joan Copjec and the graduate student cohort at the Center for Psychoanalysis and Culture at the University at Buffalo in the summer of 1995. In the intervening years, *Umbr(a)* has achieved a cult status to which few academic journals can lay claim. This reputation has been gained as much for the seminal works of psychoanalytic thinkers it has published—including Jacques-Alain Miller, Alain Badiou, Jean-Claude Milner, Étienne Balibar, Serge André, Fethi Benslama, Colette Soler, Paul Verhaeghe, Leo Bersani, Henry Corbin, Christian Jambet, Moustapha Safouan, Bruce Fink, Juliette Flower MacCannell, Alenka Zupančič, Mladen Dolar, Slavoj Žižek and numerous others (for many, in their first English translations)—as for the beauty of its typesetting and striking covers under the artistic direction of Sam Gillespie until 2003. *Umbr(a)* is now distributed in Mexico, Turkey and Korea (in the latter cases, in Turkish and Korean translation) and is available globally through online booksellers. The out of print issues are also now freely available in digital editions from the Center's website (http://www.umbrajournal.org).

We would like to thank all of the contributors and editors who have made *Umbr(a)* what it is today. We are also grateful to the Office of the Dean, College of Arts and Sciences, and the English department at University at Buffalo, which have provided the journal with financial support over the years, as well as the Graduate Student Association and various Faculty Chairs. Special thanks are due to Michael Stanish for his peerless detective work in recovering the electronic files of the back issues, as well as to Paul Ashton and Justin Clemens from re.press.

Notes

1. Sigmund Freud, "Sexuality in the Aetiology of the Neuroses" (1898), *The Standard Edition of the Complete Psychological Works of Sigmund Freud*, trans. James Strachey, et. al. (London: The Hogarth Press, 1953-1974), 3: 511-12.
2. Deleuze is speaking of Walter Benjamin and allegory. Gilles Deleuze, *The Fold: Leibniz and the Baroque*, foreword and trans, Tom Conley (Minneapolis: University of Minnesota Press, 1993) 125.
3. See Alan Sokal, "Trangressing the boundaries—towards a transformative hermeneutics of quantum gravity," *Social Text* (Spring/Summer, 1996) 217-252. See also Alan Sokal and Jean Bricmont, *Impostures intellectuelles* (Paris: Odile Jacob, 1997).

I

Hegel Unsutured: An Addendum to Badiou

Sam Gillespie

> . . . there is in all this what is called a bone. Though it is precisely what is suggested here, namely, that it is structural of the subject, it constitutes in it essentially that margin that all thought has avoided, skipped over, circumvented, or blocked whenever it seems to succeed in being sustained by a circle, whether that circle be dialectical or mathematical.
>
> —Jacques Lacan, "The subversion of the subject and the dialectic of desire"

Never known for his reserved statements, it was Lacan who stated in his tenth seminar that, "if there is anyone, I think, who does not mistake what the *Phenomenology of Spirit* brings us, it is myself."[1] This should hardly be surprising: Lacan was a man of his times and, if we are to believe Mikkel Borch-Jacobsen, no less under the scrutiny of Alexandre Kojève than any of his contemporaries. Yet Lacan does not, from the moment he claims to be the authority on Hegel, cease to underline the differences between Hegel and himself.

This again should hardly surprise: almost every other French intellectual of the period has sought, in some manner or another, to surpass the dead-locks of the dialectic. Lacan should come as no exception. But his tactics are not as predictable as one may think. Typically, the overturning of Hegelianism seeks to undercut the unity of the sublated whole—Hegel's critics never stop pointing towards the difference, or remaining end products of otherness, which are refused in the Hegelian system. Examples abound: the Derridian *supplément*, Lyotard's *différend*, the Deleuzian *fold*. One could assume as much from

Lacan—is *objet a* (that "remainder of the other") not the same as the element which disrupts a negative economy? Is it not, strictly speaking, the correlate to Derrida's *supplément*? The answer, unfortunately, is both yes and no.

What Lacan distinctly opposes is the classical, even "moralistic" dimension of the Hegelian infinity: the recurring circle completely closed in upon itself, the repetitive enfolding of the infinity in the One—the point, in short, at which the infinite ceases to be the other of the finite as One. Lacan will have little of Hegel's unity of the one and the multiple. For it does not suffice to say that the recurrence of the One—its ability to become "its own other" by becoming another One (which is nothing other than the ability of the One to sublate infinity)—exhausts the *function* of the Other. And so it would seem that Lacan would be quite at home with other criticisms of Hegel in his efforts to uphold the Other against this sublation of infinity.

If I may be forgiven for stating the obvious, Lacan makes it clear that the repetition of the One cannot exhaust the other without generating a new other in turn. Is this not what Freud teaches us in *Beyond the Pleasure Principle*? For the sake of clarity, let's assume that the entirety of my conscious life is governed by the pleasure principle. Every attempt I make to recover an earlier state—every time I "fill in" what I am missing through the sequential recurrence of signifying elements—demands that I repeat myself. In repeating myself, I am pushed forward, towards somewhere far away from the earlier state I incessantly attempt to regain. Repetition replaces the first object (the lack I fill in with various names and numbers) with a second object, the void I circumscribe when I leap from the future (from which I am guided by repetition) towards the past (in which I am guaranteed the possibility of repeating again). There are, of course, many ways in which I can apprehend *objet a*, but few are ever so tangible as this. The fact that there can be no substantial "beyond" to the pleasure principle (the fact that this beyond can only ever be supposed outside the pleasure my ego confines me to) can be attributed to the bad timing inherent in the pleasure principle. To go backwards towards an earlier state of affairs, I must make a step forwards. I repeat by necessity, creating my object anew.

Consequently, what Lacan surely means when he upholds the "function of the other" in a repetitive system is this very inclusion of a heteronomous element (the "interval," if you will) which any system aiming at continuity must invariably include. But this object does not disrupt the consistency of a perfectly closed system; by including a heteronomous element within pleasure, it is what provides that system with consistency itself. We can witness the distinctiveness of Lacan's reproach to Hegel. As Jacques-Alain Miller repeatedly states, the *objet a* is not simply a product of otherness. It is a *logical* object, that which sustains a system in the absence of the Other. It replaces the once full presence of the Other (the place from which meaning can be guaranteed) with the Other's *function*—that which repetition strives towards.[2] And it is towards this that Lacan gestures when differing from Hegel.

If it were all this simple, there would be no point to the present discussion. There are two purposes for writing this paper. One, obviously, is to sort out, at a very elementary stage, certain differences between Lacan and Hegel. This is no easy task given the variety of viewpoints on the matter. Some will say that Lacan is "bad philosophy"—*period*; there is no point in discussing him alongside Hegel. Others will read Lacan in line with contemporary, "post-structuralist," critiques of Hegel, critiques which, as I have alluded to above, for the most part, undercut the unity of Hegel's absolute through the intervention of otherness, or difference, into Hegel's system. Finally, there are those, most notably Slavoj Žižek, who will attempt to "rescue" Hegel from his critics by proclaiming him a Lacanian. If no one reading seems sufficient (although I admit a partiality to the final interpretation), it is most likely the case that any of the above agendas (saving Hegel, saving Lacan, critiquing both) overrides the difficulty—one could even say *impossibility*—of taking either Hegel or Lacan at their word.

Quite simply, it seems that distinctions need to be made, and if it is my intent to do so here, it will be for the purposes of delimiting the above example of Hegelian infinity that Lacan takes issue with. Hence, my second purpose: what I propose is not solely a reading of Hegel *avec Lacan*, but to explicate Alain Badiou's (Lacanian) critique of Hegel. Badiou's is not a simple thesis—but it does, to be sure, disclose Lacanian principles. What Badiou objects to in Hegel is the rejection of the mathematical in favor of the essential finitude of self-consciousness. Rather than viewing the mathematical as an independent foundation of truth from which various other discourses are derived (as in Plato, Descartes, or Leibniz), Hegel views the philosopher's task as being one in which the mathematical (the infinite) is placed in a subordinate relation to subjective reflection. Well, it seems clear enough where a Lacanian could differ; when acknowledging Lacan's use of cybernetics in the fifties, it is obvious that the unconscious process of counting always exceeds what the conscious subject can think at any one point. A symbolic or mathematical foundation of existence cannot be sufficiently absorbed by the essential finitude of subjective self-reflection. But to effect such an absorption seems to be Hegel's intent. This, crudely put, would be a starting point for understanding Badiou: for the latter, the mathematical imposes a structure which cannot be globally enveloped by a conscious subject.

This is only a very preliminary reading of Badiou, a reading which will be far from exhaustive. Let it suffice to say that whereas Hegel (in his efforts to subordinate the infinite to the status of the repetitive One) seeks to establish the subject as a global site of truth, Badiou's subject is always a local *part* of a logical structure in which truth is present. This subject is an indispensable part of this system, and, to be sure, there is no philosophy without a subject.

But this subject is always only a *finite* subject. There are four axioms, derived from Badiou,[3] which can be briefly given:

a. *Any finite formula expresses a subject.* The subject is not a transcendental agency or perceiving consciousness, but a point expressed by a finite number or signifier.

b. *The Subject is the local status of truth.* The subject is a point in a chain of knowledge (in Lacanian terms: S2 ... S3 ... S4 ...) which is located somewhere between an event that has been presupposed (the "supernumerary name" which inaugurates the procession of signifying elements: S1 . . .) and the point towards which that chain is directed ("signification"). The subject is caught in the chain at any one of these points. It is a part of the situation that the supernumerary name of the event constitutes.

c. *Truth is constituted by a hole in knowledge.* Truth is not qualified through an intelligible intuition. A truth is indiscernible within knowledge; it is the unnamed towards which the signifying elements which comprise knowledge as such are directed, but never reach.

a. *The subject is not this void.* The void is inhuman and a-subjective. Truth is realized through the multiplicity of elements that the void generates of which the subject is a part. The subject is, in effect, a finite part which is caught between an event and its truth. It is the local status of this situation as truth. Ultimately, saying that the subject is a local status of truth is very different from defining the subject as the hole in knowledge which is truth.

b. This final point may come as a surprise—do we not usually conceive the subject as the void which is represented by a signifier? Is this not how a subject is "sutured" into a symbolic; that is, as a void that is named? This is usually how suture is understood: the element which is sutured is the void of the subject. Badiou suggests something different, something, in fact, which comes much closer to the actual definition of suture in psychoanalysis. What is sutured, strictly speaking, is not the subject to the discursive chain, but the relation between the Symbolic as knowledge (or, to use Badiou's terms, situation) and being (the Real). It would hardly seem necessary to review the entirety of the original theory of suture that Jacques-Alain Miller wrote thirty years ago if his thesis had been sufficiently understood.[4] Since the case is otherwise, an exegesis will prove necessary. To expound both Badiou and his reading of Hegel requires that the reader devote his or her attention to the original relation between the One and the multiple.

Ordinarily, suture is read as an Imaginary process through which a subject is included in a given system while disavowing, or annulling, Symbolic difference. But in Miller's argument, the point is this: for a symbolic system to become a closed economy, it must account for the element it excludes (the subject). The agent of suturing is that which puts the Symbolic in communication with the Real, it installs "something" in the place where the subject is absent. And were it not for the inclusion of the "something" (an absence which is not nothing) within a given set (or symbolic system), distinctions between its elements could not even be drawn, since these distinctions cannot be empirically determined. This was a primary necessity for Frege's mathematics: the exclusion of an empirical thing (its substitution by number) was necessary to sustain a logical system. Yet this substitution could not occur without marking the fact that the subject has already been excluded. But if distinctions are no longer drawn between actually existing things, then there must, in that system, be some other means of differentiating its elements.

The answer appears to be easy enough: what is sutured is the lacking subject to its signifier or representative. We could imagine that a subject is sutured when it is named as an individual. Were this not possible, something would be missing from the set—there would simply be a series of empty numbers. If the reader takes further notice, however, he or she will realize that it would be contradictory to say that the subject is what *completes* the set, what provides for the missing element, since it is precisely Frege's point that the subject be excluded. The goal is something other than a merely Symbolic rewriting of the subject; for Frege, it is the formal structure of the set that interests him. The missing element, in other words, must be *logical*, not subjective.

In any event, when turning to the original problem that Miller presents, it is admittedly true that one is dealing with the inclusion of the subject within a given set. For Miller or Frege, there are two relations formed between the subject and the set: there is the relation between the subject and its given concept (*subsumption*) and there is also the relation between the subject and the number which comes to represent it in the set (*assignation*). Given a hypothetical set consisting of the "members of F," neither the concept ("member of F") of the set nor the elements (counted terms) which comprise it, comes first. The perfect logic of the system demands that the concept exist exclusively through the inclusion of the members which it subsumes. Yet these members, as objects, *are* only insofar as they fall under the given concept (that is, so long as they are no longer *things*). The paradox, or "performativity," of the set necessitates that neither assignation nor subsumption is primary: a subject is subsumed at the same time that it is assigned a number. To be included, the subject must be *counted*. So it is clear that if a thing is counted as a number, it is no longer equal *to itself* but to the number which assigns its place in the set. When counted, one does not emerge as a "member of F," but *as equal to the concept* "member of F." One is included through being equal to its representative, to the number which stands in for the self.

But a volatile loss of truth is invoked by the very principle of exclusion which founds a logical system. The subject's emergence in a set means that it is counted *as one*, and this one (1) is what becomes repeatedly representative for all members in the set. We can see clearly where the potential loss of truth occurs: how is it that one thing can be distinguished from another if they are *both* counted as one, if they can no longer be empirically differentiated as things? How is counting even possible if the distinction between "one" and "two" is no longer evident? Let me begin again: to be truly distinct, any one element must be equal to itself. One is "one" insofar as it is equal to itself: it cannot be exchanged for "two" without a loss of truth. And in order for this to be true, the number needs a "substance" of sorts, it needs a self to be equal to. But this self cannot be an empirical thing. This, in fact, is the very problem.

Something, Miller adds, must be added to the set in order to make counting possible, in order to close the set, to make each element equal to itself. This "something" is the inclusion of that which is *not equal to itself*—conceptually, zero, the empty set. We arrive at the empty set when we conceive of a set having *no members*, that is, of a set whose members are not equal to themselves. This follows (as we shall see with regards to Hegel) when we conceive of the possibility of an *empty* set: of a set which contains no elements, yet *has a property nonetheless*. Let ω represent an infinite set of which x is a member precisely when it is not equal to itself. The empty set can be written thus:

$$\varnothing = \{x \in \omega : x \neq x\}$$

Our first set ("members of F") is "sutured" through the inclusion of this other set as its member. Given this reading, our first impulse would be to inscribe the empty set between the numbers in the set, as if it is that which emerges between 1 and 2 (e.g. 1 = 1, (1≠ 2), 2 = 2). We could, in this instance, call the empty set the interval which emerges between the successive counting of elements. This is not the point for Miller: the empty set is not generated by, or even between, repetitions—it is what allows for repetition itself. There would not even be the possibility of getting from zero to one unless there were some means of counting the zero first. To get from zero to one, the set must start with nothing, the empty set Ø. In order to reach one, another empty set must be counted in addition to this—the first empty set becomes counted as one {Ø}. What sutures the set is not an "other" to its members: insofar as its members are founded upon the absence of the subject, they can only be equal to something else. This element which is not equal to itself is what allows the set's members to be exchanged for other elements without a loss of truth. Ergo: not being equal to itself, it can always equal another. Consequently, the difference between Ø and {Ø} is the difference between zero and one—one is the set of the empty set. It is even more difficult to get to two: one must add another set on top of this, the set of the set of the empty set. By the time 2 is reached, three sets have already been counted. As for 3:

$$0 = \emptyset$$

$$1 = \{\emptyset\} = \{0\}$$

$$2 = \{\emptyset\}, \{\emptyset\}\} = \{0, 1\}$$

$$3 = \{\emptyset\}, \{\emptyset\}, \{\emptyset\}, \{\emptyset\}\}\} = \{0, 1, 2\}$$

Getting to four is still more arduous since 1 is the counting, in fact, of a *nothing* which must come first. One is not primary, it is preceded by what engenders lack in the set—it accounts for the inclusive element which does not belong (the missing subject). Or, as the *counting of one* (to use Badiou's terms), the subject *as one* must seek to find its other half in the empty set which it is counted as.[5] This, in a sense, is why Lacan's subject (S̸) cannot be written without an *objet a.*

Now, where, in Hegel, does one encounter the need to produce, or include, an external object to render exceptional closure? Does the dialectic not in fact depend on the exact opposite—the exclusion of externality? Our "answer" is unclear. Perhaps this is not the question to be asked; it is well enough to suggest that Hegel excludes the Other, but this claim is not so easily made when considering that the other, in Hegel, is not really excluded as much as it is revealed in its nullity. The Hegelian knows very well that this nullity has a generative function nonetheless. In the *Science of Logic*, Hegel begins with the most basic of his categories which, of course, are being and nothing. The immediate goal is to unite the two in the "moment" of being's emergence out of nothing, but matters are confounded once Hegel speaks of *determinate* being—a being which is distinguished from mere being (where non-being is taken up in a simple unity with being). As determinate, as *something*, a posited being no longer simply has non-being as its other, it must also relate to another being, determine itself as the negative of that something. To this other being, it is equally an other. The former unity of the becoming of being had being and becoming as its moments: here, dialectical thought must grapple with *something* and *other* ("something *else*"). Each "something" is equally its other: "there is no determinate being which is determined only as such, which is not outside a determinate being and therefore is not itself an other."[6] Yet beyond this vicious circle of each being other to its other, Hegel states that a determinate being is an other to itself on its own account: "The other simply by itself is the other in its own self, hence the other of itself and so the other of the other—it is, therefore, that which is absolutely dissimilar within itself, that which negates itself, alters itself."[7] Not being a substantial other, this other is a being's own non-being.

Hegel here seems intent to unite being with non-being—to sublate otherness into a unity of self and other. In other words, the "dissimilarity" mentioned above apparently introduces a positive otherness into Hegel's system. Being would not be equal to itself since it must share equivalence with its other as well. Difference, it would seem, is not yet eradicated from Hegel's system. But Hegel insists that the dissimilarity of being with itself does not result from the immanence of otherness, but from the *lack of consistency* in the other's being. One could state this logic otherwise: being is not equal to itself because it is not *not-equal* to its other—it cannot posit, or distinguish itself from, its other. This would be the true logic of the empty set: if zero were equal to nothing, it would no longer function as the empty set, for that nothing, as equal, would then have to be marked *as something*. To be truly unequal to itself, the empty set must have no equal. For Hegelian non-being then, something becomes dissimilar to itself when its other does not possess being:

> Hence, being-in-itself is, first, a negative relation to the negative determinate being, it has the otherness outside it and is opposed to it; insofar as something is in itself it is withdrawn from otherness and being-for-other. But secondly it has also present in its own being itself, for it is itself the non-being of the being for other.[8]

This can be better understood when we consider Hegel's critique of the Kantian thing-in-itself. We believe we are saying something profound when we speak of it, when we refer to something outside the imperfections in human consciousness. But to refer to something in itself is to refer to something *apart from* that reference; as divorced from all being-for-another, it is stripped of determination, which of course means that it is nothing—that it is impossible to know what it is. Hegel then suggests that by this very realization, we know quite well what a thing-in-itself is: a truthless abstraction. But, in *truth*, for Hegel, the thing is knowable in the Notion where its determinate content is united with the *lack of being in its other* (i.e. its *positing*, which is purely empty being). The limit which separates being-in-itself from being-for-another is superceded once the split itself becomes internally constitutive *for* the Notion. What a thing is "in-itself" can only be externally determined through a being's own reflection upon its position. So while Hegel may refuse the limit which separates human consciousness from the thing-in-itself, he reaffirms it in the formation of the Notion, where the sensible conditions which affirm the content of a being are supplemented by the "sensuously unfulfilled," *internal* limitations of the remaining void of determination.[9]

It could be assumed that at this moment in the Logic, a sublation of sorts has occurred: that this determined being, in revealing the "other" for the nothing that it is, has become realized, or determinate, in itself as Notion. But there is none. What has actually transpired is that this being, in reflecting inwards on itself, has moved beyond being determined through an external limit; it now contains an internal *limitation*. That is, this being is now a *finite* being. Two consequences follow:

1. Limitation defines what something is, as opposed to the limit which determines what that being *is not*. Thus, for Hegel, this limitation is no longer separated from a finite being's being; as a term, limitation paradoxically suggests that any being is something other than the limit—that a being could "be" more than what it is were it not for its limitation. This "more" is brought to bear upon a finite being in the form of the *ought*. Something, in itself, *ought* to be more than what it is. "The ought as such contains the limitation and the limitation contains the ought."[10] Part of its being, what it ought to be, inheres elsewhere. Yet this elsewhere, while being opposed to the limitation, is implanted *by* that limitation.

2. Through its limitation, the determinate being encounters its *ought*. There is a vicious circle between the two: beyond the limitation is the *ought*, yet this *ought* is expressed by the limitation. "Limitation is determined as the negative of the ought and the *ought* is likewise the negative of the limitation."[11] There is thus a double negation at work when a finite being goes beyond itself: *the ought*, once realized, is now what the being is, yet the limitation remains nonetheless. A first negation is necessary, where the finite becomes determinate, and a second negation of this determination, where the finite becomes another finite (hence, Hegel's famous "negation of negation"). Herein lies the first emergence of the infinite: it depends on the negation of the finite. The infinite is the beyond of the finite. Of course, this is where Hegel's reader encounters the "bad infinity," where the infinite is revealed as the empty beyond of a finite being:

> In this void beyond the finite, what arises? What is the positive element in it? Owing to the inseparability of the infinite and the finite—or because this infinite remaining aloof on its own side is itself limited—there arises a limit, the infinite has vanished and its other, the finite, has entered. But this entrance of the finite appears as happening external to the infinite, and the new limit as something that does not arise from the infinite itself but is likewise found as given. And so we are faced with a relapse into the previous determination which has been sublated in vain.[12]

The infinite has no other determination than to be the empty negation of the finite. Yet when the finite being transcends its limitation, it finds that it has become another finite in turn. This would constitute infinity in the second stage, where it becomes the alternate term between two successive finites. Hegel's reader is faced with the dimension of the "tedious repetition of bad infinity." The empty infinite, {. . .}, becomes nothing less than the void of determination, the empty limit of the finite. Hegel does however realize a third moment of the infinite, when it is no longer pushed forwards from the one, but is realized within the infinite generation of the one *with itself*. Infinity would be the realization of the infinite return of the one to another one. Reflection is required—and it does of course come into play in the *Logic*. But the reader should ask, in what manner?

For Hegel, it is important to remember that each polarity realizes itself through *limitation*. The infinite (empty beyond of the finite) is itself finite by virtue of what it excludes. Similarly, the finite, while limited, would be doomed to perish were it not for the perennial *ought* which posits the finite over and against itself in the beyond. The mutual sliding into opposition of either term is what, no doubt, provides for the circularity of the infinite judgment, for the "good" infinity. The infinite is what is drawn from the repetition of either term—or better yet, from the *emptiness of the other* which either term oscillates towards. Going towards its other, it returns to itself, *the One is the infinite that is coextensive with its other in the reproduction of itself.* This is Hegel's thesis.

Over and against the image of a linear progression, the Hegelian infinite is the circle drawn within repetition. "What arises is the same as that from which the movement began, that is, the finite is restored; it has therefore united with itself, has in its beyond found itself again."[13] But even if this reflective circle is composed of two terms, it is not a disjunctive process. This is no unity of difference. In the first place, it is from the limitation of the One, which is indifferent to difference, that the infinite is drawn. The very fact that two opposed terms could become their opposites attests to the very nullity of differences, to the fact that they differ only by virtue of limitation. In other words, it is not that a limit is necessary because of the immanence of otherness, since otherness only follows from the necessity of limitation. As Hegel later writes in the *Logic*, it is only when the limitation becomes constitutive that the Notion is achieved.

If any of this exegesis on indifference, on the "bad infinity" of alterity and externality leaves something to be desired in contemporary repudiations of Hegel, I will nonetheless stop short of Hegel's critics. I will only draw two conclusions at this point:

a. That the repetition of the One, the continual reemergence of the same, does not sufficiently offer a closure onto a Notion. Jacques Lacan observed as much when he distinguished himself from Hegel: the false infinity is linked to a metonymy of recurrence, a metonymy which can luckily be drawn from the function of the repetitive One. But, as Lacan adds, "what experience shows us, is that the different fields that are proposed in it—specifically, the neurotic, perverse, and indeed the psychotic—is that the One which is reduced to the successions of signifying elements, the fact that they are distinct and successive *does not exhaust the function of the Other*."[14] It is not insignificant that Lacan calls it the *function* of the Other, for even if the Other is impossible, it still possesses a function in the object that repetition generates. It is even from the repetition of the One, from its recurrence, that the question from the other arises: "*che vuoi*?" What is it that I, the Other, demand of you? Don't get me wrong: there is not a lot of bad infinity in Lacan, this is not a radical alterity of otherness, yet there is a remainder of the Other which is buttressed through *jouissance*. And the trouble, as Lacan said in *Television*, is that this latter term cannot be inscribed in a repetitive quantum. *Jouissance* does not have a numerical constant, it does not register "in" a given repetition. A repetitive quantum is not guided by the "energy" of a human constituent: it is guided forwards by a demand that must be deciphered. To speak directly to Hegel on this count, recurrence does not exhaust, much less *explain*, the determination of a singular being's *ought*.

b. For Badiou, on the other hand, it cannot follow that the repetition of the repetitive One can be *called* infinite. Repetition, as a quantitative "bad" infinity, may indeed have qualitative being, but one may ask what it is that makes this quality "infinite" (and a "good" infinite at that)? For Hegel, the answer is simply because repetition "tires of the void," of the insubstantiality and empty beyond (or "trans-finite polarity") of the finite. For Hegel, the void does not present an obstacle because it is empty, nothing, not determinate.[15] It is because of Hegel's vehemence on this point that Badiou will fault his exclusion of the mathematical—in rejecting the bad infinity, Hegel, in effect, excludes the empty set as well: "in the numerical proliferation, there is no void, since the exterior of the One is its interior; the pure law which institutes the spreading of the same as One. *The radical absence of the Other—indifference—does not legitimize declaring that the essence of the finite number, its numericality, is infinity*." The void, the empty set, Ø, cannot simply be reduced to nothing in repetition if, as interior of the One, {Ø}, it is what is being repeated. It is only by a retroactive maneuver, (which places the empty infinite as product, rather than origin, of the One) that Hegel can then locate the good infinity *elsewhere*, outside the extimacy that the mathematical provides. In naming the true infinity, Hegel draws upon a "bad" element, the void of the finite, to make his claims. There remains an empty object in Hegel, despite his best intentions.

Paradoxically, it seems as if Badiou and Lacan are at cross-purposes in their critique of Hegel. For Lacan, Hegel's grandiose gesture exhausts, or denies, the function of the Other; for Badiou, there is too much otherness in this meeting between the finite and the infinite, in this preservation of the difference-in-the-one. For the latter, the Hegelian One is both itself (finite) and its other (void as indeterminate) which (illogically for Badiou) thinks the infinity of number from the being of One number. Why name the One "infinite," if not because the "One" (as counted, as title) must erroneously presuppose the infinite as its content? In his preservation of the other through the interiority of the One, Hegel is not Hegelian enough—he is still located on the side of Badiou's nemesis—Gilles Deleuze. For what does Deleuze designate as his formula for the subject? Precisely the "Leibnizian" formula of the One over its infinite denominator: $1/\infty$.[16] It is One *with* the infinite, or rather, the infinite folded in the One as its pure interior. But Badiou cannot, nor should his reader, think the being of the One in global terms. The One is not what contains the infinite, it is what the infinite *passes through.*

Thus, what both Hegel and Deleuze presuppose, in spite of themselves, is an anti-mathematical theory of the subject. The very "point" of punctuality which marks the One receives its consistency through being "filled out" by its infinite denominator. Prior to this, it must be asked if there can even be a subject. For Badiou, there can be a different sort of consistency for his subject: it entails that any finite point expresses a subject. This is not to say, however, that there is therefore a formula of numbers (a Symbolic) wholly sufficient onto itself which can also exist without a subject. There is, as Miller has shown, something more: the empty set, *objet a.* This does not presuppose a "substance" of the subject: on the contrary, if anything, there is too much substance in this Hegelian One. And thus, finally, we are faced with a choice; if both Hegel and Lacan presuppose a subject—which is the locus at which philosophy can persevere—it is Hegel who opts without hesitation for a multiple subject. Psychoanalysis proposes, in contrast, a subject of division, of the "cut." That the former would appear as more appealing is perhaps reducible to a refusal of the site where truth, in psychoanalysis, is to be sought. Truth is produced through *repression*, through the hole it produces in knowledge. It is here, impossibly, that the function of the Other (and, in consequence, of truth) is not exhausted. As Badou himself writes: "a truth is the principle of a subject, *by the empty set whose action it supports.*"[17]

What Descartes, Lacan, and Badiou all share is a view of the complete exteriority of the subject to its representative. With the inauguration of the "I think" comes the guarantee that "I am" must reside elsewhere. *It is in this sense that the subject is not the void.* The naming which effectuates the subject leaves its indiscernible reference, its truth, in the future anterior of the situation of which the subject is a discernibly finite part. The subject, as One, names that *which will become* the truth that precedes it, the hole in knowledge, S(Ø), which supplements its situation. It is the *finite real,* if such can be conceived, of its situation. If there can be an agreement between Badiou and Hegel, it is that the subject is indispensable for philosophy to persevere. What gets lost, however, in the latter's insistence on the interiority of the finite, is the very extimate element that any external foundation must presuppose as its truth. In subordinating the true to the interiority of a conscious subject, one may as well dispense with it altogether. It is a small step that one takes when going from a point where the true is subordinated to the "human" towards another point where philosophy realizes its end. Badiou can evince the promises that this end affords, and it embodies everything which philosophy should save us from.

Notes

1. The quote comes from Lacan's unpublished *Le séminar X, L'angoisse (1962-1962)*. From a lecture given on November 14, 1962.
2. See Miller, "To Interpret the Cause: From Freud to Lacan," *Newsletter of the Freudian Field* 3.1-2 (1989): 50. In his book, *The Lacanian Subject: Between Language and Jouissance* (Princeton: Princeton UP, 1995), Bruce Fink notes that Lacan at times has suggested much the same: that is, that ". . . all truth is mathematizable." He quotes from Lacan's unpublished *Seminar XXI, The Non-Duped Err/The Names of the Father (1973-74)*: "There is no such thing as a truth which is not 'mathematized,' that is, written, that is, which is not based, qua Truth, solely upon axioms. Which is to say that there is truth but of that which has no meaning, that is, of that concerning which there are no other consequences to be drawn but within [the register] of the mathematical deduction." Fink, 121.
3. The majority of my interpretation comes from Badiou's *Being and Event*, trans. Oliver Feltham (London: Continuum, 2006). Also see "On a Finally Objectless Subject," trans. Bruce Fink, *Who Comes After the Subject*, Connor, Cadeva and Nancy, eds. (New York: Routledge, 1991) 24-32.
4. See Jacqueline Rose's translation of "Suture (Logic of the Elements of the Signifier)" in *Screen* 18. 4 (Winter 1977-8). Also see Joan Copjec, "The Subject Defined by Suffrage," *Lacanian Ink* 7 (1993): 47-58.
5. We can thus see the primary distinction between the use that Gilles Deleuze makes of the term "suture" and the import that it has for psychoanalysis. For the former, the repression of the object proceeds *from* repetition: ". . . we cannot suppose that disguise may be explained by repression. On the contrary it is because repetition is necessarily disguised by virtue of the characteristic displacement of its determinant principle, that repression occurs in the form of a consequence in regards to the repetitions of presents: ". . . *We do not repeat because we repress, we repress because we repeat*." Deleuze, *Difference and Repetition*, trans. Paul Patton (New York: Columbia, 1993) 105. While Deleuze repeatedly drew upon Lacanian concepts throughout his career as a philosopher, it is clear that for psychoanalysis, his reading is absurd. Repetition could not even be possible without the included element—the null set—following the exclusion (repression) of something—the empirical subject.
6. Hegel, *Science of Logic*, trans. A.V. Miller (Atlantic Highlands, NJ: Humanities, 1969), 117.
7. Hegel, 118.
8. Hegel, 120.
9. See Slavoj Žižek, *Tarrying with the Negative* (Durham: Duke UP, 1993), 39.

10. Hegel, 136.
11. Hegel, 138.
12. Hegel, 141.
13. Hegel, 147.
14. Seminar X, lesson ofNovember 14, 1962.
15. This seems to be Žižek's thesis as well. See "The Wanton Identity" in *For They Know Not What They Do* (London: Verso, 1991), 51-9.
16. Gilles Deleuze, *The Fold: Leibniz and the Baroque,* trans. Tom Conley (Minneapolis: Minnesota, 1992) 130.
17. See Badiou, "Gilles Deleuze: *The Fold—Leibniz and the Baroque*," in *Gilles Deleuze and the Theater of Philosophy*, Boundas and Olkowska, eds. (New York: Routledge, 1993) 69.

2

The Elements of the Drive

Charles Shepherdson

> In no region of psychology were we groping more in the dark. Everyone assumed the existence of as many instincts or "basic instincts" as he chose, and juggled with them like the ancient Greek natural philosophers with their four elements—earth, air, fire and water.
>
> —Sigmund Freud, "Instincts and Their Vicissitudes"

The fundamental features of Freud's concept of the drive are now well known.[1] To begin with, we may recall the distinction between the instinct and the drive. Insofar as the instinct is governed by the laws of nature (survival and reproduction), while the drive is open to symbolic displacement and substitution, Freud argues that sexuality is detached from its biological foundations and subject to representation—placed, as Lacan would say, in the field of the Other. And yet, the particular character of the relation between the drive and representation (and consequently the meaning of "sexuality" as such) remains obscure and open to debate.[2] For even if it is detached from nature, this does not mean that sexuality is entirely inscribed within the circuit of representation. The Other is lacking, as Lacan says—it is "not all" and "not the whole truth" (T 3). This "lack in the Other" has decisive consequences for the theory of the drive, which will bring into play not only the imaginary and symbolic, but above all the category of the real and the object *a*, which mark the place of a certain defect in the law, a point of incompleteness in the structure of representation. The question is how we are to understand this "remainder," this element beyond representation, and why it has a privileged link to "sexuality."

At least three points may therefore be stressed at the outset. First, although contemporary accounts of psychoanalysis often speak of Freud's non-biological conception of the drive as if it coincided with historical accounts of the cultural formation of sexuality (the subject in relation to "the symbolic order"), Freud's theory remains distinct from historical and sociological arguments in several decisive respects. The "economic," "dynamic," and "topographical" points of view that Freud developed all sought to account for the logic or structure that links representation to the body—elaborating the various techniques that might allow their relations to be reconfigured, and exploring the "mechanisms" and "causes" that account for anxiety, symptoms, affective shifts and other somatic effects. Freud's work is thus quite different from historical accounts of subjectivity, although it remains clear that psychoanalysis will always require a sensitivity to the fact that in each case the "logic" of the subject unfolds within a concrete, socio-historical milieu. It is therefore insufficient to say that for Freud, "sexuality" is not a biological phenomenon, but rather an effect of the symbolic order, if this means that we can regard it as purely conventional or as the product of cultural conditions. In the face of current debates between biological determinism and cultural construction, psychoanalysis introduces the following difficulty: "sexuality" cannot be reduced to a biological fact, but neither is it a social effect. Like the incest taboo, it violates the distinction between nature and culture, not because it belongs partly to each, but because this very distinction avoids the concept of sexuality, *replacing* it with a choice between 'biology" and "social convention"—an alternative that Freudian theory contested from the start.

At the broadest theoretical level, therefore, the importance of Freud's account of the drive for contemporary discussions of subjectivity and embodiment is that it breaks with biomedical accounts of mental and bodily existence, while also refusing explanations which suggest that the "subject," having been detached from nature, is in any way a simple "product" or "effect" of contingent social conditions. This apparently obvious point is often effaced by the reception of psychoanalysis: it is sometimes supposed that Freud's work consists in exploring the relation between the "impulses" of the organism (the id) and the repressive forces of culture (the superego), and Freud himself often uses this language, as if the ego were a compromise between biological instinct and moral law. Such a view, however, collapses the distinction between the instinct and the drive, and misconstrues psychoanalysis as a confused combination of biomedical pretension and social psychology, when it would be more accurate to regard it as a distinct theoretical formation—not an attempt to patch together the forces of nature and history, but a theory with its own logic and structure. In this respect, psychoanalysis shares with phenomenology a profound commonality: both begin with a twin critique of naturalism and historicism. To consider the drive is thus to insist that Freud's account of the body and of psychic life is irreducible to both biological and socio-historical models, however dialectically intertwined one may take these two domains to be.

If the first point bears on the general theoretical arena occupied by psychoanalysis, the second point about the relation between the drive and representation bears more directly on the clinical dimension of psychoanalysis, for the concept of the "drive" always has a *bodily* significance in Freud's work. This is evident from the *specification* of the drive in terms of its corporeal location, an argument elaborated through the "oral," "anal," "scopic," and other so-called "stages" of the drive, and also in terms of the "erotogenic zones," which are understood not as biological parts of the organism, but as anatomical regions which serve as the locus for representation—regions that are not determined in advance by nature, but subject to symbolic displacement and substitution (SE 7: 183-4). Freud's purpose is not to dismiss the bodily character of the symptom in favor of a "psychological" theory of neurosis grounded in subjective "fantasies," but rather to isolate the specific character of the symptom in psychoanalytic theory, as distinct from its counterpart in organic medicine. Thus, if Freud goes on to say, five years later, that the hysteric "suffers mainly from reminiscences" (SE 2: 7), this does not mean that the hysteric is only imagining things, or that corporeality has been circumvented for the sake of an abstract discourse on "representation" and "the symbolic order." On the contrary, it means that the *body* must be distinguished from the *organism*, and understood in terms of its susceptibility to the signifier—its peculiar porousness and vulnerability with respect to the order of meaning. "The symptom," in Lacan's words, is "a metaphor in which flesh or function is taken as a signifying element."[3]

Starting from the concept of the drive, we are thus led not only to insist on the theoretical specificity of psychoanalysis (in relation to biological and historical models), but also to recognize that this specificity has two distinct but closely related aspects, which we can designate with the terms "subject" and "body": it is a matter of recognizing that, for psychoanalysis, the problem of "the subject" will be approached neither through the neurological, biochemical, materialist discourse of Helmholtz, Brücke, and Fechner (a tradition still very much alive in psychopharmacology), nor through arguments for the "social construction of subjectivity," which are often presented as the only alternative to naturalism. But at the same time, we must acknowledge that the question of the "subject" in psychoanalysis will never be clarified unless the concept of the body is also addressed, as a concrete, material domain which cannot be reduced to the level of organic life.

Lacan's formula for the drive makes this point explicit. The matheme $\$\diamond D$ designates a relation between the subject ($\$$) and the demand of the Other (D), but as a formula specifically intended to define the drive, it indicates that we are dealing, not with "subjectivity" (or with an "intersubjective" relation between the subject and the Other), but with a corporeal phenomenon. The formula thus indicates that in the drive, some part of the body has been elected as the locus of symbolic demand, the privileged place where the force of representation has had material effects. This is why, as Slavoj Žižek points out, there is a close connection between the formula for the drive and the "erotogenic zone": "certain parts of the body's surface are erotically privileged not because of their anatomical position but because of the way the body is caught up in the symbolic network. This symbolic dimension is designated in the matheme as D, i.e., symbolic demand."[4] In short, the matheme for the drive ($\$\Diamond D$), in designating a relation between the "subject" and the "demand of the Other," is neither an intersubjective nor even a linguistic matter, but is intended to address the bodily organization of libido, beyond all instinctual regularity.

One might object that Lacan's vocabulary is far removed from Freud's and that an enormous theoretical shift takes place with the introduction of the words "subject," "demand," and the "Other." This is no doubt true, and each of the terms carries a heavy philosophical load that requires detailed examination. But Freud's own discourse provides at least some basis for Lacan's terminology. For although Freud does not speak of "the demand of the Other," we may note that in describing the ego ideal—that complex formation which is both a fertile point of identification for the subject, an opening toward the future and toward the possibilities of desire, and yet also the initial form of conscience, a foothold for guilt and for the punitive agency of the superego—Freud writes that it

> is the heir to the original narcissism in which the childish ego enjoyed self-sufficiency; it gradually *gathers up* from the influences of the environment *the demands* which that environment makes upon the ego and which the ego cannot always rise to; so that a man, when he *cannot be satisfied* with his ego itself, may nevertheless be able to *find satisfaction* in the the ego ideal which has been differentiated out of the ego (SE 18: 110, emphasis added).

The ego-ideal is this strange "product," this effect of symbolic identification, this *gathering up of demands* which come from the Other and are incorporated (though not entirely integrated) within the psychic economy of the subject, where they serve as a source of both satisfaction and suffering, as the "heir" to the subject's narcissism, but also as the means by which the subject will "find satisfaction" precisely when his own ego proves deficient—in a movement of identification whose masochistic character Lacan repeatedly emphasized, while also acknowledging that desire itself only unfolds in radical dependence on this ideal, the formation of which is the mark, for Lacan, of the subject's submission to the law, understood as the law of symbolic identification (as distinct from biological identity). The ego ideal, and with it the very possibility of desire, would therefore seem to emerge only with this surplus effect, whereby the subject is submitted to the demand of the Other, so that enjoyment is constitutively marked by a masochistic or pathological element. Such is the tangled economy of desire and *jouissance*—that "pleasure in suffering" that Freud developed under the heading of the "death drive."

The ego ideal is not yet the drive, of course, and we shall have to see why this is so; but in Freud's reference to this "gathering up of demands" it is clear that the body is already at stake, and that even at the level of "symbolic identification" we cannot be content with a purely "symbolic" model, in which the unconscious would remain completely disembodied. In fact, given the peculiar economy of pleasure and suffering that organizes itself in the ego ideal (such that the ego will "find satisfaction" at the very moment when it "cannot be satisfied with . . . itself"), we should be able to provide a more adequate account of the register of "affect" that is so often said to be missing from Lacan's work—all the "moods" which characterize our bodily existence, such as guilt, anxiety, boredom (taking only the most favorite of Heidegger's terms, and leaving aside the spirits of vengeance, resentment, slavishness, and all the other modes of physiological morality that Nietzsche would have us consider). "What is the affect of ex-sisting?" Lacan asks in 1975. "What is it, of the unconscious, which makes for ex-sistence? It is what I underline with the support of the symptom" (FS 166). Thus, forged in the fire of the Other's demand, the ego ideal presents us, not with an abstract meditation on "the subject," but with an effort to understand the unnatural modes of "satisfaction" which permeate bodily existence.

Our second point is therefore clear: if psychoanalysis begins with a critique of naturalistic accounts of the symptom, it does not follow that the body is simply abandoned in favor of "imaginary" or "symbolic" matters, as if it were only a question of "representation." Rather, as Freud writes in 1888, "the material conditions" of the symptom "are profoundly altered" (1: 170). Hysteria proves to be "ignorant and independent of any notion of the anatomy of the nervous system," and we are led to conclude that hysterical (as opposed to organic) paralysis entails a different form of causality (a law that is not a law of nature) in which representation has somatic effects. Hysterical paralysis is thus located, not at the level of the *organism*, but at the level of the *body*, which has its own phenomenal specificity, its own logic and structure: in hysterical paralysis, some concrete part of the body is inaccessible, or paralyzed, or loses its function (or conversely becomes libidinally invested beyond what "nature" would dictate), according to Freud, but "without its material substratum . . . being damaged," as it would be in organic paralysis (SE 1: 170). As a result, if we wish to retain the medical language of "lesions" so forcefully analyzed by Foucault in *The Birth of the Clinic*, we have only one conclusion: "the lesion in hysterical paralysis," Freud says, "will therefore be an alteration of the *conception*, the *idea*, of the arm, for instance. . . The arm behaves as though it did not exist for the play of associations" (SE 1: 170). "Hysterical paralysis," he concludes, "is also a *representation paralysis*, but with a special kind of representation whose characteristics remain to be discovered" (SE 1: 163, emphasis added).[5]

It should come as no surprise that Heidegger drew a similar conclusion about the difference between the organism and the body. Speaking of language and the physical production of sounds, Heidegger insists on the transformation which marks the human body when it is inhabited by the possibility of speech: "Speaking implies the articulate vocal production of sound. Language manifests itself in speaking as the activation of the organs of speech—mouth, lips, teeth, tongue, larynx."[6] One might suppose that language is therefore a product of human nature, a tool that is used to express internal thoughts, and not an irremediably Other domain. One might think, Heidegger says, that "we ourselves . . . have the ability to speak and therefore already possess language" (OWL 111-12) . And yet, such a view not only conceals the nature of language, but also our own nature, and Heidegger immediately adds that these "organs" of speech are profoundly misunderstood if they are regarded from a biological standpoint, as organic structures performing natural functions of life (expressing, designating, or reasoning, which would thus be natural to the human animal): "The sounding of the voice," Heidegger writes, "is no longer only of the order of physical organs. It is released now from the perspective of the physiological-physical explanation" (OWL 101); indeed "the mouth is not merely a kind of organ of the body understood as an organism" (OWL 98). These remarks, written in commemoration of Rilke's death, were made the same year that Lacan delivered his "Proposal on Psychic Causality," which begins with a critique of Henri Ey's "organicist theory of madness," and cites Paul Elouard in the process (E 151-93). We cannot enter here into a proper treatment of Heidegger and Lacan, but it should be stressed that already in *Being and Time*, as Derrida has pointed out, Heidegger recognized that the "matter" of the body could not be understood as a natural thing, on the model of "extended substance," because the ecstatic structure of Dasein's being already entailed a "body" beyond nature. The analytic of Dasein is not an abstract or purely "spiritual" theory of "subjective" existence, but opens a corporeal "space" beyond the space of Euclidean geometry (just as it entails a death beyond all natural death). Thus, in *Of Spirit*, Derrida recalls these words from *Being and Time*: "Neither can the spatiality of *Dasein* be interpreted as an imperfection which would be inherent to existence by virtue of the fatal 'union of spirit with a body.' On the contrary, because Dasein is 'spiritual' and only because of this, it can be spatial in a way which remains essentially impossible for any extended corporeal thing."[7]

This brings us to our third point. For if the distinction between the instinct and the drive allows us to insist upon the theoretical specificity of psychoanalysis, in relation to both biological and historical analysis, and if it allows us to distinguish between the organism and the body, stressing not only the question of the symptom, but also the corporeal effects of identification (the peculiar mixture of pleasure and suffering that we find in the ego ideal), we have said little about the notorious "object relation," and nothing about the Lacanian category of the "real," which is crucial to the concept of the drive. It is not yet clear, moreover, why the drive should be understood as "sexual," and whether this means anything more than the platitude that because human sexuality is not strictly bound by the biological mandates of survival and procreation, it can therefore be said to "go everywhere." This is where the classic example of orality in Freud is still illuminating.

At first glance, the question of "sexuality" would seem to present no difficulty. Have we not already been led to expect a certain symbolic or imaginary displacement at the heart of human embodiment? Is this passage through the field of representation not what the distinction between the instinct and the drive asserted at the start? This is the lesson of *Three Essays on the Theory of Sexuality* (1905) repeated in "The Instincts and Their Vicissitudes" (1915), in both of which Freud elaborates the drive in terms of four aspects—its force, aim, object and source (*Drang*, *Ziel*, *Objekt*, and *Quelle*). With this analysis we are again on familiar ground, for in each case, the drive is revealed in its relation to representation, and thus in its fundamental difference from instinct: its *power* does not lie in a natural reserve of energy waiting to be expended, but in the force of psychic inscription, the force of an "idea" or an unconscious "thought" (a thesis which Lacan elaborates through the concept of the signifier); its *aim* is not survival or reproduction, as in the case of a natural instinct, but is rather a certain "pleasure," which is given not by the satisfaction of an organic need, but as a satisfaction obtained by the ego (a thesis which Lacan elaborates in terms of narcissism and the imaginary body); the *object* of the drive is not determined in advance as a "genital" object, in accordance with the biological laws of procreation, but is subject to displacement and substitution, as Freud suggests when he speaks of thumb-sucking, as an example of the oral drive in its detachment from organic need; and the *source* of the drive, its bodily locus, is developed in terms of the erotogenic zone, which allows us to see not only a *difference* between the organism and the body, but—in certain cases—a fundamental opposition and conflict between them. In the case of the oral drive, for example, we may find a "demand for food" that goes well beyond organic need, an "oral demand" that may even threaten and contradict the biological requirements of organic life.[8] Between anorexia nervosa and overeating, we may find that the drive is no longer governed by any natural equilibrium, any natural "relation to the object," and that this is so not only in the exceptional or pathological case, but in the very character of the drive as such. This would be the "story of genesis" according to Freud: as soon as the human animal departs from the state of nature, it can only eat "too much" or "too little," the "proper object" having always already been lost. The best one can do is to establish a "golden mean," a symbolic measure that allows the primordially lost object to be "refound" in another form, where it is regulated not by nature, but by the rule of a moral law. Taken from nature, the subject, and the entire domain of sexuality, would be placed in the field of the Other.

Such a view is not altogether mistaken, and in *Beyond the Pleasure Principle* Freud recalls this argument from his earlier work. Speaking of the child's relation to the breast in the oral phase, an example discussed at length by Jean Laplanche, Freud makes two distinctions: first, with respect to the "subjective" correlate (to put the point phenomenologically), he observes that the child's *appetite* may be satisfied by the nourishment it receives, but that *oral satisfaction* is a different phenomenon. Freud notes that the satisfaction of the oral drive can be attained through a substitute (as in the case of thumb-sucking), which is not possible in the case of hunger. This shows at one and the same time the *distinction* between the oral drive and the instinct of hunger, and also the *propping* or *leaning* of the former on the latter. Detached from the domain of "hunger," the oral drive is nevertheless located in a physical way that *departs from* this organic function (in a similar way, the scopic drive will depart from the function of sight). "Sexuality" itself, in the Freudian sense, originates in this departure.

Second, with respect to the "objective" correlate, Freud distinguishes between the *milk* which the child seeks at the *breast*, and the *breast* itself, as an "object" that is propped on the organic function of feeding, but nevertheless distinguished from it. Lacan formulates this point by distinguishing the object of need from the object of demand, the first being necessary to biological life, the second designating an object that belongs to the field of the Other. Propped on an organic function, the symbolic mobility of demand (as in the case of thumb-sucking) nevertheless thus separates it from the "unsubstitutable" aspect of need. In this example, we find a formulation of the fact that "sexuality" *emerges in the difference between need and demand*, at the level of the oral drive. At the same time, it is clear that Freud insists on the *bodily inscription of demand*, at the level of the oral drive. Thus, while we may justly assert that sexuality "goes everywhere" in Freud, it should be added that if it goes everywhere in principle, it does not do so *in fact*, in the case of a particular subject. This is where the distinction between demand and desire comes into play: if anorexia, as Lacan suggests, is a form of the oral drive in which the subject "eats the nothing," it is because lack has not been adequately established. That lack, on the basis of which the body is given, has not yet arrived, and in this respect the anorexic does not have her body. We thus have a correlation between demand and the drive: bound by the "demand for the nothing" that repeats itself mechanically at the level of the oral drive, the desire of the subject is compromised.

Thus, if it is true in one sense that sexuality "goes everywhere," and that having been detached from nature, it can appear at any point in the imaginary and symbolic network, there is also a more precise sense in which Freud speaks of "sexuality," particularly when it comes to the drive, as a particular bodily formation, a particular modality of libido. This is why we must say that "sexuality," in being detached from nature, "is not all inscribed" in the order of representation. Something remains beyond the circuit of the law, and it is here, at this limit of the law, that "sexuality" may be given a more precise meaning.

Again, it would be tempting to overlook this fact. One might think that Lacanian theory regards the subject, and indeed the unconscious itself, as a matter of the symbolic order—a "linguistic" matter, in accordance with the purely formal economy derived from Saussure and Levi-Strauss, so that the unconscious (which is "structured like a language") would therefore be explained by symbolic means. Is this not the classic explanation of "unconscious desire," which emerges in the signifying chain, disrupting the sequence of signifiers that articulate the ego's narrative with the nonsensical "material" of the lapsus, the dream, and the forgotten word—or the sudden, unexpected free association that shows where "it speaks" beyond what "I want" to say? Is not the symptom itself regarded as a "symbolic" phenomenon, the unconscious "reminiscence" or the "metaphor" in which "flesh or function is taken as a signifying element" (E 518/166)? Such is the familiar Lacanian formula, according to which "the unconscious of the subject is the discourse of the Other," a formula which allows us to distinguish between the discourse of the ego and disruptive appearance of unconscious desire. In Seminar 11, however, Lacan insists that this symbolic debris—the "discourse of the Other"—is not the whole truth, and the "unconscious" itself must be redefined, linked in turn to "sexual reality," which is irreducible to language. Neither the demand of the ego nor the discourse of the Other will be sufficient now: "This nodal point is called desire" (SXI, 154). Lacan explicitly marks this development at the very start of Seminar 11, the first sentence of which reads: "When the space of a lapsus no longer carries any meaning (or interpretation), then only is one sure that one is in the unconscious" (vii).[9]

Thus, in 1964 Lacan breaks with the received Lacanian wisdom. "I find myself in a problematic position," he writes, "for what have I taught about the unconscious?" (SXI, 149). "The unconscious is constituted by the effects of speech," he says, and "the unconscious is structured like a language" (149). Nevertheless, he now insists on a new formulation: "the reality of the unconscious is sexual reality" (SXI, 150). We are thus confronted with an aspect of the unconscious that *cannot be presented* in images or words, and it will lead Lacan to insist that Freud was right in claiming that the drive is always a "partial drive," its object *a* "partial object"—not because it involves a "part" of the subject's body (the erotogenic zone, or the anal, scopic, and other "stages"), but because it *only partly represents*: "This feature, this partial feature, rightly emphasized in objects, is applicable not because these objects are part of a total object, the body, but because they *represent only partially* the function that produces them" (E, 315, emphasis added). The same point is made in "The Subjective Import of the Castration Complex": "The drives represent the cause of sexuality in the psychic; they do so only partially and yet they constitute the only link of sexuality to our experience" (FS, 119). In short, while the drive is distinguished from instinct and detached from its natural foundations, it is not entirely inscribed in the circuit of the signifier. One might say that the drive thus poses the problem of a third alienation—beyond imaginary and symbolic alienation—insofar as it introduces the lack in the Other, and tries to grasp the bodily consequences of this lack.

Thus, if we begin with a "symbolic" conception of the unconscious, understood as the "discourse of the Other," we will have to recognize that something of the unconscious remains essentially unspeakable. As he says in "The Direction of the Treatment," "I can already hear the apprentices murmuring that I intellectualize analysis: though I am in the very act, I believe, of preserving the unsayable aspect of it" (E, 253). This "impossibility," this defect in the order of representation, leads Lacan to formulate the object *a* as a point that cannot be presented in imaginary or symbolic form (though "it is to this object that cannot be grasped in the mirror that the specular image lends its clothes" E, 316). So decisive is this development that Lacan will even begin to define the subject in terms of this "impossibility." In "Subversion of the Subject" he writes: "This cut in the signifying chain alone verifies the structure of the subject as discontinuity in the real" (E, 299).

Starting from this unspeakable point, this moment of aporia in which the Other malfunctions, we must then try to see how this "cut" or "discontinuity" of the real is able to give rise to particular bodily effects. For the "real," however lacking or "impossible" it may be (as the "phallus," a signifier of lack, as the "breast," a lost object, as the "gaze," what is missing from the visual field, etc.), can nevertheless make a difference in the structure of the body. The lack in the Other is not just an abstract "impossibility," but an "embodied aporia" (E, 265). For if the body is "untimely ripped" from nature and "gathered up" into the field of the Other, it is also here that the surplus effect of lack comes into being, giving rise to a debt that can be paid in different currency. As Lacan puts it in "The Direction of the Treatment": "This moment of cut is haunted by the form of a bloody scrap—the pound of flesh that life pays in order to turn it into the signifier of signifiers, which it is impossible to restore, as such, to the imaginary body" (E, 629-30/265). To speak of this "bloody scrap" is thus to speak of the object *a*, where we find a sacrifice of the subject, a sacrifice of desire whereby the subject throws itself into the fire, in a sacred effort to answer the Other's lack, or in movements which, though less spectacular, still leave a "mark of iron of the signifier on the shoulder of the speaking subject" (E, 265). As he says in Seminar 11, where he is concerned once again with the subject as a "discontinuity in the real," and not with symbolic "identity": "At this level, we are not even forced to take into account any subjectification of the subject. The subject is an apparatus. This apparatus is something lacunary, and it is in the lacuna that the subject establishes the function of a certain object, *qua* lost object. It is the status of the *objet a* in so far as it is present in the drive" (SXI, 185).

Let us conclude with Freud's own formulation. For Freud, the drive may initially seem to be defined at the level of *psychic inscription*. Like anything that belongs to the order of the "subject," even the most elementary "perception," so also the drive must be presented *through* the network of representation—conscious, preconscious or unconscious. The difference between the instinct and the drive would thus be nothing other than the difference between the sphere of immediate presence and biological energy, and the sphere of mediation and re-presentation. In "Instincts and Their Vicissitudes" (*Triebe und Triebschicksale*, "The Drives and their Destiny"), Freud thus offers the following definition: "an 'instinct' [*Trieb*, drive] appears to us as a concept on the frontier between the mental and the somatic, as the psychical representative of the stimuli originating from within the organism and reaching the mind" (SE 14: 121-2). But in the article on "Repression" written at the same time, Freud complicates this account: "In our discussion so far we have dealt with the repression of an instinctual representative, and by the latter we have understood an idea or group of ideas which is cathected with a definite quota of psychical energy (libido or interest) coming from an instinct" (SE 14: 152). At this point in the discussion of repression, we would seem to be concerned with a division, within the order of representation, between "instinctual representatives" that are repressed and those that are not. But Freud now adds that "some other element" has to be accounted for:

> Clinical observation now obliges us to divide up what we have hitherto regarded as a single entity; for it shows us that besides the idea, some other element representing the instinct has to be taken into account, and that this element undergoes vicissitudes of repression which may be quite different from those undergone by the idea. For this other element of the psychical representative the term *quota of affect* has generally been adopted. It corresponds to the instinct insofar as the latter has become detached from the idea and finds expression, proportionate to its quantity, in processes which are sensed as affects. From this point on, in describing a case of repression, we shall have to follow up separately what, as the result of repression, becomes of the *idea*, and what becomes of the *instinctual energy* linked to it (SE 14: 152, emphasis added).

Thus, besides the ideas which are "cathected with a definite quota of psychical energy," we must now confront a "quota of affect," an element that is "detached from the idea" and given a different destiny ("this element undergoes vicissitudes of repression which may be quite different from those undergone by the idea").

This new division between the field of representation and the "quota of affect" is not easy to grasp. We cannot simply speak of a difference between the "idea" and "energy"—as if it were a matter of separating the "psychic" domain of representation from that of "bodily" experience or affective "energy." For one thing, the "psychic" domain already entails a certain appeal to "energy" or "libido" [Freud thus speaks of "an idea or group of ideas which is cathected with a definite quota of psychical energy (libido or interest)"]; for another thing, this new "element," in being distinguished from the "idea," is not a bodily "experience" that would be altogether unrelated to the sphere of representation (Freud thus writes that "some other element *representing the instinct* has to be taken into account," and goes on to offer the following definition: "For this other element *of the psychical representative* the term quota of affect has generally been adopted" [emphasis added]). On the side of the "psychic representation" there is "energy," and on the side of the affect there is "representation." Nevertheless, if this new development is serious, we cannot simply obliterate the distinction Freud seeks to make. This much is clear: instead of a simple division between the "psychic" sphere of mediation and representation, and the "bodily" sphere of immediate presence and natural energy, we are concerned with a more complex and tangled relation, but one in which it is still possible and necessary to differentiate, and "to follow up separately," what Freud here calls—in a tentative and no doubt problematic way—the "idea" and the "instinctual energy linked to it." One might say that he seeks to isolate, not an "outside" to representation, a domain of natural immediacy that no representation would affect (the familiar notion of "instinct"), but rather a point *within* the domain of representation that remains essentially foreign, excluded, and impossible to present. Such is the relation between the symbolic and the real—the latter understood not as a "prelinguistic reality," but as an effect of the symbolic law that is nevertheless not reducible to a symbolic phenomenon. In Lacanian terms, we are concerned here with the difference between the Other and the object *a*, and it is above all the theory of the drive that forces us to acknowledge this distinction.

Notes

1. Sigmund Freud, "Instincts and Their Vicissitudes," *The Standard Edition of the Complete Psychological Works of Sigmund Freud*, trans. James Strachey, et. al. (London: The Hogarth Press, 1953-1974), 14: 117-40. Freud's works will be cited by volume and page number preceded by SE. Other abbreviations used in the text are as follows: E = Jacques Lacan, *Écrits* (Paris: Seuil, 1966). A portion of this volume has appeared in English as *Écrits: A Selection*, trans. Alan Sheridan (New York: Norton, 1977). References will be given to both volumes, whenever possible, French pagination first, English second. FS = *Jacques Lacan and the École freudienne, Feminine Sexuality,*

eds. Juliet Mitchell and Jacqueline Rose, trans. Jacqueline Rose (New York: Norton, 1985). SXI = *Le Seminaire, livre XI: Les quatres concepts fondamentaux de la psychanalyse*, ed. Jacques-Alain Miller (Paris: Seuil, 1973), and *The Four Fundamental Concepts of Psychoanalysis* (Seminar 11), trans. Alan Sheridan (New York: Norton, 1978). References will be given to both volumes, French pagination first, English second; translations are occasionally modified. T = "Television," trans. Denis Hollier, Rosalind Krauss, and Annette Michelson in *Television: A Challenge to the Psychoanalytic Establishment*, ed. Joan Copjec (New York: Norton, 1990).

2. Although the difference between "instinct" and "drive" (*Instinkt* and *Trieb*) is commonly cited in secondary literature on Lacan, where it is understood as distinguishing biological models of animal behavior from human sexuality in its relation to the symbolic order, it should be stressed that this common and obvious point of departure is not shared by other psychoanalytic schools. One has only to look at the dictionary of the American Psychoanalytic Association to find "instinct" defined as "a term introduced by biologists, mainly students of animal behavior, which has been widely applied to the behavior of humans"—a definition which is later linked to "species-typical patterns of behavior, presumed to be rooted in innate, gene-determined equipment," and that instinct theory consequently addresses "those aspects of humanness directly continuous with related species." The dictionary goes on to acknowledge that Freud's German term "*Trieb*" cannot be altogether integrated with the Latin "instinct," and that "English-speaking readers were thrown into confusion by Strachey's decision to translate *Trieb* as "instinct," since *Trieb* does not designate, as instinct does, "a motivational force that always results in a specific pattern of behavior," but rather a "sum total of the mental representations that might be associated with a given somatic process." Nevertheless, this acknowledgment of a difference between instinct and drive is not decisive, and in their definition of "instinctual drive"—a term which seems to collapse the distinction, or at least loses the decisive theoretical decision which Lacan insists upon—the editors explain that for Freud, "*Triebe* are based on innate givens, gene-determined potentials present from birth." See *Psychoanalytic Terms and Concepts*, ed. Burness E. Moore, M. D., and Bernard D. Fine, M. D. (New Haven: Yale University Press, 1990), 99-101.

3. Jacques Lacan, *Écrits* (Paris: Seuil, 1966), 518. *Écrits: A Selection*, trans. Alan Sheridan (New York: Norton, 1977), 166. References will henceforth appear in the text preceded by E, French pagination first, English (wherever possible) second. Translations are occasionally modified.

4. Slavoj Žižek, *Looking Awry: An Introduction to Jacques Lacan Through Popular Culture* (Cambridge, Mass.: MIT Press, 1991), 21.

5. *Charles Shepherdson*, "*Adaequatio Sexualis*: Is There a Measure of Sexual

Difference?" *From Phenomenology to Thought, Errancy, and Desire: Essays in Honor of William J. Richardson, S. J.*, ed. Babette Babich (Dordrecht: Kluwer, 1995), 445-71.

6. Martin Heidegger, *On the Way to Language*, trans. P. Hertz and J. Stambaugh (New York: Harper and Row, 1971), 114. Further references will appear in the text preceded by OWL.
7. Martin Heidegger, *Being and Time*, trans. John Macquarrie and Edward Robinson (New York: Harper and Row, 1962), 368. I have cited the German pagination given marginally in the English texts. For Derrida's remarks on this passage, see *Jacques Derrida, Of Spirit: Heidegger and the Question*, trans. Geoff Bennington and Rachel Bowlby (Chicago: University of Chicago Press, 1989), 25. My citation of Heidegger combines the translation of Macquarrie and Robinson with that of Bennington and Bowlby.
8. First developed in "Three Essays" (SE 7: 130-243), where one finds sections on the constitutive deviations with respect to the "object," "aim" and "source," together with a section on "the libido theory" in which "quantitatively variable force" is considered; these four terms are elaborated in "Instincts and Their Vicissitudes" (SE 14: 122-25).
9. This sentence is found only in the English edition of the seminar, in a preface written in 1976.

3

On the Proper Name as the Signifier in its Pure State

Russell Grigg

In his seminar, *Identification*, Lacan paused for a moment over the logic of the proper name as articulated by Bertrand Russell.[1] Lacan's interest was aroused by the critique of the Russellian theory of the proper name that figured in a small polemical book by Alan Gardiner.[2]

This moment is of interest to us as one of the rare occasions upon which Lacan explicitly treats the question of the *logic* of proper names, which is, as we know, a central question in analytic philosophy—and a question to which Russell's contribution is in no way insignificant. Thus it can serve as a point of departure for an exploration of the function of the proper name in psychoanalysis.

First of all, we must ask what leads Russell to advance a far-fetched thesis—which if taken literally is "obviously false from the point of view of common language"[3] —according to which only "this" and "that" are proper names.

Bertrand Russell's position, of course, lies with the Fregean theory of the proper name with its distinction between sense, *Sinn*, and reference, *Bedeutung*. According to Frege, the sense of the proper name is the means by which it determines its reference, the meaning. For example, concerning the proper name Socrates, one knows who is referred to by means of a description of this kind—"Plato's teacher."

It is for this reason that Russell can maintain that what "common language" calls a proper name—Socrates, Walter Scott—is properly speaking an abbreviated description. In using the word Socrates, one employs a description such as "Plato's teacher" or "the philosopher who drank hemlock."

Now, a proper name in the sense called "logical" by Russell absolutely cannot abbreviate a description and therefore, strictly speaking, has no sense. Only the demonstratives "this" and "that" would satisfy the requirement of being devoid of sense in a manner such that the reference would be determined without any recourse to the slightest description. Thus they are the only words worthy of being called proper names.

Gardiner aligns himself rather with J. S. Mill, for whom that which distinguishes a proper name is, on the one hand, not to have sense and on the other, to be of the order of a mark applied to a particular for the sole and exclusive reason of distinguishing it from others.[4]

Even when the name appears to have sense—Mill offers as an example "Dartmouth," the city that is located "at the mouth" of the river Dart—it is merely contingent, given that eventually the sense might no longer be true of the object to which the name refers. What distinguishes the proper name, according to Gardiner, is that it be recognized as indicating the object to which it refers itself as a *distinctive sound*, without regard to any meaning the name might possess.

Lacan mentions that this definition is not sufficient to characterize the proper name because any usage of language satisfies these conditions—it is precisely the characteristic feature of language that it be made up of distinctive sounds. This is a difficulty that Gardiner is aware of, and which leads him to rely on a psychologistic element—namely that when it comes to proper names, the speaker is particularly sensitive to the sound of the name.

In any case, this is certainly the distinctive feature of the name that Gardiner insists upon to sustain his thesis. He criticizes the reference that Mill makes to the story of Ali Baba. Mill compares the proper name to the chalkmark on Ali Baba's door that indicates his house so that the bandits can find him. His servant, Morgiana, thwarts the thieves by marking every door with the same symbol, making it impossible to figure out which house is his.

No, says Gardiner. The comparison is faulty. All Morgiana would need to do to foil the plan of the thieves would be to put a different mark on each door—leaving them unable to tell which mark was the right one. A name doesn't distinguish one door from another by the fact that it has a name whereas the others don't—but rather by the fact that its name is different from theirs.

While this critique of Mill hits its mark, a difficulty that Gardiner is aware of arises precisely at this point in his argument. As a matter of fact, what Gardiner says doesn't define the proper name, because every word is distinguished by its difference from all the others. Thus there is nothing in this definition that is specific to the proper name. And it is precisely at this point, in trying to determine the difference, that Gardiner appeals to a psychological phenomenon. This is a difficulty that he won't be able to resolve.

A proper name has no meaning. It only has a reference. Now, as it happens there are, on the one hand, proper names that do appear to have a sense—Mont Blanc, Yarmouth, Côte d'Azur—and on the other, connotations and meanings do tend to accrue to proper names. These considerations force Gardiner to maintain that the "purest" proper names are those made up of "perfectly distinctive" and "entirely arbitrary" sounds for which we have no feeling of meaning. But what are his examples? Vercingetorix and Popocatepetl! I'm not making this up.

Obviously, there is something shaky in this argument. The claim that there is a distinction between "pure" proper names and others is only required by the demands of the thesis. Plainly, it has no justification. It is difficult to distinguish psychological sensations from what belongs to the logic of the signifier and its semantic effect and borders on the psychologism that, as Frege has shown, we have good reason to reject.

Lacan doesn't hesitate to express his disagreement with the psychologism of Gardiner, considering that his account founders on a major difficulty. Gardiner's thesis miscarries because he doesn't articulate the function of the subject in any other than a psychological manner and fails to define the subject in its reference to the signifier.

More precisely, Lacan insists that what is lacking in Gardiner's approach is the function of the letter, and more particularly the function of the unary trait—"there can be no definition of the proper name except insofar as we perceive the relation of the naming utterance to something that is, in its radical nature, of the order of the letter."[5]

The sound structure is not dismissed by Lacan, since it possesses a singularity that must be respected across translations. Thus, if the proper name preserves its sound structure, it is "by reason of the affinity of the proper name and the mark."[6]

Why this insistence on the letter? Two reasons. There is on the one hand the affinity between the proper name and the letter that arises because neither possesses any meaning. Thus the proper name has the particularity of being the "signifier in its pure state." On the other hand, there is something to the fact that proper names pass directly from one language to another—"I am Lacan in any language," he tells us, while making the same observation about the names Cleopatra and Ptolemy, which played a key role in the deciphering of hieroglyphics.

How all this concerns the signifier as letter is not clear. What is incontestable, though, is that from the fact that the proper name is untranslatable, one can conclude that it has no sense—with few exceptions. The exceptions are, on the one hand, place names and, on the other, the names of celebrated persons whose celebrity rests upon a common description that serves to determine the referent for everyone. By choosing very well known names—Socrates, Cicero—as examples of his theory of descriptions, Frege thus concealed the fact that the proper name lacks meaning.

Five years later, in his seminar, *Crucial Problems for Psychoanalysis*, Lacan revisits the question of proper names. Once again, he refers to Gardiner's book. But this time, instead of appealing to the ins(is)tence of the letter in the translation of proper names, he emphasizes what he calls "the significative effects" of the proper name:

> If I present myself to you as Jacques Lacan, I say . . . something that . . . for you entails a certain number of significative effects. . . . From the moment that I introduce myself to you as Jacques Lacan, any possibility of my being a Rockefeller, for example, or the count of Paris is already eliminated."

From this, he concludes, "To say that a proper name . . . has no meaning is grossly inadequate."[7]

There is a difficulty here that arises from the fact that what Lacan says in this context evokes the Fregean theory of descriptions. For what distinguishes proper names other than the descriptions—"author of the *Écrits*," "famous French psychoanalyst," etc.—that determine that it just happens to be a matter of Jacques Lacan and not the count of Paris?

Before renouncing the thesis—which to me seems to be justified—that the proper name is the signifier in its pure state, it is necessary to take into account what Lacan says elsewhere in *Seminar XII*. It is Saul Kripke's concept of the "rigid designator" that can serve as a compass here.[8] Kripke maintains that the Fregean theory is unprovable. His insight is to see that if the sense of "Socrates" is a description such as "Plato's teacher," then "Socrates is Plato's teacher" would be necessarily true. If "Plato's teacher" is the sense of "Socrates," then Socrates just has to be Plato's teacher. However, it is obviously contingent that Socrates should ever have become a philosopher. Or, to take a more convincing example, if by "Thales" we signify "the philosopher who believed that all things are made of water," and no one ever maintained such a thesis, it is necessary to conclude that Thales never existed. To whom, then, does Aristotle refer? A person, according to the theory of descriptions. For, it must be possible that Thales was a mason, for example, and that Aristotle was deceived as to what this person did and thought.[9] It follows, therefore, that one could refer to Thales by using the proper name "Thales" even if it turns out that the only description we have of him is false. That the proper name is a rigid designator therefore means that, contrary to the theory of descriptions, no meaning is essentially tied to the proper name.

The term "rigid designator" implies therefore that no signification, no description, belongs to the proper name. And this is what Lacan seems to confirm a little later in the same seminar when he says, "I am called Jacques Lacan, but as something that can be missing, for which the name will tend to cover over another lack. The proper name, therefore, is a movable function."[10]

We better understand this "other lack" and this "fluctuating function" in the context of the concept of rigid designation of the proper name taken independently of all identifying descriptions.

It is possible to carry all of this over into the clinical context. Without going into the details—which could be developed at another time—it is very suggestive in the case of Joyce, for example, for whom the use of proper names is inscribed *against* this thesis of the proper name as "signifier in its pure state." Isn't it all the more striking that Joyce never stops playing on the function of the letter in the proper name? For example, he has only to think of the three great names of European letters, *Gouty*, *Doughty*, and *Shopkeeper*, in which his idea seems precisely to be the flooding of the signifier with an abundance of sense. On the other hand, we must wonder about the meaning of wanting "to make a name for oneself" in which all the effort consists in filling the emptiness of the essence of the proper name.

Translated by Daniel G. Collins

Notes

1. The French version of this essay was originally published in *La Cause freudienne* 39 (1998), 125-8. See Jacques Lacan, *Seminar IX, Identification* (unpublished, 1961-62).
2. Alan Gardiner, *The Theory of Proper Names: A Controversial Essay*, 2nd ed. (London: Oxford UP, 1954).
3. Bertrand Russell, "The Philosophy of Logical Atomism," in *Logic and Knowledge* (London: George Allen & Unwin, 1956), 200.
4. J. S. Mill, *System of Logic* (London, 1843).
5. Identification, session of 20 December, 1961.
6. Ibid.
7. Jacques Lacan, *The Crucial Problems of Psychoanalysis, Seminar XII* (unpublished, 1964-65), session of 6 January, 1965.
8. Saul A. Kripke, *Naming and Necessity* (Cambridge, Mass.: Harvard UP, 1980).
9. Keith Donnellan, "Proper Names and Identifying Descriptions," in *Semantics of Natural Language*, eds. Donald Davidson and Gilbert Harman (Dordrecht: Reidel, 1972), 374.
10. Lacan, Ibid.

4

The Splendor of Creation: Kant, Nietzsche, Lacan

Alenka Zupančič

In his *Critique of Judgment*, Kant approaches the question of the beautiful in four steps, with four paradoxical definitions, which all revolve around the "signifier of the lack"—the word *without* or *devoid of.* Beauty is a "liking without interest," "universality without concept," "purposiveness without purpose," and "necessity without concept." Kant's basic operation in these definitions consists in what one might call *essential subtraction*: in each of the definitions quoted above, Kant deprives the first notion exactly of that which is considered to be its essential characterization. Is it not the essence of every liking or pleasure (*Wolhgefallen*) that it is bound with interest? Is it not the essence of universality and of necessity that they are based on concepts? Is it not the essence of purposiveness that it has a purpose? The beautiful thus becomes the quality of something organized around a central void, and it is this very void which somehow dictates its organization. "Purposiveness without purpose," for example, does not simply refer to something that, while having no purpose, nevertheless strikes us *as if* (the famous Kantian *als ob*) it had one. The question is not simply that of the comparison or resemblance, and the opposition is not that of the appearance of a purpose *versus* the actual absence of any purpose. The mystery of the beautiful does not reside in the question, "How can something that has no purpose produce such a striking effect of purposiveness?" The point is rather that the absence of the purpose in the "center" and the purposiveness of what is organized around this central absence are intrinsically connected. It is not that we detect some purposiveness *in spite of* the absence of any purpose; that is, it is not that the relation between the two elements is that of contradiction, but rather the relation is that of a specific form of mutual sustaining.

What we called *essential subtraction* can be expressed even better in terms of *extimité*, defined by Lacan as the "excluded interior," as something which is "excluded in the interior." This is precisely what Kantian definitions aim at: the beauty names the effect of this excluded interior. Where the excluded dimension remains *included as excluded*, it is *via* its exclusion that it becomes operative as the organizing power of its "surroundings." It is quite remarkable that in his discussion of art in relation to the question of sublimation, Lacan accentuates almost the same structure as Kant. He stresses that in every form of sublimation, emptiness (or void) is determinative, although not in the same way. Religion consists of avoiding this void, whereas science and/or philosophy take an attitude of unbelief towards it. As for art, "all art is characterized by a certain *mode of organization around this emptiness*."[1] (Of course, the emptiness at stake is not just any kind of emptiness or void, but precisely "that excluded interior which . . . is thus excluded in the interior."[2] The other name for this void or emptiness is *das Ding*, the Thing.

Previously we took the example of "purposiveness without purpose," which might be slightly misleading since we encounter the same term (purpose) on both sides. A better example is that of "pleasure without interest," or, in another translation, "liking devoid of all interest," which will help us to clarify in detail how this "interior exclusion" actually works and what its consequences are. The notion of "pleasure devoid of all interest" also has the advantage of becoming, since Nietzsche's critique, the emblem of the Kantian conception of the beautiful and the topos of contemporary philosophical debate concerning the notion of the beautiful (and of art in general).

Nietzsche's attack on Kant's notion of "pleasure devoid of all interest" is famous enough. Nietzsche identifies Kant's position with that of Schopenhauer's (which is, in itself, a very problematic identification) and sees in it a "reactive" approach to art. According to Nietzsche, disinterested delight is an absurd notion resulting from the fact that we approach art exclusively from the standpoint of the spectator, and a non-creative spectator at this. Art and its appreciation are in no way "disinterested operations." To Kant's definition of the beautiful, Nietzsche opposes Stendhal's, which defines the beautiful as "a promise of happiness" and implies, according to Nietzsche, the recognition of the power of the beautiful to *excite the will* (and thus the interest).[3] As appealing as this critique might seem, it very much misses Kant's point, which is in fact quite close to Nietzsche's own views.[4]

But what exactly does the formula "pleasure devoid of all interest" aim at? Kant calls the pleasure that is still linked with interest (or need) "agreeableness." If I declare an object to be agreeable, this judgment "arouses a desire for objects of that kind."[5] This does not mean that with the next stage, the stage of the beautiful, or "devoid of all interest," this desire disappears—the point is that it becomes irrelevant. Let us clarify this with one of Kant's own examples, the "green meadows."

The first stage is the objective stage: the green color of the meadows belongs to objective sensation. "Meadows are green" is an objective judgment. The second stage is the subjective stage: the color's agreeableness belongs to subjective sensation, to feeling: "I like green meadows" is a subjective judgment, which also means, "I would like to see green meadows as often as possible." This is a "yes" to the object (green meadows) which is supposed to *gratify* us (Kant's term). The third stage is a "yes," not to the color, but to the feeling of the agreeable itself, a "yes" not to the object that gratifies us but to the gratification itself, i.e. a "yes" to the previous "yes." Here it is the feeling itself, the sensation that becomes the object (of judgment). "Green meadows are beautiful" is a judgment of taste, an aesthetic judgment, which is neither "objective" nor "subjective." This judgment could be called "acephalous" or "headless," since the "I," the "head" of the judgment is replaced, not with some impersonal objective neutrality as in statements of the type "the meadows are green," but with the most intimate part of the subject (how the subject feels itself affected by a given representation *as object*). "Devoid of all interest" means precisely that we no longer refer to the existence of the object (green meadows), but only to the pleasure that it gives us.

It is striking how close this third stage is to one of the central themes of Nietzsche's philosophy, the theme of the "affirmation of affirmation." As Deleuze showed very well, the point of the Nietzschean "yes" is that it has to be itself affirmed by another "yes." There has to be a second affirmation, *so that the affirmation itself can be affirmed.* For this reason the Dionysian "yes" (the "yes" to everything that provides pleasure and enjoyment) needs the figure of Ariane in order to be completed.[6] This could also be a way of understanding what is usually referred to as Nietzschean 'anesthetization of life": if life should be a "yes" to a "yes," then this means precisely that it should be "aestheticized" (in the Kantian sense of the word). Life must involve passion (engagement, zeal, enthusiasm, interest), but this passion must always be accompanied by an additional "yes"—to it, otherwise it can only lead to nihilism. This "yes" cannot be but detached from the object, since it refers to the passion itself. The great effort of Nietzsche's philosophy is to think and articulate the two together. "Yes" to the "yes" cannot be the final stage in the sense that it would suffice in itself. Alone, it is no longer a "yes" to a "yes," but just plain "yes"—the "ee-ahh," the donkey's sound of inane, empty enjoyment. Thus, for Nietzsche, the figure of affirmation can only be a figure of a *couple*, and the aesthetic detachment only a "yes" to the greatest involvement.

But how exactly does this couple function? We know that any real involvement excludes simultaneous contemplation of it. And yet they must be somehow simultaneous, they must always walk in a pair (i.e. constitute one subjective figure), otherwise we would not be dealing with the "affirmation of affirmation," but with two different types of affirmation. The figure that corresponds to this criterion is the figure of *creation*—or, in other terms, the figure of sublimation. The creation is never a creation of one thing, but always the creation of two things that go together: the something and the void, or, in Lacan's terms, the object and the Thing. This is the point of Lacan's insisting on the notion of creation ex nihilo, and of his famous example of the vase: the vase is what creates the void, the emptiness *inside* it. The arch-gesture of art is to give form to the *nothing*. Creation is not something that is situated in the (given) space or that occupies a certain space, it is the very creation of the space as such. With every creation, a new space gets created. Another way of putting this would be to say that every creation has the structure of a veil. It operates as a veil that creates a "beyond," announces it, and makes it almost palpable in the very tissue of the veil.

The beautiful is the effect of a surface which is supposed to hide something (else). One must note, however, that the beautiful here no longer remains within the frame of the Kantian definition: it is not the pleasure that we find in the harmony between a given form and an indeterminate concept of the understanding. Lacan's notion of the beautiful actually combines two Kantian notions, the beautiful and the sublime. This is why he often uses the term "sublime beauty." Beauty no longer refers to the (harmonious) form, but to the splendor, *éclat*, that seems to emanate from certain objects which may very well be "ugly" or, at any rate, "plain" if taken only in their form. What makes them "glitter" is their relation to something else, the fact that they function as a screen for something else. One of the finest examples of the beautiful image's relation to the "abyss," the background upon which it emerges, which it announces and at the same time forbids access to, is probably Poe's tale "The Facts in the Case of M. Valdemar." This relation is precisely that which exists between the repulsive and formless mass, the disgusting dissolution, the substance of *jouissance* into which Valdemar's body is transformed when he is woken up from the mesmeric trance and, on the other hand, the sublime body of Valdemar, maintained for seven months in a state of mesmeric trance, under the disguise of which it transforms irrepressibly into the Thing (in Freud's as well as John Carpenter's meaning of the word). "There lay a nearly liquid mass of loathsome—of detestable putrescence."[7] It is because of the reader's awareness of the near presence of this "liquid mass of loathsome" (long before it finally reveals itself at the end of the story) that its surface, the body of Valdemar, produces an effect of beauty: the object-body is thus "elevated to the dignity of the Thing."[8] This is why in relation to the phenomenon of the beautiful Lacan speaks of the fantasy which he formulates in terms of "*a beauty that mustn't be touched*,"[9] which is his "conceptual translation" of Kant's "devoid of all interest." The shift that this translation produces is a very subtle one: it posits the breakdown of the object, linked to the appearance of the beautiful, as the very effect of the beautiful (and not as its condition). Kant goes to the trouble of performing a kind of "phenomenological reduction," of "putting in parentheses" the existence of the object (and the pleasure or displeasure that we can find in its existence), in order to arrive at the "devoid of all interest." Whereas Lacan's point is that "putting in parentheses" the existence of the object is the effect of the beautiful on our desire and not the state of mind that we must achieve first in order to be able to appreciate the beautiful (this is, once again, closer to the Kantian conception of the sublime): "the beautiful has the effect, I would say, of suspending, lowering, disarming desire. The appearance of beauty intimidates and stops desire." [10]

We must be very careful in understanding this statement. It does not imply that beauty is on the side of the Thing and the intimidated desire on the side of the subject. On the contrary, they both refer to one and the same thing which is to be situated in the space that lies between and separates the subject and the Thing. But the appearance of the beautiful is at the same time precisely what creates this "space-in-between," this distance. The "spectator" who finds something beautiful acts, participates actively in its being beautiful and, in finding something beautiful, he re-acts in the active sense of the word. The "splendor" of beauty is a kind of shield that the artist and the "spectator" raise, in a kind of complicity, at the very point of *das Ding*. This shield is made to stop desire: desire, as it were, stops at beauty and remains with it, not wishing to go any further. It is not that the desire *for* the beautiful is suspended, but rather that desire is suspended, "frozen" within the realm of the beautiful.

This modified notion of the "devoid of all interest," which implies the engagement of desire at a certain distance, a "respect" in the sense of "do not come too close to the beautiful," is not far from Nietzsche's conception of the beautiful. In *Will to Power*, § 852, for example, he writes: "To pick up the scent of what would nearly finish us off if it were to confront us in the flesh, as danger, problem, temptation—this determines our aesthetic 'yes.' ('That is beautiful' is an *affirmation*)."[11] The opposition between the "scent" and the "flesh," in which the scent is the locus of the beautiful and flesh (or "danger") its excluded interior, is perfectly compatible with the Lacanian conceptualization of "sublime beauty" (as well as with Kant's theory of the sublime). When Nietzsche links the notion of the scent (which expresses the same idea as the veil—another word that Nietzsche likes to use) to his affirmation, this points precisely in the direction of the simultaneous appearance of two things: the involvement and the distance, the "danger" and the "pleasure," the Thing and the object. In other words, it points in the direction of sublimation.

It might seem that it is precisely the notion of sublimation that opposes Nietzsche's and Lacan's conceptions of art (and creation in general). Is not the notion of sublimation a "reactive" notion *par excellence* (reactive in Nietzsche's sense of the word, i.e. non-affirmative, non-active), implying that art can only be an "answer" and never a proposition, affirmation, invention? At best, art would be a "yes" to a "no" (i.e. to the impossibility of attaining satisfaction there where it is originally sought). Another question connected to this is the one of the "aesthetics of the ugly" (or the "explicit"): we know that not all art moves in the direction of "sublime beauty." Traditional wisdom about sublimation describes the latter as the process of converting the explicit (which is considered to be forbidden and/or impossible) into the implicit (which, because of its ambiguity, is socially acceptable and/or possible). Moreover, the explicit is supposed to be linked to the sexual, whereas in the implicit the sexual character is no longer directly visible. This is, according to Lacan—who here adopts an almost Nietzschean discourse—what "the foolish crowd thinks." Sublimation actually presupposes a change of object, yet this "change of object doesn't necessarily make the sexual object disappear—far from it, the sexual object acknowledged as such may come to light in sublimation. The crudest of sexual games can be the object of a poem without for that reason losing its sublimating goal."[12] In order to demonstrate this, Lacan stops at a poem that belongs to the literature of courtly love, while at the same time being quite sexually explicit. If our idea of courtly love (and of the sublimation that it involves) is that we are dealing with "idealization," we are now in for a big surprise. Here is a part of the poem:

> Though Lord Raimond, in agreement with Lord Truc, defends Lady Ena and her orders, I would grow old and white before I would consent to a request that involves so great an impropriety. For so as "to put his mouth to her trumpet," he would need the kind of beak that could pick grain out of a pipe. And even then he might come out blind, as the smoke from those folds is so strong.
>
> He would need a beak and a long, sharp one, for the trumpet is rough, ugly and hairy, and it is never dry, and the swamp within is deep. That's why the pitch ferments upwards as it continually escapes, continually overflows. And it is not fitting that he who puts his mouth to that pipe be a favorite.
>
> There will be plenty of other tests, finer ones that are worth far more, and if Lord Bernard withdrew from that one, he did not, by Christ, behave like a coward if he was taken with fear and fright. For if the stream of water had landed on him from above, it would have scalded his whole neck and cheek, and it is not fitting also that a lady embrace a man who has blown a stinking trumpet.[13]

This poem is a good example of the "aesthetics of the explicit," as well as proof of the fact that not all art moves in the direction of "sublime beauty." It is clear that sublime beauty with its splendor is not the only "shield" that can step in between the subject and the Thing, thus diverting the subject from feeling just pure horror or disgust or plainness. The other "shield" or way of reacting is laughter. The tragic or sublime paradigm consists in creating the surface of the Thing, creating something as the obverse of the void that can be inhabited by all sorts of projections of things that would "finish us off if they were to confront us in flesh," the surface playing the role of the "last veil."

The comic paradigm, on the other hand, is not so much a process of "tearing down the veil" and peeking on the other side, revealing the actual ridiculousness of the "sublime object," as it is a process of describing the Thing (in a certain way, of course—the poem quoted above can also be categorized as the process of describing the Thing). Good comedies do not just say, "The Emperor is naked"—they display and lay out a whole set of circumstances or situations in which the nakedness is explored from many different angles, constructed in the very process of its display. If the tragic/sublime paradigm implies that we elevate an object to the dignity of the Thing, the comic paradigm could be said to consist in elevating an object to the very indignity of the Thing.

Another commonplace about sublimation is that it provides a substitute satisfaction. Sublimation, however, should be distinguished from the symptom as compromise formation which belongs to the economy of substitution (a repressed drive returns in the form of a symptom by means of a signifying substitution). The object of "formation" that is the result of sublimation can be composed of metaphors, but is not itself a metaphor or a stand-in (for something else). This is why Lacan, following Freud, links the question of sublimation to the question of drives. Sublimation is the satisfaction of the *Trieb*. This does not mean that a drive which cannot find its satisfaction in the object that it originally aims at (because of certain social prohibitions) is then forced to find its satisfaction elsewhere, in some more "acceptable" way. The point is that the "structure" of the drives is *in itself* the very structure of sublimation: "The sublimation that provides the *Trieb* with satisfaction different from its aim—an aim that is still defined as its natural aim—is precisely that which reveals the true nature of the Trieb insofar as it is not simply instinct, but has a relationship to das Ding as such, to the Thing insofar as it is distinct from the object."[14]

When, in *The Four Fundamental Concepts*, Lacan returns to the question of the drive, he reformulates the difference between the object and the Thing in terms of the difference between *aim* and *goal*. Let us suggest an example of this difference, as well as of the difference between instinct and drive: the child's instinct to suck the nipple in order to be fed becomes the drive when the aim (or the object) of sucking is no longer milk, but the very satisfaction that it finds in sucking. Thus, a child sucking its finger already has some experience of the drive. The "change of object" that characterizes the drive, as well as sublimation, is the shift from the object that gives us satisfaction (i.e. the "natural" object, the object that can satisfy a certain need) to the satisfaction itself as an object.[15] We are not dealing with substitution, but rather with a "deviation" or "detour."[16]

Two questions arise at this point. First, can we simply say that drive equals satisfaction? And second, considering that sublimation covers a much larger field than the field of art, what is the specificity of "artistic sublimation"? In reply to the first question, we could say that if the drive is a "headless" procedure, sublimation is not. Sublimation is a kind of "navigator" of the drives, and this is why it plays such an important role in society. Collective, socially accepted sublimations "lead" the drives to certain fields where they can "relax" and "let themselves go." As Lacan points out, however, it is not simply that society approves of drives only in certain delimited fields, but also that society needs to "colonize the field of *das Ding* with imaginary schemes"[17] that sublimations tend to produce.

In answer to the second question, let us propose some general lines that can account for principal differences between science, religion, and art, as three major fields of sublimation. If we define the core of sublimation (i.e. the Thing) in terms of the Lacanian notion of the real, we can say that:

1. Science is based upon the supposition that there is no real that could not be formulated within the symbolic. Every Thing belongs to or is translatable into the signifying order. In other words, for science, the Thing does not exist; the mirage of the Thing is only an effect of the (temporal and empirical) deficiency of our knowledge. The status of the real here is the status of something not only *immanent*, but also *accessible* (at least in principle). It should be noted, however, that even though—because of this attitude of disbelief—science seems to be as far as possible from the realm of the Thing, it sometimes comes to embody the Thing itself (the "irrepressible," blind drive that may lead directly to the catastrophe) in the eyes of the public. Suffice to recall Frankenstein's monster or, from more recent times, Dolly, or the idea of clones in general.

2. Religion is founded upon the supposition that the real is radically transcendent, Other, excluded. The real is impossible and forbidden at the same time, it is *transcendent* and *inaccessible.*

3. Art is founded upon the presupposition that the real is at the same time *immanent* and *inaccessible.* The real is what always "sticks" to the representation as its other or reverse side. This reverse side is always immanent to the given space, but also always inaccessible. Each stroke always creates two things: the visible and the invisible, the audible and the inaudible, sense and nonsense, the imaginable and the unimaginable. In this manner, art always plays with a limit, creates it, shifts it, transgresses it, sends its "heroes" beyond it. But it also keeps the spectator on the "right" side of it.

In the most general terms, the limit at stake is that between pleasure and pain, the limit of the "pleasure principle." This limit is in itself a flexible, plastic limit. It can be given many different forms and it can very well include a portion of what lies beyond the pleasure principle. The example of the latter is what Kant calls the sublime: in the sublime, the Thing is not evoked by its veil, by its noticeable presence-in-absence, but instead is present in the *excess* of the forces (or magnitude) displayed before us. And yet, as Kant is careful to add, we can only enjoy it aesthetically if we are "in a safe place," if the destructive force that we admire does not reach us "physically." The distance, the "devoid of all interest," is the consequence of the fact that the object at stake concerns us at the very core of our being. Art is the very process of creating this distance. But it is crucial not to forget that there is a double movement involved in this creation. The point is not that there is first this unspeakable Thing and that art enters the scene to make it possible for us to relate to it. Art is not simply a mediator between the subject and the Thing, but rather, art is what creates this Thing in the first place. This brings us back to the notion of what is "excluded in the interior": the arch-gesture of art is precisely that of creating an "excluded interior," of producing the very void around which it spreads its "net."

Notes

1. Jacques Lacan, *The Seminar of Jacques Lacan, Book VII: The Ethics of Psychoanalysis (1959-1960)*, ed. Jacques-Alain Miller, trans. Dennis Porter (London: Routledge, 1992), 130. (Emphasis added).
2. *The Ethics of Psychoanalysis*, 101.
3. See Friedrich Nietzsche, *On the Genealogy of Morals*, trans. Walter Kaufmann (New York: Vintage, 1969), III, 6.
4. This point was already made by Heidegger. See his text, "Kant's Doctrine of the Beautiful: Its Misinterpretation by Schopenhauer and Nietzsche," in *Nietzsche: A Critical Reader*, ed. Peter R. Sedgwick (Oxford and Cambridge: Blackwell, 1995).
5. Immanuel Kant, *Critique of Judgment*, trans. W. S. Pluhar (Indianapolis: Hackett Publishing Company, 1987), 47.
6. See Gilles Deleuze, *Nietzsche* (Paris: PUF, 1965), 34-35.
7. Edgar Allan Poe, *The Complete Tales and Poems of Edgar Allan Poe* (New York: Random House, 1987), 164.
8. This is, of course, Lacan's well-known definition of sublimation.
9. Ibid., 239.
10. Ibid., 238.
11. Friedrich Nietzsche, *The Will to Power*, trans. Walter Kaufmann and R. J Hollingdale, ed. Walter Kaufmann (New York: Vintage, 1967).
12. *The Ethics of Psychoanalysis*, 161.
13. Ibid., 162.

14. Ibid., 111.

15. Jacques-Alain Miller has pointed out that the object that corresponds to the drive is "satisfaction as object." Cf. "On Perversion," in *Reading Seminars I and II. Return to Freud*, ed. B. Fink, R. Feldstein, M. Jaanus (Albany: SUNY Press, 1995), 313. So, contrary to the common belief, sublimation does not proceed from some "unnatural," "depraved," or "unacceptable" desire to something more "natural" (in the sense of being more acceptable), but rather from something perfectly natural (sucking a nipple in order to be fed) to something "unnatural" (sucking a woman's breast or a penis for the sake of sucking, for the very pleasure of sucking).

16. One could also say that the logic at stake is that of a supplement.

17. *The Ethics of Psychoanalysis*, 99.

5

Lacan between Cultural Studies and Cognitivism

Slavoj Žižek

I. CULTURAL STUDIES VERSUS THE "THIRD CULTURE"

The Struggle for Intellectual Hegemony

We are witnessing today the struggle for intellectual hegemony—for who will occupy the universal place of the "public intellectual"—between post-modern-deconstructionist cultural studies and the cognitivist popularizers of "hard" sciences, that is, the proponents of the so-called "third culture." This struggle, which caught the attention of the general public first through the so-called "de Man affair" (where opponents endeavored to prove the proto-Fascist irrationalist tendencies of deconstruction), reached its peak in the Sokal-*Social Text* affair. In cultural studies, "theory" usually refers to a mixture of literary/cinema criticism, mass culture, ideology, queer studies, and so on. It is worth quoting here the surprised reaction of Dawkins:

> I noticed, the other day, an article by a literary critic called "Theory: What Is It?" Would you believe it? "Theory" turned out to mean "theory in literary criticism."...The very word "theory" has been hijacked for some extremely narrow parochial literary purpose—as though Einstein didn't have theories; as though Darwin didn't have theories.[1]

Dawkins is here in deep solidarity with his great opponent Stephen Jay Gould, who also complains that "there's something of a conspiracy among literary intellectuals to think they own the intellectual landscape and the reviewing sources, when in fact there is a group of nonfiction writers, largely from sciences, who have a whole host of fascinating ideas that people want to read about."[2] These quotes clearly stake the terms of the debate as the fight for ideological hegemony in the precise sense this term acquired in Ernesto Laclau's writings: the fight over a particular content that always "hegemonizes" the apparently neutral universal term. The third culture comprises the vast field that reaches from the evolutionary theory debate (Dawkins and Dennett versus Gould) through physicists dealing with quantum physics and cosmology (Hawking, Weinberg, Capra), cognitive scientists (Dennett again, Marvin Minsky), neurologists (Sacks), the theorists of chaos (Mandelbrot, Stewart), authors dealing with the cognitive and general social impact of the digitalization of our daily lives, up to the theorists of auto-poetic systems who endeavor to develop a universal formal notion of self-organizing emerging systems that can be applied to "natural" living organisms and species as well as social "organisms" (the behavior of markets and other large groups of interacting social agents). Three things should be noted here: (1) as a rule, we are not dealing with scientists themselves (although they are often the same individuals), but with authors who address a large public in such a way that their success outdoes by far the public appeal of cultural studies (suffice it to recall the big bestsellers of Sacks, Hawking, Dawkins and Gould); (2) as in the case of cultural studies, we are not dealing with a homogenized field, but with a rhizomatic multitude connected through "family resemblances," within which authors are often engaged in violent polemics, but where interdisciplinary connections also flourish (between evolutionary biology and cognitive sciences, and so on); (3) as a rule, authors active in this domain are sustained by a kind of missionary zeal, by a shared awareness that they all participate in a unique shift in the global paradigm of knowledge.

As a kind of manifesto of this orientation, one could quote the "Introduction" to *The Third Culture: Beyond the Scientific Revolution*, in which the editor (John Brockman) nicely presents the large narrative that sustains the collective identification of the various scientists interviewed in the book.[3] According to Brockman, back in the '40s and '50s, the idea of a public intellectual was identified with an academic versed in "soft" human (or social) sciences who addressed issues of common interest, took a stance on the great issues of the day and thus triggered or participated in large and passionate public debates. What then occurred, with the onslaught of "French" postmodern deconstructionist theory, was the passing of that generation of public thinkers and their replacement by "bloodless academics," that is, by cultural scientists whose pseudo-radical stance against "power" or "hegemonic discourse" effectively involves the growing disappearance of direct and actual political engagements outside the narrow confines of academia, as well as the increasing self-enclosure in an elitist jargon that precludes the very possibility of functioning as an intellectual engaged in public debates. Happily, however, this retreat of the "public intellectual" was counteracted by the surge of the third culture, by the emergence of a new type of public intellectual, the third culture author, who, in the eyes of the general public, more and more stands for the one "supposed to know," trusted to reveal the keys to the great secrets that concern us all. The problem is here again the gap between effective "hard" sciences and their third culture ideological proponents who elevate scientists into subjects supposed to know, not only for ordinary people who buy these volumes in masses, but also for postmodern theorists themselves who are intrigued by it, "in love with it," and suppose that these scientists "really know something about the ultimate mystery of being." The encounter here is failed. No, popular third-culturalists do *not* possess the solution that would solve the crisis of cultural studies; they do not have what cultural studies is lacking. The love encounter is thus failed: the beloved does not stretch his or her hand back and return love.

The "Third Culture" as Ideology

It is thus crucial to distinguish here between science itself and its inherent ideologization, its sometimes subtle transformation into a new holistic "paradigm" (the new code name for "world view"). A series of notions (complementarity, anthropic principle, and so on) are here doubly inscribed, functioning as scientific *and* ideological terms. It is difficult to effectively estimate the extent to which the third culture is infested with ideology. Among its obvious ideological appropriations (but are they merely secondary appropriations?) one should, again, note at least two obvious cases: first, the often present New Age inscription, in which the shift in paradigm is interpreted as an advance beyond the Cartesian mechanistic-materialist paradigm toward a new holistic approach that brings us back to the wisdom of ancient Oriental thought (the Tao of physics, and so on). Sometimes, this is even radicalized into the assertion that the scientific shift in the predominant paradigm is an epiphenomenon of the fact that humanity is on the verge of the biggest spiritual shift in its entire history, that we are entering a new epoch in which egoistic individualism will be replaced by a transindividual cosmic awareness. The second case is the "naturalization" of certain specific social phenomena, clearly discernible in so-called cyber-revolutionism, that relies on the notion of cyberspace (or the Internet) as a self-evolving "natural" organism; the "naturalization of culture" (market, society, and so on as living organisms) overlaps here with the "culturalization of nature" (life itself is conceived as a set of self-reproducing information—"genes are memes"). This new notion of life is thus neutral with respect to the distinction between natural and cultural (or "artificial") processes—the Earth (as Gaia) as well as the global market both appear as gigantic self-regulated living systems whose basic structure is defined in terms of the process of coding and decoding, of passing information, and so on. So, while cyberspace ideologists can dream about the next step of evolution in which we will no longer be mechanically interacting "Cartesian" individuals, in which individuals will cut their substantial links to their bodies and conceive of themselves as part of the new holistic mind that lives and acts through them, what is obfuscated in such direct "naturalization" of the Internet or market is the set of power relations—of political decisions, of institutional conditions—within which "organisms" like the Internet (or the market, or capitalism) can only thrive. We are dealing here with an all too fast metaphoric transposition of certain biological-evolutionist concepts to the study of the history of human civilization, like the jump from "genes" to "memes," that is, the idea that not only do human beings use language to reproduce themselves, multiply their power and knowledge, and so on, but also, at perhaps a more fundamental level, language itself uses human beings to replicate and expand itself, to gain a new wealth of meanings, and so on.

The standard counter-argument cultural studies' proponents make to third culture criticism is that the loss of the public intellectual bemoaned in these complaints is effectively the loss of the traditional type (usually white and male) of modernist intellectual. In our postmodernist era, that intellectual was replaced by the proliferation of theoreticians who operate in a different mode (replacing concern with one big issue with a series of localized strategic interventions) and who effectively do address issues that concern the public at large (racism and multiculturalism, sexism, how to overcome the Eurocentrist curriculum, and so on) and thus trigger public debates (like the "political correctness" or sexual harassment controversies). Although this answer is all too easy, the fact remains that themes addressed by cultural studies do stand at the center of public politico-ideological debates (hybrid multiculturalism versus the need for a close community identification, abortion and queer rights versus Moral Majority fundamentalism, and so on), while the first thing that strikes one apropos of the third culture is how their proponents, busy as they are clarifying the ultimate enigmas ("reading the mind of God," as Hawking was once designated), silently pass over the burning questions that effectively occupy the center stage of current politico-ideological debates.

Finally, one should note that, in spite of the necessary distinction between science and ideology, the obscurantist New Age ideology is *an immanent outgrowth of modern science itself* —from David Bohm to Fritjof Capra, examples abound of different versions of "dancing Wu Li masters," teaching us about the Tao of physics, the "end of the Cartesian paradigm," the significance of the anthropic principle and holistic approach, and so on.[4] To avoid any misunderstanding, as an old-fashioned dialectical materialist, I am ferociously opposed to these obscurantist appropriations of quantum physics and astronomy. These obscurantist sprouts, I believe, are not simply imposed from outside, but function as what Louis Althusser would have called a "spontaneous ideology" among scientists themselves, as a kind of spiritualist supplement to the predominant reductionist-proceduralist attitude of "only what can be precisely defined and measured counts." What is much more worrying than cultural studies' "excesses" are the New Age obscurantist appropriations of today's "hard" sciences that, in order to legitimize their position, invoke the authority of science itself ("today's science has outgrown the mechanistic materialism and points toward a new spiritual holistic stance…"). Significantly, the defenders of scientific realism (like Bricmont and Sokal) only briefly refer to some "subjectivist" formulations of Heisenberg and Bohr that can give rise to relativist/historicist misappropriations, qualifying them as the expression of their author's philosophy, not part of the scientific edifice of quantum physics itself. Here, however, problems begin: Bohr's and Heisenberg's "subjectivist" formulations are not a marginal phenomenon, but were canonized as "Copenhagen orthodoxy," that is, as the "official" interpretation of the ontological consequences of quantum physics. The fact is, the moment one wants to provide an ontological account of quantum physics (which notion of reality fits its results), paradoxes emerge that undermine standard common sense scientistic objectivism. This fact is constantly emphasized by scientists themselves, who oscillate between the simple suspension of the ontological question (quantum physics functions, so do not try to understand it, just do the calculations ...) and different ways out of the deadlock (Copenhagen orthodoxy, the Many Worlds Interpretation, some version of the "hidden variable" theory that would save the notion of a singular and unique objective reality, like the one proposed by David Bohm, which nonetheless involves paradoxes of its own, like the notion of causality that runs backwards in time).

The more fundamental problem beneath these perplexities is: can we simply renounce the ontological question and limit ourselves to the mere functioning of the scientific apparatus, its calculations and measurements? A further impasse concerns the necessity to somehow relate scientific discoveries to everyday language, to translate them into it. It can be argued that problems emerge only when we try to translate the results of quantum physics back into our common sense notions of reality. But is it possible to resist this temptation? All these topics are widely discussed in the literature on quantum physics, so they have nothing to do with cultural studies' (mis) appropriation of sciences. It was Richard Feynman himself who, in his famous statement, claimed that "nobody really understands quantum physics," implying that one can no longer translate its mathematical-theoretical edifice into the terms of our everyday notions of reality. The impact of modern physics *was* the shattering of the traditional naïve-realist epistemological edifice: sciences themselves opened up a gap in which obscurantist sprouts were able to grow. So, instead of putting all the scorn on poor cultural studies, it would be much more productive to approach anew the old topic of the precise epistemological and ontological implications of the shifts in the "hard" sciences themselves.

The Impasse of Historicism

On the other hand, the problem with cultural studies, at least in its predominant form, is that it *does* involve a kind of cognitive suspension (the abandonment of the consideration of the inherent truth-value of the theory under consideration) characteristic of historicist relativism. When a typical cultural theorist deals with a philosophical or psychoanalytic edifice, the analysis focuses exclusively on unearthing its hidden patriarchal, Eurocentrist, identitarian "bias," without even asking the naïve, but nonetheless necessary questions: "OK, but what *is* the structure of the universe? How *is* the human psyche "really" working?" Such questions are not even taken seriously in cultural studies, since it simply tends to reduce them to the historicist reflection upon conditions in which certain notions emerged as the result of historically specific power relations. Furthermore, in a typically rhetorical move, cultural studies denounces the very attempt to draw a clear line of distinction between, say, true science and pre-scientific mythology, as part of the Eurocentrist procedure to impose its own hegemony by devaluating the Other as not-yet-scientific. In this way, we end up arranging and analyzing science proper, premodern "wisdom," and other forms of knowledge as different discursive formations evaluated not with regard to their inherent truth-value, but with regard to their socio-political status and impact (a native "holistic" wisdom can thus be considered much more "progressive" than the "mechanistic" Western science responsible for the forms of modern domination). The problem with such a procedure of historicist relativism is that it continues to rely on a set of silent (non-thematized) ontological and epistemological presuppositions about the nature of human knowledge and reality—usually a proto-Nietzschean notion that knowledge is not only embedded in, but also generated by, a complex set of discursive strategies of power (re)production. So it is crucial to emphasize that, at this point, Lacan parts with cultural studies' historicism. For Lacan, modern science is resolutely *not* one of the "narratives" comparable in principle to other modes of "cognitive mapping." Modern science touches the real in a way totally absent in premodern discourses.

Cultural studies here needs to be put in its proper context. After the demise of the great philosophical schools in the late '70s, European academic philosophy itself, with its basic hermeneutical-historical stance, paradoxically shares with cultural studies the stance of cognitive suspension. Excellent studies have recently been produced on great past authors, yet they focus on the correct reading of the author in question, while mostly ignoring the naïve, but unavoidable question of truth-value—not only questions such as "Is this the right reading of Descartes' notion of the body? Is this what Descartes' notion of the body has to repress in order to retain its consistency?" and so on, but also "Which, then, *is* the true status of the body? How do *we* stand towards Descartes' notion of the body?" And it seems as if these prohibited "ontological" questions are returning with a vengeance in today's third culture. What signals the recent rise of quantum physics and cosmology if not a violent and aggressive rehabilitation of the most fundamental metaphysical questions (e.g., what is the origin and putative end of the universe)? The explicit goal of people like Hawking is a version of TOE (Theory Of Everything), that is, the endeavor to discover the basic formula of the structure of the universe that one could print and wear on a T-shirt (or, for a human being, the genome that identifies what I objectively am). So, in clear contrast to cultural studies' strict prohibition of direct "ontological" questions, third culture proponents unabashedly approach the most fundamental pre-Kantian metaphysical issues—the ultimate constituents of reality, the origins and end of the universe, what consciousness is, how life emerged, and so on—as if the old dream, which died with the demise of Hegelianism, of a large synthesis of metaphysics and science, the dream of a global theory of *all* grounded in exact scientific insights, is coming alive again.

In contrast to these two versions of cognitive suspension, the cognitivist approach opts for a naïve, direct inquiry into "the nature of things" (What is perception? How did language emerge?). However, to use a worn-out phrase, by throwing out the bath water, it also loses the baby, that is, the dimension of proper philosophico-transcendental reflection. That is to say, is historicist relativism (which ultimately leads to the untenable position of solipsism) really the only alternative to the naïve scientific realism (according to which, in sciences and in our knowledge in general, we are gradually approaching the proper image of the way things really are out there, independently of our consciousness of them)? From the standpoint of a proper philosophical reflection, it can easily be shown that both of these positions miss the properly transcendental-hermeneutical level. Where does this level reside? Let us take the classical line of realist reasoning, which claims that the passage from premodern mythical thought to the modern scientific approach to reality cannot simply be interpreted as the replacement of one predominant "narrative" with another, in that the modern scientific approach definitely brings us closer to what "reality" (the "hard" reality existing independently of the scientific researcher) effectively is. A hermeneutic philosopher's basic response to this stance would be to insist that, with the passage from the premodern mythic universe to the universe of modern science, *the very notion of what "reality" (or "effectively to exist") means or what "counts" as reality has also changed*, so that we cannot simply presuppose a neutral external measure that allows us to judge that, with modern science, we come closer to the "same" reality as that with which premodern mythology was dealing. As Hegel would have put it, with the passage from the premodern mythical universe to the modern scientific universe, the measure, the standard that we implicitly use or apply in order to measure how "real" what we are dealing with is, has itself undergone a fundamental change. The modern scientific outlook involves a series of distinctions (between "objective" reality and "subjective" ideas/impressions of it; between hard neutral facts and "values" that we, the judging subjects, impose onto the facts; and so on) which are *stricto sensu* meaningless in the premodern universe. Of course, a realist can retort that this is the whole point: only with the passage to the modern scientific universe did we get an appropriate notion of what "objective reality" is, in contrast to the premodern outlook that confused "facts" and "values." Against this, the transcendental-hermeneutic philosopher would be fully justified to insist that, nonetheless, we cannot get out of the vicious circle of presupposing our result: the most fundamental way reality "appears" to us, the most fundamental way we experience what "really counts as effectively existing," is always already presupposed in our judgments of what "really exists." This transcendental level was very nicely indicated by Kuhn himself when, in his *Structure of Scientific Revolutions*, he claimed that the shift in a scientific paradigm is *more* than a mere shift in our (external) perspective on/perception of reality, but nonetheless *less* than our effectively "creating" another new reality. For that reason, the standard distinction between the social or psychological contingent conditions of a scientific invention and its objective truth-value falls short here: the very distinction between the (empirical, contingent socio-psychological) genesis of a certain scientific formation and its objective truth-value, independent of the conditions of this genesis, already presupposes a set of distinctions (e.g., between genesis and truth-value) that are by no means self-evident. So, again, one should insist here that the hermeneutic-transcendental questioning of the implicit presuppositions in no way endorses the historicist relativism typical of cultural studies.

Knowledge and Truth

In what, then, does the ultimate difference between cognitivism and cultural studies consist? On the one hand, there is neutral objective knowledge, that is, the patient empirical examination of reality. Cognitivists like to emphasize that, politically, they are not against the Left—their aim is precisely to liberate the Left from the irrationalist-relativist-elitist postmodern imposter; nonetheless, they accept the distinction between the neutral theoretical (scientific) insight and the eventual ideologico-political bias of the author. In contrast, cultural studies involves the properly dialectical paradox of a truth that relies on an engaged subjective position. This distinction between knowledge inherent to the academic institution, defined by the standards of "professionalism," and, on the other hand, the truth of a (collective) subject engaged in a struggle (elaborated, among others, by philosophers from Theodor Adorno to Alain Badiou), enables us to explain how the difference between cognitivists and proponents of cultural studies functions as a shibboleth: it is properly visible only from the side of cultural studies. So, on the one hand, one should fully acknowledge the solid scholarly status of much of the cognitivist endeavor—often, it is academia at its best; on the other hand, there is a dimension that simply eludes its grasp. Let me elaborate this relationship between truth and the accuracy of knowledge by means of a marvelous thought experiment evoked by Daniel Dennett in his *Darwin's Dangerous Idea*: You and your best friend are about to be captured by hostile forces, who know English but do not know much about your world. You both know Morse code, and hit upon the following impromptu encryption scheme: for a dash, speak a truth; for a dot, speak a falsehood. Your captors, of course, listen to you two speak: "Birds lay eggs, and toads fly. Chicago is a city, and my feet are not made of tin, and baseball is played in August," you say, answering "No" (dash-dot; dash-dash-dash) to whatever your friend has just asked. Even if your captors know Morse code, unless they can determine the truth and falsity of these sentences, they cannot detect the properties that stand for the dot and dash.[5] Dennett himself uses this example to make the point that meaning cannot be accounted for in purely syntactic inherent terms: the only way to ultimately gain access to the meaning of a statement is to situate it in its life-world context, that is, to take into account its semantic dimension, the objects and processes to which it refers. My point is rather different. As Dennett himself puts it, the two prisoners, in this case, use the world itself as a "one-time pad." Although the truth-value of their statements is not indifferent but crucial, it is not this truth-value as such, in itself, that matters; what matters is the translation of truth-value into a differential series of pluses and minuses (dashes and dots) that delivers the true message in Morse code. And is something similar not going on in the psychoanalytic process? Although the truth-value of the patient's statements is not indifferent, what really matters is not this truth-value as such, but the way the very alternation of truths and lies discloses the patient's desire—a patient also uses reality itself (the way [s]he relates to it) as a "one-time pad" to encrypt his or her desire. And, in the same way, theory uses the very truth-value (accuracy) of post-theoretical knowledge as a medium to articulate its own truth-message.

On the other hand, politically correct proponents of cultural studies often pay for their arrogance and lack of a serious approach by confusing truth (the engaged subjective position) and knowledge, that is, by disavowing the gap that separates them, by directly subordinating knowledge to truth (say, a quick socio-critical dismissal of a specific science like quantum physics or biology without proper acquaintance with the inherent conceptual structure of this field of knowledge). Essentially, the problem of cultural studies is often the lack of specific disciplinary skills: a literary theorist without proper knowledge of philosophy can write disparaging remarks on Hegel's phallogocentrism, on film, and so on. What we are dealing with here is a kind of false universal critical capacity to pass judgments on everything without proper knowledge. With all its criticism of traditional philosophical universalism, cultural studies effectively functions as a kind of *ersatz*-philosophy, and notions are thus transformed into ideological universals. In postcolonial studies, for instance, the notion of "colonization" starts to function as a hegemonic notion and is elevated to a universal paradigm, so that in relations between the sexes, the male sex colonizes the female sex, the upper classes colonize the lower classes, and so on. Especially with some "progressive" interpreters of contemporary biology, it is popular to focus on the way the opposing positions are overdetermined by the politico-ideological stance of their authors. Does Dawkins' "Chicago gangster theory of life," this reductionist determinist theory about "selfish genes" caught in a deadly struggle for survival, not express the stance of a competitive, bourgeois individualist society? Is Gould's emphasis on sudden genetic change and ex-aptation not a sign of the more supple, dialectical and "revolutionary" Leftist stance of its author? Do those who emphasize spontaneous cooperation and emerging order (like Lynn Margulis) not express the longing for a stable organic order, for a society that functions as a "corporate body"? Do we thus not have here the scientific expression of the basic triad of Right, Center and Left—of the organicist conservative notion of society as a whole, of the bourgeois individualist notion of society as the space of competition between individuals, and of the revolutionary theorist notion of sudden change? (Of course, the insistence on a holistic approach and emerging order can be given a different accent: it can display the conservative longing for a stable order, or the progressive utopian belief in a new society of solidary cooperation where order grows spontaneously from below and is not imposed from above.) The standard form of the opposition is the one between the "cold" mechanist probing into causality, displaying the attitude of the scientific manipulator in the service of the exploitative domination of nature, and the new "holistic" approach focused on spontaneously emerging order and cooperation, pointing toward what Andrew Ross called a "kinder, gentler science." The mistake here is the same as that of Stalinist Marxism, which opposed "bourgeois" to "proletarian" science, or that of pseudo-radical feminism, which opposes "masculine" to "feminine" discourse as two self-enclosed wholes engaged in warfare. We do not have *two* sciences, but *one* universal science split from within, that is, caught in the battle for hegemony.[6]

Theoretical State Apparatuses

The academically-recognized "radical thought" in the liberal West does not operate in a void, but is indeed a part of power relations. Apropos of cultural studies, one has to ask again the old Benjaminian question: not "How does one explicitly *relate* to power?" but "How is one *situated within* predominant power relations?" Does cultural studies not also function as a discourse that pretends to be critically self-reflective, to render visible the predominant power relations, while it effectively obfuscates its own mode of participating in them? So it would be productive to apply to cultural studies itself the Foucauldian notion of productive "bio-power" as opposed to "repressive"/ prohibitory legal power: what if the field of cultural studies, far from effectively threatening today's global relations of domination, fits within this framework perfectly, in the same way that sexuality and the "repressive" discourses that regulate it are fully complementary? What if the criticism of patriarchal/ identitarian ideology betrays an ambiguous fascination with it, rather than a will committed to undermining it? There is a way to *avoid* responsibility and/or guilt precisely by emphasizing one's responsibility or too readily assuming guilt in an exaggerated way, as in the case of the politically correct white male academic who emphasizes the guilt of racist phallogocentrism, and uses this admission of guilt as a stratagem *not* to confront the way he, as a "radical" intellectual, perfectly fits the existing power relations of which he pretends to be thoroughly critical. Crucial here is the shift from British to American cultural studies. Even if we find the same themes and notions in both, the socio-ideological functioning is thoroughly different: we shift from the effective engagement with working class culture to the academic radical chic.

However, despite these critical remarks, the very fact that there is resistance to cultural studies proves that it remains a foreign body unable to fit fully into the existing academy. Cognitivism is ultimately the attempt to get rid of this intruder, to re-establish the standard functioning of academic knowledge—"professional," rational, empirical, problem-solving, and so on. The distinction between cognitivism and cultural studies is thus not simply the distinction between two doctrines or two theoretical approaches; it is ultimately a much more radical distinction between two totally different modalities or, rather, *practices* of knowledge, inclusive of two different institutional apparatuses of knowledge. This dimension of "theoretical state apparatuses," to use the Althusserian formulation, is crucial: if we do not take it into account, we simply miss the point of the antagonism between cognitivism and cultural studies. It is no wonder that cognitivists like to emphasize their opposition to psychoanalysis: two exemplary cases of such non-academic knowledge are, of course, Marxism and psychoanalysis. Psychoanalysis differs from cognitivist psychology and psychotherapy in at least three crucial features: (1) since it does not present itself as empirically-tested objective knowledge, there is the perennial problem (in the United States, where psychiatric care is sometimes covered by medical insurance) of the extent to which the state or insurance will reimburse the patient; (2) for the same reason, psychoanalysis has inherent difficulties in integrating itself into the academic edifice of psychology or medical psychiatry departments, so it usually functions as a parasitic entity that attaches itself to cultural studies, comparative literature or psychology departments; (3) as to their inherent organization, psychoanalytic communities do not function as "normal" academic societies (like sociological, mathematical or other societies). From the standpoint of "normal" academic societies, the psychoanalytic society cannot but appear as a "dogmatic" discipline engaged in eternal factional struggles between sub-groups dominated by a strong authoritarian or charismatic leader; conflicts within psychoanalytic communities are not resolved through rational argumentation and empirical testing, but rather resemble sectarian religious struggles. In short, the phenomenon of (personal) transference functions here in an entirely different way than in the "standard" academic community. (The dynamics in Marxist communities are somewhat similar.) In the same way that Marxism interprets the resistance against its insights as the "result of the class struggle in theory," as accounted for by its very object, psychoanalysis also interprets the resistance against itself to be the result of the very unconscious processes that are its topic. In both cases, theory is caught in a self-referential loop: it is in a way *the theory about the resistance against itself.* Concerning this crucial point, the situation today is entirely different than, almost the opposite of, that of the '60s and early '70s when "marginal" disciplines (like the cultural studies' version of psychoanalysis) were perceived as "anarchic," as liberating us from the "repressive" authoritarian regime of the standard academic discipline. What cognitivist critics of cultural studies play upon is the common perception that, today, (what remains of) the cultural studies' version of psychoanalysis is perceived as sectarian, Stalinist, authoritarian, engaged in ridiculous pseudo-theological factional struggles in which problems over the party line prevail over open empirical research and rational argumentation. Cognitivists present themselves as the fresh air that does away with this close and stuffy atmosphere—finally, one is free to formulate and test different hypotheses, no longer "terrorized" by some dogmatically imposed global party line. We are thus far from the anti-academic/establishment logic of the '60s: today, academia presents itself as the place of open, free discussion, as liberating us from the stuffy constraints of "subversive" cultural studies. And although, of course, the "regression" into authoritarian prophetic discourse is one of the dangers that threatens cultural studies, its inherent temptation, one should nonetheless focus attention on how the cognitivist stance succeeds in unproblematically presenting the framework of the institutional academic university discourse as the very locus of intellectual freedom.

II. IS FREEDOM NOTHING BUT A CONCEIVED NECESSITY?

You Cannot, Because You Should Not!

So, how does Lacanian theory enable us to avoid the impasse of cultural studies and to confront the challenge of the cognitivist and/or evolutionary naturalization of the human subject? In Andrew Niccol's futuristic thriller *Gatacca* (1998), Ethan Hawke and Uma Thurman prove their love for each other by throwing away the hair each partner provides to be analyzed in order to establish his or her genetic quality. In this futuristic society, authority (access to the privileged elite) is established "objectively," through genetic analysis of the newborn—we no longer have symbolic authority proper, since authority is directly grounded in the real of the genome. As such, *Gatacca* merely extrapolates the prospect, opened up today, of the direct legitimization of social authority and power in the real of the genetic code: "by eliminating artificial forms of inequality, founded on power and culture, socially egalitarian programs could eventually highlight and crystallize natural forms of inequality far more dramatically than ever before, in a new hierarchical order founded on the genetic code."[7] Against this prospect, it is not enough to insist that the democratic principle of what Etienne Balibar calls *egaliberté* has nothing to do with the genetic-biological similarity of human individuals, but aims instead at the principal equality of subjects qua participants in the symbolic space. *Gatacca* confronts us with the following dilemma: is the only way to retain our dignity as humans by way of accepting some limitation, of stopping short of full insight into our genome, short of our full naturalization, that is, by way of a gesture of "I do not want to know what you objectively/really are, I accept you for what you are"?

Among the modern philosophers, it was Kant who most forcefully confronted this predicament, constraining our knowledge of the causal interconnection of objects to the domain of phenomena in order to make a place for noumenal freedom, which is why the hidden truth of Kant's *"You can, therefore you must!"* is its reversal: *You cannot, because you should not!* The ethical problems of cloning seem to point in this direction. Those who oppose cloning argue that we *should not* pursue it, at least not on human beings, because it is *not possible* to reduce a human being to a positive entity whose innermost psychic properties can be manipulated—biogenetic manipulation *cannot* touch the core of human personality, so we should prohibit it. Is this not another variation on Wittgenstein's paradox of *prohibiting the impossible*: "What we cannot speak about we must pass over in silence"? The underlying fear that gains expression in this prohibition, of course, is that the order of reason is actually inverted, that is, that the ontological impossibility is grounded in ethics: we should claim that we cannot do it, because otherwise *we may well do it*, with catastrophic ethical consequences. If conservative Catholics effectively believe in the immortality of the human soul and the uniqueness of human personality, if they insist we are not just the result of the interaction between our genetic code and our environs, then why do they oppose cloning and genetic manipulations? In other words, is it not that *these Christian opponents of cloning themselves secretly believe in the power of scientific manipulation, in its capacity to stir up the very core of our personality?* Of course, their answer would be that human beings, by treating themselves as just the result of the interaction between their genetic codes and their environs, freely renounce their dignity: the problem is not genetic manipulation as such, but the fact that its acceptance signals how human beings conceive of themselves as just another biological machine and thus rob themselves of their unique spirituality. However, the answer to this is, again: but why should we not endorse genetic manipulation *and* simultaneously insist that human beings are free responsible agents, since we accept the proviso that these manipulations do not really affect the core of our soul? Why do Christians still talk about the "unfathomable mystery of conception" that man should not meddle with, as if, nonetheless, by pursuing our biogenetic explorations, we may touch some secret better left in shadow—in short, as if, by cloning our bodies, we *at the same time also clone our immortal souls?*

So, again, we are back at the well-known conservative wisdom that claims that the only way to save human freedom and ethical dignity is to restrain our cognitive capacities and renounce probing too deeply into the nature of things. Today's sciences themselves seem to point toward a way out of this predicament. Does contemporary cognitivism not often produce formulations that sound uncannily familiar to those acquainted with different versions of ancient and modern philosophy, from the Buddhist notion of Void and the German Idealist notion of reflexivity as constitutive of the subject up to the Heideggerian notion of "being-in-the-world" or the deconstructionist one of *différance?* The temptation arises here to fill in the gap by either reducing philosophy to science, claiming that modern naturalizing cognitivism "realizes" philosophical insights, translating them into acceptable scientific form, or, on the contrary, by claiming that, with these insights, postmodern science breaks out of the "Cartesian paradigm" and approaches the level of authentic philosophical thought. This short-circuit between science and philosophy appears today in a multitude of guises: Heideggerian cognitivism (Hubert Dreyfuss), cognitivist Buddhism (Francisco Varela), the combination of Oriental thought with quantum physics (Capra's "Tao of physics"), up to deconstructionist evolutionism. Let's take a brief look at the two main versions of this short-circuit.

1. Deconstructionist Evolutionism

There are obvious parallels between the recent popularized readings of Darwin (from Gould to Dawkins and Dennett) and Derridean deconstruction. Does Darwinism not practice a kind of "deconstruction," not only of natural teleology, but also of the very idea of nature as a well-ordered positive system of species? Does the strict Darwinian notion of "adaptation" not claim that, precisely, *organisms do not directly "adapt,"* that there is *stricto sensu* no "adaptation" in the teleological sense of the term? Contingent genetic changes occur, and some of them enable some organisms to function better and survive in an environment that is itself fluctuating and articulated in a complex way, but there is no linear adaptation to a stable environment: when something unexpectedly changes in the environment, a feature which hitherto prevented full "adaptation" can suddenly become crucial for the organism's survival. So Darwinism effectively prefigures a version of Derridean *différance* or of the Freudian *Nachträglichkeit,* according to which contingent and meaningless genetic changes are retroactively used (or "exapted," as Gould would have put it) in a manner appropriate for survival. In other words, what Darwin provides is a model explanation of how a state of things which appears to involve a well-ordered teleological economy (animals doing things "in order to ..."), is effectively the outcome of a series of meaningless changes.

The temporality here is future anterior, that is, "adaptation" is something that always and by definition "will have been." And is this enigma of how (the semblance of) teleological and meaningful order can emerge from contingent and meaningless occurrences not also central to deconstruction?

One can thus effectively claim that Darwinism (of course, in its true radical dimension, not as a vulgarized evolutionism) "deconstructs" not only teleology or divine intervention in nature, but also the very notion of nature as a stable positive order—this makes the silence of deconstruction about Darwinism, the absence of deconstructionist attempts to "appropriate" it, all the more enigmatic. Dennett, the great proponent of cognitivist evolutionism, himself acknowledges (ironically, no doubt, but nonetheless with an underlying serious intent) the closeness of his "pandemonium" theory of human mind to cultural studies deconstructionism in his *Consciousness Explained:* "Imagine my mixed emotions when I discovered that before I could get my version of the idea of 'the self as the center of narrative gravity' properly published in a book, it had already been satirized in a novel, David Lodge's *Nice World.* It is apparently a hot theme among the deconstructionists."[8] Furthermore, a whole school of cyberspace theorists (the best known among them is Sherry Turkle) advocate the notion that cyberspace-phenomena render palpable in our everyday experience the deconstructionist "decentered subject." According to these theorists, one should endorse the "dissemination" of the unique self into a multiplicity of competing agents, into a "collective mind," a plurality of self-images without a global coordinating center, that is operative in cyberspace and disconnect it from pathological trauma—playing in virtual spaces enables individuals to discover new aspects of "self," a wealth of shifting identities, and thus to experience the ideological mechanism of the production of self, the immanent violence and arbitrariness of this production/construction.

However, the temptation to be avoided here is precisely the hasty conclusion that Dennett is a kind of deconstructionist wolf in the sheep's clothing of empirical science. There is a gap that forever separates Dennett's evolutionary naturalization of consciousness from the deconstructionist "meta-transcendental" probing into the conditions of (im)possibility of philosophical discourse. As Derrida argues exemplarily in his "White Mythology," it is insufficient to claim that "all concepts are metaphors," that there is no pure epistemological cut, since the umbilical cord connecting abstract concepts with everyday metaphors is irreducible. First, the point is not simply that "all concepts are metaphors," but that the very difference between a concept and a metaphor is always minimally metaphorical, relying on some metaphor. Even more important is the opposite conclusion, that the very reduction of a concept to a bundle of metaphors already has to rely on some implicit *philosophical, conceptual* determination of the difference between concept and metaphor, that is to say, on the very opposition it tries to undermine.[9] We are thus forever caught in a vicious circle: true, it is impossible to adopt a philosophical stance freed from the constraints of naïve, everyday life-world attitudes and notions; however, although *impossible*, this philosophical stance is at the same time *unavoidable*. Derrida makes the same point apropos of the well-known historicist thesis that the entire Aristotelian ontology of the ten modes of being is an effect/expression of Greek grammar. The problem is that *this reduction of ontology (of ontological categories) to an effect of grammar presupposes a certain notion (categorical determination) of the relationship between grammar and ontological concepts which is itself already metaphysical-Greek.*[10]

We should always bear in mind this delicate Derridean stance, through which the twin pitfalls of naïve realism and direct philosophical foundationalism are avoided: "philosophical foundation" for our experience is *impossible*, and yet *necessary*—although all we perceive, understand and articulate, is, of course, overdetermined by a horizon of pre-understanding, this horizon itself remains ultimately impenetrable. Derrida is thus a kind of metatranscendentalist, in search of the conditions of possibility of this very philosophical discourse. If we miss this precise way in which Derrida undermines philosophical discourse *from within*, we reduce deconstruction to just another naïve historicist relativism. Derrida's position here is thus the opposite of Foucault's. In answer to a criticism that he speaks from a position whose possibility is not accounted for within the framework of his theory, Foucault cheerfully retorted: "These kinds of questions do not concern me: they belong to the police discourse with its files constructing the subject's identity!" In other words, the ultimate lesson of deconstruction seems to be that one cannot postpone *ad infinitum* the *ontological* question, and what is deeply symptomatic in Derrida is his oscillation between, on the one hand, the hyper-self-reflective approach that denounces in advance the question of "how things really are" and limits itself to third-level deconstructive comments on the inconsistencies of philosopher B's reading of philosopher A, and, on the other hand, direct "ontological" assertions about how *différance* and arche-trace designate the structure of all living things and are, as such, already operative in animal nature. One should not miss here the paradoxical interconnection between these two levels: the very feature that prevents us from forever directly grasping our intended object (the fact that our grasping is always refracted, "mediated," by a decentered otherness) is the feature that connects us with the basic proto-ontological structure of the universe.

Deconstructionism thus involves two prohibitions: it prohibits the "naïve" empiricist approach ("let us examine carefully the material in question and then generalize hypotheses about it ..."), as well as global ahistorical metaphysical theses about the origin and structure of the universe. This double prohibition that defines deconstructionism clearly and unambiguously bears witness to its Kantian transcendental origins. Is not the same double prohibition characteristic of Kant's philosophical revolution? On the one hand, the notion of the transcendental constitution of reality involves the loss of a direct naïve empiricist approach to reality; on the other hand, it involves the prohibition of metaphysics, that is, of an all-encompassing world-view providing the noumenal structure of the universe as a whole. In other words, one should always bear in mind that, far from simply expressing a belief in the constitutive power of the (transcendental) subject, Kant introduces the notion of the transcendental dimension in order to answer the fundamental and insurpassable deadlock of human existence: a human being compulsorily strives toward a global notion of truth, of a universal and necessary cognition, yet this cognition is simultaneously forever inaccessible to him or her.

2. Cognitivist Buddhism

Is the outcome any better in the emerging alliance between the cognitivist approach to mind and the proponents of Buddhist thought, where the point is not to naturalize philosophy, but rather the opposite, that is, to use the results of cognitivism in order to (re)gain access to ancient wisdom? The contemporary cognitivist denial of a unitary, stable, self-identical self—that is, the notion of the human mind as a pandemonic playground of multiple agencies, that some authors (most notably Francisco Varela)[11] link to the Buddhist denial of the self as the permanent substance underlying our mental acts/events—seems persuasive in its critical rejection of the substantial notion of self. The paradox upon which cognitivists and neo-Buddhists build is the gap between our common experience that automatically relies on and/or involves a reference to some notion of self as the underlying substance that "has" feelings and volitions and to which these mental states and acts "happen," and the fact, well known even in Europe at least from Hume onwards, that, no matter how deeply and carefully we search our self-experience, we encounter only passing, elusive mental events, and never the self as such (that is, a substance to which these events could be attributed). The conclusion drawn by cognitivists and Buddhists alike is, of course, that the notion of self is the result of an epistemological (or, in the case of Buddhism, ethico-epistemological) mistake inherent to human nature as such. The thing to do is to get rid of this delusive notion and to fully assume that there is no self, that "I" am nothing but that groundless bundle of elusive and heterogeneous (mental) events.

Is, however, this conclusion really unavoidable? Varela also rejects the Kantian solution of the self, the subject of pure apperception, as the transcendental subject nowhere to be found in our empirical experience. Here, though, one should introduce the distinction between egoless/selfless mind events or aggregates and the subject as identical to this void, to this lack of substance, itself. What if the conclusion that there is no self is too quickly drawn from the fact that there is no representation or positive idea of self? What if self is precisely the "I of the storm," the void in the center of the incessant vortex/whirlpool of elusive mental events, something like the "vacuola" in biology, the void that is nothing in itself, that has no substantial positive identity, but which nonetheless serves as the irrepresentable point of reference, as the "I" to which mental events are attributed. In Lacanian terms, one has to distinguish between the "self" as the pattern of behavioral and other imaginary and symbolic identifications (as the "self-image," as that what I perceive myself to be) and the empty point of pure negativity, the "barred" subject ($). Varela himself comes close to this when he distinguishes among: (1) the self qua the series of mental and bodily formations that has a certain degree of causal coherence and integrity through time; (2) the capitalized Self qua the hidden substantial kernel of the subject's identity (the "ego-self"), and, finally; (3) the desperate craving/grasping of the human mind for/to the self, for/to some kind of firm bedrock. From the Lacanian perspective, however, is this "endless craving" not *the subject itself*, the void that "is" subjectivity?

Neo-Buddhists are justified in criticizing cognitivist proponents of the "society of mind" notion for endorsing the irreducible split between our scientific cognition (which tells us that there is no self or free will) and the everyday experience in which we simply cannot function without presupposing a consistent self endowed with free will. Cognitivists have thus condemned themselves to a nihilistic stance of endorsing beliefs they know are wrong. The effort of neo-Buddhists is to bridge this gap by translating/transposing the very insight that there is no substantial self into our daily human experience (this is ultimately what Buddhist meditative reflection is about). When Ray Jackendoff, author of one of the ultimate cognitivist attempts to explain consciousness, suggests that our awareness-consciousness emerges from the fact that we are, precisely, *not* aware of the way awareness-consciousness itself is generated by worldly processes—that there is consciousness only insofar as its biological-organic origins remain opaque[12]—he comes very close to the Kantian insight that there is self-consciousness, that I think, only insofar as *"das Ich oder Er oder Es (das Ding), welches denkt"*[13] remains impenetrable for me. Varela's counter-argument that Jackendoff's reasoning is confused, that these processes we are unaware of are just that—processes that are not part of our daily human experience but totally beyond it, hypostatized by the cognitivist scientific practice[14]—thus misses the point. This inaccessibility of the substantial-natural self (or, rather, of the substantial-natural base to my self) *is* part of our daily non-scientific experience, precisely in the guise of our ultimate failure to find a positive element in our experience that would directly "be" our self (the experience, formulated already by Hume, that no matter how deeply we analyze our mental processes, we never find anything that would be our self). So what if one should here apply to Varela the joke about the madman who was looking for his lost key under a street light and not in the dark corner where he effectively lost it, because it was easier to search under the light? What if we are looking for the self in the wrong place, in the false evidence of positive empirical facts?

The Inaccessible Phenomenon

Our result is thus that there is effectively no way to overcome the abyss that separates the transcendental *a priori* horizon from the domain of positive scientific discoveries. On the one hand, the standard "philosophical reflection of science" (positive sciences "do not think"; they are unable to reflect on their horizon of pre-understanding accessible only to philosophy) more and more resembles an old automatic trick losing its efficiency; on the other hand, the idea that some "postmodern" science will attain the level of philosophical reflection (say, that quantum physics, by including the observer in the observed material objectivity, breaks out of the frame of scientific objectivism/naturalism and reaches the level of the transcendental constitution of reality) clearly misses the proper level of transcendental *a priori*.

It is true that modern philosophy is in a way "on the defensive" against the onslaught of science. Kant's transcendental turn is linked to the rise of modern science not only in the obvious way (providing the *a priori* of Newtonian physics), but in the more radical way of taking into account how, with the rise of modern empirical science, a direct metaphysical "theory of everything" is no longer viable and cannot be combined with science. So the only thing philosophy can do is to "phenomenalize" scientific knowledge and then to provide its *a priori* hermeneutic horizon, given the ultimate inscrutability of the universe and man. It was Adorno who had already emphasized the thorough ambiguity of Kant's notion of transcendental constitution: far from simply asserting the subject's constitutive power, it can also be read as the resigned acceptance of the *a priori limitation* of our approach to the real. And it is our contention that, if we think to the end the consequences of this notion of the transcendental subject, we can nonetheless avoid this debilitating deadlock and "save freedom." How? By reading this deadlock as its own solution, that is, by yet again displacing the epistemological obstacle into a positive ontological condition.

To avoid any misunderstanding: we are not aiming here at illegitimate short-circuits in the style of "the ontological undecidability of the quantum fluctuation grounds human freedom," but at a much more radical pre-ontological openness/gap, a "bar" of impossibility in the midst of "reality" itself. What if *there is no "universe"* in the sense of an ontologically fully-constituted cosmos? That is to say, the mistake of identifying (self)consciousness with misrecognition, with an epistemological obstacle, is that it stealthily (re)introduces the standard, premodern, "cosmological" notion of reality as a positive order of being. In such a fully-constituted, positive "chain of being," there is, of course, no place for the subject, so the dimension of subjectivity can only be conceived of as something which is strictly codependent with the epistemological misrecognition of the true positivity of being. Consequently, the only way to effectively account for the status of (self)consciousness is to assert *the ontological incompleteness of "reality" itself:* there is "reality" only insofar as there is an ontological gap, a crack, in its very heart. It is only this gap that accounts for the mysterious "fact" of transcendental freedom, that is, for a (self)consciousness that is effectively "spontaneous" and whose spontaneity is not an effect of the misrecognition of some "objective" causal process, no matter how complex and chaotic this process is. And where does *psychoanalysis* stand with regard to this deadlock? In a first approach, it may seem that psychoanalysis is the ultimate attempt to fill in the gap, to re-establish the complete causal chain that generated the "inexplicable" symptom. However, does Lacan's strict opposition between cause and the law (of causality) not point in a wholly different direction? Lacan states:

> Cause is to be distinguished from that which is determinate in a chain, in other words from the law. By way of example, think of what is pictured in the law of action and reaction. There is here, one might say, a single principle. One does not go without the other .... There is no gap here .... Whenever we speak of cause, on the other hand, there is always something anti-conceptual, something indefinite .... In short, there is a cause only in something that doesn't work.... The Freudian unconscious is situated at that point, where, between cause and that which it affects, there is always something wrong. The important thing is not that the unconscious determines neurosis—of that one Freud can quite happily, like Pontius Pilate, wash his hands. Sooner or later, something would have been found, humoral determinates, for example—for Freud, it would be quite immaterial. For what the unconscious does is to show the gap through which neurosis recreates a harmony with a real—a real that may well not be determined.[15]

The unconscious intervenes when something "goes wrong" in the order of causality that encompasses our daily activity: a slip of the tongue introduces a gap in the connection between intention-to-signify and words, a failed gesture frustrates my act. However, Lacan's point is, precisely, that psychoanalytic interpretation does not simply fill in this gap by way of providing the hidden complete network of causality that "explains" the slip: the cause whose "insistence" interrupts the normal functioning of the order of causality is not another positive entity. As Lacan emphasizes, it belongs rather to the order of the *nonrealized* or *thwarted,* that is, it is *in itself structured as a gap,* a void insisting indefinitely on its fulfillment. (The psychoanalytic name for this gap, of course, is the death drive, while its philosophical name in German Idealism is "abstract negativity," the point of absolute self-contraction that constitutes the subject as the void of pure self-relating.)

And the psychoanalytic notion of fantasy accounts precisely for the illusory/failed attempt to fill in this ontological gap. The basic paradox of the

Freudian notion of fantasy resides in the fact that it subverts the standard opposition of "subjective" and "objective." Of course, fantasy is by definition not "objective" (in the naïve sense of "existing" independently of the subject's perceptions); however, it is also not "subjective" (in the sense of being reducible to the subject's consciously experienced intuitions). Fantasy rather belongs to the "bizarre category of the objectively subjective—the way things actually, objectively seem to you even if they don't seem that way to you."[16] When, for example, the subject actually experiences a series of fantasmatic formations that interrelate as so many permutations of each other, this series is never complete; rather, it is always as if the actually experienced series presents so many variations of some underlying "fundamental" fantasy that is never actually experienced by the subject. (In Freud's "A Child Is Being Beaten," the two consciously experienced fantasies presuppose, and thus relate to, a third one, "My father is beating me," which was never actually experienced and can only be retroactively reconstructed as the presupposed reference of—or, in this case, the intermediate term between—the other two fantasies.) One can go even further and claim that, in this sense, the Freudian unconscious itself is "objectively subjective." When, for example, we claim that someone who is consciously well-disposed toward Jews nonetheless harbors profound anti-Semitic prejudices he is not consciously aware of, do we not claim that (insofar as these prejudices do not render the way Jews really are, but the way they appear to him) *he is not aware how Jews really seem to him?*

Furthermore, does this not allow us to throw a new light on the mystery of Marxian commodity fetishism? What the fetish objectivizes is "my true belief," the way things "truly seem to me," although I never effectively experience them this way—Marx himself here uses the term *"objektiv-notwendiges Schein"* (a necessarily objective appearance). So, when a critical Marxist encounters a bourgeois subject immersed in commodity fetishism, the Marxist's reproach to him is not, "A commodity may seem to you a magical object endowed with special powers, but it really is just a reified expression of relations between people"; the Marxist's actual reproach is rather, "You may think that the commodity appears to you as a simple embodiment of social relations (that, for example, money is just a kind of voucher entitling you to a part of the social product), but *this is not how things really seem to you*—in your social reality, by means of your participation in social exchange, you bear witness to the uncanny fact that a commodity really appears to you as a magical object endowed with special powers."

This is also one of the ways of specifying the meaning of Lacan's assertion of the subject's constitutive "decenterment." The point is not that my subjective experience is regulated by objective unconscious mechanisms that are "decentered" with regard to my self-experience and, as such, beyond my control (a point asserted by every materialist), but rather something much more unsettling: I am deprived of even my most intimate "subjective" experience, of the way things "really seem to me," of the fundamental fantasy that constitutes and guarantees the core of my being, since I can never consciously experience it and assume it. According to the standard view, the dimension that is constitutive of subjectivity is that of the phenomenal (self)experience. In other words, I am a subject the moment I can say to myself: "No matter what unknown mechanism governs my acts, perceptions and thoughts, nobody can take from me what I see and feel now." Say, when I am passionately in love, and a biochemist informs me that all my intense sentiments are just the result of biochemical processes in my body, I can answer him by clinging to the appearance: "All you're saying may be true, but, nonetheless, nothing can take from me the intensity of the passion that I am experiencing now ...." Lacan's point, however, is that the psychoanalyst is the one who, precisely, *can* take this from the subject, insofar as his or her ultimate aim is to deprive the subject of the very fundamental fantasy that regulates the universe of the subject's (self)experience. The Freudian subject of the unconscious emerges only when a key aspect of the subject's *phenomenal* (self)experience (his or her fundamental fantasy), becomes *inaccessible* (that is, is primordially repressed). At its most radical, the unconscious is the *inaccessible phenomenon,* not the objective mechanism, that regulates my phenomenal experience. So, in contrast to the commonplace that we are dealing with a subject the moment an entity displays signs of "inner life"—that is, of a fantasmatic self-experience that cannot be reduced to external behavior—one should claim that what characterizes human subjectivity proper is rather the gap that separates the two, that is, the fact that fantasy, at its most elementary, becomes inaccessible to the subject; it is this inaccessibility that makes the subject "empty" ($). We thus obtain a relationship that totally subverts the standard notion of the subject who directly experiences him or herself, and his or her "inner states": an "impossible" relationship between the *empty, nonphenomenal subject* and the *phenomena that remain inaccessible to the subject*—the very relation registered by Lacan's formula of fantasy, $◇a.

Geneticists predict that in about ten to fifteen years, they will be able to identify and manipulate each individual's exact genome. Potentially, at least, each individual will thus have at his or her disposal the complete formula of what (s)he "objectively is." How will this "knowledge in the real," the fact that I will be able to locate and identify myself completely as an object in reality, affect the status of subjectivity? Will it lead to the end of human subjectivity? Lacan's answer is negative: what will continue to elude the geneticist is not my phenomenal self-experience (say, the experience of a love passion that no knowledge of the genetic and other material mechanisms determining it can take from me), but the "objectively subjective" fundamental fantasy, the fantasmatic core inaccessible to my conscious experience. Even if science formulates the genetic formula of what I objectively am, it will still be unable to formulate my "objectively subjective" fantasmatic identity, this objectal counterpoint to my subjectivity, which is neither subjective (experienced) nor objective.

Notes

1. John Brockman, *The Third Culture: Beyond the Scientific Revolution* (New York: Simon and Schuster, 1996), 23.
2. Ibid., 21.
3. Ibid., "Introduction."
4. See, as one among the thousand paradigmatic passages: "Is there, as David Bohm says, an 'implicate order' to matter that is beyond our present comprehension and presumes a 'wholeness' to all things? Can we conceive of a 'Tao of physics,' as Fritjof Capra's million-selling book terms it, in which Eastern philosophies parallel the mind-wrenching paradoxes of the quantum world?" (Pat Kane, "There's Method in the Magic," in *The Politics of Risk Society*, ed. Jane Franklin [Oxford: Polity Press, 1998], 78-79.)
5. See Daniel C. Dennett, *Darwin's Dangerous Idea* (New York: Simon and Schuster, 1995), 421.
6. It is interesting to note how the opposition of "hard" science, whose conceptual structure embodies the stance of domination, and "gentle" science bent on collaboration and so on, comes dangerously close to the New Age ideology of two mental universes, masculine and feminine, competitive and cooperative, rational-dissecting and intuitive-encompassing. In short, we come dangerously close to the premodern sexualization of the universe, which is conceived of as the tension between the two principles, Masculine and Feminine.
7. Perry Anderson, "A Sense of the Left," *New Left Review* 231 (September/October 1998): 76.
8. Daniel C. Dennett, *Consciousness Explained* (New York: Little, Brown and Company, 1991), 410.
9. See Jacques Derrida, "La mythologie blanche," *Poetique* 5 (1971): 1-52.
10. See Jacques Derrida, "Le supplement de la copule" in *Marges de la philosophie* (Paris: Minuit, 1972).
11. See Francisco Varela, Evan Thompson, and Eleanor Rosh, *The Embodied Mind* (Cambridge: MIT Press, 1993).
12. See Ray Jackendoff, *Consciousness and the Computational Mind* (Cambridge: MIT Press, 1987).
13. "The I/Ego or He or It (the Thing), which thinks."

14. See Varela, op. cit., 126.

15. Jacques Lacan, *The Four Fundamental Concepts of Psycho-Analysis,* trans. Alan Sheridan (New York: Norton, 1978), 22.

16. Dennett, *Consciousness Explained,* 132. (Dennett, of course, evokes this concept in a purely negative way, as a nonsensical *contradictio in adjecto.*)

6

The Enjoying Machine

Mladen Dolar

In his seminar *The Ethics of Psychoanalysis*, Lacan writes the following remarks on the function of the chorus in Greek tragedy:

> When you go to the theater in the evening, you are preoccupied by the affairs of the day, by the pen that you have lost, by the check that you will have to sign the next day .... Your emotions are taken charge of by the healthy order displayed on the stage. The Chorus takes care of them. The emotional commentary is done for you .... Therefore you don't have to worry; even if you don't feel anything, the Chorus will feel in your stead. Why after all can one imagine that the effect on you may be achieved, at least a small dose of it, even if you didn't tremble that much? To be honest, I'm not sure if the spectator ever trembles that much.[1]

This is indeed a most curious device: we can delegate our terror and pity onto the chorus, who feels for us, grieves for us, trembles for us, and frees us of our burden of participation and emotion. Whatever we may be thinking or feeling while attending the performance, we "objectively" experience terror and pity via our stand-ins. This point was taken up by Slavoj Žižek in *Enjoy Your Symptom!*, where he proposed some other instances of the same device such as the women hired to mourn and cry over the dead in the place of the mourner, a practice still followed in certain parts of the world; the prayer wheels of the Buddhist monks; and, to come closer to our everyday experience, the canned laughter that accompanies various TV sitcoms. In this bizarre phenomenon, the machine laughs instead of us and frees us, so to speak, of the burden of enjoyment. The moment one starts to look, the examples keep springing up; the phenomenon suddenly appears to be widely present without bearing a name. It was finally given a name by Robert Pfaller with his felicitous invention of the concept of interpassivity, and under this banner a gradually spreading international discussion followed.[2]

Among the advantages of this term, interpassivity, is that it counteracts interactivity and points out its reverse side. Interactivity is one of the slogans of the day, the password for dealing with the new media and praising their alleged advantages, as well as the motto of a series of new artistic forms and practices that involve participation by the audience. On the other hand, interpassivity aims at a certain kind of enjoyment disguised by interactivity. What kind of enjoyment can be derived from something like canned laughter? Surely it's rather an unavowable sort of pleasure to be indulged in private, something clearly bordering on perversion, a guilty pleasure, a secret enjoyment. One can present oneself as a hero of interactivity, taking things into one's own hands, not letting oneself be imposed on, striking back, as it were, that is, being a subject (although in the rather dubious sense of a peasant in the global village). But interpassivity? This notion hardly seems glamorous; moreover, there is even something shameful about it. For it seems that, in order to be a subject, one must at least oppose passivity. One could say that interpassivity is the reverse side of the subject, a constant peril that could engulf subjectivity—and also something presenting itself as a lure, the song of the Sirens, a constant temptation to submit to this unavowable enjoyment. (However, in order not to be passively seduced by the song of the Sirens, the active strategy, in this case, strangely consists in being helplessly tied to a mast. So there you are.)

Ultimately, there seems to be a dilemma, an alternative: either you are a subject, actively shaping the world around you, interacting with it, or you give way to enjoyment, entrust yourself to (inter)passivity, let the things laugh and cry instead of you. Either the subject or the (passive, perverse) enjoyment.

ROUND ONE: LA CLAQUE

Let me start with a brief prehistory of interpassivity. There is a short piece that can perhaps be seen as the birthplace of canned laughter and of the entire idea of interpassivity. It is a brief text called "*La machine à gloire*" ("The glory-producing machine"), written by the nineteenth-century author Villiers de l'Isle-Adam. He was of aristocratic origin, a fact which seems to have defined his basic stance and demeanor throughout his life and work. For the one thread that runs through virtually all his writing is a horror and rejection of bourgeois civilization (for him a contradiction in terms), its spurious values, its idea of progress, and its lack of spirit, character, or valor.

The piece on the glory machine tells us about a marvellous invention by Baron Bathybius Bottom, an English engineer (whose English name, apart from the obvious anal allusion, also recalls the immortal ass-headed Bottom of *A Midsummer Night's Dream*). This new machine, which infallibly produced nothing less than glory, is an extension of a very old phenomenon, which I suspect might be as old as the invention of theater itself, and which in French has an unmatchably economical and evocative name, *la claque*. It designates organized applause, the group of "hired hands" in the audience who applaud by prearrangement, most often for financial reward. The French word is so excellent that the English and the German had no choice but to borrow it.[3] Quite appropriately, its primary meaning in French is "a smack, a slap in the face, a box on the ear," and among its other meanings we also find "the brothel"—to say nothing of its vicinity to the cloaca (*la cloaque*).

The claque, to be sure, doesn't involve just applause: it can cover a vast variety of reactions, both positive and negative. A well-organized claque can proffer, in Villiers' picturesque terms,

> Cries of frightened ladies, muffled Sighs, telling True Tears, sudden Small Chuckles, immediately contained, of a spectator who is slow in getting the point (six pounds extra), Clicking of tobacco boxes, into whose generous depth the raptured man must take refuge, Clamour, Suffocations, Encores, On-calls, silent Tears, Threats, On-calls with Yelling, Signs of approbation, divulged Opinions, Crowns, Principles, Convictions, moral Tendencies, epileptic Attacks, Childbirths, Hissing, Suicides, the Crackle of discussion (Art for Art's sake, the Form and the Idea), and so on.[4]

This hilarious inventory is immediately followed by a warning: "Let us stop here. The spectator might be led to imagine that he himself, unwittingly, is part of the claque (which is an absolute and incontestable truth); but it is better to leave some doubt in his mind about that" (100).

The claque presents a strange logical counterpart to the chorus of Greek tragedy, which served as one of the paramount instances of interpassivity. The chorus is the spectator's stand-in or representative on stage, relieving her of terror and pity, which it feels and expresses in her place. The claque is her representative in the audience taking care of her appropriate reactions off stage—clapping, booing, laughing and crying for her, taking the burden of feeling and enjoyment off her shoulders. The spectator can relax; the claque will attend to the rest. But then, can one ever draw the line between the claque and the audience? Does not the claque surreptitiously infiltrate the audience and its reactions, so that finally the two coincide? Is there an audience outside the claque? Villiers sees very well that the claque is not unrelated to the unconscious: the spectator is part of it without knowing it; he is bound against his will to this Other sitting next to him with which he shares the space and the time of the spectacle and from which he cannot simply disentangle himself. One could say that in the unconscious *ça claque*, perhaps even before *ça parle*, or that *ça claque* is the model and the epitome of *ça parle*. Can the spectator ever say, "Away with the claque! I want to rely on my own authentic reactions!"? But this turn has already been anticipated by the claque itself: "The latest stage of the Art is proffered when the claque itself cries out: 'Away with the claque!' and then pretends to have been itself moved (*entraînée*) and applauds at the end of the play, as if it were the real Audience and the roles reversed; it then restrains the overzealous exaltation and imposes restrictions" (100).

So the claque is intractable because its boundaries are constantly blurred and it cannot be assigned to a limited space. It can incorporate its own criticism and perhaps functions at its best when it shouts, "Away with the claque!," taking on the battle-cry against itself. The claque is itself and also its own negation, and the self-negation makes it stronger and omnipresent. The spectator can indeed relax, since even her feelings against the claque are taken care of by the claque. One may frown at Villiers' inveterate contempt for the crowd and its inability to make up its own mind or form its own judgment, but the mechanism of the claque goes well beyond his bias. For the question is: how does one extricate the authentic from the contrived? Is there an unequivocal line? Hasn't one always already been part of the claque? Has there ever been a theater without the claque, or indeed any form of art without some counterpart of it? Can one be rid of the claque?

One must extend the notion of the claque even to that which surrounds the performance—the publicity, the reviews, the criticism, the media coverage—and which has driven us to the theater in the first place. But its forms are far more insidious: there are people, forming strange groups of *claqueurs* over the centuries, who have seen the plays, read the books, admired the paintings, and listened to the music all before us, and who have produced an inaudible claque. They have seen it all, heard it all, and enjoyed it all before us. Would one ever set foot in a theater without the invisible claque spreading the rumor that this is what one should do? Isn't the claque another name for tradition? Is there a culture without the claque? Are there any standards of authenticity that would not, at some point, have recourse to the claque? Can one ever form an authentic judgment independently without some support of the claque even when one imagines to oppose it? Opposition to it, as we have seen, has already been taken care of by the claque.

So there is an organized applause that has been going on for centuries and there is no easy way of discerning its bias and partiality. What would we be without that bias? Can there be an enjoyment of art without some backdrop of the claque enjoying it for us? Without being *entraîné*? The point is not that there are no intrinsic values, but rather that the very notion of intrinsic values has to rely, at some point, on the claque. One has to suppose that the claque knows. And if one replaces a certain value, induced by the claque, by another supposedly more genuine one, it is perhaps the case of substituting one claque for another. The claque is "supposed to know," but it is also in its nature to contradict itself.

Only a small step separates this from interpassivity: why bother going to the theater at all, since the claque, past and present, has been and is enjoying it in our place? Perhaps the only authentic stance would be to stay at home, relying on the claque to attend to the troublesome business of culture instead of us, delegating our enjoyment to it, while we can relax at home and do—what? Watch the sitcoms with canned laughter? Is there an enjoyment outside the claque?

This doesn't apply solely to art and culture. The claque produces glory in all its forms: "Every glory has its claque, that is, its shadow, its part of artifice, of mechanism and of nothingness" (97). So any glory is constantly and inextricably accompanied by its claquing shadow, the applauding double, which might have become invisible and inaudible as the background noise of history despite the fact that it has been long since forgotten who hired it, and for what reward. Or rather perhaps it has never been properly hired at all: perhaps it has itself been always already *entraînée*; it was always just following the claque whose origin escapes us. Instead of asking the paranoid question, "Who hired the claque?," one should rather ask, "How does the claque function so well without being hired?" This is the part of glory that dooms its valor to contrivance, fabrication and deceit, its shining to darkness, its being to nothingness, while at the same time securing its success and survival. The claque is glory's part of spanking, of the brothel, and of the cloaca. Culture, tradition, and history all seem to be permeated with the claque. La claque—what a formidable name for the big Other!

Returning to Villiers' text, the ingenious Baron Bottom had the brilliant idea to turn the claque into a machine—something that it had always already been anyway: "In fact, the claque is a machine made of humanity, and hence perfectible" (97). The imperfect human machine can be perfected, its contingencies eliminated, and its human material replaced by the accuracy and predictability of a mechanical device. The machine could be incorporated into the theater hall itself, into its very architecture: phonographs would be placed into the orifices of statues and decorations, and at the appropriate moment they would emit "the wow-wows, the Cries, the 'Out with the cabal!,' the Laughter, the Sighs, the Encores, the Discussions, the Principles, the Clicking of tobacco boxes, and so on, all the sounds of the audience, but *perfected*" (102, italics added). The machine could be further perfected by the emission of gases, dispersing in turn tear gas and laughing gas as the occasion demanded; by the attachment of wooden hands to every seat; by the installation of devices that throw flowers and laurels on the stage, and so on. All this would be operated from a sophisticated control room placed in the prompter's pit, which would thus turn into a veritable "cock-pit." There can be no doubt that once any play had entered this tremendous machine, it would be condemned to success; there could be no accidents. All resistance would be in vain.

On top of that, an extension of Bottom's machine could also take care of theater criticism. The recycled clichés and commonplaces could be mechanically assembled, with the appropriate names being inserted in the blank spaces, and the ensuing results would by far surpass all modest human endeavours. Criticism has always been part of the claque anyway; it is just as mechanical in nature. The spirit is a machine, and the claque can be seen as another instance of Pascal's advice: first the machine, and the spirit will follow.

It is no coincidence that Bottom has been named after Shakespeare's Bottom, the weaver. Like the new Bottom, the old one was also a mastermind of theatrical trickery. But there is a crucial difference: the old Bottom believed in theater's intrinsic magic and its sway over the audience, which turned him into a Brechtian *avant la lettre*. He wanted to disenchant the audience: "This is only a play, these are not real swords and lions."[5] He believed, with infinite credulity, in the infinite credulity of the audience. For him the theater was too convincing in itself to need a claque, so the duty of the actors was quite the opposite: to fend off too much enthusiasm, to break down the illusion. Whereas the new Bottom, knowing very well that all magic is contrived, has the opposite concern: how to arouse the audience and make it believe. His tricks are no less crude and obvious than the old Bottom's, but one cannot but be taken in. The audience, under a spell like the fairy Queen Titania, has no choice but to fall head over heels in love with the ass's head.

So the enigma of glory has found its final resting place with our bottomless Bottom: "This Sphinx has found its Oedipus" (107).

ROUND TWO: DESIRE

Several problems arise from Villiers' text. First of all, are we dealing with a genuine case of interpassivity? There is a fine line between true interpassivity and what one finds in the case of the claque, though the question is whether the demarcation line can be maintained all the way through. It can be approached through Villiers' crucial term *entraîner*—to induce, to impose, to provoke, or to prompt. The point of the machine, for him, is to induce in the audience the reactions first emitted by the claque (whether in its human or mechanical shape). The claque has to contaminate the spectator with laughter, tears, and opinions, which first arise in their artificial forms pretending to be "the real things." The claque applauds in order to make me applaud; it laughs to make me laugh. The spectator's "authentic" feelings are provoked by artifice, so that she herself is no longer able to tell the difference. The point of interpassivity, however, is slightly different from that of this apparatus: in interpassivity, the devices, whether human or mechanical, take upon themselves the reactions *instead of us*; they feel for us, so that we are freed from the burden of enjoyment, or rather, so that we can indulge in the bizarre enjoyment of delegating enjoyment to the (human or mechanical) other. Canned laughter doesn't make us laugh; rather it prevents us from laughing. Villiers stops short at this twist.

There is nothing extraordinary in delegating a human activity; indeed one could say that an activity first becomes specifically human by being delegated, either to a thing, such as a tool—man often being defined precisely as a "tool-making" animal—or, to another man, a "speaking tool," Aristotle's designation of the slave. These two ways of transferring one's activity to another are the very stuff of history, the substance of the progression of technology and the concomitant development of class relations (the means of production and the relations of production, to nostalgically recall the Marxist terms). The gesture of delegating an activity both defines man's nature and, by the mediation it introduces, exposes it to alienation. So human activity is, by definition, always "inter."

That one could delegate one's passivity is far less obvious, and one of the many problems it involves is knowing if a clear limit could be set up between activity and passivity. Can one unproblematically put such things as laughing, crying, or praying under the simple heading of passivity? Where does passivity start, and activity stop? Is laughing passive? Surely it is generally provoked: it is by its nature a reaction to something, but then again, is there ever an action that would not also be a reaction? Can one perform an unprovoked action? *Like the Kantian* causa noumenon *of the notorious third antinomy in the Critique of Pure Reason, a cause that wouldn't itself be an effect? Even in the extreme case of perception, with our senses merely being affected by external stimuli, one can hardly maintain, at least after the Kantian turn, that it is simply passive—Kant's point being precisely that the subject always already contributes to the constitution of what she perceives.* Delegating laughter to another is certainly paradoxical, but perhaps not primarily by virtue of its passivity. It is rather laughter's incalculable character that makes it so, the way in which it can be seen as intimately human (and indeed another common definition of the human is "the laughing animal"), so irreducibly human that it cannot be delegated. Whereas "the tool-making" animal necessarily delegates, "the laughing animal" doesn't—at least not until the recent invention of canned laughter. So is feeling ever simply passive? If it is initially a reaction (but this is true of any activity), it is itself only palpable by "actively" expressing itself, by being "acted out," made visible, externalized in one way or another, worked-through, and thus by itself becoming a cause for other reactions, so that the line is always blurred.

Perhaps the crux of the matter doesn't lie so much with passivity, whose boundaries can never be strictly established, but rather with the concept of enjoyment. Enjoyment is what lies at the bottom of those intimate feelings enumerated in the catalogue of interpassivity. On the one hand, enjoyment is something untransferable (ultimately incalculable and immeasurable),[6] and on the other, a bonus, a reward, a gain, a benefit, a blessing—so why on earth would one want to delegate it at all? Perhaps instead of interpassivity one should speak of "inter-enjoyment." This brings us back to the point with which we started: enjoyment (in passivity) as the reverse side of the subject (as activity). The crux of passivity is the enjoyment it involves. Nevertheless the problem is thus displaced, since one can easily conceive of getting enjoyment from activity, but is it of the same kind as the unavowable and shameful enjoyment in passivity? And is enjoyment simply passive?

Here the intervention of psychoanalysis is called for, and I suppose inevitable. To be brief, let's say that if enjoyment is what people are after, then it can and should be complemented by the concept of desire. We thus obtain the conceptual pair, desire and enjoyment, which can perhaps substitute the somewhat dubious pair, activity and passivity. But do they fit? Is desire really after enjoyment? Does desire seek enjoyment? In the *Écrits*, we find the following brief sentence, one of Lacan's notorious proverbs: "*For desire is a defence, a defence against the transgression* (outre-passer) *of a limit in enjoyment*."[7] This elementary psychoanalytic insight—desire is a defence against enjoyment—seems considerably to complicate our problem, or perhaps to utterly simplify it.

The very nature of desire is to be interactive. There is no desire that is not *entraîné*, provoked by the other. One desires by relying on the desire of the other, so there has to be an elementary identification with the other for desire to emerge. Lacan never tired of repeating that the subject's desire is the desire of the Other, and we can paraphrase: the subject's desire is the desire of the claque. One can easily see that with the claque one's reactions, judgments, and opinions are always framed in some way by the claque, which offers the entries, the attitudes, the proper ways of responding, and which instigates our wish to participate in the first place. One has always already unwittingly started participating. If desire necessarily takes support in identification, its crucial form is the identification with the desire of the other. Surely there is a paradox here. If one only desires what one lacks, the identification with the desire of the other entails an identification with what the Other lacks. In desire, one is dragged into activity in order to figure out what has dragged the other into activity (this is at the core of its interactivity). What makes the Other tick? What is it after? How and why does it desire? How does it enjoy? Or does it enjoy at all? One can only find this out by adopting the desire oneself, which is thus indeed nothing but the desire of the Other. Apart from assuming that the Other (of the claque) knows, there is also the supposition that the Other enjoys, so one follows the claque, one goes through the motions indicated by the claque, in the hope of being awarded the prize of enjoyment. But here is the rub.

Desire is coupled with identification, but it doesn't result in enjoyment—it is maintained by being perpetually dissatisfied. The supposition that the Other enjoys does not lead to enjoyment; it prevents it. The lack has to be maintained if desire is to be sustained. The subject loves her lack; she would give up anything to keep it. Should she attain enjoyment, her very status as subject would collapse, insofar as subject and desire are here synonymous.

The first form of interpassivity follows from this. If desire is but a defence against enjoyment, then an ingenious way of defending oneself consists in entrusting enjoyment to the other. "The other enjoys, so I want to enjoy as well" leads directly to "The other enjoys, so thank God I don't have to!" Let the claque do what it is supposed to do anyway, that is, enjoy—instead of me. Let the video watch my favorite movies for me, for otherwise I would have to enjoy them myself, and that would be unbearable. I can see in advance the disappointment that this would bring; I can see that I can never measure up to the supposed enjoyment. By leaving satisfaction to the other, I can continue to suppose that there is such a thing as the satisfaction of desire. Were I to enjoy myself, hope would vanish, so if the other enjoys for me, I can maintain and preserve my desire by defending myself against enjoyment, in accordance with the nature of desire.

It is not difficult to recognize here the strategy of the obsessional neurotic, the direction that Pfaller has admirably explored.

ROUND THREE: DRIVE

Yet, this line of reasoning still places interpassivity in the realm of interactivity: it is a possible strategy to circumvent the impasse of desire and a way to prolong it. It is the point where desire, as essentially interactive, presents its limit-case, but which follows from its logic as one of its possible outcomes. Desire mimes passivity in order to deal with the deadlock of its inherent interactivity. It mimes passivity to avoid enjoyment, but does it not yield some enjoyment nevertheless? If the subject is by definition the subject of desire, and if desire is a defence against enjoyment, can the subject nevertheless obtain some bit of enjoyment? Does she get what she defends herself against? Can one enjoy by letting the other enjoy and thus resign oneself to one's own incurable dissatisfaction? And since I propose to replace interpassivity with "inter-enjoyment," one can further ask: is enjoyment "inter"? If desire is essentially "inter," does the same go for enjoyment?

It is here that the psychoanalytic concept of drive should be introduced. To put my thesis in somewhat simplified terms, I would say that *the key to interactivity lies with desire, while the key to interpassivity lies with the drive.* And since we disposed desire and enjoyment in a neat pair of opposites, it follows that enjoyment is placed on the side of the drive. For if desire is maintained by being constantly unsatisfied, then drive is something which, alarmingly, always finds its way to enjoyment and satisfaction.[8]

Let's take an example from Lacan, which in fact faithfully follows Freud's argument: "Even when you stuff the mouth—the mouth that opens in the register of the drive—it is not the food that satisfies it, it is, as one says, the pleasure of the mouth."[9] What satisfies hunger? Apart from the trivial necessity of eating in order to survive, how can we place hunger in our dichotomy of desire and drive? It might seem rather strange to treat hunger as an instance of desire, but once the need to eat becomes inflected with demand, as it necessarily does in the earliest stage—demand for attention, demand for love—it gets inextricably caught in the web of desire. The argument has been made often enough; it forms the backbone of the well-known dialectical progression need-demand-desire.[10] One could well ask if hunger, insofar as it involves desire, depends on the claque. This may appear a bizarre suggestion, but there is indeed the massive presence of "the mother's claque" (the mother being the first instance of the Other), her approval and delight with the baby's eating. One eats not simply to satisfy one's need, but also to satisfy the mother's desire, which ultimately coincides with the subject's own. One can't even eat without some applause, as it were. But insofar as hunger is desire, it is always unsatisfied; whatever and however much one eats, it is not "it." The various bulimic and anorexic disorders present spectacular proof of this. However much one stuffs the mouth of desire, it never gets enough; any food turns out to be the wrong kind of food and the satisfaction of hunger highlights all the more the falling short of enjoyment. Desire is that which remains hungry despite the amount or quality of food.

Drive is different: it is a satisfaction, an enjoyment that one gets as a by-product, so to speak, of the dissatisfaction of desire. One hasn't satisfied desire, but one has enjoyed anyway—it is a surplus enjoyment, an additional enjoyment surreptitiously sneaking into the very process of vainly seeking enjoyment. In the case of the oral drive, oral pleasure has been added regardless of the dissatisfaction of desire and even because of it. The object consumed is never it, the real thing, but some part of it is necessarily produced in the very act of consumption—and this bit is the object of drive.[11] So if desire can never reach enjoyment (indeed it does everything to avoid it through the pretense of pursuing it), then the problem of the drive is the very opposite: *one can never be rid of enjoyment.* It is a curious kind of enjoyment provided by the drive's not reaching its goal and by an object that is indifferent. Freud has already seen this in his famous paper on the drives: "[The object] is what is most variable about an instinct and is not originally connected with it .... It may be changed any number of times in the course of the vicissitudes which the [drive] undergoes during its existence...."[12] If the object is not important, then how does the drive get its satisfaction? The oral drive may seem to be firmly coupled with the breast as its object, but the breast is ultimately not essential to it; rather, the drive is satisfied by circling it, as Lacan says, without reaching its goal.[13] The drive is satisfied through its being thwarted, "inhibited in its goal" (*zielgehemmt*), but nevertheless it doesn't miss its aim. Lacan actually uses the English distinction between aim and goal, which is indiscernible in the French *le but*:

> Here we can clear up the mystery of the *zielgehemmt*, of that form that the drive may assume, in attaining its satisfaction without attaining its aim.... When you entrust someone with a mission, the aim is not what he brings back, but the itinerary he must take. The aim is the way taken. The French word *but* may be translated by another word in English, goal .... If the drive

> may be satisfied without attaining what ...would be the satisfaction of its end ... it is because ... its aim is simply this return into circuit .... The *objet petit a* is not the origin of the oral drive. It is not introduced as the original food, it is introduced from the fact that no food will ever satisfy the oral drive, except by circumventing [circling around] the eternally lacking object....[14]

The drive reaches its aim without attaining its goal; its arrow returns from the target, like a boomerang. However, contrary to what Lacan suggests, it doesn't return back to the subject because the subject is essentially the subject of desire, as we have seen, while the drive, with its bit of surplus enjoyment, has no subject (at least not in any ordinary sense, not even the Lacanian one).[15] There is no subject at the origin of the drive; there is only the subject of desire emerging from its entanglement with the Other and enjoyment is but its by-product. The drive has no origin and no end; its only subsistence is in the circular movement yielding a tiny bit of enjoyment—but an enjoyment that cannot satisfy desire or fill the lack, an enjoyment from which desire flees.

All this appears to be at odds with the usual representation of the drive as a biological or somatic pressure, as a reservoir of energy or a field of forces—the notions that we find abundantly scattered throughout Freud's writing. Lacan proposes another model, that of the drive as an organ. It is a strange kind of organ, "situated in relation to the true organ,"[16] but nevertheless an "ungraspable organ, [an] object that we can only circumvent, in short, [a] false organ ... whose characteristic is not to exist, but which is nevertheless an organ."[17] Lacan continues: "This organ is unreal. Unreal is not imaginary. The unreal is defined by articulating itself on the real in a way that eludes us, and it is precisely this that requires that its representation should be mythical ...."[18]

So Lacan produces his own myth, a parody of Aristophanes' myth of the missing half: the missing half that would complement a human being (as sexed) and make him or her whole, is a lamella, "something extra-flat, which moves like the amoeba .... It goes everywhere ... survives any division ... can run around ...."[19] Furthermore, "If you want to stress its joky side, you can call it *l'hommelette* .... And it is of this that all the forms of the *objet a* ... are the representatives, the equivalents."[20] So in order to imagine the object of the drive, one has to conceive of an organ that is lost or missing, but that nevertheless prolongs the body, being moulded by the body's orifices and borders (all the objects *a* stem from there). The object is infinitely pliable, yet never fitting and never graspable, except through the circuit of the drive. So in our case of the oral drive, the breast is not the organ of libido; rather, the lamella is this extra-flat, extra-thin foil that always comes to interpose itself between the open mouth and the breast. It is *l'hommelette* that always prevents us from simply eating an omelette.

One can provisionally sum up with another Lacanian proverb: "Desire comes from the Other, and enjoyment is on the side of the Thing."[21]

ROUND FOUR: THE KNOCKOUT

So where does that leave us with our problem of interpassivity? By approaching the problem in our terms of drive and enjoyment, as opposed to desire, it appears that both sides of inter-passivity—"inter" and "passivity"—have to be transformed or abandoned.

To start with, it seems that the drive can't be reduced to the division between active and passive. To be sure, Freud, when considering the vicissitudes of the drives, shows that some of their major transformations consist in reversals between activity and passivity, but he nevertheless maintains that at the core "every [drive] is a piece of activity; if we speak loosely of passive [drives], we can only mean [drives] whose *aim* is passive."[22] Passivity would thus figure as a derivative subdivision of drives' inherent activity. Lacan seems to agree: "In fact, it is obvious that, even in their supposedly passive phase, the exercise of a drive, a masochistic drive, for example, requires that the masochist give himself … a devil of a job."[23]

Yet, I think it can be argued, on the basis of Lacan's own account, that the proper mode, or the proper "voice," of the drive is the middle, a grammatical notion between the active and the passive voices. The drive evolves neutrally, indifferently, though it can bring about both active and passive expressions. It is something that happens or takes place without a subject actively striving for it or passively submitting to it: perhaps both activity and passivity pertain to the realm of desire and its vicissitudes, whereas passivity figures as the limit-case of activity. One can perhaps cautiously propose another classification of the verbal voices. Whereas, at first sight, the major division appears to be between the active and passive voice, with the middle as an awkward appendix, a second look reveals a more crucial divide between inclusion and non-inclusion of the subject into what the verb describes. On that account, both the active and the passive voice (with the subject either acting or being acted upon) would fall into one category, while the middle voice would form the other one.[24]

Second, enjoyment is perhaps not "inter" at all. Drive doesn't care about the Other; it doesn't worry about the claque. Neither does the drive need the claque to show it the way nor does it call for any identification. It doesn't get entangled in the desire or (supposed) enjoyment of the Other; it rather refuses and dismisses the Other as such, utterly indifferent to its tricks. So there is an enjoyment outside the claque and it is precisely this enjoyment that psychoanalysis seeks. This is what causes the problem. If interpassivity in the first sense, in its obsessional neurotic variety, remains inherently "inter," delegating enjoyment to the other, then in the second sense, it keeps all enjoyment for itself—except there is no self for which it would be kept or to which it could be ascribed. Thus, there is no sense in keeping it, both because it is not a quantum to be stocked, and because one gets it anyway whether one wants it or not.

So in this second sense interpassivity, deprived of both "inter" and "passivity," appears indeed as the shadow of interactivity. In this second sense *one cannot delegate enjoyment, but one cannot keep it either*. There is an "it enjoys" where both the subject and the Other vanish. To be sure, there is a delegation of enjoyment in a sense—but not to the Other (other subjects, machines, or the phantom of the big Other)—a delegation to an it that eludes the Other, as it also eludes our own body. The lever of enjoyment, as it were, is that unreal bodily organ that one doesn't possess, but of which one also cannot be rid.

With this second sense of interpassivity, it seems that our topic has disappeared. Interpassivity, instead of being localizable, limited to certain curious, rare, and outstanding phenomena, has become omnipresent and universal. If we thus make it synonymous with the basic mechanism of the drive, if it coincides with the drive altogether, then one may well ask whether there is any human phenomenon that wouldn't fall under the heading of interpassivity.[25] Is eating, to prolong our example, a case of interpassivity? In our second sense, yes, and indeed very prominently, since it is the very earliest one, and perhaps a model for all others to come. Insofar as drive can be seen as the shadow side of desire, interpassivity sneaks into every human endeavor as its hidden reverse. While in the first sense, it only appeared in some select instances, as a peculiar, but consequential extension of the obsessional logic, in this second sense one cannot be rid of it at all. One cannot choose enjoyment in the drive; one doesn't enjoy the way one would like to.

Can the two senses be brought together? Is there a possible transition, a bridge between the two? One could say that the very process of psychoanalysis is precisely such a bridge. Lacan sees it along those lines when he conceives of analysis as a transition from the structures of desire to those of drive.

First of all, drive introduces a dimension "beyond the pleasure principle," while desire, with its defense against enjoyment, remains firmly within the realm of the pleasure principle, all its dissatisfaction notwithstanding. Lacan says, "What is at issue in the drive is finally revealed here—the course of the drive is the only form of transgression that is permitted to the subject in relation to the pleasure principle. The subject will realize that his desire is merely a vain detour with the aim of catching the *jouissance* of the other…."[26]

The aim of analysis is to inflect desire toward this point from which it has been fleeing—to produce something that cannot be directly desired, since desire is indirect by its very nature (it can indeed be epitomized by the formula, "the desire to desire"). That something produced is precisely enjoyment, in which the by-product comes to the fore and is laid bare from under the cover of fantasy. As Lacan explains, "After the mapping of the subject in relation to the *a*, the experience of the fundamental fantasy becomes the drive. What, then, does he who has passed through the experience of this opaque relation to the origin, to the drive, become? How can a subject who has traversed the radical fantasy experience the drive? This is the beyond of analysis, and has never been approached."[27]

It is perhaps a bit too much to tackle the tricky problems of fantasy at this late stage. In brief, one can say that fantasy is the support of desire, and the point of analysis is to traverse the fantasy that has been supporting desire, that is, to take that support away. And what is left then, without that buttress, is the drive. Both the traversing of the fundamental fantasy and the destitution of the subject (should one say the knockout of the subject?)—two formulas Lacan gives for the end of analysis—coincide in the drive. In the final analysis, that is, at its end, fantasy is dislodged by the drive. Desire as the defense against enjoyment collapses, and what emerges is the unthinkable beyond of desire, which is also beyond analysis, something that has so far never been approached, according to Lacan.

One can conceive of the beginning of analysis as interactive: the patient enters it with the supposition that the analyst is the other who knows, and who in particular knows the way to enjoyment. There is an attempt at identification with that other and at figuring out his desire. But here the analytic mechanism departs from the common ways of desire: there is no claque. The analyst, that figure of the Other, doesn't applaud, although he is admittedly being hired and rather well paid. *The analyst is anti-claque*—someone not to applaud. And since there is no claque to follow (or to oppose), no claque on which to base one's desire, interactivity eventually loses its footing and desire is referred back to itself, to its own vagaries that lose their ground. It emerges as groundless, that is, grounded only in the contingency of fantasy, and once this is shattered, the only thing remaining is the by-product, the drive: something that is not interactive at all, that is without substance and without a subject, in a manner of (Hegelian) speaking.

The first sense of interpassivity may well appear within the first part of this process, as a defense against what analysis is after. One defends oneself against the analyst, that horrible alien, and one of the strategies of doing this can be the interpassive one. One not only assigns enjoyment to the other, but one also offers oneself as the tool of it. As long as the other enjoys, I don't have to, so I must secure his enjoyment. One's mission is to be in the analyst's secret service. The analysis is at some point always on the edge of a love affair, or a master-slave liaison.[28] Should it really turn into one, the subject's desire would have scored a victory, and one would eventually wind up with a new marvel of interpassivity, *the canned analyst.*

But if analysis is up to its task, then it should dismantle this mechanism of interpassivity in order to make it pass into the other one, the one aligned with the drive. The emergence of the drive is the endpoint of analysis, and what lies beyond has never been approached, as Lacan said in 1964. But a few years later, he will propose a very precise mechanism for envisaging that beyond: the mechanism known as *la passe*, the passage from the position of the analysand to that of the analyst. And this is the ultimate point: the emergence of a new kind of desire from the drive, the desire of the analyst. One of Lacan's key papers on the problem appropriately bears the title "On Freud's 'Trieb' and the psychoanalyst's desire."[29] One could say: the birth of the analyst's desire from the spirit of the drive, or rather from its complete lack of spirit.

Does this new desire avoid the traps of the old desire? Is it a desire liberated from the claque, or is it necessarily accompanied by a new variety of the claque, one that has formed the very substance of the history of psychoanalytic movement through the past century?

Notes

1. Jacques Lacan, *The Seminar of Jacques Lacan, Book VII: The Ethics of Psychoanalysis (1959-1960)*, ed. Jacques-Alain Miller, trans. Dennis Porter (New York: Norton, 1992), 252.
2. See *Interpassivität*, ed. Robert Pfaller (Vienna: Springer, 2000), which summarizes his long-standing efforts on this theme. Two international conferences were organized about it in Linz and Nürnberg in 1998, and Pfaller provides the best summary of this discussion. For Žižek's further reflections on the theme, see *The Plague of Fantasies* (London: Verso, 1998).
3. Brewer's *Dictionary of Phrase and Fable*, always up to its task, gives the following description: "A body of hired applauders at a theatre etc. said to have been originated or first systematized by M. Sauton who in 1820 established an office in Paris to secure the success of dramatic performances. The manager ordered the required number of *claqueurs*, who were divided into *commissaires*, those who commit the piece to memory, and noisily point out its merits; *rieurs*, who laugh at the puns and jokes; *pleureurs*, chiefly women who hold their handkerchiefs to their eyes at the emotional parts; *chatouilleurs*, who are to keep the audience in good humour; and *bisseurs*, who are to cry bis (encore)." The phenomenon appears to have been so ubiquitous in the nineteenth century that numerous authors have spoken about it well before Villiers (most extensively Emile Souvestre in *Le monde tel qu'il sera* in 1846). In December 1842 an anonymous note in *Revue et gazette musicale* already suggested the replacement of the claque by a machine, pretending that this device already existed in England and should be imported.
4. Villiers de l'Isle-Adam, *Contes cruels*, ed. Pierre Citron (Paris: Garnier-Flammerion, 1980), 100. Subsequent references will appear parenthetically within the text.

5. See Shakespeare, *A Midsummer Night's Dream*, Act III, Scene 1. Bottom says, "Write me a prologue; and let the prologue seem to say, we will do no harm with our swords, and that Pyramus is not killed indeed: and for the more better assurance, tell them that I Pyramus am not Pyramus, but Bottom the weaver; this will put them out of fear."
6. The fact that enjoyment is essentially incalculable presses us all the more to attempt to calculate it. There has been a whole line of thinking, during the Enlightenment, obsessed with "the calculus of enjoyment," with some hilarious results. See, for instance, Jeremy Bentham.
7. Lacan, *Écrits* (Paris: Seuil, 1966), 825.
8. See Jacques-Alain Miller, "Commentary on Lacan's Text," in *Reading Seminars I and II*, eds. Richard Feldstein, Bruce Fink, and Marie Jaanus (Albany: SUNY Press, 1996), 426: "What Freud calls the drive is an activity which always comes off. It leads to sure success, whereas desire leads to a sure unconscious formation, namely, a bungled action or slip: 'I missed my turn,' 'I forgot my keys,' etc. That is desire. Drive, on the contrary, always has its keys in hand." I will come back to the question of the drive being an "activity."
9. Lacan, *The Four Fundamental Concepts of Psychoanalysis,* ed. Jacques-Alain Miller, trans. Alan Sheridan (New York: Norton, 1978), 167.
10. See Lacan, *Écrits*, 691: "Thus the desire is neither the appetite for satisfaction [as in need] nor the demand of love, but the difference resulting from the subtraction of the former from the latter ...." The simplest formula is: desire is demand minus need.
11. For many insights concerning this issue I am very much indebted to the work accomplished by Alenka Zupančič in *Ethics of the Real* (London: Verso, 2000), 238 ff. and passim, and in a more elaborate form in her work published so far only in Slovene. See also Miller.
12. Sigmund Freud, "Instincts and Their Vicissitudes," in *The Standard Edition of the Complete Psychological Works of Sigmund Freud*, trans. James Strachey, et. al. (London: The Hogarth Press, 1953-1974), 14: 122-123. Note, I have modified Strachey's translation of *Trieb* to drive.
13. See Lacan, *Four Fundamental Concepts*, 168: "As far as the oral drive is concerned ... it is obvious that it is not a question of food, nor of the memory of food, nor the echo of food, nor the mother's care, but of...the breast .... If Freud makes a remark to the effect that the object in the drive is of no importance, it is probably because the breast, in its function as object, is to be revised in its entirety. To this breast in its function as object ... we must give a function that will explain its place in the satisfaction of the drive. The best formula seems to me to be the following—that *la pulsion en fait le tour .... Tour* is to be understood here with the ambiguity it possess-

es in French, both turn, the limit around which one turns, and trick." In the footnote in the English translation, the proposed English equivalents for the French phrase are "the drive moves around the object" and "the drive tricks the object."

14. Lacan, *Four Fundamental Concepts*, 179-180.
15. I am here leaving aside the tricky problem of the subject of the drive. The least one can say is that it is not a subject in the standard Lacanian sense of the barred subject, but something that Lacan somewhat mysteriously calls "a headless subject," for want of a better word: "what I have metaphorically called a headless subjectification, a subjectification without a subject, a bone … " (Lacan, *Four Fundamental Concepts*, 184). One cannot but recall here Hegel's notorious dictum that "the Spirit is a bone"—should one say the bone of headless enjoyment seeking a subject? The headless subject as a by-product of a by-product?
16. Lacan, *Four Fundamental Concepts*, 196.
17. Ibid., 196-198.
18. Ibid., 205.
19. Ibid., 197.
20. Ibid., 197-198.
21. Lacan, *Écrits*, 853.
22. Freud, "Instincts and Their Vicissitudes," 122.
23. Lacan, *Four Fundamental Concepts*, 200. The example doesn't quite work by Lacan's own standards, since he has spent much time and effort demonstrating that the drive is not to be confused with perversion. Masochism, like any perversion, proceeds from a subject seeking enjoyment, and as in every perversion, the dimension of the Other looms very large, since the enjoyment that is at stake in perversion is the enjoyment of the Other. (See, for example, Lacan, *Four Fundamental Concepts*, 185: "the sadist himself occupies the place of the object, but without knowing it, to the benefit of an other, for whose *jouissance* he exercises his action as sadistic pervert.") The drive's bondage, on the other hand, is not with the Other.
24. I am well aware that I am twisting Benveniste's famous account of the "medium," or "middle," here for the current purpose.
25. See Lacan, *Four Fundamental Concepts*, 166: "It is clear that those with whom we deal, the patients, are not satisfied, as one says, with what they are. And yet, we know that everything they are, everything they experience, even their symptoms, involves satisfaction. They satisfy something that no doubt runs counter to that with which they might be satisfied, or rather, perhaps, they give satisfaction *to* something. They are not content with their state, but all the same, being in a state that gives so little con-

tent, they are content. The whole question boils down to the following—*what* is contented here?"

26. Lacan, *Four Fundamental Concepts*, 183. See also *Écrits*, 851: "This gap is the gap desire encounters at the limits imposed upon it by the principle ironically called the pleasure principle, which relates it to a reality for which one can say it is here but the field of praxis. It is from precisely that field that Freudianism rends desire, whose principle essentially consists in impossibilities."

27. Lacan, *Four Fundamental Concepts*, 273.

28. The master-slave relationship, at least the way Lacan reads it, can be taken as a case of obsessional interpassivity. See Lacan, *Écrits*, 314: "In fact the obsessional subject manifests one of the attitudes that Hegel did not develop in his dialectic of master and slave. The slave has given way in the face of the risk of death in which mastery was being offered to him in a struggle of pure prestige. But since he knows that he is mortal, he also knows that the master can die. From this moment on he is able to accept his laboring for the master and his renunciation of enjoyment in the meantime; and, in the uncertainty of the moment when the master will die, he waits." It is perhaps rather ironic to see interpassivity in the attitude of someone who works very hard, who is indeed "slaving," and appears to be anything but passive, but the hard work is conditioned and framed by the delegation of enjoyment—that is what keeps it going: "Let the other enjoy so that I don't have to." If striving for enjoyment demands strenuous activity, this is but a trifle compared to the hard labor one has to perform in order to prevent enjoyment.

29. Lacan, *Écrits*, 851-854.

7

Pierre Loves Horranges
Lévinas-Sartre-Nancy: An Approach to the Fantastic in Philosophy

Catherine Malabou

In this essay, I will try to situate the question of the fantastic in philosophy. Upon this road, there are three great predecessors, three decisive approaches to the question: Lévinas, Sartre, Nancy. Rather than beginning with a discussion of what the fantastic in philosophy is not or cannot be (for example, a "genre," as in literature), I will open by indicating what it is susceptible to become: a new category, designed to characterize what I will name *the real of ontological difference*. Indeed, the fantastic designates a certain modality of the real—a real that, we will see, exceeds the real and outstrips it; like every self-respecting version of the fantastic, the fantastic in philosophy is the real irruption of the extraordinary, something foreign to the real, in the real. Accordingly, this in-excess-of-the-real must lead back to the ontological problematic from which it arises and to the phenomenon that it characterizes: the appearance *in reality* of ontological difference. What is fantastic is this appearance; what is fantastic is the reality of the difference between Being and beings. This reality is what all three of Lévinas, Sartre and Nancy call *existence* – and this is precisely what authorizes their strange grouping.

What is fantastic is existence conceived as the reality of the difference between Being and beings. The "definition"—if it is one—is now complete. And since our conference is oriented by "sense," the question of sense, you will have understood that I intend, in my own way, to question the sense of existence or, at least, of *that* existence.

I turn back to my "definition": the fantastic is existence conceived as the reality of the difference between Being and beings. Two aspects of this definition are particularly noticeable. First, it entails a relation to the image, contained in the etymology of the word "fantastic"—*fantasma, fantastikè*. Second, it entails a reference to Heidegger. The reference may be oblique or contorted, but this torsion precisely situates the distance and the proximity of Lévinas, Sartre, and Nancy from Heideggerian philosophy. In my definition of the fantastic, the reference to Heidegger is indirect in more than one manner. On the one hand, Heidegger never spoke of a *reality* of ontological difference. He perhaps never spoke of reality at all—since, as we know, the two concepts of *Realität* and *Wirklichkeit* were deconstructed in *Being and Time*. Accordingly, on the other hand, Heidegger never thought that existence could continue to designate, as it is does within the metaphysical tradition, something like "reality." Finally, even though he was intent upon elucidating the status of the image and imagination, Heidegger never confused the image, *das Bild*, with the simple "phantasm," nor imagination, *die Einbildung*, with fantasizing (*Phantasie*). But, one will object, Lévinas, Sartre and Nancy did not either! Nevertheless, a sustained reading of their works will show that they displaced the Heideggerian thinking of the image and the imagination; that, at the same time, they displaced the sense of ontological difference; and that they thereby displaced the sense of existence toward another imagination, another difference, another existence.

The fantastic, conceived as the reality of the difference between Being and beings, thus names a certain *Heideggerian inheritance* that displaces what it inherits. Lévinas, Sartre, Nancy, as faithful and unfaithful inheritors, seek to bring to light, that is also to produce, *the effect of Heidegger's thought in the real;* the way in which ontological difference now constitutes the real of philosophy, *what there is to think*. The fantastic thus characterizes the effect in the real of deconstruction (*Destrucktion, Abbau*)—the deconstruction of the image, of the real. Further, this effect, the effect of Heideggerian thought in the real, is *existence*, the emergence of a new signification of existence, which is no longer *stricto sensu* Heideggerian and no longer simply designates *Dasein*'s mode of being, but rather *the irruption of ontological difference in the real and as the real*. Existence should here be understood as the concretion or concreteness of difference. Lévinas, Sartre and Nancy all speak of the *materiality* of difference. Existence is what returns, *materially*, after Heidegger's disappearance: the fantastically real inheritance of Heidegger.[1]

Everything begins with a contrasense: Sartre translates *Dasein* by "human reality" and thus transforms the ontological difference, which Heidegger explicitly presented as the difference between Being and beings, into the difference between existence and the existent. What Heideggerian did not decry the scandal! This or these "constrasenses," among other things, meant that Sartre would be purely and simply excluded from the circle of "true" philosophers. However, it is ever more apparent to me that this or these "contrasenses" are not in fact contrasensical, at least not entirely; and that Sartre's "translations" are pregnant—even their author knows nothing about it—with a truth whose sense could only appear later, much later—today, when what there is to think is precisely existence as the *reality* of ontological difference, the fantastic return of existence after Heidegger, after Heidegger's existence.

Reading a passage from *Being and Nothingness* will confirm that, when it came to the matter of the fantastic, Sartre knew what he was talking about.

To engage or reengage the truth of Sartre's "contrasenses," I have decided to let Lévinas speak first; for, starting with his earliest texts, Lévinas also turns the difference between Being and beings into the difference between "existing" and "existents." In *Time and the Other*, for example, he declares: "We return again to Heidegger. One cannot ignore his distinction… between *Sein* and *Seiendes*, Being and beings, but which, for reasons of euphony, I prefer to render as *existing* and *existent*, without ascribing a specifically existentialist meaning to these terms."[2]

The question of the fantastic, for Lévinas, is linked to the difference between "existing" and "existents." The fantastic, for him, is the mode of being of what does not exist… and thus of existing itself. "I would gladly say," the author continues in *Time and the Other*, "that existing does not exist."[3] This declaration is easy to understand to the extent that "existing" characterizes the mode of being of something that is not a being, the mode of being of Being itself, or of the being—*Dasein*—which has an understanding of its own Being.

Even as the Lévinasian concept of existence presents itself, at first, as the translation of Heidegger's concept, it will very quickly be distinguished from that concept. As Lévinas comments on Heidegger in *Time and the Other*, he insists upon the fact that it is not possible to think Being and beings without one another; that their difference unites them; and that Being is always the being of a being. "Existing," he says, "is always grasped in the existent."[4] There is no existence or existing "without existents."[5]

Accordingly, it is at the moment when he elucidates the meaning of *Geworfenheit* that Lévinas bifurcates, as it were; it is at this moment that he parts company with Heidegger and displaces difference for reasons other than "euphony." He begins by recalling that "*Geworfenheit* should be translated as 'the-fact-of-being-thrown-in'… existence." Therefore, there is no existing without existents. Nonetheless, he adds:

> It is as if the existent appeared in an existence that precedes it, as though existence were independent of the existent, and the existent that finds itself thrown there could never become master of existence. It is precisely because of this that there is desertion and abandonment. Thus dawns the idea of an existing that occurs without us, without subject, an existing without existents.6

The fantastic enters into play at the precise point of this paradoxical dissociation between existing and existents, between Being and beings—a dissociation that does not appear in Heidegger. There where existing cannot exist without existents, it still cuts itself away from them and it is this cut that is fantastic. Lévinas thus seeks to show how difference is susceptible to becoming ontological separation and then ontological indifference.

When existing shows that it is separated from existents, the frightful and the horrible make their appearance. The philosopher asks: "How can we approach this existing without existents?" And his response is, for my argument, extremely interesting: "by an act of the *imagination*."

Let us imagine all things, beings and persons, returning to nothingness. What remains after this imaginary destruction of everything is not something, but the fact that there is. The absence of everything returns as a presence, as the place where the bottom has dropped out of everything, an atmospheric density, a plenitude of the void, the murmur of silence. There is, after this destruction of things and beings, the impersonal 'field of forces' of existing. There is something that is neither subject nor substantive. The fact of existing imposes itself when there is no longer anything. And it is anonymous: there is neither anyone nor anything that takes this existence upon itself. It is impersonal like 'it is raining' or 'it is hot.' Existing returns no matter with what negation one dismisses it. There is, as the irremissibility of pure existing.[7]

"Let us imagine all things returning to nothingness." But what imagination is capable of this feat? Such an imagination must be capable of nothing less than *imagining being, imagining existing,* which does not exist. One thinks immediately of the Heideggerian interpretation of productive imagination in Kant. Imagination, Heidegger says, is not creative within the ontic order, but rather within the ontological.[8] Has one ever reflected on the vertigo opened up by the idea of a creative imagination within the ontological order—an imagination that no longer operates within the register of beings or non-beings, but rather of Being, and that even gives the expression 'that does not exist' a sense entirely other than the ontic sense?

For Heidegger, as we know, the imagination's ontological power of "creation" is the schematism, still called originary temporalization. The schemas are pure images—that is, determinations of time. Being's manner of being is time. But Lévinas, who recognizes that the anonymity of existing reveals time as such, the "soldering" that holds the temporal exstases together (as he says in the same text), insists at the same time upon the hallucinatory effect produced by the very possibility of an image of Being. What Lévinas seeks to describe here is the reverberation of the schema in the real, the fantastic image that appears like an atmosphere, a hypervigilance, an insomnia without limit, an incessant murmur—other names, the author says, for the "basis of beings." Everything happens as if the schema itself was right there. Radicalizing and profoundly transforming the Heideggerian analysis of anxiety, and thus displacing its problematic, Lévinas devotes himself to describing the *shockwave* provoked by what he calls "the return of absence within presence," the ontic mirage of the ontological image, which is, in a sense, one being's response to the annihilating solicitation of its own image. It is the phenomenon of this response that is "fantastic." The ontological image becomes real—like a profound night or darkness, something that becomes possible to describe. In *Existence and Existents*, Lévinas says: "Nocturnal space delivers us to Being." And, he continues, it is from darkness that things "acquire their fantastic character."

> Darkness does not only modify their contours for vision; it reduces them to undetermined, anonymous being, which they exude.
>
> One can also speak of different forms of night that occur right in daytime. Illuminated objects can appear to us as though in twilight shapes. Like the unreal, inverted city we find after an exhausting trip, things and beings strike us as though they no longer composed a world, and were swimming in the chaos of their existence. Such is also the case with the 'fantastic,' 'hallucinatory' reality in poets like Rimbaud, even when they name the most familiar things and the most accustomed beings. The misunderstood art of certain realistic and naturalistic novelists, their prefaces and professions of faith notwithstanding, produces the same effect: beings and things that collapse into their 'materiality,' are terrifyingly present in their destiny, weight and shape. Certain passages of Huysmans or Zola, the calm and smiling horror of de Maupassant's tales do not only give, as is sometimes thought, a representation 'faithful to' or exceeding reality, but penetrate behind the form which light reveals into the materiality which, far from responding to the philosophical materialism of the authors, constitutes the dark background of existence. It makes things appear to us in a night, like the monotonous presence that bears down on us in insomnia.
>
> The rustling of the *there is*... is horror.[9]

The unreal, the hallucinatory, horror: such are the ontic responses to the paradoxical appeal of ontological indifference.

Ontological indifference, in Lévinas, primarily designates the mode of being of Being, of existing without beings or without existents. It is the indifference of Being with regard to beings, which find themselves abandoned. But ontological indifference also characterizes the mode of Being of the beings or of the existents thereby deserted; it characterizes the existent itself insofar as it has become an *intruder* in relation to its own existence. This effect of mutual foreignness produced between Being and beings thereby opens another dimension of indifference, that of indistinction or non-difference. Even as the difference between existing and existents is stretched to the limit, to the point of separation, existing and existents become paradoxically confused with one another; they become impossible to distinguish. Existing and existents become foreign to one another; and they curiously allow the community of this very foreignness to appear in one flesh, one matter, one basis, one real image, one schema. This matter, other than matter, ontico-ontological matter, is the very consistency of difference: "this materiality that... constitutes the obscure basis of existence."

On the one hand, the fantastic inheres in the hallucinatory dimension of apprehending such a materiality—neither ontic nor ontological, but both at the same time; and this hallucinatory dimension becomes the necessary dimension of philosophical thought. On the other hand, it inheres in the mode of being of this materiality or reality, whose stuff, this strange flesh, Heidegger never thought. This reality thus appears at once as a materialization of Being *insofar as it is different from beings* and as the effect of *the suspension of the beingness of beings or existents,* which thereby become unreal or really unreal. The fantastic (whence its name) can thus appear as an image supplement—or a phantasm, if one likes—whereby the ontological image is embodied; whereby the schema and time make their non-existence exist.

In the same movement, beings vanish and being is embodied—which is to say, along with Sartre, that it is "qualified."

With this analysis in mind, one should read the magnificent chapter from *Being and Nothingness* entitled "Of quality as a revelation of being." One should also reread *Nausea* and, this time around, accuse Lévinas of a contrasense when he declares: "'Nausea,' as a feeling for existence, is not yet a depersonalization; but horror turns the subjectivity of the subject, its particularity *qua* entity, inside out."[10] Because nausea is only the way in which the *there is* ever rises into the mouth.

The chapter, "Of quality as a revelation of being," begins—once again, and this point is particularly interesting for my argument—with an analysis of the imagination that emerges from a critique of "Bachelard's material imagination." According to Sartre, this imagination, material as it may be, remains a property of the psyche; it remains subjective and thus lacks the "ontological reality" to which any true "psychoanalysis of things" must return. What is this psychoanalysis? Psychoanalysis makes it possible, Sartre says, "to establish the way in which each thing is the *objective* symbol of being and of the relation of human reality to this being."[11]

"Each thing is the objective symbol of being." This phrase, without playing on words, is fantastic. It transforms the meaning of the symbol. If all things are symbols, then it is not because they are sensible representations, metaphors, the images of states of the soul, or an intelligible reality that would transcend them. Referring to being, these symbol-things do not refer to anything, to anything other than themselves. Insofar as they exist, things let what does not exist, being or existence, appear in them, materially and objectively. This strange appearance is once again a sort of real image, existence brushing up against *what is there.* This is to say that things are not symbols, if one understands a symbol—according to the traditional definition of the term—to be an image detached from the thing of which it is the image; an image that one can grasp in itself, in the psyche, which can do without its body. Insofar as it is *objective,* however, forming a single body with what it symbolizes—in some sense, with itself—the symbol is no longer a symbol, but the real—if one understands the real, following Lacan's elaboration of it during the same period, as something that resists symbolization or idealization. According to what only seems to be a paradox, the "objective symbol," in Sartre, designates the incoercible resistance of the real, and thus of existence, to the symbol. It is precisely this resistance of existence to the symbol that Sartre calls "the existential symbolism of things," thereby affirming that the symbol exists—which is to say that it is not a symbol. Or that the symbol is what is.[12]

The task of the "psychoanalysis of things" is thus to "establish the manner in which each thing is the objective symbol of being and of the relation of human reality to this being." This psychoanalysis must take the psyche into account—whence its name; but it must do so in a very particular manner. Sartre immediately gives an example: "take… the particular quality which we call *viscous*."[13] "The viscous," he will say later, "does not symbolize a psychic attitude a *priori*; it manifests a certain relation of being with itself and this relation has an originally psychic quality [*et cette relation est originellement psychisée*]."[14] In fact, Sartre is in the process of redefining the schema: "this relation has an originally psychic quality" signifies that the viscous is a schema originarily given to the mind, inscribed within it *a priori* as a pure image: "I am enriched," Sartre writes, "by a valid ontological schema… which will interpret the meaning of being of all the existents of a certain category,"[15] that is, all viscous existents. But, much as in Lévinas, this schema *enters into presence within what it schematizes*; that is, the viscous, as schema, is itself viscous, and it is in this sense that it shows itself as the relation of being to itself—this phenomenon going beyond imagination properly speaking: "a phenomenon of constant *hysteresis* in relation to itself." The being of the viscous and the viscous entity thus exist in a relation that resembles the relation between the honey in my spoon and the honey in the pot upon which I pour it:

> The honey which slides off my spoon on to the honey contained in the jar first sculptures the surface by fastening itself on it in relief, and its fusion with the whole is presented as a gradual sinking, a collapse which appears at once as a deflation (think, for example, of children's pleasure in playing with a toy which whistles when inflated and groans mournfully when deflated) and a spreading out—like the flattening of the full breasts of a woman who is lying on her back.[16]

Honey upon honey: as in Lévinas, this image translates ontological indifference; it comes on stage as the very reality of the commonality of being and beings, existing and existents. What meets up in this indifferent sugared difference, in this ontological difference at once annulled and revealed by the honey, is, Sartre tells us, the "there is" and "the facticity of being-thrown." Things thus literally *take part* in finitude. And I remain persuaded, contrasense or not, that the genius of Sartre's writing and its fantastic power consist in the way in which it makes ontological difference exist; that is, the way in which it invites things to bear witness to the question of Being. Only then, for example, could there be a "metaphysical coefficient of lemon."

> In each apprehension of quality, there is in this sense a metaphysical effort to escape from our condition so as to pierce through the shell of nothingness about the 'there is' and to penetrate to the pure in-itself. But obviously we can apprehend quality only as a symbol of a being that totally escapes us, even though it is totally there before us; in short, we can only make revealed being function as a symbol of being-in-itself. This means that a new structure of the 'there is' is constituted which is the meaningful level although this level is revealed in the absolute unity of one and the same fundamental project. This structure we shall call the metaphysical purport of all intuitive revelation of being; and this is precisely what we ought to achieve and disclose by psychoanalysis. What is the metaphysical purport of yellow, of red, of polished, or wrinkled? And after these elementary questions, what is the metaphysical coefficient of lemon, of water, of oil, etc.? Psychoanalysis must resolve all of these problems if it wants to understand someday why Pierre loves oranges and has a horror of water, why he gladly eats tomatoes and refuses to eat beans, why he vomits if he is forced to swallow oysters or raw eggs.[17]

In this text, a language is sought that would attain this very particular level of ontico-ontological reality, the level on which philosophical analysis has neither to do with beings or with being, but with both at the same time, different-indifferent, soldered together in the matter of existence. This text resonates as an echo of the famous scene in *Nausea* when the root of the chestnut tree, flesh of Being and beings, fantastically appears in a public park, much like the unreal cities that Lévinas speaks of:

> And then all of a sudden, there it was, clear as day: existence had suddenly unveiled itself. It had lost the harmless look of an abstract category: it was the very paste of things; this root was kneaded into existence. Or rather the root, the park gates, the bench, the sparse grass, all that had vanished: the diversity of things, their individuality, were only an appearance, a veneer. This veneer had melted, leaving soft, monstrous masses, all in disorder—naked, in a frightful, obscene nakedness.[18]

One must be attentive here to the motif of unveiling: "existence was suddenly unveiled." Sartre's novel envisages the effects in the real of the Heideggerian unveiling of existence; *aletheia* comes on stage, the effective unveiling that calls ontological difference to come into appearance, to enter into existence. It is as if the real underscores its own deconstruction, modifies itself in service of this deconstruction; as if it were ready to bend to its new philosophical and phenomenological destiny, *taking ontico-ontological form*, giving itself to be differently seen, letting *existing* difference be seen as the very matter of this form, at once existence become "paste" and nothing.

For this reason, existence, for Sartre, as for Lévinas, does not ultimately have much to do—despite what they both affirm—with the existence of *Dasein*. It is something other than what comes into play when the two authors retranslate the couple Being-beings into "existing-existents." Existence appears in their work as the *real effect* of ontological difference and not simply as the mode of being of an entity that is not a thing. And it is paradoxically this real effect that is fantastic, to the extent that this real exceeds the real, as it is generally understood. At stake is the incursion of existence into things, the incursion of difference into the night or the sadness of a garden, surreality or hypermateriality of being after Heidegger: a post-Heideggerian real.

The academic character of my exposition so far—firstly Lévinas, secondly Sartre, thirdly Nancy (I could not find a better method for what I intended to present here)—masks the fact that it was through reflection on the work of Nancy that I came to see a unity—an unsettled and perhaps contestable unity, he will say to me—between the thought of these three authors. I am currently in the process of writing on Heidegger and I have had to confront, like so many others before me, the unavoidable question of the changes in his work after *Being and Time*, and to reflect upon the fact that the category of existence very quickly loses the central role that it obviously played at the heart of the analytic that bears its name. Accordingly, it has always struck me that *existence* remains, in the thought of Nancy who is a great reader of Heidegger, a major concept, and that it continues to insist, to exist after its ontological disinheritance, after the failure of existentialism, and finally, after the work of Derrida—within whose work, to my knowledge, existence is not a fundamental philosopheme. I thus began with this question: why does existence resist and what is existence for Nancy? While I was rereading his texts, I noticed a certain "family resemblance" between his analyses and those of Lévinas and Sartre. If the context of his analyses is very different, something, within existence conceived as an ontological effect, remains deeply identical—which raises, once again, the question of the fantastic.

Existence is not thinkable, for Nancy, outside of a double structure, that of the "right on" (*à même*)—"*an*" in German—and that of the "being-caught-within." To exist is being-right-on, like Sartre's honey is right on the honey when its ecstasy takes it from the spoon to the pot. "The being of existence takes place right on existence," Nancy declares in "The Decision of Existence," one of the articles that make up *Une pensée finie*. He continues: "*There is no* existentiale *that is not immediately and as such caught in the* existentiell."[19]

"The Decision of Existence" presents itself as a reading of *Being and Time* that attempts to understand how Dasein passes from improper existence—everydayness, the "One"—to proper or authentic existence. It is this passage itself that is the "decision of existence." However, once again, this reading of Heidegger displaces Heidegger; and existence acquires, as it were, a new existence.

Nancy thus insists upon the fact that the decision of existence takes place *right on* existence. This signifies, and paragraph 38 of *Being and Time* affirms, that "existence in its ownness is not something which floats above falling everydayness; existentially, it is only a modified grasp (*ein modifiziertes Ergreifen*) in which such everydayness is seized upon."[20] In other words, decision, the passage from the improper to the proper takes place as a kind of slippage—"without changing ground," Nancy says; it is very much existence that modifies itself, right on itself. Nancy thus asks how there can be decision, a pure cut—*Entscheidung*—where there is precisely nothing to cut, since existence remains caught in itself, flows from itself toward itself, as it were, without rupture. Nancy's insistence upon this existential paste and this existential vice grip deports the Heideggerian definition of existence toward something other than itself, toward another future. How can there be a decision, therefore, if decision always implies the cutting edge of an opening? How to open and what is opening when one is caught? To cut, Nancy responds, can only signify this: to open existence *upon its incision*. "The essence of the decision [of existence]... is itself cut, exposed, opened—on its very incision, so to speak."[21] What begins to appear here is, indeed, the slice of existence—that is, a thickness that lets itself be sliced, or cut, to the quick. A reality, here again, of ontico-ontological being: "*nothing* that is—but only of Being-delivered-over to beings, which is existence."[22] The "modified grasp" of existence by itself—which, Nancy mentions, Heidegger tells us "nothing more" about—implies a mutability, and thus a certain malleability, and thus a certain materiality, or plasticity, of existence. The double structure of existence's relation to itself, the structure of the "right on" and that of "being-caught-in," marks the upsurge of an understanding of existence as the reality of difference. Difference starts to exist.

This existence of existence is not night, nor is it the viscous or the root of a chestnut tree; it is all that at the same time; it is the body. The body is the existence of existence; it is the existence of the body. "The body," Nancy writes in *Corpus*, "*is* the being of existence."[23] With this word, "the body," so simple and so old, Nancy gives a name to the simplest apparatus of ontico-ontological materiality. This body is indeed the "ontological body," the body of ontico-ontological difference.

Does that mean that it is the *incarnation* of ontico-ontological difference? No. Nancy says that the ontological or ontico-ontological body is not the "incarnation" of difference, but its "carnation," or rather its "local color."

> ... another name for local color is *carnation* [...] Not *in*carnation, where the body is filled with the breath of Spirit, but simple carnation, like the scansion, color, frequency and nuance, of a place, of the event of existence.[24]

"Incarnation" and "carnation" are analyzed as two "versions of coming to presence." The one is metaphysical, traditional; the other is the apparition, real and recent, of difference. But how would this carnation, this ontological body, be apprehended if not as fantastic phenomena? The singular body can be seen, as in Lévinas, at once detached and attached, delivered and redeemed, inseparable and separated from the ontological body that is the basis of existence, this "compact thickness," this "continuity of sense": the body "does not inhabit either the 'spirit' or the 'body.' They take place at the limit [upon the cutting edge], *as the limit itself*: limit—outer edge, fracture and intersection of the foreign within the continuity of sense, within the continuity of matter. Opening, *discretion*."[25] The being of existence and existence itself are at once united and separated, soldered together, right on one another, both caught up in one another and strangers, each an *intruder* for the other. There again, the community of this foreignness takes place, bodies forth, makes space, time, and matter, and produces vertigo. Nancy does not speak literally of horror, or of the fantastic, but he does have his own word, a very beautiful word: *areality*. The ontico-ontological real is "areal."

"Areality" is also the title of one of the slices of *Corpus*:

> "Areality" is an old word that signifies the property of having an *air* (*area*). By accident, the word can also suggest a lack of reality, or rather a tenuous, light, or suspended reality: that of the distance that localizes a body, or within a body. The paucity of reality, indeed, which is at the "basis" of substance, matter or the subject. But this paucity of reality makes up the entire *areal real* in which the architectonic of the body (as it has been called) articulates itself and plays itself out. In this sense, areality is the *ens realissimum*, the maximal potentiality of existing, within total extension of its horizon. Simply put, the real as areal unites the *infinite* of the maximum of existence... to the absolute *finitude* of the areal horizon.[26]

Areality—this beautiful word speaks of space, space as reality. At the same time, it speaks of this reality as the "paucity of reality," as non-thing (the *a* being understood as a privative prefix); a-real as the contrary of the real, but still appearing right on the level of things. Areality is also a form of the schematism. An "air" renders bodies homogeneous with the concept. There is no apprehension of bodies without the mediation of an air. At the same time, the schema itself comes on stage, assumes a body itself, and thus provokes the effect of a real, a surreality, the maximum of the real—a fantastic image. "Comes the world of bodies," Nancy writes. But what comes with this world?

> First of all, it is perhaps nothing other, nothing more than *this*: what comes is *what images show us*. Our billions of images show us billions of bodies—as bodies have never been shown. Crowds, masses, melees, packages, files, troupes, swarms, armies, gangs, disbanded particles, panics, tiers, processions, collisions, massacres, mass graves, communions, dispersions, full to the brim, overflowing with bodies always both in compact masses and pulverizing divagations, always collected (in streets, ensembles, megalopolises, banlieues, centers of transit, surveillance, care, or forgetting) and always

> abandoned to a stochastic mixture of these same places, to an agitation that structures them, an incessant generalized departure. This is the world of worldwide departure: the spacing of *partes extra partes*, with nothing that overarches it or upholds it, without Subject of its destiny, taking place only as a prodigious press of bodies.[27]

The world overflows right on itself, one body against another; difference compacts, compresses itself. And the hallucinatory reality that surges up from this congregation or this agglomeration given in images calls thought to open itself to this (surreal, a-real, areal) effusion, to think the real of another age, the real of ontico-ontological difference, to make itself available to the possibility of apprehending a fantastic reality, existence that exists, existence that does not exist: the effect of the real of Heidegger's legacy.

While rereading Heidegger, I understood that the destiny of ontological difference was indeed "carnation," the name given to what should become an effect of a real—of another real, of course, but still a real—beings and Being together, which does not limit itself to the existence of Dasein, but enters into presence everywhere, always, there, like the root of the chestnut tree, viscous paste, night without sleep, body in departure, areola. And Nancy taught me much; for, he never sought to ontologize the body or to affirm it as an ontico-ontological bastard child. This body does not give itself "in flesh and blood;" it arealizes itself. And, in a film about Sartre, I found something that he says very profound: "It is not a matter of being an idealist or a materialist, but rather a realist." Ontological realism thus appears as the future of a certain phenomenology.

Forging a real alliance between the work of three thinkers, whose differences I have decided not to exhibit, I have insisted upon the fantastic dimension of this objectivity, this materiality, or this reality, which confronts philosophy with a new challenge and obliges thought to economize otherwise the distinction between existent and non-existent, between "this exists" and "this does not exist." Heidegger made possible this fantastic dimension of the real; and this opening of philosophical thought to strange phenomena of Being; but he did not undertake their analysis—which thus becomes our task.

I have elsewhere elaborated how what I call "plasticity" could designate this place of an always already "psychicized" being, as Sartre says, where philosophy encounters itself; where metaphysics and an other thought cross and organize the modalities of their exchanges; where, for example, the trace of ontological difference forms itself, materializes itself in forms: forms of the real, but also artistic forms, heretofore unknown forms of philosophical writing—a writing evidenced in texts such as *Nausea*, certain passages from *Being and Nothingness*, *Existence and Existents*, or *Corpus*, the first examples of a fantastic philosophy.

How could one not think, finally, of Nancy's *L'Intrus*, where the fantastic is born from the impossibility of distinguishing between "the organic, the symbolic, and the imaginary"?

> From the moment that I was told that I must have a heart transplant, every sign could have vacillated, every marker changed: without reflection, of course, and even without identifying the slightest action or permutation. There is simply the physical sensation of a void already open [*déjà ouvert*] in my chest, along with a kind of apnea wherein nothing, strictly nothing, even today, would allow me to disentangle the organic, the symbolic, and the imaginary, or the continuous from the interrupted—the sensation was something like one breath, now pushed across a cavern, already imperceptibly half-open and strange; and, as though within a single representation, the sensation of passing over a bridge, while still remaining on it.[28]

And later:

> I become like an android from science-fiction, or rather one of the living dead, as my youngest son said to me one day.[29]

To conclude, I turn to Roger Caillois, a great thinker of the fantastic, who has silently accompanied me throughout this exposition and whom I admire very much. In *Cohérences aventureuses,* Caillois excludes from the category of the fantastic all pictural or poetic works that deliberately intend to produce the fantastic: "The first rule that I give myself is to exclude what I call the fantastic that tries too hard: those works of art purposely created in order to surprise"[30]: the marvels of fairy tales, legends and mythology, the painting of Hieronymus Bosch, "delusions of the demented mind, indulgent fancies, the masks of Tibetan demons, the avatars of Vishnu,"[31] skeletons, hells, sorcerers. "I let myself entertain," he pursues, "the dream (unreasonable, I am afraid) of a permanent and universal fantastic."[32]

What Caillois calls the "permanent and universal fantastic" closely resembles what I have here tried to approach under the name of the philosophical fantastic. This fantastic, Caillois says, is a "coherent and unavoidable" fantastic that is always born from the intrusion of a foreign element at the heart of the familiar—this element not coming from outside, but from within being. "The fantastic in my sense does not come from an element outside the human world: composite monsters, infernal fauna, the irruption of demonic, grotesque or sinister creatures. It emerges from a contradiction that bears upon the very nature of life and that obtains nothing less than the appearance of momentarily abolishing, by means of its vain but troubling prestige, the border that separates life from death."[33]

Translated by Steven Miller – The essay translated here originally appeared as "Pierre aime les horranges: Lévinas-Sartre-Nancy—une approche du fantastique en philosophie," in *Sens en tous sens: autour des travaux de Jean-Luc Nancy*, eds. Francs Guibal and Jean-Clet Martin (Paris: Galilée, 2004), 39-57.

Notes

1. One could also say it in this way: existence, that is the fantastic, is what returns even when the category of "existence" has disappeared from Heidegger's thought—which happens very quickly, right after *Being and Time*.
2. Emmanuel Lévinas, *Time and the Other*, trans. Richard A. Cohen (Pittsburgh: Duquesne University Press, 1987), 44.
3. Ibid, 46.
4. Ibid, 45.
5. Ibid, 45.
6. Ibid, 45-6.
7. Ibid, 46-7.
8. See in particular, *Phenomenological Interpretation of Kant's* Critique of Pure Reason, trans. Parvis Emad and Kenneth Maly (Bloomington: Indiana University Press, 1997), 283: "Now we see that, if the productive power of the imagination plays a leading role in the structure of human finite knowledge, nay, if the power of imagination is the very unifying root of intuition and thinking, then in finite knowledge too there is something original in the sense *originarium*. But this original faculty does not concern beings themselves, as does *intuitus originarius*, which is *ontically creative* and brings things as such into extantness. By contrast the *exhibito originaria* of the productive synthesis of the power of imagination is merely *ontologically creative*, in that it freely 'figures' the universal horizon of time as the horizon of a priori resistance, i.e., of objectness" [Translation slightly modified].
9. Émmanuel Lévinas, *Existence and Existents,* trans. Alphonso Lingis (Pittsburgh: Duquesne University Press, 1988), 54-5.
10. Ibid, 56.
11. Jean-Paul Sartre, *Being and Nothingness*, trans. Hazel E. Barnes (New York: Washington Square Press, 1956), 768.
12. Ibid, 769.
13. Ibid, 770 [Translation slightly modified].
14. Ibid, 779 [Translation slightly modified].
15. Ibid.
16. Ibid, 775.
17. Ibid, 770.
18. Jean-Paul Sartre, *Nausea*, trans. Lloyd Alexander (New York: New Directions, 1964), 127.

19. Jean-Luc Nancy, *The Birth to Presence,* trans. Brian Holmes et. al. (Minneapolis: University of Minnesota Press, 1993), 99.

20. Ibid, 99.

21. Ibid, 85.

22. Ibid, 91.

23. Jean-Luc Nancy, *Corpus* (Paris: Métailié, 2000), 17.

24. Ibid.

25. Ibid, 18.

26. Ibid, 39.

27. Ibid, 37.

28. Jean-Luc Nancy, *L'Intrus*, trans. Susan Hanson, *CR: The New Centennial Review* 2.3 (Fall 2002): 3.

29. Ibid, 3.

30. Roger Caillois, *Cohérences aventureuses (Esthétique généralisée; Au cœur du fantastique; La Dissymétrie)* (Paris: Gallimard, 1962, 1965, 1973), 72.

31. Ibid, 74.

32. Ibid, 74.

33. Ibid, 173.

8

Sameness without Identity

Tim Dean

> There are times in life when the question of knowing if one can think differently than one thinks, and perceive differently than one sees, is absolutely necessary if one is to go on looking and reflecting at all .... [W]hat is philosophy today—philosophical activity, I mean—if it is not the critical work that thought brings to bear on itself? In what does it consist, if not in the endeavor to know how and to what extent it might be possible to think differently, instead of legitimating what is already known?
>
> —Michel Foucault[1]

THINKING DIFFERENTLY

This passage, from Foucault's introduction to the second volume of *The History of Sexuality*, captures exactly what contemporary criticism values about difference. To think differently is to think beyond or against the status quo; the political significance of philosophy consists in its thinking otherwise, its refusing to authorize the "already known," and thus its functioning as something other than a discourse of legitimation or conservation. According to this logic, critical thinking cannot hope to solve the crises of legitimation that characterize modernity, but instead must intensify them by persistently questioning that which is "already known." Philosophical activity assumes its political dimension by functioning at certain historical moments, certain "times in life," as an avant garde. At such moments the challenge lies in resisting the lures of self-authorization and self-consolidation; it is a question not of developing but of changing, of "dispers[ing] one toward a strange and new relation with himself," as Foucault puts it in his original preface to *The Use of Pleasure*.[2] With the practice of thinking differently comes the promise—or, depending on one's point of view, the threat—of change.

In the passage above Foucault is explaining why the second and third volumes of his *History of Sexuality* appear so discontinuous with the first. During the course of establishing how individuals recognize themselves as subjects of something called sexuality, Foucault found it necessary to return to the more basic question of how individuals come to recognize themselves as subjects in the first place; hence his decision to "reorganize the whole study around the slow formation, in antiquity, of a hermeneutics of the self."[3] What draws Foucault to the period of antiquity is the disjunction between its techniques of the self and our hermeneutics of desire—the fact that for the Greeks one exercises an elaborate relation to himself without concern for deciphering one's own truth, much less tending to locate that truth specifically in desire. Another way of putting this would be to say that while in his introductory volume of *The History of Sexuality* Foucault attempts to think sexuality outside the framework of psychoanalysis (which he tacitly identifies with the repressive hypothesis), in subsequent volumes he commits himself to the more basic project of trying to think *subjectivity* non-psychoanalytically. Or, more accurately yet, *The Use of Pleasure* and *The Care of the Self* represent Foucault's most sustained attempts to think subjectivity apart from psychology; and in so doing he refused to countenance psychoanalytic antipsychologism as a viable method for this project.

Thus in "thinking differently" Foucault is doing two things at once. First, he is measuring his distance from conceptualizations of subjectivity and sexuality that, at the time of his writing the preface, had dominated the Parisian intellectual landscape since the 1950s. Lacan remains central to the status quo against which Foucault is thinking, because from the latter's perspective psychoanalysis represents the "already known," the taken-for-granted paradigm of subjectification. No doubt this positioning of psychoanalysis involves misrecognizing what Lacan was doing, as suggested by Foucault's reductive critique of the concept of repression. More significantly, however, in "thinking differently" Foucault is measuring the distance from his own conceptualizations of subjectivity and sexuality too. The "already known" that the second and third volumes of *The History of Sexuality* refuse to legitimate should be understood as encompassing the first volume. Thinking differently entails being deliberately discontinuous with oneself. And this discontinuity involves more than simply changing one's mind or backtracking; it is a matter not of self-contradiction but of becoming other than what one was.

The species of self-transformation that Foucault describes in the course of rationalizing his attempt to "think differently" in the second and third volumes also constitutes his object of analysis in those works. According to his account, Greek "arts of existence" consist not in discovering or realizing one's subjective identity, but in departing from it. Thus in taking the occasion to anatomize ancient techniques of the self that exhibit little preoccupation with identity, Foucault departs from his own intellectual identity and its itinerary, to such an extent that publishing conventions necessitate some explanation of the evident discontinuity. Yet in this resistance to identity we can discern a larger continuity structuring Foucault's entire *oeuvre*, namely, his ongoing commitment to the critique of identity as a classificatory mechanism indispensable to regimes of normalization. Since for Foucault identities represent forms of imprisonment, it makes sense that he would resist those classifications through which we identify and position intellectuals and their work too. The most basic way of thinking differently is thus to think against identity, particularly one's own.

Thinking differently counts as political activity because it promises a kind of freedom: "The object was to learn to what extent the effort to think one's own history can free thought from what it silently thinks, and so enable it to think differently."[4] Here the phrase "one's own history" refers to both the history of one's epoch and one's own specific trajectory within that context. The possibility of liberating thought "from what it silently thinks" suggests achieving some distance from unspoken assumptions—one's own as well as those of others. But the idea of a form of thinking that operates silently within thought itself conjures the specter of something akin to the unconscious; indeed, it is not difficult to read Foucault's sentence as an allegory of psychoanalysis: *the object is to learn to what extent the effort to think one's own history can free thought from what it silently thinks, and so enable it to think differently*. Psychoanalysis, too, represents a practice of self-transformation, of becoming other to oneself by doing substantially more than merely switching self-identifications. From this vantage point, to think differently would be to think psychoanalytically, even if in certain contexts that entailed thinking against psychoanalytic orthodoxy or counter psychoanalytic institutionalization.

In making this argument, I do not wish to assimilate Foucault to Lacan, or to nullify the former's critique of psychoanalysis. Rather, I am interested in how, for both Foucault and Lacan, thinking seems antithetical to identity—how, that is, "thinking differently" may be considered a redundancy, insofar as thinking entails introducing a difference to what otherwise appears seamlessly self-identical. As Lacan put it in one of his many revisions of the Cartesian formula, "I think where I am not, therefore I am where I do not think."[5] For both Lacan and Foucault (albeit differently), *thinking ruptures identity*. Within a psychoanalytic framework, thinking ruptures identity because there can be no thinking, no movement of consciousness, that is not divided by the unconscious. When we regard the unconscious as an effect of language, we grasp how the linguistic sign's division between signifier and signified renders impossible any psychical identity that would remain untroubled by slippage. Lacan thus establishes psychoanalysis on an antipsychologistic basis, rejecting psychology as a science of identities.

It is not only psychological presuppositions that are challenged by this basic psychoanalytic move, but also philosophical and sociological conceptions of identity. We should not forget that philosophy, psychology, and sociology all employ different senses of the term: while for psychology *identity* designates a self-conscious sense of selfhood, for philosophy the term refers to a non-psychological principle of unity or indiscernibility; sociologically *identity* betokens social categories of classification—for instance, those of gender, race, and sexuality—that variably inform an individual's psychological identity while remaining irreducible to it. I note these extremely schematic distinctions merely to observe that critiques of identitarianism often draw inconsistently on discourses of identity (for example, by using a philosophical sense of non-identity to try to undermine oppressive social identities), and that Lacan's account of subjective division, while it carries far-reaching implications for all these discourses, rarely employs the term *identity*.[6]

If thinking ruptures identity, then we must entertain the possibility that in this formula the term *thinking* might be substituted with *deconstruction*—deconstruction ruptures identity—insofar as the latter has shown how every identity is fissured from within by differences that are not merely contingent upon, but rather constitutive of, identity. Jacques Derrida's early neologism *différance* articulates this principle, suggesting how writing ceaselessly betrays the semantic identities that it is supposed to secure.[7] While attributing disruptions of identity specifically to writing, Derrida also aligns the differential and deferring properties of inscription with the Freudian unconscious, arguing famously that "writing is unthinkable without repression."[8] Drawing on Freud's model of the psychical apparatus as a "mystic writing-pad," Derrida contends that writing cannot be conceptualized apart from a self-division or internal difference that is identifiable with the unconscious. In pursuing this line of thought he is, of course, mounting a tacit critique of Lacan's account of the unconscious as an effect of *spoken* discourse. My purpose in recalling these old debates, however, is not to negotiate Derrida's complex and ongoing engagement with psychoanalysis, but rather to emphasize how for several decades the critical avant garde has been inseparable from a multivalent critique of identitarianism, whose implications we still are in the midst of assessing. Whether in psychoanalytic, deconstructive, or historicist guise, critiques of identity politics have found in the concept of difference a powerfully unsettling critical tool.

If poststructuralism may be distinguished by its focus on the disruptive effects of internal difference, then the political consequences of such disruption have been exploited most avidly by various minoritarian schools of thought, in which attention to internal differences fruitfully complicates analyses of gender, sexuality, race, ethnicity, and postcoloniality. As a critique of sexual identitarianism, queer theory emerges from this nexus, based philosophically on Foucault's genealogy of sexual classifications in the first volume of *The History of Sexuality*. Unlike Foucault, however, queer theorists have expressed considerable ambivalence about "the loss of specificity" attendant upon a rigorous dismantling of sexual identity categories. The danger is that demonstrating the historical contingency of identity categories and thereby evacuating their contents will cancel the hard-won recognition of differences and reinstate a universal norm, with disastrous political consequences for those whose identities are defined by their distance from the norm.

Anxiety over "specificity" in queer theory thus takes the following form. Foucault has shown how the category of homosexuality emerged toward the end of the nineteenth century as an instrument of regulatory power that was designed to identify, isolate, and control those whose erotic behavior failed to conform to a certain reproductive ideal associated with capitalism. Homosexuality's becoming an identity, a new kind of pathological selfhood, forms part of the larger process of differentiation that constrains human life by binding us to any number of psychological classifications. As a result sexual identities—no matter how ostensibly liberatory—come to be understood as problems rather than solutions. Or, rather, liberatory sexual identities, such as the categories lesbian and gay, become necessary only in response to severely pathologizing identitarian classifications. The process of differentiation that enabled homosexuality to emerge as a quasi-permanent difference from heterosexuality—and thus ultimately to challenge the latter's normative universality—remains contaminated by the regulatory intentions that inspired differentiation in the first place.

Once seen from this perspective, the political potential of proliferating erotic identities appears distinctly limited. Yet the counter-response to these problems of differentiation—for which the term *queer* has come to stand in the field of erotic politics—risks returning sexual minorities to the invisibility they suffered before sex and gender universals were challenged. In short, critiques of identitarianism provoke the fear, for both individuals and groups, that too much will be lost if identity is lost. Minoritarianism cannot survive a full-scale assault on identity politics, a fact that helps explain the ambivalence surrounding anti-identitarianism. There are limits to how far a complete dismantling of identity categories can be sustained, in part because the structures of imaginary recognition through which we make sense of ourselves depend on these categories. Without some baseline minimum of identity, the ego dissolves. And hence too much internal difference tends to be experienced as intolerable.

We thus encounter two related problems: first, that the introduction of differences can undermine identity categories to the point of disabling incoherence; but second, and conversely, that difference always threatens to reestablish itself *as* identity and thereby to generate a new status quo, which inhibits recognition of further differences. Bisexuality provides a good example of this Janus-faced conundrum, in that most lesbian and gay thinking tends to regard full acknowledgment of bisexuality as dangerously compromising to gay politics, whereas most bisexual thinking feels marginalized by the hegemony that lesbian and gay identities assume beyond the ambit of normative heterosexuality. If one is bisexual, gayness or lesbianism can seem like the status quo that one is struggling against, quite as much as heteronormativity.[9] When difference coalesces into identity—when it becomes reified or essentialized—one is no longer "thinking differently" in the way that Foucault describes. Instead, once difference congeals into identity, one ends up thinking against the other rather than against oneself—and this is infinitely easier to do. Thus difference rapidly appears as an external problem, a question of the boundary between oneself and others, rather than figuring an internal inconsistency that renders one other to him- or herself.

Another way of framing this problem would involve pointing out that the relation between identity and difference tends to be conceived in imaginary or binary terms, such that difference effectively denotes merely a *different identity*. To forestall this recentering of difference as identity, a third term that remains inassimilable to either pole of the binary, while also refusing to function as a compromise between them, is needed. Elsewhere I have argued that Lacan's distinguishing among registers of alterity offers one way of thinking the identity-difference relation in non-imaginary terms, since the otherness of language remains irreducible to social differentials. That is to say, Lacan's theory of the symbolic order maintains a distinction between otherness and difference that is both conceptually and ethically beneficial.[10] Linguistic alterity functions as a third term mediating different identities or subject positions in such a way that no identity can claim to be unfractured; no subject position can achieve complete self-identity once language is taken into account. Derridean *différance* functions in approximately this way too, as an unregulatable force of differentiation that perpetually prevents the recentering of difference as identity. It is by employing versions of this logic that poststructuralist queer theorists, such as Judith Butler and Lee Edelman, critique the assumption of sexed and gendered identities.[11]

The poststructuralist emphasis on difference has often led to a collapsing of otherness with difference, and thus to a neglect of the specificity not so much of social differentials as of linguistic alterity. But even when the specificity of representational mediation is observed scrupulously, the doubleness of this mediating alterity tends to go overlooked. By this I mean that identity is troubled not only by the fissuring of linguistic alterity, but also by what language misses. To put this in explicitly Lacanian terms: subjective identities are compromised by both symbolic and real axes of mediation. The language through which we express and thereby create ourselves fractures selfhood doubly, since it not only proliferates signification beyond our control, but also fails to signify completely in spite of its generativity. Lacan calls linguistic excess *the unconscious*; linguistic deficiency he calls *the real*. The pertinence of the Lacanian real lies less in its undermining of identity than in its sabotaging of difference. That is to say, the real represents a zone of undifferentiation—a place where difference cannot exist—because it is devoid of signifiers; the real is defined negatively as nothing other than this void. If it betokens a logical space that is equally inhospitable to difference and identity, then perhaps the Lacanian real could be conceived in terms of sameness—a sameness that is distinct from, indeed resistant to, identity.

Generally conceived in terms of its resistance to meaning, the real has been aligned most commonly with trauma and hence with what hurts. This emphasis was necessary in part as a corrective to facile appropriations of French psychoanalysis that perceived in the category of *jouissance* a liberatory pleasure conveniently separable from the difficulties attendant upon psychic negativity. Yet as an instance of the failure of imaginary and symbolic differentiations, the real may be aligned hypothetically with ontological sameness—and thus thought apart from the primarily negative dimension of trauma, impossibility, and pain. To "think differently" at this juncture in the history of psychoanalysis may be, paradoxically, to think more about sameness than about difference, to become temporarily indifferent to difference, and to resist assimilating sameness too readily to the imaginary register. While I do not wish to attribute to psychoanalytic discourses of sexual difference all the problems of identitarianism, thinking sameness may entail bracketing or demoting sexual difference as an explanatory category. Thus it would be less a question of supplementing the analytic paradigm of sexual difference with consideration of racial difference or postcolonial difference (to invoke two of the directions pursued recently in psychoanalytic studies) than of thinking in an entirely different register—that of undifferentiation. Rather than multiplying differences and discriminating ever finer particularities, we might suspend temporarily the differentiation machine in order to consider forms of existence for which the distinction between identity and difference is largely irrelevant.

While queer theory emerged as part of the ongoing pluralist project of "difference studies," it has a stake in resisting the sexual differentiations of modernity. Critical emphasis on sexual difference, valuable though it has been, tends to reinforce heteronormativity by tying erotic relationality too closely to differences between the sexes. As I have argued elsewhere, the psychoanalytic preoccupation with sexual difference often leads to an elision of otherness with difference, such that one's subjective relations to alterity get figured primarily in terms of relations with "the Other sex."[12] Consequently queer theory stands to gain from investigating how non-imaginary sexual sameness—a sameness irreducible to identity—may represent more than merely the mythic prehistory or default of sexual difference.

But perhaps it is misleading to speak in terms of *sexual* sameness, as if the category of sexuality—or, indeed, any category—could still signify meaningfully at the level of ontological undifferentiation that concerns us here. It may be more accurate to hypothesize instead that the sexual grants access to states or relations that dissolve the already troubled distinction between sexual and non-sexual. Certainly it is the case phenomenologically that relations of apparent sameness in homosexuality adumbrate some possibilities for the de-differentiating imagination. For example, Leo Bersani's recent work suggests that the sameness of gender in homosexuality points toward an ontological solidarity of being that makes the ostensible failure of difference ethically exemplary. Rather than betraying a disavowal of difference or a narcissistic immaturity (as some psychoanalytically inspired homophobes have claimed), homosexuality would lay bare, as it were, the relational potential of dissolving the boundaries between oneself and others, or of apprehending those boundaries as illusory. From this perspective the gay clone appears less as a model of stifling conformism than as an allegorical figure of what Bersani calls "inaccurate self-replication." The idea is not that we should start trying to look alike after all, or should aspire to a single gendered ideal, but rather that the critique of queer culture's manifestations of sameness may be missing something that a notion of the erotic "clone" makes visible. The critique of the clone—that it perpetuates an exclusionary ideal of masculinity—comes from the gay left as well as the antigay right: whereas the latter sees in sameness a narcissistic disavowal of difference, the former often regards the clone's idealization of butch, self-sufficient masculinity as a racist, misogynist, and ultimately homophobic formation. Apart from the arousal he stimulates in many gay men, surely there is nothing good to be said for this figure?

CLONES

In order to distinguish cultural manifestations of sameness from the ontological de-differentiation that interests Bersani, it may be helpful to meditate further on the gay clone. The term refers to a post-Stonewall norm of masculinity, a particular "look" adopted in the 1970s primarily by American gay men, at a historical moment when it seemed newly possible to embrace gay and masculine identities simultaneously.[13] Before Stonewall, being openly gay usually meant being flamboyant (conforming to the model of gender inversion), whereas sexual liberation ostensibly disentangled gender from sexuality, such that one could conform to normative gender expectations while nevertheless acknowledging one's non-normative sexual identity. To put it in vernacular terms, after Stonewall the macho gay man and the lesbian femme came to supplement the nelly queen and the butch dyke as more readily available identities for non-heterosexual men and women. In this context the gay clone appropriated the insignia of American westernism—faded denim, flannel shirts, leather boots, often a bandanna, and the *de rigueur* mustache—to affect a look of rugged masculine individualism: think the Marlboro Man or, in its campier version, the Village People. It seemed ironically fitting that the model photographed in the 1970s as the Marlboro Man, that icon of American masculinity, happened to be gay.

Gay men adopted with such alacrity the visual styles of normative masculinity—and, increasingly, hypermasculinity—that it made perfect sense to speak of the clone look. While the term connotes a critique of gender homogenization—we endured the struggles of sexual liberation so that all gay men could try to look alike?—more often than not the clone functioned as an index of desirability, even for those who employed the term disparagingly. When discussing the clone's commitment to masculinity, Foucault connected his recent cultural emergence to the significance of "monosexual relations," remarking on the lack of precedence for sexual intimacy between two adult men (rather than between an older man and a youth) outside the context of single-sex institutions such as prisons and the military.[14] Here I am not interested in either praising the gay clone as subversive of sex-gender hierarchies or blaming him as conformist; neither am I especially concerned with what made this image so potent an erotic stimulant in the first place. Rather, I'm interested in how the clone has mutated in gay culture—how he has replicated inaccurately, we might say—and, ultimately, how the desire for sameness, or what Foucault speaks of in terms of monosexuality, may represent more than a stubborn refusal to move beyond the securities of the imaginary into the grown-up world of difference.

Of course, the term *clone* was always hyperbolic in gay culture, since no two persons can be visually identical unless they happen to be twins (and in that case the appearance of identity must be carefully cultivated if visual indistinguishability is to be sustained into adulthood). Rather than signaling visual identity, then, the clone signified a shared erotic ideal—albeit one that was subject to endlessly proliferating differentiations as gay men discovered they were each looking for something quite specific in bed. When we get down to the nitty gritty, a collective erotic ideal rapidly disintegrates into divergent preferences that vastly exceed any binary system yet devised. It is not just that desire divides along hetero- and homo- lines, but also that within each category numerous subcategories proliferate, in a manner that spurs the taxonomic imagination to redouble its classificatory efforts.

Perhaps as a result of experiencing the negative effects of erotic classification, gay men have become particularly adept at elaborating complex sexual typologies—a project in which the clone's sartorial accessories were enlisted without hesitation. I refer here to the gay "hanky code," a signifying system whereby differently colored bandannas signal the specific erotic activity one is pursuing. The hanky code is sufficiently complicated to warrant some explaining—even to rather experienced gay men. Worn on the left-hand side, a bandanna generally indicates that the wearer wishes to assume a dominant position during sex; worn on the right, it indicates the wearer's desire to be dominated. However, even if one were content to remain positionally consistent and therefore in some sense *non*-promiscuous during a given erotic encounter, the array of bandanna hues is so variegated as to induce vertigo.

A card I carry in my wallet lists no less than 59 different bandanna colors, each of which subdivides into two meanings depending on whether it is worn left or right. To ensure that one is getting what one is looking for, he must be able to distinguish, often under dim lighting, light blue from robin's egg blue from medium blue from navy blue from teal blue—and be able to tell left from right consistently, a faculty not closely correlated with the gay gene.[15] And naturally one needs to be sure of what one is looking for in the first place. Needless to say, gay folklore is as replete with tales of erotic misrecognition as is Shakespearean comedy; despite their carefully choreographed signals, gay men often end up with a surprise once they make it into the bedroom. Paying attention to the gay clone, we thus discover a bewildering multiplicity of erotic differentiation associated with this icon of erstwhile sameness. The taxonomic imagination frequently risks defeat at the hands of its own classificatory zeal. This would be one way of understanding what Foucault meant by his thesis that there is no power without resistance—that obstructions to power come not from some outside force but rather from inside power itself.

While the gay hanky code promotes differentiation based on the kind of erotic activity desired, it also militates against the clone's monopoly on desirability by subdividing potential partners into any number of types. That is to say, the hanky code differentiates not only according to behavior (do you like to fist or to get fisted?), but also according to identity (are you looking for a black lover or a Latino? a cop or a cowboy or a Daddy?). By differentiating along the axis of identity and appearance, as well as along that of activity, gay semiotic systems permit virtually anybody to become a type. You might have considered yourself too nondescript to qualify as a clone (or a cowboy or a leatherman); so much the better for perfecting that "boy next door" look. Haven't set foot inside a gym since high school? All the more likely that you'll qualify as a chubby, drawing the ardent devotion of "chubby chasers," men who prefer their sex partners very overweight (wear an apricot bandanna). Whatever your race, age, or body-type—and whether you're hirsute or smooth, circumcised or not, tattooed or not, bald or not—you will qualify as some stranger's erotic ideal. Increasingly HIV-seropositivity qualifies as an erotic type too.[16] Even the condition of being without observable distinction carries its own distinction: it is considered sexy to be generic, since the generic counts as yet one more erotic type. In the gay world, being unmarked is itself remarkable. Thus while Bersani is right to insist—against those who idealize queer desire as utopianly democratic—on "the ruthlessly exclusionary nature of sexual desire,"[17] nevertheless queer culture offsets desire's exclusionary commitments by its paradoxical diversification of exclusivity.

From a psychoanalytic perspective we could say that if virtually anybody can be seen as a type and therefore as sexually attractive *to someone*, then this is because practically anything can be fetishized. Just as conventionally unappealing acts—defecating, urinating, spitting, hitting—can come to be regarded as erotically stimulating, so too can conventionally unappealing physical traits.[18] Doubtless this fetishistic aptitude compensates for the impossibly demanding ideals of physical beauty that circulate so intensively in gay male culture: once slotted into type, even strikingly unprepossessing men can get as much sex as the most handsome Adonis. We might say that gay men represent the most resolute fetishists, capable of transforming *any* physical attribute or activity into an object of desire. But when we consider Lacan's claim that desire is structurally fetishistic (insofar as its cause is the shape-shifting, multiform *objet petit a*), we see that the gay aptitude for fetishism represents nothing more than an intuitive grasp of the workings of desire *tout court*. In practice if not in theory, North American gay men are mostly Lacanians.

One of the more unlikely hanky codes is the grey flannel bandanna: worn on the right, it signifies "likes men in suits"; worn on the left, "actually owns a suit." This example suggests some kinship between the aptitude for making anything into a sexual fetish and the capacity for regarding any identity as a form of drag—a capacity represented most famously in *Paris Is Burning*, Jennie Livingston's documentary about Harlem drag balls, and theorized most persistently by Judith Butler. Multiplying fetishistic "types" undermines normative objects of desire in the same way that expanding drag beyond female impersonation undermines essentialized identities. Thus what seems politically appealing about gay fetishism is its potential anti-identitarianism: fixating on one particular trait dissolves the culture's fixations on normative objects of desire by proliferating the possible activities and sites of eros. Further, in highlighting the partiality of desire's objects, fetishism throws into relief how human desire originates not in heterosexuality—nor even in the attractiveness of other persons—but in the impersonal operations of language on corporeality. Lacan's theory of the *objet a* offers an account of how symbolic existence disintegrates human bodies, leaving intangible objects of desire in its wake.

When we characterize *objet a* as Lacan's principal contribution to the study of fetishism, we see that the psychoanalytic account of objects forms part of what I have designated as the differentiating imagination. Perhaps originally psychoanalysis participated in the insidious project of differentiation that I termed taxonomic, namely, the attempt to classify sexual perversions with the aim of curing or at least regulating them. But, as I have suggested, Lacan's account of the object differentiates and proliferates causes of desire to a point that confounds heteronormativity. As with the psychoanalytic account of the unconscious, the theory of *objet a* counters sexual identitarianism and therefore provides queer critique with potent conceptual ammunition. However, as with Butler's appropriation of drag for counteridentitarian purposes, difficulties arise as soon as one endeavors to harness these psychically implicated concepts to political agendas. Too often the capacity for differentiation that undermines identity is understood in voluntarist terms, as if it were a matter simply of choosing one's identities, fetishes, or objects of desire.

Besides the issue of voluntarism, which has sparked such critical animus, there is a further problem here. This problem stems from the assumption that the only viable response to identitarianism or essentialism originates in the differentiating imagination—that, for example, the ostensibly homogenizing figure of the gay clone must be demystified to reveal an agent of diversification. To phrase this problem at its most basic, I would suggest that criticism has been misled in its conviction that difference, rather than sameness, represents the best weapon against identitarian regimes. Instead of deconstructing sameness to reveal the differentiations that constitute and thereby internally fracture it, we might distinguish between registers of sameness in the manner that (following Lacan) I previously argued for distinguishing between registers of otherness. Doubtless there is something paradoxical in attempting to distinguish likenesses, just as there is in Bersani's call for "an emphasis on the *specifics* of sameness," which also conjures the perverse prospect of differentiating sameness.[19] Yet the example of the gay clone remains useful in helping us to distinguish imaginary sameness from the ontological de-differentiation that Bersani has been investigating under the rubrics of "homoness" and "inaccurate self-replication."

Ultimately the clone represents an *image* of sameness, as well as of desirability, and thus a figure for imaginary identity. He makes the image of what one might have and the image of what one might be the same image. The clone is a figure for imaginary identity because, in narrowing the distance between self and other, his appeal is fundamentally narcissistic. Whereas Lacan's account of narcissism emphasizes the subject's alienation in a specular image, the clone seems to promise that one may embrace rather than remain alienated from oneself. From a psychoanalytic perspective, this sounds like claiming that somehow imaginary alienation—and the aggressivity that accompanies it—could be overcome. What a transparent fantasy, that one would surmount one's psychic difficulties through the body of the sexual partner!

Yet what does Lacan's notion of imaginary alienation mean, other than that the subject *mis*recognizes him- or herself through the intermediary of the image of another? The point is that imaginary individuation is a giant mistake, and that we are not separately bounded monads struggling to find our way in the world, but rather profoundly connected beings whose interdependence we repeatedly fail to grasp. Lacan's account of the symbolic order indicates this interdependence, though in a differentiating register. The symbolic cuts through imaginary illusions, dividing us against ourselves and undermining our identities. But the real cuts through the differentiating illusions of the symbolic, reminding us that language cannot totalize the effects it aspires to master. Beyond the symbolic lies a realm about which we can *say* very little without denaturing it. Thus our accounts of what Lacan calls the real are always necessarily fictions of one sort or another. It is a new set of fictions about the real that Bersani has been generating in his recent work, suggesting ways of thinking about relational being beyond our comparatively familiar imaginary and symbolic coordinates.

In books such as *The Freudian Body*, Bersani offered a powerful account of how imaginary identities are disrupted and yet survive—even take a kind of pleasure in—that disruption. Developing Laplanche's notion of *ébranlement*, he described the erotic in terms of "self-shattering" and anatomized the paradoxes of trying to erect a politics on that which defeats the coherent self.[20] Albeit from a non-Lacanian vantage point, Bersani was charting the illusoriness of the human ego, and he therefore could be regarded as a fellow traveler with respect to a certain Lacanian project. More recently, however, the focus of his work has shifted from self-shattering to self-extension, or what we might call subjective mobility beyond the confines of the ego. I see a parallel here with Lacan's shift from investigating symbolic disruptions of the imaginary to his later emphasis on real disruptions of the symbolic. Once the illusory carapace of the individuated self is broken, it is only a particular brand of face-to-face intersubjectivity that falters. Without the myth of imaginary differentiation, relationality might not be quite so terrifyingly difficult as intersubjective problems suggest. Bersani's contention is that a happier, less antagonistic relationality is perpetually in process at an ontological level that mostly eludes us. Far from representing a merely occasional occurrence, however, this communication of being—where the term *communication* is understood more in Bataille's sense than in Lacan's—happens all the time, and it is only our jealously guarded imaginary selves that prevent us from registering it more clearly.

Bersani argues that ontological relationality becomes visible in certain artworks and certain manifestations of homosexuality; the question of Caravaggio's sexuality brings these two dimensions together.[21] When considering Bersani and Ulysse Dutoit's analyses of painting and film, we should bear in mind that—unlike most art critics—they are discussing images in a non-imaginary way and focusing on how images corrode rather than secure identity. In this respect, their art criticism shares something fundamental with the work of more explicitly Lacanian critics such as Parveen Adams, Joan Copjec, and Graham Hammill, all of whom in varying ways analyze images not for their thematization of the real (as Slavoj Žižek does) but for their formal dislocations of imaginary recognition.[22] The issue of recognition—how we recognize ourselves as dispersed in the world, and thereby recognize the communication of being as always already having begun—poses a central problem here. What does "recognition" without imaginary identification mean? Is there a non-imaginary form of recognition that would not be susceptible to the vicissitudes of *mis*recognition?

Certainly the term *misrecognition* implies the possibility that, perhaps in a register beyond the ego, a less delusional kind of subjective contact might occur, one in which preoccupations with mastery and possession—of oneself and others—would seem less urgent. If this kind of contact occurs without the rivalry that structures imaginary relations, it must be because boundaries demarcating self from other have dissolved. In this zone of ontological de-differentiation or sameness, it no longer makes any sense to speak of the self. After a certain point, a de-individuated self is no self at all, and I think it promotes misprisions of Bersani's project to retain vocabularies of selfhood when describing the communication of being. Thus it is less a question of ascertaining how inexact are the "inaccurate self-replications" that Bersani and Dutoit identify, than it is of grasping how selfhood figures only a corner of being—how being comprehends while vastly exceeding the ego, and how therefore our selves are but aberrations within the world's impersonal ontology.[23]

In his effort to account for what draws us to this ontological register, Bersani has developed an oxymoronic model of non-imaginary narcissism, locating in the lures of sameness a rationale for our participation in the communication of being. Reading the psychoanalytic critique of homosexuality against itself, he has argued that gay narcissism—or homoness—represents not a troubling disavowal of difference but an enlightening demonstration of how the distinction between difference and identity dissolves in another ontological register. Thus he hypothesizes how imaginary sameness, as exemplified by the figure of the gay clone, might give way to a non-imaginary world of contact that is so drained of antagonism as to qualify as a space of true solidarity. Given that the communication of being involves contact without barriers, it is perhaps inevitable that we think about it through metaphors of bodily intimacy. The ontological relatedness of which Bersani speaks offers an unlimited intimacy that most people seek (if they do seek it) through sex. But the problem with sex is that it tends to limit intimacy to other persons, when what is at stake in the communication of being is impersonal relationality—or what Bersani elsewhere calls "our already established at-homeness in the world."[24]

The metaphor of worldly at-homeness differs from the more overtly erotic figures through which we might explain the attractions of ontological de-differentiation. Despite its interest in narcissism, psychoanalysis has not been especially helpful in rationalizing this attraction, primarily because it pictures de-differentiation as almost exclusively terrifying or traumatic. Yet there is something tautological in the insistence that what threatens the ego is felt to be threatening; what about those aspects of subjectivity that exceed the ego? Why not view the cultural phenomenon of creating a shared "look" and the related phenomenon of a sexuality based on sameness of gender as but superficial instances of a more profound sameness that de-individuates subjectivity less threateningly than the loss of boundaries usually is understood to imply?

Without such an over-developed psychology of selfhood, we might be slower to cast de-differentiation in negative terms. In this respect, both Foucault's and Lacan's antipsychologism remains to be exploited.

Doubtless the prospect of treating Foucault and Lacan as companion ethicists of the impersonal raises potential methodological problems concerning the loss of distinctions between significantly different thinkers. Bersani recently has suggested, however, that "distinctions between ideas are perhaps grounded in assumptions of a difference of being between the self and the world."[25] There is always a danger that our carefully elaborated distinctions among thinkers and ideas might be based on—or at least fueled by—imaginary identifications that misrecognize deeper interdependencies. Our commitments to individuation make the identifiability and ownership of ideas a high priority, as if thought respected the imaginary boundaries that we place around persons. Yet if, as I hypothesized earlier, thinking ruptures identity, perhaps thinking ultimately corrodes distinctions in favor of analogies that correspond to analogies among worldly forms. From this perspective, "thinking differently" would conduce to sameness (though not to identity), and thus to an ontological realm at least partly independent of epistemological anxieties—a realm, that is to say, in which thinking would be coterminous with being. Faced with such a prospect we might well ask: What have we got to lose but our selves?

Notes

1. Michel Foucault, *The Use of Pleasure*, trans. Robert Hurley (New York: Random House, 1985), 8-9.
2. Foucault, "Preface to *The History of Sexuality*, Volume Two," trans. William Smock, in *Essential Works of Foucault 1954-1984, vol. 1: Ethics: Subjectivity and Truth*, ed. Paul Rabinow (New York: New Press, 1997), 205.
3. Foucault, *The Use of Pleasure*, 6.
4. Ibid., 9.
5. Jacques Lacan, "The Agency of the Letter in the Unconscious or Reason since Freud," in *Écrits: A Selection*, trans. Alan Sheridan (New York: Norton, 1977), 166. A couple of sentences later, Lacan immediately rewrites this formulation: "I am not wherever I am the plaything of my thought; I think of what I am where I do not think to think." On Lacan's rewriting of Cartesianism, see Mladen Dolar, "Cogito as the Subject of the Unconscious," in *Cogito and the Unconscious*, ed. Slavoj Žižek (Durham: Duke University Press, 1998), 11-40.
6. Strictly speaking identity is not a psychoanalytic concept, although *identification* is, of course, central to psychoanalytic theory. Devoting his seminar of 1961-62 explicitly to the topic of identification, Lacan is particu-

larly keen to discriminate registers of identification—imaginary, symbolic, and real—and the relations among them. A decade later, in seminars XIX and XX, he approaches this issue through the idea of "the One," meditating on the gnomic formula "*Y a d' l'Un*"—"There's something of the One"—to advance his ongoing critique of identitarianism, in this case with respect to sexual identification, narcissism, and love. See Lacan, *The Seminar of Jacques Lacan, Book XX: On Feminine Sexuality: The Limits of Love and Knowledge: Encore (1972-1973)*, ed. Jacques-Alain Miller, trans. Bruce Fink (New York: Norton, 1998).

7. See Jacques Derrida, "Différance," in *Speech and Phenomena, and Other Essays on Husserl's Theory of Signs*, trans. David B. Allison (Evanston: Northwestern University Press, 1973), 129-160.

8. Derrida, "Freud and the Scene of Writing," in *Writing and Difference*, trans. Alan Bass (Chicago: University of Chicago Press, 1978), 226. See also Derrida, "Différance," 149-150.

9. A representative gay political reservation about bisexuality is encapsulated in David M. Halperin's claim that the category of queerness "invites the kind of hostile political manipulation that already is all too familiar to lesbians and gay men from the deployment of the label 'bisexual': it provides a means of de-gaying gayness. Like 'bisexual,' though for different reasons, 'queer' would seem to provide a ready-made instrument of homophobic disavowal: inasmuch as it reconstitutes sexual identity under the sign of the political, it has the capacity to despecify the realities of lesbian and gay oppression, obscuring what is irreducibly *sexual* about those practices and persons most exposed to the effects of sexual racism" (Halperin, *Saint Foucault: Towards a Gay Hagiography* [New York: Oxford University Press, 1995], 65). Coming from a spokesperson for queer theory, this critique of bisexuality necessarily qualifies the widespread assumption that *queer* betokens an expanded rubric of inclusivity for sexual minorities. Substantial counter-arguments to this negative view of bisexuality may be found in Marjorie Garber, *Vice Versa: Bisexuality and the Eroticism of Everyday Life* (New York: Simon and Schuster, 1995); and Jonathan Dollimore, *Sex, Literature and Censorship* (Cambridge: Polity, 2001).

10. See Tim Dean, "Two Kinds of Otherness and Their Consequences," *Critical Inquiry* 23:4 (Summer 1997): 910-920.

11. See Lee Edelman, *Homographesis: Essays in Gay Literary and Cultural Theory* (New York: Routledge, 1994) and the work of Judith Butler, who stages confrontations with the impasses of anti-identitarianism in book after book.

12. Dean, "Homosexuality and the Problem of Otherness," in *Homosexuality and Psychoanalysis*, ed. Tim Dean and Christopher Lane (Chicago:

University of Chicago Press, 2001), 120-143.

13. The term *clone* does not appear in a comprehensive lexicon of gay slang originally published in 1972, an omission suggesting that its earliest argot usage must have been the mid-1970s. See Bruce Rodgers, *The Queens' Vernacular* (San Francisco: Straight Arrow Books, 1972); reprinted as *Gay Talk: A (Sometimes Outrageous) Dictionary of Gay Slang* (New York: Paragon, 1979).

14. Foucault writes: "We were right to condemn institutional monosexuality that was constricting, but the promise that we would love women as soon as we were no longer condemned for being gay was utopian. And a utopia in the dangerous sense, not because it promised good relations with women but because it was at the expense of monosexual relations. In the often-negative response some French people have toward certain types of American behavior, there is still that disapproval of monosexuality. So occasionally we hear: 'What? How can you approve of those macho models? You're always with men, you have mustaches and leather jackets, you wear boots, what kind of masculine image is that?' Maybe in ten years we'll laugh about it all. But I think in the schema of a man affirming himself as a man, there is a movement toward redefining the monosexual relation. It consists of saying, 'Yes, we spend our time with men, we have mustaches, and we kiss each other,' without one of the partners having to play the nelly [*éphèbe*] or the effeminate, fragile boy ....We have to admit this is all something very new and practically unknown in Western societies. The Greeks never admitted love between two *adult men*" (Foucault, "The Social Triumph of the Sexual Will," trans. Brendan Lemon, in *Essential Works*, vol. 1, 161-162, brackets in original).

15. Blue bandannas break down like this:

Worn on LEFT		*Worn on RIGHT*
Wants Head	Light Blue	Expert Cocksucker
Sixty-Niner	Robin's Egg Blue	Sixty-Nine
Cop	Medium Blue	Cop-Sucker
Fucker	Navy Blue	Fuckee
Cock and Ball Torturor	Teal Blue	Cock and Ball Torturee

Clearly the implications of failing to distinguish, say, light blue from teal blue can be quite dramatic. Today, however, the hanky code has fallen into desuetude, supplanted by the greater convenience and explicitness of online cruising, in which participants spell out directly what they desire. Nevertheless, as in newspaper personals, a form of shorthand has developed in online cruise ads that is sufficiently complex to warrant the kind of translations offered by my hanky code card. For instance, Barebackcity.com, a website for gay men who want sex without protection, offers a handy glossary covering the 60 or so abbreviations and acronymic terms that one is likely to encounter while cruising its site (see http://misc.barebackcity.com/abbreviations.asp). What fascinates me is how—whether with the hanky code or in online cruise ads—the semiotic system tends to outstrip the competence of its users, thereby verging on a specifically *symbolic* order in which, as Lacan says, "man is always cultivating a great many more signs than he thinks" (Lacan, *The Seminar of Jacques Lacan, Book II: The Ego in Freud's Theory and in the Technique of Psychoanalysis (1954-1955)*, ed. Jacques-Alain Miller, trans. Sylvana Tomaselli [Cambridge: Cambridge University Press, 1988], 122). That is to say, in these subcultural semiotic worlds there is an unconscious.

16. See Dean, *Unlimited Intimacy: Reflections on the Subculture of Barebacking* (Chicago: University of Chicago Press, 2009).

17. Bersani, *Homos* (Cambridge: Harvard University Press, 1995), 107.

18. For scat, piss, spit, or "heavy S&M," wear brown, yellow, pale yellow, or black bandannas, respectively.

19. "Only an emphasis on the specifics of sameness can help us to avoid collaborating in the disciplinary tactics that would make us invisible" (Bersani, *Homos*, 42).

20. Bersani, *The Freudian Body: Psychoanalysis and Art* (New York: Columbia University Press, 1986); see also Bersani, "Is the Rectum a Grave?," in *AIDS: Cultural Analysis/Cultural Activism*, ed. Douglas Crimp (Cambridge: MIT Press, 1988), 197-222.

21. Bersani and Ulysse Dutoit, *Caravaggio's Secrets* (Cambridge: MIT Press, 1998).

22. See Parveen Adams, *The Emptiness of the Image: Psychoanalysis and Sexual Differences* (London: Routledge, 1996); Graham L. Hammill, *Sexuality and Form: Caravaggio, Marlowe, and Bacon* (Chicago: University of Chicago Press, 2000); and Joan Copjec, *Imagine There's No Woman: Ethics and Sublimation* (Cambridge: MIT Press, 2002).

23. In a brilliant meditation on Ralph Waldo Emerson's impersonality, Sharon Cameron claims that "there cannot help but be resistance to the idea of the impersonal since the consequences of the impersonal destroy being the only way we think we know it" (Cameron, "The Way of Life by Abandonment: Emerson's Impersonal," *Critical Inquiry* 25:1 [Autumn 1998]: 31). I would argue instead that the impersonal shows the extent to which the way we think we know being is mistaken. What the impersonal destroys is not being but selfhood. Having suggested how Bersani could be read as Lacanian, I am not about to suggest that we now read him as

Emersonian, but rather that his work could be considered within a genealogy of impersonality that would include Emersonian philosophy.

24. Bersani, "Genital Chastity," in Dean and Lane (eds.), 366.

25. Bersani, "Against Monogamy," in *Beyond Redemption: The Work of Leo Bersani*, ed. Timothy Clark and Nicholas Royle, a special issue of *Oxford Literary Review*, 20:1-2 (1998): 19.

9

Lacan at the Limits of Legal Theory: Law, Desire, and Sovereign Violence

Steven Miller

CIVIL DISOBEDIENCE AND THE LAW OF GOD

The best place to seek the concept of law is not in the theory of law itself but in the praxis of civil disobedience. More than a political strategy, civil disobedience manifests—or rather "demonstrates"—the disjunction between the existence of the law and its essence, that is, between the existence of an unjust law and the essence from which this law should derive its authority. This disjunction has been articulated primarily in terms of the dualism of natural law theory, which holds that any given terrestrial law ("the law of the land") ultimately derives its authority from the law of God or the moral law. The clearest theoretical presentation of the connection between civil disobedience and the law of God occurs in Martin Luther King, Jr.'s theologico-political epistle, "Letter from Birmingham City Jail":

> One may well ask, "How can you advocate breaking some laws and obeying others?" The answer is found in the fact that there are two types of laws: there are *just* and there are *unjust* laws. I would agree with Saint Augustine that "An unjust law is no law at all."
>
> Now what is the difference between the two? How does one determine when a law is just or unjust? A just law is a man-made code that squares with the moral law or the law of God. An unjust law is a code that is out of harmony with the moral law...Any law that uplifts human personality is just. Any law that degrades human personality is unjust. All segregation statutes are unjust because segregation distorts the soul and damages the personality.[1]

In this context, the law of God has a strictly political importance; it is the name for the principle of justice (universal equality and liberty) whereby terrestrial laws can be legitimately contested. For King, in accord with the tradition of Kantian-Christian morality, this principle is inseparable from the sanctity of human personality; every law must recognize the inviolability of human personality in order to be recognized as a law of the land. Rather than standing for a value unto itself, however, the primary value of what King calls the "moral law" inheres in its function as a test of the lawfulness of positive law. The moral law can thus be reduced to the "virtue" or "sense" of justice—reduced, in other words, to the categorical imperative that unjust laws must always be actively contested. The famous opening lines of John Rawls' *A Theory of Justice* (written contemporaneously with the civil rights struggles of the 1960s) articulate just such an imperative: "Justice is the first virtue of social institutions, as truth is of systems of thought. A theory however elegant and economical must be rejected or revised if it is untrue; likewise laws and institutions no matter how efficient and well-arranged must be reformed or abolished if they are unjust. Each person possesses an inviolability founded on justice that even the welfare of society as a whole cannot override."[2] If virtue is the political actualization of morality, then civil disobedience would be the political act that manifests the sense of justice.

The absolute value of the person, however, need not be the only test of the lawfulness of the law, just as the meaning of civil disobedience need not depend upon reference to such a value. This form of political action has an import that goes beyond its theoretical justification. Civil disobedience remains a decisive and relevant practice because it manifests the possibility of legitimate contestation—the contestation of unjust state action—that does not depend upon deference to a sacred principle (be it the Good, the Person, or the Law, along with their historical corollary, the economy of private ownership). Indeed, it is my initial working hypothesis that the question of law cannot even be posed as such until it is emancipated from its traditional complicity with the economy of personhood and private ownership. On this point, my discussion follows certain basic theses of the legal thought of both Hans Kelsen and Jacques Derrida.[3] The works of these seemingly incompatible thinkers are linked through their fidelity to the Kantian tradition—or rather, through their attempt to inherit the Kantian tradition in a way that takes it beyond its entrenchment in the values of personhood and property.[4]

The attempt to think such an emancipation of law from the property system involves two major difficulties. First, *contestation*: if the law can no longer be conceived on the basis of its adherence to a transcendent principle, what is the basis for its legitimate contestation—that is, a possible contestation of legalized injustice that does not abrogate fidelity to the rule of law as such? In the name of what does one contest injustice if not the inviolability of the person and his property? Second, *violence*: the price of affranchising the question of the law from its complicity with a legal system designed to protect private property is a more complex engagement with the relation between law and violence. Kelsen's theory is exemplary on this point: he holds that the only possible concept of law, a concept that would transcend the relation between juridical institutions and specific politico-economic systems (capitalist or communist), would be a concept that defines law according to the horizon of its enforcement, that holds the force of law to be intrinsic to law as such. As such, for Kelsen, law is what he calls a "coercive norm."[5] Derrida makes an analogous argument: he elaborates both the genealogy, from Montaigne and Pascal to Kant, and the political horizon of such a concept of law as the "force of law."[6]

In contemporary political thought, the answer to the first set of difficulties takes the form of an attempt to discover if the *universal* has a place beyond the theological determination of politics, and thus to think the universal in terms of the contestation of personality, the division of the subject, the death of God, expropriation, or arche-violence. The second set of difficulties is linked to the first through the question of civil disobedience. The wager implied in the traditional praxis of civil disobedience is that the violence of law—and even the most revolting implementation of this violence in the form of "law enforcement"—presupposes such a universal. The wager is that *this* law, no matter how unjust, can only ever be enforced as *the* law—that the active enforcement of *a* law (the law of a specific land) necessarily implies the claim that it is *the* law and thus universal. In the case of an unjust or discriminatory statute, the enforcement of the law will always entail a presupposition that contradicts the letter of the law. At the moment of enforcement, the state can no longer avoid the universality presupposed by the fact of its own institutions, and thus unavoidably exposes itself to claims that contest their justice.

The legitimacy of civil disobedience does not ultimately depend upon the principle that the act claims to uphold, but rather inheres in the specific theater of its public gesture. On the one hand, as Rawls writes in his chapter on the topic, the act of civil disobedience "addresses the sense of justice of the majority of the community"[7]; it openly insists on the disjunction between the existing laws and the law of law. On the other hand, the same act has a scope that exceeds the open airing of a principle of justice. Its function is not to transform the community into a theater of the beautiful soul, to represent an exclusive adherence to a law that transcends the law of every land. The paradoxical "civility" of civil disobedience inheres in the fidelity of this public action not to a higher law, but to the very same unjust law of the land that it openly disobeys. The gesture that represents such fidelity is in fact the most dramatic moment in any act of civil disobedience: the moment at which the actors submit to the legal consequences of their action, allowing themselves to be arrested. As Rawls writes, "[c]ivil disobedience...expresses disobedience to law within the limits of fidelity to law, although it is at the outer edge thereof. The law is broken, but fidelity to law is expressed by the public and nonviolent nature of the act, by the willingness to accept the legal consequences of one's conduct."[8] Beyond demonstrating the contradiction between the law of God and the law of the land, the theater of civil disobedience would thus body forth this other contradiction between the universal implied by law enforcement and the discrimination written into the law or otherwise manifest in state action. This activist "willingness to accept the legal consequences of one's conduct" displays an adherence to the sheer *fact* of the law beyond the set of its specific dictates.

For Rawls, this fidelity to law remains subordinate to the task of addressing the community, to the expression of conscience. To some extent, he advocates a kind of "responsible" activism, designed both to advance its claims and to reassure the state that disobedience is neither an act of war, juvenile resentment, or pathological compulsion, but is rather "conscientious and sincere." To accept the legal consequences of one's conduct (arrest, bodily injury) would thus function as a pledge of allegiance to the rule of law as such, that the act for which one is being punished has been undertaken in the name of a sense of justice (or even "a theory of justice"): "This fidelity to law helps to establish to the majority that the act is indeed politically conscientious and sincere, and that it is intended to address the public's sense of justice. To be completely open and nonviolent is to give bond of one's sincerity, for it is not easy to convince another that one's acts are conscientious, or even to be sure of this before oneself."[9] It is important to be clear on this point: fidelity to law—to the rule of law or the mere fact of law—does not necessarily imply allegiance to constituted authorities, but rather to the possibility of contestation from which such authorities derive their own claims to legitimacy. The rule of law does not name the sovereignty of the prevailing order, but rather the point at which sovereign power *loses control of itself*—both in the sense that, in defense of unjust laws, state violence becomes constitutively illegitimate and excessive, and in the sense that it is at precisely the point of such excess that state action unavoidably exposes itself to contestatory interventions.

In the courtroom, the oath invokes the law of God as the guarantor of the truth. In the theater of civil disobedience, Rawls claims that one would "invoke" one's own present acquiescence to punishment (for example, going limp upon seizure by the police) as an attempt to guarantee ("to give one's bond") that one acts in accordance with the law of God itself. This is precisely the rhetorical situation of King's letter written from prison. In other words, civil disobedience presents a situation in which God is not the ultimate guarantee, a situation in which one must establish one's credibility and sincerity according to an immanent criterion in order to make others believe that one truthfully acts in the name of God or a rational sense of justice. This criterion is what Rawls calls simply "fidelity to law," but would more appropriately (and problematically) be called fidelity to the consequences of law, fidelity to the "force of law," or even fidelity to the violence of law. The disobedient protester does not simply contest state violence in the name of a higher principle of nonviolence, but rather openly (and contemptuously?) "swears" on the violence to which he submits at the very moment he is acting out of respect for a higher law.[10] The force of law thus opens a space in which it becomes possible to claim adherence to a universal principle, in which it becomes possible to expose one's adherence to the universal *as* universal, rather than as an unverifiable private predilection. Indeed, the universal only becomes thinkable within the horizon opened with such exposition.

THE FULFILLMENT OF THE LAW

Civil disobedience thus manifests an unavoidable and fundamental engagement with the law, without this law being reducible either to the statutes of a determinate legal order or to a law that transcends all legal orders. The law at stake emerges rather at the point where the "sincerity" of the act turns into a theatrical ironization of violence. It is not a coincidence, therefore, that the law in this sense should occur as a poetic *topos.*

One of Schönberg's choral song cycles (*Sechs Stücke für Männerchor*, op. 35), from 1930, includes the following lyrics:

> That there is a law
> which all things obey
> the way you follow your Lord:
> a law which is master of all things the way
> your Lord is your master:
> this is what you should recognize as a miracle!
> That someone decides to rebel
> is an obvious banality.[11]

These lines not only reduce the act of rebellion against the law to the status of banality, but also implicitly expose the limits of any theoretical attempt to elaborate a concept of law as such. The tonality of exhortation in general arises from a rupture—in this case, that rupture with the regime of sufficient reason called the "miracle." Accordingly, this exhortation asks its addressee to accept this rupture as the condition for thinking the law. It asks one to begin with the illegitimate fact of a law without concept.

Any discourse that attempts to theorize the law will be beset by the suspicion that its ultimate purpose is to uphold the preservation of an illegitimate and coercive legal system. When speaking of the law, one opens oneself to the accusation that this term represents merely the aspiration of a specific system of law to legitimate status, that one keeps an entire penal code in reserve for those who need convincing in order to accept that *this* law is *the* law. To speak of *the* law is always illegitimate simply because there is no such thing: there are only *laws* in the plural whose aspiration to the status of law will always be infinitely contestable. This plurality of laws, however, does not in itself invalidate the claim of each law or system of law to be lawful, does not make it impossible for each law to present itself as *the* law. On the contrary, this plurality is irreducible because *the* law is nothing other than the mere fact—the miracle of which Schönberg's song urges us to recognize—"that there is *a* law." Law as such thus becomes inseparable from the withdrawal of the concept or principle of law, from the fact that there is a law beyond any access to what law is. What Schönberg calls the "miracle" of the law's existence would thus name its essential excess, the event of its presentation beyond its own concept. The decision to rebel thus becomes a banality, amounting to nothing other than the claim that a given law is illegitimate because it has no right to call itself law, while such illegitimate nomination is in fact inseparable from the structure of law as such.

The same problems arise when one attempts to take up the philosophical question, "What is the law?" On the one hand, the question seems to refer to the essence of law or the concept of law. On the other hand, this version of the question will always be displaced by another. To ask "What is the law?" can always amount to asking "What is the law that applies to this case?" "What does the law *say* in this situation?" Further, the problem of what the law says is not limited to knowing which law applies in any particular case, but extends to the problem of understanding what the specific applicable law means. Indeed, it is possible to become so absorbed with knowing what the law says that the question of its essence is indefinitely deferred, if not forgotten. The miracle of the law, therefore, would not so much occur as an epiphany before which one stands paralyzed with wonder; rather, it would lie in this engaged relation to the saying—the "jurisdiction"—that will have always carried the law beyond the question of its essence.

What both the Jewish and the Christian traditions call *the fulfillment of the law* names the way in which this engaged relation to the saying of the law has always already been folded into the law itself. According to one rabbinical tradition, for example, Moses does not only deliver the Torah to the Israelites at Mount Sinai, but at the same time he is also supposed to have "revealed" to them every eventual commentary on the Torah and all the commentaries upon those commentaries.[12] The commentary on the saying of the law, in other words, comes "before the law" itself. Saint Paul predicates the Christian event upon the same tradition when he postulates that love for the neighbor is the fulfillment of the law: "The commandments, 'You shall not commit adultery; You shall not murder; You shall not steal; You shall not covet'; and any other commandment, are summed up in this word, 'Love your neighbor as yourself.' Love does no wrong to a neighbor; therefore, love is the fulfilling of the law" (Rom. 13:8-10). Paul departs from the rabbinic tradition only to the extent that he emancipates the relation to the law from the historical revelation of the law itself (from the tradition of Sinai). Instead, he finds the relation to the law in the praxis of love for the neighbor: love *does* no wrong to the neighbor. The law is "revealed" in the love for the neighbor, and this love reveals itself as the "miracle" of an engagement with the law (its "summation") that is both "older" and "newer" than the gift of the law itself.

DIVINE VIOLENCE

If the attempt to present *a* law as *the* law can never be upheld without reference to a coercive or punitive power, the point of the decision to rebel would be to contest this power (especially in cases where its deployment is manifestly unjust). The problem with such rebellion, however, is that it presumes the possibility of purifying law of its association with sovereign power. It can only contest the injustice of the power that is supposed to uphold the law in the name of the law "itself," or rather, in the name of the pure principle of a law whose legitimacy would not be contaminated by an appeal to violence. In other words, acts of rebellion remain effective only so long as they engage determinate systems of law, acts for which the responsible parties can be prosecuted. But such acts would lose their basis if a punitive violence, perhaps even of the most extortative variety, were inseparable from the pure concept of law as such—if this concept were nothing other than a "fact" to whose acceptance there is no alternative but the pain of death.

In "The Temptation of Temptation," his Talmudic lesson on the relation between law and reason, Emmanuel Levinas elaborates a tradition according to which the horizon of coercion and punishment emerges inseparably from the original gift of the law itself. Levinas' text is devoted to a passage from the Tractate *Shabbat* (88*a* and 88*b*) that comments on the simple lines of Exodus 19:17: "Moses brought the people out of the camp to meet God. They took their stand at the foot of the mountain." But the Talmudic passage immediately reinscribes these lines within a kind of rabbinical fiction that opens the horizon of a divine violence. Yahweh threatens to destroy his own people, using the mountain itself as an implement, if they decide not to accept the law that he presents to them. Rabbi Abdimi bar Hama bar Hasa comments that the lines from Exodus "teach us that the Holy One, Blessed be He, inclined the mountain over them like a titled tub and that He said: If you accept the Torah, all is well; if not here will be your grave." The miracle "that there is a law" thus happens as a violent extortion that divides the life of the people to whom the law is delivered. The revelation of the law only becomes a historical event to the extent that the very life of the people suddenly depends entirely upon its acceptance. The threat of divine violence places the Israelites in the position of making the impossible choice between the law and their own extinction.

For Levinas, however, this decision is not simply a forced choice because it occurs before it becomes possible to distinguish between freedom and coercion (unless the "force" in the forced choice names precisely the status of force or violence beyond their determination according to the distinction between freedom and coercion). One significant section of his reading revolves around the apparently nonsensical promise, which the Israelites were supposed to have offered Yahweh once he presented them with the law: "we will do and we will hear." The nonsense of the promise inheres in its inversion of a normative temporal order that the divine commandment generally functions to preserve. To the extent that the commandment prescribes certain deeds that should follow its word, it also prescribes in general that the deed as such should follow the word, that the deed is only possible based on a clear preliminary understanding of the word, and further, on the presupposition that the word is inherently understandable. Conceived in this way, the form of the commandment inscribes the primacy of reason with respect to the law, the primacy of metalanguage with respect to language. How, then, could one *do* the law without first having *heard* its requirements, or without having scrutinized the ground for its claim to adherence? The praxis that pertains to this inversion, as Levinas elaborates it, fulfills the law; and this fulfillment of the law takes place within the horizon of divine violence: "To receive the gift of the Torah—a Law—is to fulfil it before consciously accepting it...Not only does acceptance precede examination but practice precedes adherence. It is as if the alternatives liberty-coercion were not the final ones, as if it were possible to go beyond the notions of coercion and adherence due to coercion by formulating a 'practice' prior to voluntary adherence."[13] The gift of the law is already the fulfillment of the law; the miracle of the law lies in its being accepted without being understood; the fact of the law lies in an act that goes beyond freedom and beyond the will.

Saint Paul's elaboration of "the fulfillment of the law" can be read as both an extension and a transformation of the same tradition. The love for the neighbor fulfills the law in that it constitutes a fundamental praxis from which the authority of the commandment itself would derive. What distinguishes the Christian love for the neighbor from the tradition from which it emerges, however, is that this love moves beyond the threat of every possible violence upon the life of the one to whom the law is addressed. Paul thus opens the trajectory, which culminates in Kant, that makes love for the neighbor into the movement whereby law is detached from the event of its revelation and the threat of sovereign violence that it implies. *Rather than commanding what cannot be done, the prescription to love the neighbor commands what can only be done without being commanded.* "Love *does* no wrong to a neighbor; therefore, love is the fulfilling of the law." The impossibility of the command paradoxically bears witness to a fundamental stratum of possibility, what Kant calls the "practicability" or even the "feasibility" (*Tunlichkeit*) of the moral law.[14] Even where the command has been articulated, the praxis of love itself should always have come before the law that makes it imperative: "For, as a commandment [to "*Love God before all, and your neighbor as yourself*"] it requires respect for a law that *commands love* and does not leave it to one's discretionary choice to make this one's principle. But love for God as inclination (pathological love) is impossible, for he is not an object of the senses. The same thing toward human beings is indeed possible but cannot be commanded, for it is not within the power of any human being to love someone merely on command. It is, therefore, only *practical love* that is understood in that kernel of all laws."[15] Love thus becomes synonymous with an ethical courage: one must always love without fearing for one's life. Love is not love that admits the extortion of the violence that subtends every commandment. At the limit, such true unforced love (even the love of God himself) necessarily entails the death of God since its horizon exceeds the reach of his power. If the death of God shows that death itself has an omnipotence beyond the power of divine violence, then love belongs to the horizon of death.

LACAN AND THE DEATH PENALTY

Lacan locates the facticity of *the* law (the fact that there is *a* law) in analytic experience: "The hard thing we encounter in the analytic experience is that there is one, there is a law."[16] If the rudiments of a legal theory could be found in Lacan's writings, they would thus be largely consistent with the tradition that accepts the "hard thing" (or the "miracle") that "there is a law" without concept and without theory, and that makes this thing itself the basis for the contestation of injustice. Moreover, like Levinas, Lacan finds that this "hard thing" is inseparable from a sovereign violence, and he shows that this violence emerges where the law itself can no longer account for its own existence.

Despite readings that emphasize its analysis of the moral law, Lacan's "Kant with Sade" is as much an engagement with questions of positive legality. According to a tradition that conceives law as divided between these two—moral and positive—poles, Lacan never examines questions of the former without measuring their impact upon the paradigm of the latter. Although the reading of the *Critique of Practical Reason* and its determination of the "doctrine of virtue" belong to the explicit program of Lacan's essay, it also implicitly opens the way for an elaboration of the relation between psychoanalysis and the problems of legal institutions that pertain to the "doctrine of right." Indeed, the proper names invoked by the title itself might well bear witness to such a concern with both major divisions of the *Metaphysics of Morals*: whereas Lacan makes Kant into the name for the determination of the subject by the moral law, he makes Sade into the name for the institution of the moral law as the foundation of right and the possibility of justice. The perverse virtue of the Sadian maxim is not only to introduce the division of the subject (*enoncé, enonciation*) there where this division is repressed in Kant by the voice of conscience, but also to introduce the claim upon a *right* there where Kant limited himself to positing a *fact*, that is, the moral law as the "fact" of reason that constitutes the inviolable dignity of the person. In other words, Sade shows that even this universal fact takes place within the horizon of sovereign violence; he demonstrates that, politically speaking, a systematic and potentially infinite *violation* (*jouissance*) can occupy the place of what Kant calls dignity. The challenge of Sade is his claim that the universal is inseparable from violation and thus that *jouissance* is inseparable from the possibility of justice. Lacan responds to this challenge by revising both Kant and Sade. On the one hand, he locates the fact of law in desire rather than reason; on the other, like Sade (but also Levinas) he situates this fact within a sovereign violence. For Sade, sovereignty lies in the freedom of transgression, but the sovereignty that matters for Lacan is manifest in the cruelty of the death penalty. Whereas the sovereignty of transgression inheres in the violation of the law, Lacan shows that the death penalty is a paradoxical corollary of Christian charity, and thus that its sovereignty inheres in the fulfillment of the law. Lacan reinscribes this fulfillment as the "autonomy" of desire.[17]

In a discussion of censorship from his seminar of 1954-1955, Lacan examines a law that is formally analogous to the ultimatum that Yahweh delivers to the Israelites. Lacan addresses what he calls a "primordial law": "any man who says that the King of England is an idiot will have his head cut off."[18] The law is primordial because it excludes the position from which its acceptance could be the result of a deliberative act. The death penalty is thus the point at which the possibility of such an act is excluded. The law is accepted to the precise extent that its non-acceptance entails the death of its addressee.

> I want to show you that any similar law, any primordial law, which includes the specification of the death penalty as such, by the same token includes, through its partial character, the fundamental possibility of being not understood. Man is always in the position of never completely understanding the law, because no man can master the law of discourse in its entirety.
>
> I hope I'm giving you a feeling of this final, unexplained, inexplicable mainspring upon which the existence of the law hangs. The hard thing we encounter in the analytic experience is that there is one, there is a law. And that indeed is what can never be completely brought to completion in the discourse of the law—it is this final term that explains that there is one. [*Et c'est bien ce qui ne peut jamais être complètement achevé dans le discours de la loi—c'est ce dernier terme qui explique qu'il y en a une.*][19]

How does Lacan's version of the death penalty differ from the divine violence that Levinas locates in the rabbinical tradition? The answer to this question can be found in the closing pages of "Kant with Sade": the sovereign violence of the death penalty emerges on the far side of the commandment to love the neighbor. It is, as Lacan writes, "one of the corollaries of Charity."[20] In other words, the death penalty is the sovereign violence that survives the death of God, that goes beyond the divine violence which binds the people to the law. The death penalty is also a violence that binds one to the law, but, whereas divine violence comes from the same God who gives the law itself, the death penalty would come from a different god—or it would name, rather, the sovereign power of death itself freed from reference to any determinate authority. Whereas Yahweh threatens his people with the death that he has the power to administer, the recourse to the death penalty amounts to the deployment of death itself as a power. Although the death penalty remains inseparable from the incomprehensible fact that there is a law, it has a scope that far exceeds the limits of this fact. For Lacan, the problem of the death penalty only emerges with the fulfillment of the law in the love for the neighbor. In fact, following Freud, he describes this roving death as the repressed truth of the love for the neighbor—such that it becomes possible for him to understand the fulfillment of the law starting from the death penalty rather than from love. Rather than the revelation of the law in its praxis, the fulfillment of the law thus exposes the dimension of a sovereign violence that is irreducible to the law. The fulfillment of the law exposes that the fact of the law does not belong to the horizon of the law, and thus what Lacan calls *ethics* corresponds to the fulfillment of the law in this sense.

These considerations might help to measure the complexity of Lacan's assessment of Sade's position in the last pages of "Kant with Sade." Lacan's basic point is that, despite Sade's systematic apology for transgression and destruction, the logic of his demonstration remains bound to what Saint Paul called the "curse of the law." Lacan limits himself entirely to the closed set of "opportunities" opened by the explicit prohibitions (rather than the mere fact) of the law. The logic of the argument thus gestures toward that fulfillment in which tradition upholds the event of a miraculous rupture with this malediction:

> Sade thus stopped, at the point where desire is knotted together with the law. If something in him held to the law, in order there to find the opportunity Saint Paul speaks of, to be sinful beyond measure, who would throw the first stone? But he went no further.
>
> It is not only that for him as for the rest of us the flesh is weak, it is that the spirit is too prompt not to be lured. The apology for crime only pushes him to the indirect avowal [*aveu détourné*] of the Law. The supreme Being is restored in Maleficence.[21]

This avowal of the law does not amount to a confession of sin. Lacan is not saying that Sade's apology for crime ultimately becomes an elaboration of guilt and thus a personal appeal for forgiveness. The apology for crime as such can only be an avowal of the fundamental sin of subjection to the law and an appeal for expiation from this sin—an appeal, in other words, for expiation from the malediction of the law itself. In this sense, the avowal of the law restores the supreme Being to the extent that it functions as a demand perhaps addressed to the power of what Walter Benjamin calls "divine violence," which constitutes a form of retribution that "purifies the guilty, not of guilt, however, but of law." "For with mere life," Benjamin writes, "the rule of law over the living ceases. Mythical violence is bloody power over mere life for its own sake, divine violence pure power over all life for the sake of the living."[22]

For Lacan, however, the confession that appeals to the power of such expiation implies a disavowal of what Schönberg called the *miracle* of the law, what Kant called the *fact* of the moral law, or what Lacan himself (in the last lines of "The Subversion of the Subject and the Dialectic of Desire," which immediately follows "Kant with Sade" in the *Écrits*) called "the Law of desire." *Desire is the facticity of the law from which expiation is not possible.* (And the dictum from the *Ethics* seminar, "do not give up on your desire," would have a similar status to Schönberg's exhortation). The death penalty is the point at which the possibility of such expiation definitively withdraws. The fulfillment of the law toward which Lacan's analysis of Sade gestures would be nothing other than the mere presentation of the law beyond expiation.

Much like Saint Paul, Lacan situates the "Christian commandment" ("love your neighbor as yourself") beyond the logic of transgression to which the curse of the law restricts the subject. And he makes clear that Sade, in staging his apology within the parameters of the law's dictates, keeps a distance from the implications of this commandment unto Christian charity. For Lacan, however, this commandment does not imply a pacified love between men, but rather the absolute hostility that Freud associated with it in *Civilization and Its Discontents.* Sade's extensive apology for crime functions to recoil from this dimension of *méchanceté*: "We believe that Sade is not close enough to his own wickedness to recognize his neighbor in it. A trait which he shares with many, and notably with Freud. For such is indeed the sole motive of the recoil of beings, sometimes forewarned, before the Christian commandment."[23] As evidence of this recoil, Lacan cites Sade's rejection of the death penalty. "For Sade, we see the test of this, crucial in our eyes, in his refusal of the death penalty, which history, if not logic, would suffice to show is one of the corollaries of Charity."[24] Much as Levinas finds that the fulfillment of the law is overdetermined by a relation between the people and the threat of divine violence, Lacan finds that the history and logic of the death penalty is internal to the fulfillment of the law in the love for the neighbor. To oppose the death penalty, as Sade does, amounts to rejecting the facticity of the law, and thus to repressing the autonomy of desire. In other words, desire as such becomes legible only within the horizon of a sovereign violence. Carl Schmitt famously identifies such violence with the contingent possibility of a decision on the exception embodied by the person of the sovereign—the decision to suspend the validity of the entire law in states of emergency. For Lacan, this horizon becomes the "sinuous" line that constitutes the topology of the fantasy.

Notes

1. Martin Luther King, Jr., *A Testament of Hope: The Essential Speeches and Writings of Martin Luther King, Jr.*, ed. James M. Washington (San Francisco: Harper & Row, 1986), 293.
2. John Rawls, *A Theory of Justice*, rev. ed. (Cambridge: Harvard University Press, Belknap Press, 1970), 3.
3. See Hans Kelsen, *Introduction to the Problems of Legal Theory*, trans. Bonnie Litschewski Paulson and Stanley L. Paulson (Oxford: Clarendon Press, 1992); and Jacques Derrida, "Force of Law: 'The Mystical Foundation of Authority,'" trans. Gil Anidjar, in *Acts of Religion*, ed. Gil Anidjar (New York: Routledge, 2002). For a discussion of Kelsen and Derrida, see Margaret Davies, "Derrida and Law: Legitimate Fictions," in *Jacques Derrida and the Humanities: A Critical Reader*, ed. Tom Cohen (Cambridge: Cambridge University Press, 2001). Throughout this paper, I am further indebted to Juliet Flower MacCannell's reading of Rousseau with Lacan—especially her understanding of the social contract as the "negative law" of universal dispossession. What seems ultimately at stake in such a reading is the determination of whether democracy is essential to the concept of the political, or whether, as Carl Schmitt decided, the concept of the political only emerges with the suspension of the regime of democratic legality. See Juliet Flower MacCannell, *The Hysteric's Guide to the Future Female Subject* (Minneapolis: University of Minnesota Press, 1999). See also Willy Apollon's "Introduction" to *Lacan, Politics, Aesthetics*, ed. Willy Apollon and Richard Feldstein (Albany: State University of New York Press, 1996).
4. The list of attempts to emancipate legal theory from such an entrenchment would also have to include the psychoanalytic teaching of Jacques Lacan, which I will address later in the paper, and Antonio Negri's communist theory of the state. See Antonio Negri, *Insurgencies: Constituent Power and the Modern State*, trans. Maurizia Boscagli (Minneapolis: University of Minnesota Press, 1999); and Michael Hardt and Antonio Negri, *Labor of Dionysus: A Critique of the State-Form* (Minneapolis: University of Minnesota Press, 1994).
5. Kelsen, 26.
6. Derrida's elaboration of the question is incompatible with Kelsen's theory, however, in that, for Derrida, the force of law can never be theorized simply as a "norm," comprehended in terms of a generic attribute. The epistemological aspirations of the theory of law will always encounter insuperable obstacles in the force of law. For Derrida, as for Walter Benjamin, whose text provides the occasion for his intervention, the theory of law must always begin—and perhaps end—with a critique of violence. I will return to this point later, but in connection with a discussion

of the presentation of law in psychoanalysis.

7. Rawls, 320.
8. Ibid., 322.
9. Ibid.
10. This aspect of civil disobedience is perhaps not far from the Stoic "contempt" that, at one point in his analysis of Kant and Sade, Lacan levels against the Sadian experience of *jouissance*. "What [pain] is worth for Sadian experience will be better seen by approaching it through what, in the artifice of the Stoics, would dismantle this experience: contempt... Imagine a revival of Epictetus in Sadian experience: 'See, you broke it,' he says, pointing to his leg. Lowering *jouissance* to the destitution of such an effect where its pursuit stumbles, isn't this to turn it into disgust?" Lacan, "Kant with Sade," trans. James B. Swenson, Jr., *October* 51 (winter 1989): 60. (This translation will be slightly modified throughout.)
11. Arnold Schönberg, *Das Chörwerk*, Sony 2K44571. For an important discussion of the law in Schönberg's opera *Moses und Aron*, see Massimo Cacciari, *Icônes de la loi*, French trans. Marilène Raiola (Paris: Christian Bourgois, 1990). (English translation forthcoming from Stanford University Press.)
12. See Gershom Scholem's essay, "Revelation and Tradition as Religious Categories in Judaism" in *The Messianic Idea in Judaism, And Other Essays on Jewish Spirituality* (New York: Schocken Books, 1971).
13. Emmanuel Levinas, *Nine Talmudic Readings*, trans. and intro. Annette Aronowicz (Bloomington: Indiana University Press, 1990), 40.
14. Immanuel Kant, *Critique of Practical Reason*, ed. and trans. Mary Gregor (Cambridge: Cambridge University Press, 1997), 66. "Fontenelle says: *'I bow before an eminent man, but my spirit does not bow.'* I can add: before a humble common man [*einem niedrigen bürgerlich-gemeinen Mann*] in whom I perceive uprightness of character in a higher degree than I am aware of in myself *my spirit bows*, whether I want it or whether I do not and hold my head ever so high, that he may not overlook my superior position. Why is this? His example holds before me a law that strikes down my self-conceit when I compare it with my conduct, and I see observance of that law and hence its *practicability* proved before me in fact."
15. Ibid., 71.
16. Lacan, *The Seminar of Jacques Lacan, Book II: The Ego in Freud's Theory and in the Technique of Psychoanalysis (1954-55)*, ed. Jacques-Alain Miller, trans. Sylvana Tomaselli (New York: Norton, 1991), 129. (This translation will be slightly modified throughout.)
17. See Lacan, *Écrits* (Paris: Seuil, 1966), 814.
18. Lacan, *The Ego in Freud's Theory*, 128.

19. Ibid., 128, 129.
20. Lacan, "Kant with Sade," 74.
21. Ibid.
22. Benjamin, *Reflections: Essays, Aphorisms, Autobiographical Writings*, ed. and intro. Peter Demetz, trans. Edmund Jephcott (New York: Schocken Books, 1978), 297.
23. Lacan, "Kant with Sade," 74.
24. Ibid.

10

When Love is the Law: On *The Ravishing of Lol V. Stein*

Dominiek Hoens

In this divine ravishing the centuries pass by more quickly than the hours.
—François Fénelon, *Télémaque* (1699)

In the recent work of Slavoj Žižek, "love" has taken on a politically revolutionary meaning by coming to name the event that breaks with the normal order predicated on a dialectic of Law and Sin (or desire).[1] Though not exclusively, the Christian notion of *agape* functions as the primary source of inspiration for this renewed conceptualization of the unconditional point that goes beyond a given state of affairs. Along similar lines, of course, is the pivotal intervention of Alain Badiou, who argues in favor of, on the one hand, an understanding of love as "evental" and, on the other hand, Saint Paul as the model for any militant ethics. Extrapolating from these two lines of reasoning, it should not be surprising to find *agape* again as the central point around which many other contemporary critiques of ideology have begun to revolve.

Taking a Lacanian step back, however, might give us the opportunity to ask whether the glad tidings of *agape* overlook one crucial "logical" moment. In order to address this question I will make use of one of Lacan's most important texts, "Logical Time and the Assertion of Anticipated Certainty,"[2] which has proven to be most inspiring and useful for demonstrating the precise moment of rupture, or what Žižek has qualified as "the act."[3] Returning to this text will hopefully clarify that this moment of love is not exclusively the moment of the act, nor simply the fidelity to a truth, but also the possible moment of being reduced to waste.

In close connection to the problem of love and desire, this moment of being reduced to waste—a certain falling out of the world—has been explored by Marguerite Duras. While returning to Lacan's article I will thus read it in conjunction with Duras' *The Ravishing of Lol V. Stein*. Lacan himself has focused on Duras' novel in another text, "Homage to Marguerite Duras, on *Le ravissement de Lol V. Stein*," where the informed reader can discern two allusions to his commentary on Antigone: "splendor" [*éclat*] and "between-two-deaths" [*entre-deux-morts*].[4] Indeed, is Lol V. Stein not as splendorous and *apolis* as Antigone? Is she not "this wounded figure, exiled from things, whom you dare not touch, but who makes you her prey"?[5] Does she not take up the function of beauty, as the last protection against the horror of *jouissance*? The two figures of Antigone and Lol share the distinction of being the main characters of their tragedies, but not without contaminating others with a "leprosy of the heart."[6] It is therefore possible to raise the question: who, in fact, is the tragic figure? If pressed to answer, one might be tempted to argue that the tragic figure is not Lol, but Jacques Hold (and not Antigone but Creon). Perhaps this lack of clarity prevents the reader from identifying with Lol, and instead implicates one in the triangles that she organizes, whereby one comes to occupy a position that she herself has set in place—her own. While caught within this ambiguity, the reader is made attentive to the temporal unfolding of a structure, and the "place" that a character takes within it. The effect of occupying such an awkward position, for the reader, is not unlike the effects taking place in the narrative itself, most significantly during the crucial scene at the Casino, where Lol loses her fiancé Michael Richardson to the mysterious *femme fatale* Anne-Marie Stretter. It is at this precise point, the superficial or "impotent" changes of the narrative itself, that the drama of Duras' novel should be located. Lol, I would argue, is not the passive subject of painful events, but rather someone who remains faithful to the place she comes to occupy during the event at the Casino.

Being ravished means being taken away, being displaced, being raptured, being dispossessed. The "of" in *The Ravishing of Lol V. Stein* is not without ambiguities. Is it an objective or subjective genitive? As objective, we could understand "of" as Lol being ravished by the scenes that she witnesses, including both the passively observed encounter between Michael Richardson and Anne-Marie Stretter, as well as the amorous meetings she *actively does not see* between Jacques Hold and Tatiana Karl. If we read "of" as a subjective genitive, this implies that Lol is the one who ravishes others, or is at least the cause of others' ravishment. Quite clearly, at the level of the narrative, it is Jacques Hold who has been ravished. From this second perspective, the relation between Jacques Hold and Lol is similar in many respects to the relation between female mystics and their confessors, in which the female subject is ravished and the male confessor, for his part, is ravished by this ravishment, only to subsequently attempt to guide her in such ravishment.

But this guidance is ambiguous: while based on trust in the divine truth of the mystic inspirations, the confessor often attempts to bring the inspirations into conformity with existing theology. Or, as in the case of Fénelon and Madame Guyon, the male confessor struggles to formulate new theological theses and defend them in relation to an existing tradition.[7]

The title of Duras' text is open to these possible readings, and with the title everything is made present: one person causes/is overwhelmed by ravishment. In this respect *Lol V. Stein* is a turning point in Duras's *oeuvre* (which eventually leads her to construct one-scene works like *Agatha*, *The Malady of Death*, and *The Man Sitting in the Corridor*). The scene Lol witnesses at the Casino, which structures the entire novel, is not simply the starting point of a narrative, nor simply its traumatic origin, but has within it the power to render any narrative impossible: like a black hole it absorbs each of the characters and their histories. The scene has an implosive effect, making any attempt at spatial or temporal expansion extremely precarious. It was Foucault who compared the characters in Duras' *récits* to the figures painted by Bacon[9]: rendering the space of a void, or exposing an open mouth, both reveal the disappearing or dissolution of the body.[9]

LOGICAL TIME

One could use the expression "absence of time" to describe this eternal moment in which Lol is caught. The narrative that follows the scene at the Casino is nothing but the description of this timelessness. What do we mean, however, when we say "timelessness"? Positing an opposition between the presence and absence of time would be much too easy, especially since it would take for granted that we know what "time" is. Lacan, in "Logical Time," describes three modalities of time: the instant of the glance, the time for comprehending, and the moment of concluding. It would be a mistake to think that one can "be" in one of these moments. As it becomes clear in Lacan's presentation, it is only retroactively, after one has concluded, that it makes sense to differentiate between the three modalities.

To demonstrate this retroactive differentiation of the three modes, Lacan analyzes a logical problem.[10] A prison warden can free one of three prisoners, and decides to subject them to a test. He shows them five disks—three white and two black—and tells them that he is going to put one disk on each of their backs. They cannot see which one it is, and are not allowed to communicate in any way with the other prisoners. The first to come to him and tell him what color disk he has on his back will be freed. But the warden adds another condition. The conclusion must be based on logical, and not simply probabilistic reasons. That is, the prisoners cannot just make a lucky guess, but must give sound reasons for why they have come to their conclusion.

The warden proceeds to put a white disk on each prisoner's back. How do they come to the right solution? Let's give the three prisoners names—A,

B, and C—and let's adopt A's perspective. A sees two whites, and knows there are five disks in play: three white and two black. If A saw two blacks, then he would know right away that he is white. But A sees two whites. From this situation, nothing can be concluded directly. So, he is forced to make a hypothesis. He supposes that he is black, and then considers what B and C would see, and what kind of hypothesis they would make in this case. If A is black, and if, for example, B supposes that he were black, then C, according to B, would be able to leave immediately, because C would see two blacks. Now, because C does not leave immediately, B should arrive at the conclusion that he is white (supposing A is black). But B also does not leave, thus A is able to conclude that he is white.

The "solution" of this problem, however, can only be qualified as "sophistic," since, strictly speaking, none of the prisoners can conclude anything concerning their identities (the color of the disk each is wearing on their back) when confronted with two white disks. The logical reasoning is only possible on the basis of an interpretation of the situation. What Lacan calls the *instant of the glance* concerns what one sees at the beginning: two white disks. If the two other prisoners were wearing black disks, then the time to come to a conclusion would indeed only last an instant, "a lightening-flash time, so to speak, being equal to zero."[11] Since one cannot come to an immediate conclusion, one has to think and make a hypothesis about one's own identity as it is perceived by the others. Lacan's major point is that this *time for comprehending* is, in itself, endless and can only be put to an end by making a conclusion. This conclusion is based on a necessary but insufficient logical reasoning. The active intervention by the prisoners consists in understanding the other's *standing still* as a *hesitation*. This addition to the initial hypothesis (and what can be derived from it) is motivated by an anxiety which seizes the prisoner. This anxiety cannot be attributed to the thought that one could possibly lose the game (and remain imprisoned), but the realization that the entire process of reasoning is based on the other's standing still. As a consequence, as soon as they move, each one must not only stop thinking, but must understand that a conclusion is no longer possible.[12]

The importance of the analysis of this sophism resides in the specific way that time, identity, and intersubjectivity are thought together. Lacan's thesis is that one can only acquire an identity through a decisive subjective act based on the introduction of time into an intersubjective dynamics. This action consists in "pulling a certitude out of anxiety."[13] The dimension of time is anticipatory: one anticipates a conclusion for which there are no sufficient reasons. It is only the act of conclusion that will make it possible to investigate afterward whether or not the reasoning was sound. The one who does not conclude has nothing to investigate.[14]

LOL V. STEIN

The resemblances between the game the prisoners have to play and the scene at the Casino in S. Thala are striking.[15] Both situations involve three people, and the *telos* seems to reside in an escape. In the "Logical Time" situation the prisoner supposes him/herself to be black, which is different from the two others, who are white. As we have seen, this supposition is the first step of a reasoning that will create the conditions within which a decisive act can be made (since if one supposed him/herself to be white, like the others, nothing could be deduced). At the same time this supposition brings about anxiety, since if one were *really* black the others have to make one fewer suppositions. This is why Lacan gives the following account of the act: "*I hasten to declare myself white, so that these whites, whom I consider this way, do not precede me in recognizing themselves for what they are.* We have here the *assertion about oneself* through which the subject concludes the logical movement in the making of a *judgment.* The very return of the movement of comprehending, before which the temporal instance that objectively sustains it has vacillated, continues on in the subject in reflection. This instance reemerges for him therein in the subjective mode of a *time of lagging behind* the others in that very movement, logically presenting itself as the urgency of the *moment of concluding*."[16] The act (as the moment of concluding) comes down to making a performative declaration: identifying oneself with a signifier. It is this act that puts an end to the time for comprehending, effectively grounding sense and meaning. If one misses the moment of concluding then the time for comprehending is reduced to its initial moment of the hypothesis concerning how the others see me—a black object under their gaze. The initial hypothesis links me *qua* object to the gaze of the others, but delinks me from them *qua* subject, for I am what they are not.[17]

It is in this moment of the initial hypothesis that Lol appears to be caught. From the moment that Anne-Marie Stretter enters the Casino, Lol is ravished, and everything else loses significance—to the extent that even in regard to Michael Richardson, her fiancé, Lol can state, "from the first moment that woman walked into the room I ceased to love [him]" (126). We have seen how the starting point, of finding oneself opposite two others, returns just before the last moment, the moment of concluding. The anxiety evoked in being the object of two others, which is the anxiety of being left behind[18]—like a "dead dog on the beach at high noon, this hole of flesh"—could potentially propel one to make a decision.[19]This decision requires the making of an *anticipatory* identification with a signifier.[20] One could say that this identification is an *imagined* identity based on an *intersubjective* dynamics. Lol appears to be aware of this possibility but does not know how to make use of it, as when she says: "I have plenty of time, oh, how long it is" (19). Or, for instance, when Michael Richardson and Anne-Marie Stretter are about to leave, Lol tries to convince them to stay longer, since "it wasn't late it was only the early summer dawn that made it seem later than it really was" (12). She has the infinite time of one who is convinced of the absence of the single word, the one signifier, which could represent her in a symbolic universe. She never ceases to await the arrival of this signifier. What was effectively revealed in one moment casts a shadow on Lol that is longer than life. As the narrator[21] describes it:

> Again it begins: the windows closed, sealed, the ball immured in its nocturnal light, would have contained all three of them, and they alone. Lol is positive of that: together they would have been saved from the advent of another day, of one more day at least. What would have happened? Lol does not probe very deeply into the unknown into which this moment opens. She has no memory, not even an imaginary one, she has not the faintest notion of this unknown. But what she does believe is that she must enter it, that that was what she had to do, that it would always have meant, for her mind as well as her body, both their greatest pain and their greatest joy, so commingled as to be undefinable, a single entity but unnamable for lack of a word. I like to believe—since I love her—that if Lol is silent in her daily life it is because, for a split second, she believed that this word might exist. Since it does not, she remains silent. It would have been an absence-word, a hole-word, whose center would have been hollowed out into a hole, the kind of hole in which all other words would have been buried. It would have been impossible to utter it, but it would have been made to reverberate. (38)

This absence of the word, a signifier that would represent Lol in a symbolic universe, coincides with a radical detachment from all others. As Lol says to Jacques Hold: "When I say that I no longer loved him, I mean to say that you have no idea to what lengths one can go in the absence of love" (126-127).

LOVE

Thus far analogies have been made between "Logical Time" and *Lol V. Stein*: an intersubjective triangular scheme, time as a logical factor, and the event as a *prior* and necessary condition for any subjectivity. This has allowed us to highlight an essential point in the logic of reasoning that is presented in "Logical Time": a subjectivity is only gained through "inventing" or "jumping to" a subjective position from out of an object position. At the moment I presuppose a reasoning in an other, and thus secretly identify myself with this other, I will be confronted with an initial hypothesis—my difference from the other. This difference is not only factual, but is fully implied in the logical process that unfolds, and it is on the basis of this difference that the others can come to a decision and leave me behind. The drama does not consist in being left behind, then, but in the fact that one is left behind as an object. Even further, this object in the drama is effectively a non-object to the extent that in order for it to truly be an object one needs the gaze of others.[22] An exchange between Jacques Hold and Lol testifies to this: "'For ten years I've been under the impression that there were only three people left: the two of them, and me.' I ask again: 'What is it you wanted?' With precisely the same hesitation as before, the same interval of silence, she replies: 'To see them'" (96).

This triangular dynamic leads to an impossible position, which in its very impossibility is the only way of arriving at a subjectivation. Lacan's publication of "Logical Time," and his frequent return to it throughout his *oeuvre*, stems from the underlying question of how such a subjectivation is possible, and how it is possible for one to think, or conceptualize its occurrence. It was in the 1950s that Lacan emphasized the necessary condition of a symbolic order. Briefly put, the intervention of the symbolic castrates the object from itself, leaving the "itself" only to be found in the interval between the elements that constitute this order. Despite this "solution" the question still remains whether it is final, or even sufficient.

Readers familiar with Lacan's *Seminar VIII, Le transfert*, will have noticed that what is at stake in the subjectifying of an object position that is explicated both in "Logical Time" and *Lol V. Stein* is similar to what Lacan calls the miracle of love. To explain love, Lacan makes use of what he names "a metaphor of love." Metaphor, in this instance, should be understood in the loose sense as "the use of an image." In a rare moment in Lacan's teaching he tells us a "myth," as he calls it, in order to illustrate an aspect of his theory. This myth is as follows:

> This hand—which extends its gesture of awaiting, attracting, and stirring toward the fruit, the rose, and the bush suddenly enflamed—is closely tied to the maturation of the fruit, the beauty of the flower, and the enflaming of the bush. But when the hand has gone far enough in this movement of awaiting, attracting, and stirring, and a hand comes out of the fruit, the flower, and the bush, and stretches itself toward your hand, at that moment it is your hand that freezes in the closed plenitude of the fruit, the opening of the flower, and the explosion of a hand that enflames—well, what produces itself there is love.[23]

Two moments are discernible. First, the hand that stretches out toward the object changes the object in a surprising way, becoming mature, beautiful, or enflamed. In this moment the attractive qualities of the object become clearer, and one could even say they are created by the hand that reaches—which, as one can imagine, makes the hand even more eager to hold the fruit in its palm. The second moment is more difficult to discern. At first sight it looks as if one hand stretches out for an object and, along its path, encounters another hand. This would suggest that love consists of a desire for an object that humanizes itself. Love, if this were true, would be the meeting of two hands. Lacan warns his audience, however, that he is not talking about what happens when two hands meet, rather he is describing when and where love takes place. The *moment* of love, according to Lacan, is not in the meeting of the two hands, but the moment when out of the fruit, the flower, the bush, a hand *rises*. As we will see, Lacan's idea of love is contrary to any idea that takes it as something that happens between "equal partners" for whom love would be, simultaneously, the effect as well the cause that makes it possible for an amorous meeting to take place. According to Lacan, in love there must be a fundamental *disparity* at work.

Lacan constructs this short parable amidst his reading and analysis of Plato's *Symposium*. In order to explain love he adopts the Greek terminology of *eromenos* (the beloved) and *erastes* (the lover), given that "love" is at the root of both words, which nicely parallels his double understanding of the term. The *eromenos* is the one confronted with the Other's desire, who positions himself and is positioned by another as a beautiful object. From this perspective, one could equate *eromenos* with Lacan's idea of narcissistic love. The beloved is the one who, in thinking of himself as lovable, interprets the Other's desire, thus reducing love to an infantile stage of wanting to be loved. Things get more interesting, however, when we follow what Lacan has to say about the *erastes*. Strictly speaking, the *erastes* is not this desiring Other (to whom I can position myself as the beloved object) but the one who can emerge only after first being placed in the position of the beloved. This is what Lacan calls the miracle of love: that someone who is positioned as the object of desire for the Other is able to subjectify this object position and desire in return.

TRINITY

The status of this object position can now be questioned. In *Seminar XX*, Lacan returns to his argument in "Logical Time" during his discussion of the work of Richard de Saint Victor, a twelfth-century mystic and theologian.[24] In his *De Trinitate*, Richard de Saint-Victor asks the question whether God needs to be thought as one or as a trinity. Starting from the thesis that love is an essential aspect of God and that love always concerns an other,[25] he believes there must be a second divine being who would be worthy of this divine love, namely the Son. The Son, insofar as he too is a divine being, must love God in return. This relation sounds like a perfect dyad, but according to Saint Victor this love can only be qualified as *pleasing*, but not as *perfected*. Perfect love—and, it must be emphasized, divine love cannot be but perfect—implies that one wants to share the love one receives from the other. If the Son receives divine love from God, his own love can be pleasing when it loves God in return. His love, however, is perfected when the love that he receives is shared. According to Saint Victor, one needs a third person, namely a *condilectus* (a co-loved), that comes to be identified as the Holy Spirit. When Lacan refers to this passage in Saint Victor's work he emphasizes that this third term, the Holy Spirit, is not a subject but an object—more precisely, an object *a*. This object *a* is necessary insofar as it is the one factor that functions as the condition of possibility for the love relation between the One and the Other.

In the moment of falling in love, the fantasmatic support for the lack-of-being (the desire that one effectively is) is temporarily suspended, as one is placed in the position of the object of desire for the Other. The metaphor of love *qua* creative act is a response that pulls one out of that object position—that is, through our very lack. One needs two operations for this to occur. First, it is necessary to fantasize what that object position could, in fact, be. Second, one needs to castrate (or bar) oneself from that position.[26] Lol V. Stein, as we have seen, is caught in an endless inquiry concerning this object position. After the eventful night at the Casino she slumbers for years, until she meets her old friend Tatiana Karl and her secret lover, Jacques Hold. Whereas Lol was fascinated by Anne-Marie Stretter's black dress, or more precisely what it envelopes, Lol later becomes attached to watching the secret meetings between Tatiana and Jacques. What now intrigues her is Tatiana's nudity "under her black hair." Parallel to the infinite quest to know what one is in the desire of the Other, Lol is convinced that one word is missing. This lack, however, is not to be understood as pointing toward a signifier that could name what it means to be desired. Rather, the only effect the missing signifer would have is the separation of her from such an object position.

Lol's investigation can now be understood as a quest for divinity and pure love. As soon as Anne-Marie Stretter enters the scene with Michael Richardson, Lol is able to take up the position of the object *a* that is necessary to install a relation between the three of them. Just as in the prisoner's sophism, where one of the prisoners thinks of himself as radically different from the others, he is still needed in order to allow the others to relate to one another. This position leaves two options: either one remains in that object position, and is left behind, or one joins the others by leaving the position behind. The first option remains within the (divine) infinity of the time for comprehending, but comes upon an obstacle when encountering the finitude of the others (the fact that they will leave, and act as if time is not infinite). In the second option, one embraces finitude by subjectifying this infinity. To assume finitude requires the operations of separation and castration: abandoning one's position as object, one must subject oneself to an order in which one can only persist as a lack-of-being.

Reading Lacan through *Lol V. Stein* demonstrates how the most problematic moment, the moment of concluding, is made present in the logic of love. Love consists in the switching of position, from the *object* to the *subject* of desire. This is why love cannot exist without a loss: in order "to give what one does not have" one must invent what one *could be* in the desire of the Other, and thus lose what one "really" is. To love is to desire *with* this loss. Lol reveals that in order for this work of mourning to be possible there must be a basic, unjustifiable, belief in a point of identification. To love is to question this point, realizing that one can only perform its existence.

CONCLUSION

I hope to have shown how an obscure, "third" position of objective waste is inherent to any "miracle of love." In order to do something *with* this object position one must perform an anticipatory identification with an element, a signifier, from an existing symbolic order. In addition, what Lol V. Stein shows us is that remaining faithful to this object position is possible. What we cannot learn from Lol is her mystical dereliction, or her way of escaping the "hold" of Jacques Hold's understanding. Nor can we come to know how she was able to experiment with "love" in such a way that she turned the notion of a "love relation" into a ridiculous oxymoron, effectively qualifying it as "true" in contradistinction to the normal, married, adulterous couples that surround her. What we can learn from Lol is that her position is a logical and necessary moment in any love-event. If we consider the formal structure of this love as equivalent to any "true" political act, it is Lol who forces us to ask these final questions: Where is the object in the "act"? Is it to be found *as* the militant who, in a tragic way, is exploited by an obscure desiring Other? Is it to be found *as* "the Jew" (Rom. 11) who functions as the necessary exclusion to the positing of a universal, Pauline truth?

I wish to thank Marc De Kesel, Sigi Jöttkandt, and Andrew Skomra for their valuable comments on an earlier draft of this text.

Notes

1. See Slavoj Žižek, *The Fragile Absolute—or, Why is the Christian Legacy Worth Fighting for?* (New York: Verso, 2000), 113-130; *The Puppet and the Dwarf: The Perverse Core of Christianity* (Cambridge: MIT Press, 2003), 92-121.
2. Jacques Lacan, "Logical Time and the Assertion of Anticipated Certainty: A New Sophism," *Écrits: The First Complete Edition in English*, trans. Bruce Fink (New York and London: W.W. Norton & Company, 2006), 161-175.
3. See Ed Pluth and Dominiek Hoens, "What if the Other is Stupid? Badiou and Lacan on 'Logical Time,'" in *Think Again: Alain Badiou and the Future of Philosophy*, ed. Peter Hallward (London: Continuum, 2004), 182-190.
4. Lacan, "Homage to Marguerite Duras, on *Le ravissement de Lol V. Stein*," trans. Peter Connor, in Marguerite Duras, *Marguerite Duras* (San Francisco: City Lights Books), 125, 129. [Translation modified.] This text is notorious for Lacan's remark that "Duras knows, without me, what I teach" (124). It has been said that upon meeting Duras, Lacan's introductory exclamation was: "You do not know what you are saying." It was Michèle Montrelay who brought *The Ravishing of Lol V. Stein* to the attention of Lacan's group,

giving a presentation on the novel in the last session of *Seminar XII.* See Lacan, *Problèmes cruciaux pour la psychanalyse* (1964-1965), unpublished seminar, 23 June 1965. This paper was revised for publication as the first chapter of her *L'ombre et le nom. Sur la féminité* (Paris: Minuit, 1977), 9-23. A very informative chapter on Lacan's reading of *Lol V. Stein* can be found in Jean-Michel Rabaté, *Jacques Lacan: Psychoanalysis and the Subject of Literature* (New York: Palgrave, 2001), 115-134.

5. Lacan, "Homage to Marguerite Duras," 125.
6. The others are Creon and Jacques Hold, but such leprosy affects the reader as well. Julia Kristeva has warned that "Duras's books should not be put into the hands of oversensitive readers," in *Black Sun: Depression and Melancholia*, trans. Leon S. Roudiez (New York: Columbia University Press, 1989), 227. Recall Jacques Hold admitting that, Lol, "has us in her hands." Marguerite Duras, *The Ravishing of Lol Stein,* trans. Richard Seaver (New York: Pantheon, 1966), 82. Subsequent references will appear parenthetically within the text.
7. Fénelon's theses, for instance, were condemned by Pope Innocent XII in his *Cum alias,* 12 March 1699. For the relation between Fénelon and Madame Guyon, see Jacques Lebrun, *Le pur amour de Platon à Lacan* (Paris, Seuil, 2002), 131-160. One could perhaps argue that Lacan positions himself in a similar relation to Duras.
8. Michel Foucault, *Dits et écrits. Tome II, 1970-1975* (Paris: Gallimard, 1994), 765.
9. Another important shift for Duras are the films she made in the 1970s, which are known for their disjunction of sound and image. This shift was anticipated, in my opinion, by *Lol V. Stein,* which is clearly marked by a preoccupation with visuality—one could even argue that the gazes are the agents of the novel. One should not overlook, however, the importance of the aural. After her illness, Lol gets married. Her highly structured, empty life takes a new turn the moment a couple passes her house, when she hears the woman say, "Dead maybe." At that moment, the reader is unclear to whom or what this refers, but Lol seems to understand it as a message concerning her own existence. Later on, when Lol is speaking of what happened at the Casino, she claims that she heard Michael Richardson and Anne-Marie Stretter saying, "'maybe it will kill her.'" Duras, *The Ravishing of Lol Stein,* 28, 95. At that moment, Lol's friend Tatiana insists that this is impossible, since she was with her the entire night and is certain they were too far away to hear what the couple was saying. But Lol, indeed, seems to hear what others cannot, or do not want to hear. The scene "made" by the visual contains an additional, auditive element that opens it up and refers it to a future. The book version of Duras' *India Song* is also organized around a scene, between the vice-con-

sul and the same Anne-Marie Stretter, but this scene appears amidst "rumours" (voices that tell the story of their own love, the love stories of others, as well as the comments made by other guests at the party). See *India Song*, trans. Barbara Bray (New York: Grove Press, 1976). Finally, having watched the film version of *India Song*, there is one element that cannot be forgotten: the vice-consul's cry.

10. The presentation and interpretation of Lacan's article borrows from David Blomme and Dominiek Hoens, "Anticipation and Subject: A Commentary on an Early Text by Lacan," in Computing Anticipatory Systems: CASYS'99—Third International Conference, ed. Daniel Dubois (New York: American Institute of Physics, 2000), 117-123.
11. Lacan, "Logical Time," 167.
12. "Having surpassed the *time for comprehending the moment of concluding*, it is *the moment of concluding the time for comprehending*. Otherwise this time would lose its meaning. It is not, therefore, because of some dramatic contingency, the seriousness of the stakes, or the competitiveness of the game, that time presses; it is owing to the urgency of the logical movement that the subject *precipitates* both his judgement and his departure ("precipitates" in the etymological sense of the verb: headlong), establishing the modulation in which temporal tension is reversed in a move to action [*tendance à l'acte*] manifesting to the others that the subject has concluded." Ibid., 169.
13. Jacques Lacan, *Le Séminaire, Livre X. L'angoisse (1962-1963)*, ed. Jacques-Alain Miller (Paris: Seuil, 2004), 93. [My translation.]
14. After the moment of concluding in the prisoner's sophism (often erroneously referred to as "the prisoner's dilemma"), when the three of them go to the door, they immediately have to stop again (because the conclusion was based on the standing still of the others). It can be proven, however, that with three prisoners there will be only two halts needed for them to acquire absolute certainty about the color of the disk on their respective backs. In these halts the subjective interpretation of the other's standing still as a hesitation becomes objectified and is empirically verifiable.
15. This is not the first time *Lol Stein* has been compared with the prisoner's sophism. Erik Porge was the first to highlight the expression "count oneself three" [*se compter trois*] in "Homage to Marguerite Duras," 122. See Porge, *Se compter trois. Le temps logique de Laçan* (Toulous: Erès, 1989), 146-149. More recently, Eric Laurent has discussed *Lol Stein* from a "logical time perspective" in "A Sophism of Courtly Love," *Lacanian Ink* 20 (2000): 45-61.
16. Lacan, "Logical Time," 168.
17. See Lacan, *The Seminar of Jacques Lacan, Book XX: Encore: On Feminine Sexuality, The Limits of Love and Knowledge, (1972-1973)*, ed. Jacques-Alain

Miller, trans. Bruce Fink (London and New York: W.W. Norton & Co., 1998), 49: "But what warrants a closer look is what each of the subjects sustains (*supporte*), not insofar as he is one among others, but insofar as he is, in relation to the two others, what is at stake in their thinking. Each intervenes in this ternary only as the object *a* that he is in the gaze of the others."

18. "Among the many aspects of the Town Beach ball, what fascinates Lol is the end. It is the precise moment when it comes to an end, when dawn arrives with incredible cruelty and separates her from the couple of Michael Richardson and Anne-Marie Stretter, forever, forever." Duras, *The Ravishing of Lol Stein*, 36-37.

19. Ibid., 38. See also Ibid., 174. Asked about Lol, Duras replied that she could show her on screen, but only as hidden, "as when she is lying on the beach like a dead dog, covered in sand." Marguerite Duras and Michelle Porte, *Les Lieux de Marguerite Duras* (Paris: Minuit, 1977), 100. [Editor's translation.] The absence of shame indicates that Lol does not take a subjective distance from this sudden appearance of herself *qua* object *a*, incarnated by Anne-Marie Stretter.

20. The identification is "anticipatory" because there is no sufficient ground for it, since it must await the recognition by the Other. Lol seems to be paralyzed by this moment of jumping to a conclusion—her phrases are often unfinished and left in suspension. See Duras, *The Ravishing of Lol Stein*, 17, 85, 102, 127, 128, 141, 142, 146, 160, 161, 165.

21. One can later identify Jacques Hold as the narrator: "Tatiana introduces [Pierre] Beugner, her husband, to Lol, and [Jacques] Hold, a friend of theirs—the distance is covered—me." Ibid., 65.

22. Lol, like prisoner (A), finds herself in the gaze of Michael Richardson (C), which is mediated by Anne-Marie Stretter (B), who was born, as we learn in *India Song*, under the name Anne-Marie Guardi. "Guardi" (*son nom de Venise*) means "to look" (many thanks to John Murphy for pointing this out). When the two leave, Lol does not lose her lover, Michael Richardson, but Michael Richardson *and* Anne Marie Stretter, resulting in her long illness: "When I woke up, they were gone. (Je me suis retrouvée sans eux.)." Ibid., 127.

23. Jacques Lacan, *Le Séminaire, Livre VIII. Le transfert (1960-1961)*, ed. Jacques-Alain Miller (Paris: Seuil, 2001), 67. [Editor's Translation.]

24. See Lacan, *Seminar XX, Encore*, 40.

25. To keep this divine love for Himself would make God a miser, which should make Him ashamed in front of the "angels and the other beings." The other person involved should engage in this *ménage à trois*, and even desire it, for if they do not this would be considered a "lack of charity"

[*defectus caritatis*] and, again, would cause shame. See Richard de Saint-Victor, *La trinité*, trans. Gaston Salet (Paris: Sources Chretiennes, 1969), 176, 197. [My translation.]

26. Thus the metaphor of love repeats the formula of the fantasy: $\$\lozenge a$.

11

Antigone's Kind: The Way of Blood in Psychoanalysis

Petar Ramadanovic

> These cultures, Freud says, already revealed the true function of the father as symbolic: the child, he says, will call by the name of "father" anyone who might have lawfully married her or his mother, anyone with the right clan name, the right totemic affiliation, and will address as "mother" any woman who might lawfully have born her or him. This marks an explicit separation between biological origin and symbolic identity. One might even say that these "primitive" institutions reveal more clearly the true structure of culture, whereas our "modern" family retains a confused and misleading resemblance to the "biological unit," thereby sustaining an illusion of "nature" that conceals the true function of the family as a cultural institution.
>
> —Charles Shepherdson[1]

INTRODUCTION

In Freud's opus, there are two basically different kinds of response to war. The first consists of his direct, timely texts on war, the 1915 "Thoughts for the Times on War and Death," and the 1935 exchange of letters with Albert Einstein entitled "Why War?" The second kind, involving a riskier strategy, is best represented in the critique of Jewish identity in *Moses and Monotheism*. In this 1939 work, written amid the mounting persecution of Jews in Austria and Germany, Freud's intention is to expose Jewish identity and show that Moses, the father of the race, was in fact an Egyptian. His critique of a Jewish fantasy of racial purity, despite its factual inaccuracies, is still an unparalleled theoretical gesture precisely because of the unusual direction it takes. To be sure, it applies no less to Germans who, identifying with a failed Austrian painter, had begun to see themselves as a new race of chosen people with an epochal mission.[2]

Instead of speaking of any particular armed conflict, I will follow this second, self-reflective strategy in this essay. After briefly introducing Jacques Lacan's understanding of the father function, I will focus on Sophocles' *Oedipus Tyrannus* and *Antigone* in order to recall that the fundamental psychoanalytic figure—the figure of Oedipus—is grounded in a peculiar, restrictive notion of true fatherhood.[3] I am turning to the familiar territory of Oedipus because literary analyses of the Theban tragedies have not explained what a father is in these plays,[4] just as psychoanalytic discussions of the father function have come short of examining in sufficient detail the blueprint (Sophocles' drama of Oedipus) after which the Oedipus complex is named.[5]

In addressing the tangle revolving around truth, the meaning of Oedipus' blood, and fatherhood, this essay will revisit the nature/culture opposition in the form that Jacques Derrida's "Structure, Sign, and Play in the Discourse of the Human Sciences" gives to it. With the help of Claude Lévi-Strauss, Derrida shows that this binary rests on the incest prohibition, which emerges as the condition for the possibility of both the notion of "nature" and the notion of "culture." The conclusion to be drawn, however, is not that the incest prohibition is neither strictly natural nor cultural. Through the ban on incest, culture—or, rather, Culture—asserts itself as the only universal, the only possible human system over and against any other system, including "nature." Thus, the prohibition (just like the nature/culture binary) constitutes the culture's groundless or arbitrary, but still essential, defining ground.

Derrida's text is particularly relevant for our present purposes because it gives a name to the shift Lacan makes when he explains, in the seminar on ethics to which we will turn below, that the father in psychoanalysis is not the actual father but the father function. In Derrida's terms, this shift to the father function corresponds to a switch from one philosophical system (one cultural system as well) to another, from one notion of truth to another. In its movement from classical metaphysics and classical psychoanalysis (which supposes that there is a fixed center and an "actual" father) toward structuralism (which supposes that there is no center, that the center is displaced, and that the function of the father is not reducible to the actual father), philosophy, Derrida suggests, goes from understanding the system (the system of knowledge) as a spatial entity to attempting to think it as a functional entity. In his words: "it was necessary to begin thinking that there was no center...that the center had no natural site, that it was not a fixed locus but a function, a sort of nonlocus in which an infinite number of sign-substitutions came into play."[6]

Lacan's critique of the biological father, the former center of the family, is less than precise about the stakes of this differentiation between the so-called father progenitor or father begetter and the father function. Here is an example of the shift that accompanies Lacan's reading of *Antigone* in *Seminar*

VII. Just after finishing his analysis of the tragedy, Lacan pauses to emphasize that, for psychoanalysis, "father" is a function not reducible to the actual, biological father. In support of this distinction, he cites the Latin proverb according to which the "father is he who acknowledges us," *pater is est quam justae nuptiae demonstrant.* But then he adds that in psychoanalytic theory, "the sole function of the father is to be a myth, to be always only the Name-of-the-Father, or in other words nothing more than the dead father."[7]

If mentioning the dead father is supposed to explain the notion of fatherhood by convention presented in the proverb, Lacan's formulation also endows the function with the sense of an inescapable, indomitable, ultimate principle that manifestly contradicts the proverb's spirit of arbitrariness. The dead father is not simply a patriarch who is no longer potent, but now a mythical figure. He is, better put, a ghost, a mental function whose significance is crucially transformed by the fact that he is now an *it*, and *it* is no longer alive although *it* is still active. *It* is beyond remedy, reach, response—a perfect monument to the formerly living man.

The example of Oedipus that Lacan references only strengthens the equivalence between death and fatherhood and makes the stakes of the distinction between the biological father and the function even less clear. That the "father is he who acknowledges us" means, Lacan says, that "we are at bottom in the same boat [*au même point*] as Oedipus" (309). But, in Oedipus' boat there are, at least from the perspective of Greek culture, two vastly different fathers. There is a true father and then there is an adoptive father. There is a dead father and a living one. There is a father whom Oedipus knows and a father whom he does not know. The aim of Sophocles' tragedy is nothing less than to distinguish between the two fathers: on the one hand, the king of Corinth, who receives Oedipus as a gift, and, on the other hand, Laius, who turns out to be *phuteusas pater*, the father progenitor or begetting father—though Oedipus never met him as his father.

The tragedy defines fatherhood not as a matter of acknowledgment, not as a matter of convention or metaphor, but as a hidden truth that can be discovered if one persists in a difficult, catastrophic search.[8] The tragedy's understanding of what makes a father runs counter to the quality of chance that the proverb identifies as proper to fatherhood. The play, further, relies on a notion of search celebrated in interpretations of *Oedipus Tyrannus* as the intellectual search *par excellence*, though this search is conducted with the blind faith that truth, itself endowed with an agency, does necessarily eventually reveal itself.

How and why I am turning to psychoanalysis in this essay should be obvious then: because the scene that is usually identified as central to psychoanalysis—the familial, Oedipal drama—and the law of the father that proceeds from this scene, decide the significance, the "nature" of family relations, as well as the nature of what is considered to be a true blood tie. I would like to dwell on the fact that Oedipus' story is not only about unconscious desires and the incest prohibition. It is, *firstly*, a story that determines the basis for identifying true fathers and true blood, and only as such is it a story of patricide and incest.

What, indeed, is the boat that we are in if an Oedipus who killed his adoptive father would not, could not, be a psychoanalytic or a tragic hero?

PART I. ANTIGONE

Unique Value

On the assumption that it is children who define parents as parents, I will begin with Lacan's reading of *Antigone*, leaving *Oedipus Tyrannus* for the second part of the essay. I will contend that it is the daughter who ultimately defines the kind of father Oedipus is, and that she does this in the last significant act of the Labdacid family saga, when she buries her brother Polynices.[9]

Commenting on Antigone's act, Lacan says: "Because he [Polynices] is abandoned to the dogs and the birds and will end his appearance on earth in impurity, with his scattered limbs an offense to heaven and earth, it can be seen that Antigone's position represents the radical limit that affirms the unique value of his being without reference to any content, to whatever good or evil Polynices may have done, or to whatever he may be subjected to" (279). By covering the corpse, Lacan observes, Antigone affirms her brother's unique value. Lacan then explains what he means by unique value, adding to his commentary something that does not obviously follow from Sophocles' play. Expanding on his assumption that Antigone "affirms the advent of the absolute individual" (278), Lacan states that this unique value of Polynices' being has no "reference to any content," that is, to any deed Antigone's brother performed while he was alive. Further, his value has nothing to do with "whatever he may be subjected to."[10] And this son of Oedipus was subject to, for instance, the punishment that he should have received, had he survived, for attacking the city.

According to Lacan, what "the unique value of his being" is should also make the corpse replaceable in the sense that, contentless, *this* body is just like any other unburied body precisely because it is outside of the web of social relations that made the son of Oedipus into a *particular* individual. Separated from all the details of Polynices' life, the corpse is now all that remains of the human, mortal being, merely a bearer of a proper name. That the corpse still has a name means simply that there is someone (anyone, not necessarily his sister) to recognize and claim it. Antigone could even mistake his remains for another's, and not tend to the corpse that was Polynices (presumably, there is a whole army of unburied enemy dead lying around Thebes?). Regardless, the act would have the same symbolic significance because the unique value, the absolute individuality, consists in nothing other than the recognition of human mortality—the *having been* of him who once was Oedipus' son. To honor Polynices means, in Lacan's line of thinking, to acknowledge that these remains are not a mere object, certainly not an animal carcass, but the mortal remains of the man who answered to the name of Polynices.

From the same perspective, Creon's ban on burying the corpse goes too far because it orders what is, in Lacan's terms, the "second death" of a man, the debasement of his remains to the level of an object, and thus the man's erasure from the symbolic. The purpose of the burial is to reverse the effect of this ban and to restore the being, without necessarily restoring any of the being's attributes. The purpose, in other words, is to acknowledge Polynices' singularity. But, as we well know, Antigone would not have defied Creon's pronouncement just because it ordered the debasement of *a* corpse. By the end of his lecture Lacan himself shifts from the argument concerning the absoluteness of the individual being to the claim that Antigone protects the family being, not human singularity.[11]

What we are dealing with here are two different values (and value systems) that Lacan does not, in the Antigone lectures at least, distinguish as essentially different.[12] The first is the absoluteness of the corpse, which is separated from all particularities of Polynices' life, and represents the "ineffaceable character of what is" (279). This notion is of interest to Lacan only for a brief moment (in this lecture, at least) while he discusses Polynices' remains and before he returns to Antigone. A second issue concerns what, in Sophocles' play, constitutes a sufficient reason for the heroine to break Creon's order. For the play, the question is whose corpse it has to be in order for Antigone to defy Creon and the city.

I am discussing the unique value here in order to suggest, even before we approach Sophocles' text, that Antigone's act has nothing to do with human singularity. It has nothing to do with the difference between human and animal deaths that, for instance, Heidegger asserts in *Being and Time*—a work that may have inspired Lacan, either directly or indirectly, to claim that the corpse is at the limit of subjecthood, that it is beyond "reference to any" moral, personal, or historical content.

Antigone is concerned only with the family, which she considers the very ground that confers upon one what one *is*. She does not act because she believes that leaving a human corpse to rot is an insult to the gods (as not only Lacan, but also the Chorus, Tiresias, and some Theban citizens may think), but because the corpse of *her* brother has not been properly honored—and this has certain implications for her family, all of whose members, as we shall see in a moment, are dead.

To what end, and how she buries this last male offspring of Cadmus' line, if she does not bury him either *as* a human being or *as* an absolute individual, remains to be seen below.

THE FAMILY'S ESSENTIAL BEING

When she acts, Antigone is more than clear that she honors her dead brother, and she would not do the same for anyone else. After she is sentenced to death, addressing herself to Polynices, she utters these crucial words:

> Polynices, for burying your body I get this reward! Yet in the eyes of the wise I did well to honour you; for never, had children of whom I was the mother or had my husband perished and been mouldering there, would I have taken on myself this task, in defiance of the citizens. In virtue of what law [*nomos*] do I say this? If my husband had died, I could have had another, and a child by another man, if I had lost the first, but with my mother and my father in Hades below, I could never have another brother. Such was the law for whose sake I did you special honour.[13]

She would not have defied Creon's law for anyone who is replaceable, but she has to do it for the one—her brother—who cannot be replaced by another, since her parents are dead.

Antigone's mother is dead because continuing her life would have meant prolonging an unbearable incest. Her father, afraid to die because he would meet in the afterlife the father he murdered and his mother, who is also his wife, is no longer alive because, as Sophocles tells us at the end of *Oedipus at Colonus*, the gods took pity on him and bore him away. Antigone must have a particular reason for mentioning the offensive impossibility of another son of her parents, a reason beyond recalling that her parents are dead, or explaining that she has buried Polynices because she could not have another brother. The latter is a necessary but not sufficient reason for her to defy Creon. In and of itself, it does not adequately account for the significance of her act.

The fact that Oedipus' children and their father share the same mother makes an identification of what distinguishes him from them—namely, *the different fathers*—the implicit task of this speech (one of the final words that a living Labdacid utters). At any rate, Antigone devotes the central part of the speech precisely to deciding who and what her kin are and what her place in that family is. By saying that she would not have defied the city for anyone but a brother, she first separates kin from everyone else. She then goes on to define what the family is by distinguishing between three different families: one belonging to the dead Oedipus, to which she is related by blood; another possible family belonging to her husband, to which she would be related by law, that is, by marriage; and, of course, the family in which her mother has the organizing role, the family in which her father is her brother. She gives primacy to the first of these three, choosing Oedipus' family for herself. She then identifies her mother and father (as those who cannot have children again), implicitly separating the incestuous parents from their children, her father from her brothers. Finally, she singles out one family member, an impossible brother, thus properly defining a brother as a male offspring of the same parents who bore her. She makes these distinctions to order the relations between family members, between parents and children, sister and brothers, relations that were disrupted by the incest of Jocasta and Oedipus. And she does so understanding that she is the last of her kind and that her burial of Polynices is the *final* act in the entire saga of Cadmus' unfortunate line.

In her own eyes, Antigone is, literally, the last among "those of me": "O tomb, O bridal chamber, O deep-dug home, to be guarded for ever, where I go to join those who are *my own*, of whom Persephassa [Persephone] has already received a great number, dead, among the shades! Of these *I am the last* [the one left behind] and my descent will be the saddest of all" (87; emphases added).

The rule she lays down in the process of defining kinship dictates that her unburied dead brother—precisely because he is not yet buried—is her only remaining relation in this world to her *own*. Her own are members of Oedipus' family with whom she hopes to reunite in the afterlife. Otherwise—if she did not believe that the family were a patrilineal bond with the dead Oedipus' kind, but a relation established through marriage or another conventional rule—Antigone would consider even Creon her kin. He is her uncle, after all. And, more importantly, she would not so easily renounce her living sister, Ismene. (Below, we shall see why Ismene is not a part of the family that Antigone is trying to define and protect through the burial of Polynices.)

If Antigone is not honoring the singularity of being we described above, neither is she honoring just any version of kinship relations, any Law of the Father. She favors what she understands to be the true family, her *own* dead people, that is, a father's line (not a husband's or a mother's), the father figure being the disseminator of the family's seed as well as of its name, which only one of his daughters chooses to bear. For it is this father's *Atè*, as Lacan says, that Antigone is following. In her act Antigone is thus honoring one specific, patrilineal family bond, which is the bond with her own who are now dead. She is placing this bond (and also the logic of true blood that underwrites it) before and above all other relations, including her relation to the living female sibling. Lacan, needless to say, recognizes that Antigone buries her brother as her father's son (and not as a singular being). He goes on to conclude his analysis of the tragedy by claiming that Antigone "is required to sacrifice her own being in order to maintain that essential being which is the family *Atè*, and that is the theme or true axis on which the whole tragedy turns" (283). In other words, Lacan asserts that in burying her brother, Antigone maintains the unique value not of a human being (as *a* human being), but of her family. The unique value, this "essential being," is identified by Lacan as the family's *Atè*. But the meaning of *Atè* as a concept ("the limit that human life can only briefly cross," as Lacan says [262-263]), or its particular content, is not, I will argue against Lacan, what constitutes the essential being of Oedipus' family. The essential being is the fact that this family has an *Atè* and that Antigone is there to follow it and thus confirm that Oedipus' dead kin are her true blood relations.[14]

The essential being that was, in our first approach to Lacan, emptied of content and divorced from all context, is now related to the family to which Antigone is "essentially" attached and for which she dies. If above we thought with Lacan that there was such a thing as a unique value of the singular being, as *a* mortal being irrespective of its history, by the end of the Antigone lectures, Lacan replaces this idea with the notion that the characters in the play derive their uniqueness from their position in the family. The family itself is identified *post facto*, in retrospect, after the death of the parents. The source of the family—its "center," as Derrida might call it—is placed, in Antigone's belated recognition, simultaneously here and elsewhere. The actual father is displaced into the afterlife where, dead, he becomes unassailable. Having been transformed into a function, the "father" is also removed into the past. After her parents die, the only thing Antigone actually needs to do is to take upon herself the "impossible" role of being her father's daughter. Her burial of Polynices is meant to affirm, to honor this logic, this indomitable law of Oedipus that is established through her act. Such is her *nomos*. To cite her words again: "In virtue of what law do I say this? If my husband had died, I could have had another, and a child by another man, if I had lost the first, but with my mother and my father in Hades below, I could never have another brother. Such was the law for whose sake I did you special honour."

We can conclude then that Antigone buries Polynices not merely because she can have no more brothers or because the unburied corpse is her brother. The burial of Polynices is a means to the end of defining what family is *hers* and what *her family* is. She chooses, let me repeat, between, on the one hand, the future and the family of a husband she might have and, on the other hand, the past and the dead Labdacid line, electing the latter. Burying the brother is her way of distinguishing her dead father from her dead brother, and of honoring her own dead stock as her *own*, of whom she is the last in line. The reason for her sacrifice is thus not only that her act makes it possible for her to become a true member of the accursed family of Oedipus, as Lacan says, but also that it allows her to do what her father did—namely, to define what precisely a ("natural") family is. For her, as for her father, family is a matter of the past, an unalterable, true blood tie spanning at least two generations, each of which is defined by its male members.

The burial of the dishonored corpse of Polynices has, then, a very precise value and content. Finally, it identifies Antigone as the last living, true offspring, the true blood of Oedipus.

THE GOOD OF ALL

If Antigone's act is supposed to challenge the "good of all" of classical ethics, as Lacan emphasizes, it is because she separates the members of her family from everyone else—because she discriminates against the *all*, in favor of the *one*. However, since she ultimately sacrifices herself not for a singular being (nor for Polynices, nor for the "ineffaceable character of what is") but for the *nomos* that is the father function, she, in fact, affirms a certain logic that can itself be universalized. She offers a good whose basis differs from Creon's law only in the limited sense that the latter is meant to protect the city and the king who is the city's symbol, while Antigone's act is meant to honor the *true* father's name. (That it is, indeed, the "true" father that she affirms, we shall see below, in the second part of this essay.)

When Antigone invokes the unwritten laws, she is saying, in effect, that Creon's ordinance did not come from Zeus, nor from Dike and the older, chthonic generation of gods as, one assumes, all other pronouncements by the Theban kings did because, simply, they were legitimate kings and Creon is not. Here we should understand that Creon is not merely an autocratic ruler concerned for the well-being of all living Thebans. He is, more essentially, a ruler who has come to the throne not as the King's direct descendant, but as the Queen's brother. Related to the royal family by Jocasta's marriage, Creon has no direct blood ties to the previous king, Oedipus. He is technically a usurper who needs to impose himself and prove that he is capable of being the city's leader. And *this* he tries to do, first, by issuing an edict that defines the city's friends and foes, and then by sticking to his ruling despite growing approval of Antigone's act among the citizens.

If, then, this tragedy situates the ground of a community between justice and law, between unwritten customs and modern laws, between family and state (as post-Hegelian interpretations tell us), we should recognize that the belief-system so situated is itself circumscribed by a more general symbolic act, an act that too often goes unregistered: Antigone's attempt to affirm (fix, secure) Oedipus' central position in her family. Whatever the city of Thebes will believe kinship relations to be, whatever the kind of rule the city will adopt, Oedipus (and his notion of what a family is, which is affirmed by Antigone) will be at the heart of its symbolic system. Here Oedipus is not merely a father figure but a father with a specific history—a dead king who unknowingly killed his father and committed incest. He is, in short, a criminal who committed no crime, a criminal only in the sense that, *post facto*, after the discovery of what a "true" identity is, he pronounced himself the killer of his father and husband to his mother.

What *Antigone* does, and what Lacan's reading repeats after it, is to *inscribe Oedipus' law* as *the Law of the Father*. As such, *Antigone* has the conservative purpose of confirming that the paternal function is modeled on Oedipus. What Oedipus himself stands for, what the divisions and assumptions inaugurated in his tragedy are, we shall see in the second part of this essay, after a brief look at Antigone's sister, Ismene.

ISMENE

For the tragic audience, the family circle is closed at the end of *Antigone.* The rupture signaled by the exposed corpse at the opening of the play is covered over, and the cycle of the family curse that moved the Theban tragedies forward is now finished. There are no more sons or strange daughters to continue the *Atè* into the next generation. The community can leave behind (that is, bury and forget) this terrible disturbance at the very heart of what makes it one political entity.

For the analytic audience, on the other hand, the message of the play is often said to be "do not give up on your desire." After the interpretation we have offered, it is hard to see what giving up on one's desire would mean in this context. In his reading of *Antigone,* Lacan defines the law of Oedipus as itself constitutive of desire, without allowing that a negation of this law, or an alternative to it, is possible. The two options Lacan presents are, in fact, either to follow desire, as Antigone does, or to exist without an essential determination, as Ismene does.

In not going after what is for Antigone "her desire" (Oedipus' *Atè*), Ismene does not, however, simply give up on hers. Since at the very beginning of the play Ismene does not rise to the status of Oedipus' true daughter, it seems that she is never again in a position to act (or not to act) according to her desire. Ismene is not the *kind* of daughter who could pursue the *Atè*, though she accompanies her father to his death and is ready to join Antigone now and share "the blame." She even offers to die with her beloved sister ("But in your time of trouble I am not ashamed to make myself a fellow voyager in your suffering") and is rejected by Antigone ("And I do not tolerate a loved one who shows her love only in words" [53]).

But neither is Ismene Oedipus' rejected, illegitimate offspring. She is, simply, the *other one* (as Creon refers to her when he orders that both daughters should be punished, before changing his mind). Ismene, we can say, is the forgotten one, to whom neither ancient Greek myth and poetry, nor psychoanalysis, devotes attention. We have to say, then, that the alternative to the legal sphere that appears in the play, an alternative to the culture defined by Oedipus' *Atè* and its repetition (including Ismene's fear of *Atè*), is something altogether other than legality and civility as they are constituted in this play and reconstituted in Lacan's reading.

This "altogether other" legality and civility are not some forgotten past forms, some more originary organization of the law—matriarchy, for instance, as Luce Irigaray claims. For instance, in *Speculum of the Other Woman*, Irigaray identifies Sophocles' play as the "historical bridge between matriarchy and patriarchy."[15] Her *Sexes and Genealogies* expands on the same thought:

> What is the nature of the laws that Antigone respects? They are religious laws relating to the burial of her brother who has been killed in a war

> among men. These laws have to do with the cultural obligations owed to the *mother's blood*, the blood shared by the brothers and sisters in the family. The duty to this *blood* will be denied and outlawed as the culture becomes patriarchal. This tragic episode in life—and in war—between the genders represents the passage into patriarchy. The daughter is forbidden to respect the blood bonds with her mother.[16]

It is not, however, Creon's ban or any other political edict that stands between Antigone and her mother, as Irigaray indicates. It is the incest taboo that forces Antigone to affirm the law of the father and the logic of blood, where blood is a symbolic, rather than a biological tie. Otherwise, without this reinterpretation, her father would remain her brother.

With respect to *Antigone*, the other legality does not stand as savagery to civility, as pre-Oedipal to post-Oedipal, or as crime to law. Savagery, at any rate, as we learn from Shepherdson, is always younger than civility and is born of it.[17] This legality, this culture is, simply, other than the law of the father constituted as Oedipal law, itself understood as the law of true blood ties. Like Ismene, this other legality may be Oedipus' child but is not Oedipus' true blood in the sense that Antigone is. But what are true blood ties exactly?

PART II. OEDIPUS

Blood Ties

Here I will offer only an introductory account of the significance of blood in *Oedipus Tyrannus*, which should nevertheless suffice, since the notion of blood I am going to identify is neither obscure nor new to the reading of Sophocles' plays, only a radically different concept from the one to which psychoanalysis is accustomed.[18]

Basically, there are two instances of "blood" that are crucial for our reading. The first concerns the definition of the difference between Laius and Polybus, and the second concerns the definition of the Theban royal lineage. The first takes place after the Messenger from Corinth tells the King that Polybus was not his father. I will paraphrase their conversation in order to emphasize the difference between the two fathers defined in this scene.

Polybus, the Messenger says, *was not your* genos (kin, stock, or race). *But, what are you saying?* Oedipus asks. *How is it possible that he and I are not of the same kind if he is the one I came from, if he is my source? No*, says the Messenger, *he is no more your kind than I am.* Oedipus then asks the crucial question concerning fatherhood, which brings together the two competing notions of what a father is: *how is it possible that he who was my lord and my guardian was not the one who brought me forth? How is it possible*, he asks, *that Polybus is my progenitor but that he is not of my race? Well*, the Messenger responds, *it is not possible. Polybus was not your begetter, not your original procreator.*

Why then, Oedipus asks, surprised, *did he call me his son? He called you his son*, the Messenger explains, *because he received you as a gift from me. But*, Oedipus adds desperately, *he loved me dearly. He loved me as a father loves a son. The reason for that*, the Messenger suggests, *is that he had no children of his own. He did not have any descendants of his kind to whom he could compare you.*[19] The first piece of the puzzle is thus solved: Polybus is not Oedipus' father. In order to unravel the second secret—who fathered Oedipus?—the play traces in reverse the hands through which he was passed as a baby, starting with the Messenger who gave the baby to Polybus. The chain leads all the way back to Jocasta, who, the Shepherd suggests a bit later, is the beginning of the chain. As the baby's mother, she is the only one who would know whether or not Oedipus' real father was Laius, the former king of Thebes.

The mother does not herself confirm the veracity of the Shepherd's words and the father's identity. Instead, her suicide does so implicitly, suggesting that Laius is, indeed, Oedipus' father. Oedipus, in a recognition of his own, storms into the palace saying, "All is now clear! O light, may I now look on you for the last time, I who am revealed as cursed in my birth, cursed in my marriage, cursed in my killing!" (453). When he comes back, he gives his final commentary on what he has done. Addressing his children for the last time, he says: "Your father killed his father and bore you from the source of his own being" (479).

The result of the differentiation of the two kinds of father is that Laius was a true father and had a child of his own *genos*. Polybus, on the other hand, was not a true father and did not have offspring of his own blood. Oedipus is indeed, as he himself concludes, "of the race of Laius" (469). While Laius is the begetting father, to whom Oedipus traces his lineage, Polybus is just another man to whom Oedipus is related in the same way that he is related to the Messenger. That is, Oedipus is no relation of his. Polybus merely handled the baby on its route from the mother to a definition of *what*, not only who, the real father is. Laius' *haima*, his blood, runs in Oedipus' veins. It is Oedipus' blood, as well as the blood Oedipus spills, and it is this blood that needs to be avenged in order to lift the plague ruining the city of Thebes.[20]

The understanding of progeneration that Oedipus accepts at the end of the play holds that the true father deposits his seed (*spermata*) in the mother's womb, which is itself the receptacle where the seed grows. Thus, Oedipus is Laius' *spermata* grown, and Laius is Oedipus' true father because he is the source of the seed. We should notice, however, that even in Oedipus' case, the son is produced by an illocutionary act, enacting what it names. That is to say, even in *Oedipus Tyrannus*, biological origin is, in fact, a cultural origin. No matter what reason Oedipus gives to prove that Laius and not Polybus is his true father, the son is the one whom the father claims (which in this case happens when Laius identifies Oedipus as the future patricide). And the father is, as we see at the end of the play, the one whom the son claims last.

LAIUS

The second example of blood concerns Laius' lineage identified in the very first line of the play: "Children, latest to be reared from the stock of Cadmus" (327). Laius has a place in the family because he is, in Oedipus' words, "the son of Labdacus, [who] sprung from Polydorus and from Cadmus before him and Agenor long ago" (349). The blood line that Oedipus thus identifies spreads from one generation of true-begetting fathers to the next, starting with the oldest, Agenor, who begot Cadmus, who begot Polydorus, who begot Labdacus, who begot Laius, who, as Oedipus discovers, begot the last king. Or, rather, since it is the son who names a certain man as a begetter, the right order of Laius' lineage is, as Oedipus himself indicates, the reverse, from the youngest to the most ancient. *When there are no living sons, a daughter, as we saw above, has to take upon herself the impossible symbolic act of making the father.*

The same point concerning blood relations can be made starting from the beginning of Oedipus' life. When Laius receives the prophecy, he does not understand it as, to paraphrase Jocasta, just another revelation of every man's unconscious and recognizes that he and his son will rival in competition for the mother. Instead of hearing the prophecy as an indeterminate message (announcing, for instance, the possibility that the son may even go so far as to rise up against and kill his father), Laius, being a Labdacid, behaves as if the prophetic words did not need to be interpreted. As if it were absolutely certain and clear that his son *would* kill him, he desperately tries to prevent the patricide from taking place, all the while unconsciously working to make his murder and the incest possible. (For instance, we learn that Laius did not see to the baby's end himself. Instead, it was Jocasta who handed the child to the Shepherd.) It is his belief in a certain kind of truth, the strength of his unconscious desire, and his blindness to what he is doing that make Laius into the father of the son who will kill him.

If this makes Laius into a figure for the father's unconscious desire, or for the father's castration anxiety, he can be that only if he is also a figure for literal interpretation, a figure for the belief in blood bonds as indomitable and true ties.

TOWARD A CONCLUSION

Reading Oedipus' story backwards, from Antigone's death toward Oedipus' birth, has allowed us to develop an understanding of what a father is that is fundamentally different from the basic psychoanalytic notion developed in relation to the Theban plays. Staying close to Lacan, Pietro Pucci defines the father as follows: "The Father figure is the figure of the anchorage of any discourse to a fixed origin, to a transcendental signified, and therefore, in the play, he is not simply the figure of Oedipus's real biological origin, but the figure around whose constitution and fabrication the possibility of truth pivots for every discourse in our world."[21]

According to Pucci, the father is not simply a begetter; he is—*rather miraculously*—the figure that can be two things at the same time: a biological origin, an actual father, as well as the center, the function, around which the very possibility of truth circles. What Pucci identifies in the above quotation as the truth is Oedipus' truth, not a father's truth or the truth of fatherhood in general. It is the truth that becomes possible when Oedipus recognizes Laius as his legitimate father and rejects Polybus, who is not his *genos* and who cannot be called the true begetting father.

Surprisingly, given her feminist and queer investments, in *Antigone's Claim* Judith Butler accepts Lacan's understanding of Oedipus, which is, at bottom, the same as Pucci's suggestion that Oedipus is the organizing principle that sets the rule "for every discourse in our world."[22] She writes, for instance: "For the Oedipus complex to be universal by virtue of being symbolic, for Lacan, does *not* mean that the Oedipus complex has to be globally evidenced for it to be regarded as universal .... Rather, where and when the Oedipus complex appears, it exercises the function of universalization: it *appears* as that which is everywhere true."[23] Precisely. But, the figure of Oedipus can *appear* as universal only if two additional assumptions also appear as true. First, that there is such a thing as true fatherhood, and second, that the system of signs—the entire system of signs—follows the rules that Oedipus, and Antigone after him, rely on when deciding what constitutes a proper father function.[24] Butler, to do her reading of Oedipus justice, does go on to ask if the understanding of universalization she has formulated "work[s] to usher in God (or the gods) through another door."[25] But she all too quickly equates the contingency of the Oedipus complex with its "ungroundedness," and does not pursue the implication.

Even if seen as contingent, the figure of Oedipus (and the complex with his name) depends on a certain ground, namely, on the distinction between true and arbitrary blood, legitimate and illegitimate family ties. The drama institutes a binary (true/false, indomitable/arbitrary) on which the protagonist's destiny and the meaning of the figure of Oedipus rest. In differentiating between his two fathers, Oedipus, and Greek culture with him, choose one genealogy, one logic of truth, one legality over a possible alternative. In relying on the Oedipus myth the way we commonly do—the way Lacan does in the lectures on *Antigone*, the way Pucci does in *Oedipus and the Fabrication of the Father*, the way Butler does in *Antigone's Claim*—we are reiterating this election.

Through *Antigone* Oedipus *imposes* itself as a universal model, making certain family forms appear insignificant or, in the worst case, illegitimate. As is to be expected, what is taken to be the drama at the very origin of Western culture—the myth of Oedipus—also sets the limitations to what can legitimately be called a family within that system.

Although the father figures are mutually interchangeable in the three plays by Sophocles, it is important to emphasize that the principal father figure of the tragedies is not Laius but Oedipus: I do not mean Oedipus the king who finds his true father, but the Oedipus who is the father of the truth that there is such a thing as a true father. Antigone the daughter is the one who confirms and fixes this figure for the future, which will see no more sons of the Labdacid line. She is, in other words, the first one with the complex.

Following this line of thinking, to have the complex means to accept the father in the terms that define Oedipus as a father. As such, the Oedipus complex is more a rite of initiation than a complex, a tangle of unconscious, unarticulated desires. It is a deed or act that a child *must* perform, just like Antigone, in order to become a member of a specific (Western?) family. Through the rite, the child becomes what it (already) is and, in the process, makes its parents into who they (already) are, namely, parents.

That fatherhood and family are defined based on Oedipus' choice is the problem with the complex and with any reading—including Sophocles' three plays, Lacan's lectures on *Antigone*, Butler's *Antigone's Claim*[26]—of the Oedipus myths as an originary cultural drama.

FREUD

For his part, Freud states clearly that we do not share Oedipus' fortune. In one of the few places in his work where he does actually address Sophocles' tragedy (which is of little consequence for his building of psychoanalysis),[27] he says: "King Oedipus, who slew his father Laius and married his mother Jocasta, merely shows us the fulfilment of our own childhood wishes. But, more fortunate than he, we have meanwhile succeeded, in so far as we have not become psychoneurotics, in detaching our sexual impulses from our mothers and in forgetting our jealousy of our fathers."[28] What Freud indicates in this passage is that *we* are more fortunate than Oedipus was. Unlike *us* and unlike neurotics, the poor king did not feel jealousy toward the dead man he identified, at last, as his father. In this sense, he never had a chance of becoming neurotic.

But, more importantly, in *The Interpretation of Dreams* Freud refers to the myth of Oedipus and to Sophocles' play in the hope of identifying the nascent science of psychoanalysis with classical Greek culture. On the one hand, the myth illustrates, for a wide, general audience, his hypothesis of children's sexuality. On the other hand, *Oedipus Tyrannus* offers a hyperbole for the work of psychoanalysis, for, according to Freud, the play "consists in nothing other than the process of revealing … *a process that can be likened to the work of a psychoanalysis*."[29] The result of the comparison is that psychoanalysis appears capable of explaining the most puzzling misfortune related in Greek mythology.

Its work of explanation, Freud suggests indirectly, runs as ineluctably as destiny in Sophocles' famous play or, perhaps, as persistently as the tragedy's uncovering of the truth. Freud does not indicate, however, whether psychoanalysis too moves towards blinding the patient (as Chase suggests),[30] or if it runs toward some kind of catharsis. By the end of his life, as we learn from Freud's late text on the terminal point of analysis, his belief in the potency of psychoanalysis—which is what the early reference to Oedipus expresses—is, however, significantly revised.

In this essay I have attempted to continue Lacan's project of emptying the paternal metaphor, which I take to be the defining task of psychoanalysis after Lacan. I have also tried to suggest that an interrogation of a certain form of identification, and of a certain notion of family within which this identification is formed—in short, the logic of blood—should be the very focal point of our psychoanalytic thinking about wars. I should add in closing that there is, perhaps, an even more fundamental type of *genos* than the one (blood) to which this essay is devoted. It is found in relation to the status of psychoanalysis conceived as a body of knowledge and, specifically, in the investigation of the *kind* of knowledge that psychoanalysis pretends to be. Both Freud and Lacan claim for it that it is a science, a discourse about family (and not so much a science about the individual), without devoting much analysis to their supposition (their fundamental scientific but also cultural notion) that there is a *genos*—be it natural or cultural—in the first place.

Notes

1. Charles Shepherdson, *Vital Signs: Nature, Culture, Psychoanalysis* (New York: Routledge, 2000), 140.
2. In a recent essay on Freud's "Thoughts for the Times on War and Death," Samuel Weber singles out identification—an "identification with the hero, the star, the individual … and against the enemy, the foreigner, the mass"—as the prime mobilizer for war. "Wartime," in *Violence, Identity, and Self-Determination*, ed. Hent de Vries and Samuel Weber (Stanford: Stanford University Press, 1997), 102.
3. Among Judith Butler's primary tasks in *Antigone's Claim* is reenvisioning what a family is. To the extent that Butler challenges in this work the figure of Oedipus, whose law is "the law of psychoanalysis itself," my exposition on Antigone and Oedipus fully agrees with hers. In my reading of the plays, however, I will depart significantly from her interpretation. For Butler, the two Greek plays are *still* the primary model dramatizing the human transition into culture, even though she wants to radically examine "whether the incest taboo has also been mobilized to *establish* certain forms of kinship as the only intelligible and livable ones." *Antigone's Claim: Kinship Between Life and Death* (New York: Columbia University Press, 2000), 21, 70.
4. Though the classical scholarship on Sophocles' Theban tragedies is overwhelming, to the best of my knowledge, no work, not even Pietro Pucci's

psychoanalytically informed *Oedipus and the Fabrication of the Father:* Oedipus Tyrannus *in Modern Criticism and Philosophy* (Baltimore: Johns Hopkins University Press, 1992), explains what it is that Oedipus is choosing when he begins to consider Laius, and not Polybus, his father. Literary scholars seem to be so invested in the established understanding that they are unwilling to examine closely the crucial differences between Sophocles' Oedipus and the psychoanalytic function that bears the king's name. For instance, in "Beyond Oedipus," Shoshana Felman presents a theory of self-recognition without noting that in the play Oedipus' self-recognition is predicated on an understanding of what a true father is. See "Beyond Oedipus: The Specimen Story of Psychoanalysis," in *MLN* 98 (December 1983): 1021-1053.

5. Citing George Steiner's *Antigones*, Butler asks in *Antigone's Claim* what psychoanalysis would be if it took the figure of Antigone, and not Oedipus, as its point of departure (57; see also 76). In this text I will suggest that such a psychoanalysis would not be fundamentally different. This is what Lacan's interpretation of *Antigone*, when read in the way we are going to read it here, shows. But the stakes of analyzing Antigone and Oedipus are quite beyond what Steiner would want to wager—at stake is psychoanalysis itself as a body of knowledge whose organizing principle is the castration theory (and not the figure of Oedipus or, for that matter, Antigone). For Freud, and Lacan as well, castration is the crucial psychic mechanism underpinning the desire and rivalry that the figure of Oedipus represents.
6. Jacques Derrida, "Structure, Sign, and Play in the Discourse of the Human Sciences," in *Writing and Difference*, ed. and trans. Alan Bass (Chicago: University of Chicago, 1978), 280.
7. Jacques Lacan, *The Seminar of Jacques Lacan, Book VII: The Ethics of Psychoanalysis, 1959-1960*, ed. Jacques-Alain Miller, trans. Dennis Porter (New York: Norton, 1993), 309. Subsequent references will appear parenthetically within the text. While I will be arguing against one Lacan in this article—the Lacan of the dead father—I consider my reading Lacanian because it agrees with, and indeed follows, the Lacan for whom fatherhood is a matter of linguistic utterance, a matter, as he says, of acknowledgment.
8. Commentators agree that Sophocles' text does not provide enough evidence that the man whom Oedipus murdered at the crossroads was Laius. The other crucial identification—namely, the identification of Oedipus, who is the king of Thebes, with the son Laius wanted killed—is a combination of two firsthand testimonies, one by the Shepherd and one by the Messenger, and Jocasta's tacit admission that Oedipus is, indeed, Laius' offspring. Given this background, it should be easy to conclude that what is at stake in reading or retelling Oedipus' drama is not only the nature of

fatherhood but, primarily, the nature of truth.

9. In her 1979 essay "Oedipal Textuality," Cynthia Chase writes, "Sophocles' play portrays Oedipus as the one person in history *without* an Oedipus complex in the conventional sense: he has murdered his father and married his mother in an appreciation of expediency rather than in satisfaction of a desire. The one person who actually enacts patricide and incest completely misses the experience—until after the fact." "Oedipal Textuality: Reading Freud's Reading of *Oedipus*," in *Diacritics* 9 (Spring 1979): 53-68. This after-the-factness of his complex is, for Chase, the reason why *Oedipus Tyrannus* should be read in terms of Freud's deferred action. But what is the "final act" in Oedipus' story? The crucial, if not also the last, revision of what the figure of Oedipus stands for takes place when the last of Cadmus' true offspring dies, and my contention in this article will be that the significance of Oedipus' history becomes decidable only in relation to the ultimate event in the drama of his life, which is Antigone's burial of Polynices. The act, as we shall see, is a symbolic burial of Oedipus, who dies a mysterious death at the end of *Oedipus at Colonus*.
10. The original French is even more emphatic in stressing the contentlessness of the corpse than the Porter translation cited above. Lacan refers to the unique value of being as beyond any content, beyond, indeed, anything good or evil: "*au-delà de tous les contenus, de tout ce que Polynice a pu faire de bien et de mal, de tout ce qui peut lui être infligé.*" *Le Séminaire de Jacques Lacan, Livre VII: L'Ethique de la psychanalyse, 1959-1960* (Paris: Seuil, 1986), 325.
11. Serge Leclaire offers an exquisite psychoanalytic account of the "unique value" of being. See "The Dream with the Unicorn," in *Psychoanalyzing: On the Order of the Unconscious and the Practice of the Letter*, trans. Peggy Kamuf (Stanford: Stanford University Press, 1998), esp. 81-87.
12. Lacan, as Alenka Zupančič claims in *Ethics of the Real: Kant, Lacan* (London: Verso, 2000), would have seen these two values as archaic and modern forms of the same essential determination. Suffice it to indicate here that the differentiation between what we have called a singular being (the modern being-toward-death) and what will be identified later in the text as a family being (the archaic being-for-another) is crucial for understanding the ethics of the situation presented in the play.
13. Sophocles, *Antigone*, in *Sophocles: Works, English and Greek*, vol. 2, ed. and trans. Hugh Lloyd-Jones (Cambridge: Harvard University Press, 1994), 87-89. Subsequent references will appear parenthetically within the text.
14. As far as classical studies are concerned, Lacan's usage of the concept of *Atè* is unusual, but not unique. An understanding close to the one presented by Lacan was introduced by Josef Stallmach in his 1950 dissertation *Atè: Beitrag zur Frage des Selbst- und Weltverständnisses des frühgriechis-*

chen Menschen. The work was published as Heft 18 of *Beiträge zur klassischen Philologie* (Meisenheim am Glan, 1968). I have not been able to locate any information regarding Lacan's direct or indirect knowledge of Stallmach's work. See Leon Golden, "*Hamartia*, *Atè*, and Oedipus," in *Classical World* 72 (September 1978): 3-12.

15. Luce Irigaray, *Speculum of the Other Woman*, trans. Gillian C. Gill (Ithaca: Cornell University Press, 1985), 217.
16. Irigaray, *Sexes and Genealogies*, trans. Gillian C. Gill (Ithaca: Cornell University Press, 1993), 2.
17. Shepherdson, 140.
18. A typical psychoanalytic account of Oedipus does what Freud did not do himself; it reorganizes Oedipus' story to correspond to Freud's understanding of child sexuality. If unconscious knowledge is to mean anything, either Oedipus can have the complex retroactively, in the form of a deferred action (as argued by Chase), after he realizes who his parents were, or he cannot have it at all. When Chase concludes that Oedipus is the instance when "parrincest ... becomes readable for the first time," she repeats the common assumption that itself ignores the fact that for Freud Oedipus' myth is a convenient example of what became readable in his self-analysis and what appeared in the analyses of his patients. Chase, 58.
19. See Sophocles, *Oedipus Tyrannus*, in *Sophocles: Works, English and Greek*, vol. 1, ed. and trans. Hugh Lloyd-Jones (Cambridge: Harvard University Press, 1994), 429-431. Subsequent references will appear parenthetically within the text.
20. The two other instances in which *haima* appears in *Oedipus Tyrannus* refer to Lauis' blood, spilled by Oedipus. One is the prophecy that Oedipus relates to the Messenger, that he would "spill my father's blood [*patroon haima*] with my own hand" (425). The second is the confirmation of the prophecy: "O three roads, hidden glade, coppice and narrow path where three ways meet, ways that drank my own, my father's blood [*toumon haima*] shed by my hands" (471). The second instance also carries the sense that Oedipus has, literally, shed his own blood. In *Antigone*, Creon identifies Polynices' attack on Thebes as the spilling of his own blood. He says that Polynices came back from exile to the land of his fathers and the gods of his race to feed on the blood of his own kind (*haimatos koinou*). See *Antigone*, 21.
21. Pucci, 9.
22. Ibid.
23. Butler, 45.
24. The fact that the Oedipus complex only "*appears* as that which is every-

where true" does not, for Lacan, lessen the hold of the father figure, but increases it. As "factually" true, the Oedipus complex would be a natural law (a biological fact, we might say), with as little symbolic consequence for a family as gravity has. The complex would be a given and not a matter of the economy of the truth—not the grounding myth of this economy.

25. Butler, 45.

26. I would also include Zupančič's reading of Oedipus in her book *Ethics of the Real.* She says, for instance, "he [Oedipus] travels the path of initiation (of 'symbolization') in reverse and, in so doing, he experiences and demonstrates the radical contingency of the Meaning borne by the symbolic." If the difference between Polybus and Laius were, indeed, one of contingency, and not one of status, we would not need to disagree with Zupančič's account. But the question is not, as Zupančič seems to think, whether or not "the Father," the superman of our fantasies, the king of Thebes, "is also the father (a man with all his weaknesses)." The paternity in question is much more precise: why is it that even "a man with all his weaknesses" can be Oedipus' Father, but Polybus cannot? Zupančič goes so far as to suggest that Oedipus is not guilty. Of course he is. He is guilty because he identifies Laius with the father from the prophecy. Zupančič, 193.

27. Voicing a common assumption, Chase claims that "the drama of Oedipus is his [Freud's] most recurrent and insistent reference" (54). Yet, since Oedipus is, in fact, a rare reference for Freud, when Chase has to explain what Oedipus' "psychoneurosis" is, she has to map him onto another of Freud's cases and draw the implications for Oedipus' unusual and not thoroughly considered (by Freud) situation. *The Concordance* lists only one instance in *The Standard Edition* where Freud discusses Oedipus and Sophocles' drama—the famous passage in *The Interpretation of Dreams.* In all other instances, and there are fewer than one would think, the complex carrying the name of the mythological father is a shorthand for a theory of sexuality that Freud formulated independently from the tragedy and the myth.

28. Sigmund Freud, *The Interpretation of Dreams* in *The Standard Edition of the Complete Psychological Works of Sigmund Freud*, ed. and trans. James Strachey et al. (London: Hogarth, 1953-1974), 4:262.

29. Ibid., 261-262; emphasis added.

30. Chase, 58.

12

The Aim of the Analytic Act

Colette Soler

What is promised as an end of analysis?[1] This question has been present from the beginning of psychoanalysis. Is it to cure what Freud called the "illness" of neurosis, that is, to reduce the dissidence of the symptom and reestablish "normality"—and, in particular, sexual "normality"? Freud was not far from this idea when he claimed that the capacity to love and work were the best we could hope to obtain, as well as when he ironically explained that the goal was to transform neurotic misfortune into common misfortune. Lacan, on the contrary, when interrogating the end of analysis in 1968, claimed that the aim was to produce an incurable subject. But in 1975, in contrast, he linked the end of analysis with identification with the symptom. It is this apparent change of perspective that I will investigate.

THE ILLNESS OF MANKIND

Psychoanalysis, via Freud and Lacan, has produced the formula for the sexual illness of mankind. Due to the unconscious, "there is no such thing as a sexual relationship." With this thesis, the status of the symptom is altered, and consequently the status of the therapeutic act. Let me follow this thread.

The thesis that the unconscious is structured like a language, and the symptom as a message, or metaphor, was suggested by Freudian technique. But as Lacan never ceased to re-elaborate in his later years, with the unconscious understood as the "treasure of the drive"—which implies a wedding of the signifier and the living being—the symptom is the response of *jouissance*. Thus, Lacan came to the point where he recaptured the fundamental Freudian thesis: the symptom is a mode of satisfaction. It can be deciphered like a message, but it is not only a way of speaking, but above all it is a way of enjoying. This is why, years ago, I did not hesitate to evoke Lacan's second step as a "second return to Freud."[2] The language of the symptom is, so to speak, incarnated, embodied; it organizes and regulates *jouissance*. Even further, the unconscious is made real through *jouissance*. Hence the surprising formula from *Encore*: "The real, I will say, is the mystery of the speaking body, the mystery of the unconscious."[3] In psychoanalysis, however, therapeutic effects testify to the grasp of language on what is most real in symptomatic disorders; one verifies that the least verbal of symptoms (anxiety, somatization, thought disturbances) can be transformed by the sole means of language. The curious docility of the symptom in an analytic session supports this conception of the unconscious.

Freud thus confronted the following problem: how can a mode of *jouissance* that is so self-centered, even autistic, come to be reconciled with the relationship of desire and love for another body, which is obviously necessary for the constitution of the sexual couple, whatever it may be, but especially of the heterosexual couple? The discovery of the drive, far from leading to pansexualism, rather posed the question, from its very origin, of the libido that was apt to sustain the sexual link. If Freud opened this perspective, he did not carry it to its logical conclusion. To answer the question, finally, he has nothing to offer but his elaboration of the Oedipus complex, with the various identifications that it entails. With this, he tried to explain one thing and its reverse, I mean the norm of heterosexual desire and what differs from it. And when he admitted that he did not know, it was the concept of "constitution"—that is, nature—so often referred to by him, that remained his last resort. I certainly realize that Freud's texts are always more subtle than the mere enunciation of his theses and that the number of nuances with which he corrects each of them defies any easy summary. Nonetheless, after having clearly located the link between the symptom and sex—and it is precisely on this point that he broke decisively with Jung—Freud turned the symptom into an anomaly of the sexual, more precisely a distorted substitute of the so-called normal sexual satisfaction. Hence, in this case, it was obvious that the symptom could only be conceived within the sphere of an individual pathology of *jouissance*.

It must be said that this point of view is strongly suggested by the most elementary clinical experience of hearing the subject's complaint. A symptom is presented to the analyst as that which does not stop imposing itself. Whether it is in the form of not being able to refrain from certain thoughts or from a feeling in the body, or from experiencing certain troubling affects, a symptom is experienced as a disturbance, an anomaly, a deviation or constraint. In this respect, the only difference between the patient and Freud is that the former does not immediately perceive the symptom's sexual implications, although from the very beginning, transference makes him aware of the incidence of the unconscious.

The primary affect of the symptom as dysfunction is a fact no clinician could deny, Lacan no more than any other. But what does psychoanalysis reveal when it deals with the "psychology of the love life," in both its happy and unhappy forms, if not this: the unconscious is captain of the ship, presiding over what we call the mysteries of love, specifically over the choice of object insofar as it causes desire and/or *jouissance*. To put it in another way, the love partner, in the sexual sense of the term, and more generally any partner inscribed in a social link, is no less a product of the unconscious, no less coded than an obsession or a somatization. Thus between a man and a woman, and more generally between any two bodies, the unconscious is present, simultaneously separating and linking them. Freud perceived this when he exposed the fact that both love life and group formations are produced by repetitive choices. Repetition means that it is not all women that interest a man, but only some, that is, those who are linked with his unconscious. In other words, there is no such thing as sexual "instinct."

THERE IS THE SYMPTOM

The general formula could be stated as follows: if there is no such thing as a sexual relationship, there is the symptom. The symptom is a substitute built from the unconscious.

Between these two formulas a third one remains implicit, a concept at which Lacan hammered away for a whole seminar through the famous phrase, "There is (the) One." This formula is not as simple as it seems, whether it refers to the "One" of the signifier One as opposed to Two, or the "One" of the saying, the One-saying (*l'Un-dire*), or the "One" of the *jouissance* of the body beyond all ties. In each case, this formula underscores the exile of the speaking-being (*parlêtre*) from any relation with the *jouissance* of the sexual partner. The symptom that achieves a union between the discrete elements of the unconscious and that other thing which is *jouissance*, as I have said, provides a replacement. Given that an appropriate or natural partner for *jouissance* is lacking, the symptom is put in place of something else, a substitute, an element seized from the unconscious, or a letter (as Lacan claimed in 1975), which fixes the privileged *jouissance* of the subject, this subject, who is subjected otherwise to the great law of the want-to-be. Lacan went so far to say: the symptom is the way by which everyone "enjoys the unconscious" (*jouit de son inconscient*).[4]

I designate the *fundamental symptom*, just as we speak of the fundamental fantasy, as the singular symptom which establishes a link where there is no established social link, that is to say, at the level of love affairs. As Lacan says in *Television*, love affairs are cut from any social link. This means, in the same way that the psychotic subject confronts his organs and even his life without the assistance of a discourse, every speaking being is forced to confront the other sexed body without the help of an established discourse. The fundamental symptom is the symptom which compensates for this fundamental lack, it determines a singular mode of relating to a sexual partner, a modality that is always enigmatic, produced by the unconscious as operating on the real. At this level, every one is without equal (*sans pareil*), and this is why Lacan can say that, for a man, "a woman is a symptom." I have called this the "fundamental symptom," but could also call it the last symptom, for it is the symptom that compensates for the lack of the final term in the field of libido language.

The fundamental symptom is no longer the problem but the solution—and this is without any paradox. The solution is proper to everyone, the response to the non rapport imposed on all, the universal illness for beings who are affected by the unconscious. "There is no such thing as sexual relationship" means that any partner is a symptomatic one. This symptomatic solution can be more or less uncomfortable for the subject, more or less common, but in any case it responds to the lack which is at the core of language, the lack stemming from the impossibility of inscribing the Other *jouissance*.

A solution is invented, case by case, according to the accidents of history. But what can be said of the inventor? It is difficult to say that the symptom is the subject's invention, since it constrains him. Shall we say that it is an invention of the unconscious? This would be too simple, for it would also be necessary to bring up the response of *jouissance*—the subject of *jouissance*—which creates what Freud called a "fixation." Let us say then that this marriage of the unconscious element and *jouissance* is the fruit of the conjuncture of first encounters—which, as Freud would say, are traumatic. According to him, these encounters have either touched one's own body or the other's body. Therefore, the unconscious in the symptom-letter is not the discourse of the Other, it is the trace of the contingency of a fateful encounter (*rencontre fatale*)—just as we say *femme fatale*—with a being of *jouissance* that the subject did not know, but which had already begun to respond.

I therefore conclude that invention was at the beginning. Invention is found not only in the act that is reiterated as always new, without Other—and this is why I have elsewhere spoken of "actheism" to play on "atheism"—and also not only in the ciphering that makes unexpected statements appear. In the beginning there is no subject, for the subject is an effect. There is, however, the symptom, which is the choice of a singular *jouissance*, in the double sense of the term (as individual and strange). The speaking being must recognize itself in the very opacity of this *jouissance*. This, indeed, is why inventions, especially those in the arts, can be homologous to the symptom. We can also conceive, if the symptom is invented in the gap of the Other, that a new symptomatic invention can expel another. Therefore, the first encounter, which I called fateful, is not fatal.

The spectrum of consequences that the symptom entails is vast, but the foremost one is this: there is no subject without a symptom. It is through the symptom that everyone has access to his or her *jouissance*. Its functions as a prosthetic device, given the foreclosure of sex. In other words, every subject invents or adopts—if the term invents is too strong—an alternative, something which comes into the place of the empty rapport. One should never dream of eliminating it, and with it we can defend the incurable Lacan spoke of in 1968. An analysis which starts with the symptom will also end with the symptom, but with an obvious transformation. A key question now emerges: how does the act operate on this necessary function of the symptom, and how can we situate the therapeutic effect?

SYMPTOM(S)

If the symptom is a substitution, not all substitutions have equal value. The problem is then to define the value in question. Given that the ethic of psychoanalysis is not an ethic of norms, what would provide the criterion of values? *Jouissance*? This is problematic, given that *jouissance* is subject to several paradoxes. We would have to ask the question, "*Jouissance* for whom?" since the value of *jouissance* for the speaking being is linked to its exchange value. The Other cannot be eliminated here. On a practical level, this means that autism is not a tenable position. There are certainly instances of autistic *jouissance*, but they are strictly local: Freud noticed this early on, amazed at how one can fall ill from not being able to love, in other words, from not being able to transfer one's libido outside oneself. More than that, we know that it is not any *jouissance* whatsoever that is compatible with the social link.

There are clearly many different types of symptoms. On the one hand, the Other of discourse proposes a symptom to the subject. The symptom that the Other proposes is normality. This normality consists in imposing norms as a remedy for the non-rapport, and typically these are male norms (*normes mâles*), as Lacan would say. Normality is the compensation par excellence that satisfies the Other, and when it is also able to satisfy the subject—here is the key reservation—it is clearly an incurable symptom. On the other hand, at the other extreme, there is perversion. Perversion is a satisfying symptom, in the sense that it is enough—*satis* means "enough" in Latin—of a compensation of *jouissance*. It compensates well enough for the absence of the sexual relation.

This satisfaction does not mean that the pervert will not complain or suffer. Fritz Lang's marvelous film, *M*, is as a prototype in this regard. The compensation function is seen here in all its simplicity: the protagonist, unable to have intercourse with women, strangles little girls. The first people to suffer from his symptom are the others, his victims and their families, but he is also subjected to a very real suffering, because he is divided by the diabolical truth of his *jouissance*, which is his own *jouissance* at the same time as being alien to him. This example shows in an exemplary way how a symptom that satisfies as much as a compensation, despite the pain that the subject might have to pay as its price, is not susceptible to analysis. In other words, Jack the Ripper is not a subject for analysis even if he is really unhappy and really sorry for the consequences of his actions. A warning to those analysts who work in prisons: remember that there are acts which do not involve an appeal to the Other. This, at least, is how I understand Lacan's advice against taking a subject into analysis who has killed his father, a recommendation that is given without knowing any more information about the case.

Between the symptom of normality that satisfies the Other and the symptom of perversion that goes against the Other, there is, of course, a third form: the neurotic symptom. This neurotic symptom, which Freud qualified as a compromise, is unsatisfying both with respect to norms and to *jouissance.* In this sense, it is abnormal, but it does not succeed in becoming perverse: the neurotic only dreams of being a pervert, for the precise reason that he is not one. Caught between these two dissatisfactions, the subject complains. In this respect, I believe the neurotic symptom par excellence is what Lacan, at one time, called hysteria without symptoms, in the classical and nosographic sense of the term. Hysteria without symptoms is when the subject gives his complaint the dignity of a symptom. This shows us the true source of the symptom, since it involves the subject's yearning for the missing rapport and, at the same time, refusing any substitute for this place that he marks simply with his incessant complaint. This is a position which is, in fact, opposed to the supplementary character of any compensation or substitution of *jouissance.* When it is stubborn, this refusal may go as far as beauty itself or even death, which is not without its link to beauty. We may recall here the example of Socrates.

THE SYMPTOM OF TRANSFERENCE

What is the impact of the act on the symptom at the start of analysis? The act's first effect is to render the symptom analyzable. This involves a change, and the term "to render" here should be understood in the sense of producing something. The symptom will change its use, that is, it will exchange its value as insufficient *jouissance* for a value as knowledge: this is the induction to the transference. At the start of analysis, one might say that the analytic act has the effect of dissociating the symptom, of producing a separation between its core of *jouissance* and its formal envelope. This is the initial change, which we can make more precise with Lacan's term *dés(a)ification*, in the sense of an extraction of *object a* as surplus *jouissance.* Through this operation, the act serves as a catalyst for speech, allowing what will produce the work of transference to emerge, that is, fragments of unconscious knowledge. This is the situation at the start of analysis.

Transference, however, is a reconstitution of the symptom. The analysand binds himself to the couple analyst-analysand, which went unknown until Freud. It is important in this coupling that the analyst knows what determines him at the level of *jouissance.* As the cause of transference work, he is also the cause of another *jouissance*, that of deciphering. For it is true, as Freud clearly witnessed, that the speaking being never really gives up anything.

The problem is that the symptom in the treatment needs to be transitory, and that if it is the name of the analyst, it is a name that is to be lost, like the

Name-of-the-Father. In others words, the efficacy of the act is as an operation of the symptom, but at the same time against the symptom. After having constructed the analytic symptom, it must be deconstructed to produce an exit from the process; otherwise, the analysis is interminable.

The exit still has to be a good one. The good one is the one that satisfies. As Lacan put it, "the main aim of analysis is to give this urgently needed satisfaction," thus positing a final urgency to match the subjective urgency that motivates the entry into the treatment.[5] I would define the exit that is not good as the one which fails to satisfy. Perhaps the form it most often takes is that of the exit due to wear and tear, due to the long passage of time, to weariness; the one which is made on the basis of the "I've had enough" of pure resignation. The proper exit, on the other hand, is the one that satisfies. But how should we understand this if not by linking it to the final identification with the symptom?

The incurable subject that I have evoked is a subject identified with its own symptom, at least the symptom I have called fundamental, which defines the symptomatic sexual partner. Is this a return to the *status quo ante*? Certainly it is not, given that it supposes a change insofar as we come to relate to the transference included in the neurotic symptom.

We must not forget that, if the symptom is a way to enjoy the unconscious, there are different ways to do so. With respect to the marriage between the signifier and *jouissance*, ciphering is one mode while the fundamental symptom is another. The latter is a function of exception—a logical function—in relation to the infinite labor of ciphering. This symptom anchors or fixes a configuration of constant *jouissance*, whereas ciphering, which is sporadic, never ceases to displace this *jouissance* in the series of signs, thus opening up the way to surprise and even innovation.

The identification with the fundamental symptom puts a stop to the symptom of transference, and we can say that it exposes the true name of the subject, the name of its own identity of *jouissance*—an incurable identity.

To illustrate this distance between the symptom as a sign to the analyst in the transference and the symptom as a name, I will return to *M.* The film allows me to situate a difference between neurosis and perversion. It is astonishing how clearly Lang's film shows us the difference between the symptom as sign and the symptom as name. What makes a sign for M. is the little melody that accompanies his outings and signals the murders, but which only the blind, those who are not captured by the *jouissance* of vision, can hear. This is the sign of the symptom. Then there is the letter M that is marked on M.'s back: this is the name of the accursed, a name with which he does not identify himself, but which the other uses to identify him, since M. is obviously neither an analysand nor a neurotic. I will return, then, to the incurable at the end of analysis.

Lacan has left us many formulas for a finite or terminable analysis: the end marked by assuming "being for death," by subjectivizing castration, by the subjective destitution of the pass, and finally by identifying with the symptom. Amidst this variety, which follows from his structural elaborations, we are left with a question: what is the "saying," the unique saying, which is to be inferred from the multiple things that have been said (*dits*)?

If we juxtapose Freud's position on a finite analysis, it seems that according to what can be disengaged from what he said (*ses dits*), the actual end is a matter of simple pragmatism. This is not the case with Lacan, who at each stage situates the end in terms of structures, and even of the matheme. At the end, we have the identification with the symptom. Is this a theoretical upset, as some have said? It is certain that Lacan's work between 1970 and 1975 is marked by changes: the new Borromean schematism and its clinical advances, the redefinition of the symptom, the devaluation of the hegemony of the symbolic, the reevaluation of the real. Yet, to what extent do these shifts of perspective alter what is to be obtained from the end of an analysis?

I shall argue that the formula is new but the saying is not, for it never varied. This identification with the symptom is not to be confused with what I will call the identifications of alienation—identifications via the Other—which go from the ideals of the Other, I(A), to the phallic signifier. These identifications certainly try to "crystallize" into an identity, but they are merely elaborate facades that hide a subject that is only supposed, who cannot be identified in the Other, and thus functions only as a lack (-1). The symptom as singular, as Lacan had once said about the Thing, is not on the side of the Other but rather comes from the real, from *jouissance*. This identification consists, he says, in "recognizing oneself in it." What does this mean? This expression should be weighed against another, from the same period, that says that one can never recognize oneself in one's unconscious.

Obviously, in order to recognize oneself in one's symptom, one must have identified the symptom at a distance; one must have recognized—beyond the therapeutic changes occurring throughout the analytic elaboration—the specific modalities of *jouissance* that do not cease to be written for the subject and which define his partner. This is the condition for dealing with the symptom, or as Lacan put it, "knowing how to do it" (*savoir faire avec*). For the neurotic—who, by definition, does not recognize himself in his symptom and continues to deny and complain about it, even when he gives himself the air of a cynic—this is progress.

To recognize oneself in one's symptom is to take upon oneself what must be called a *jouissanceidentity*. This has nothing to do with identifying with the Other. Thus the symptom that does not cease to write itself responds to the "What am I?" of the entry into analysis. The end by means of identifying with the symptom is an end through identity, not by identification; or, more precisely, it is an end achieved by what I will call a separation-identity. There is, indeed, no other identity.

The explicit precursor of this thesis can be found at the end of *The Four Fundamental Concepts of Psychoanalysis*, where Lacan, in mentioning an identification of a special type with the *object a*, was already aiming at a separation-identity by *jouissance*. More essential still, this Borromean symptom determines not only the subject that is supposed in relation to the signifier, but on the contrary, the "real subject" that Lacan designated in 1975 as the one who is irrefutably there: the individual speaking being that has a body and is substantial.

This saying about the end of analysis by separation-identity can be generalized. Regarding the end and the result of the analytic metamorphosis, there is no other saying of Lacan's than this, as I have more extensively demonstrated elsewhere. This saying has moved from the ineffable identity that is affirmed by the ecstatic "you are that" in the 1949 text on the Mirror Stage, through the subjective destitution, to the famous identification with the *jouissance*-letter of the symptom in 1975. This letter, however, uproots the end from the ineffable, since within language it alone is identical to itself.

Identity is the contrary of mental perplexity and turmoil; separation is the contrary of alienation. It is astounding to witness the extent to which Lacan produced misunderstandings and was grossly misinterpreted by his first students. In a manner that was increasingly pathetic, and thus idealized, these followers put forth, in succession, notions of lack, castration, de-being, destitution, and—of course—non-knowledge. Hence they were stupefied by the appearance of the identification with the symptom, which served only as the final quilting point of the thesis that had been present from the beginning. Lacan himself diagnosed this misunderstanding by evoking those analysts who authorize themselves only by their perplexity.

Without this fundamental thesis of the end by separation-identity, how can we acknowledge an important clinical fact (which, moreover, the enemies of psychoanalysis enjoy pointing out), that those who are called "analyzed," and for whom analysis has sometimes changed everything, have nonetheless, at a certain level, remained the same and even become more incorrigible?

ETHICS IS NEVER INDIVIDUALISTIC

That the time for understanding has taken so long has its drawbacks. These disadvantages are clinical, of course, but are not confined to the clinic insofar as the conception of the end of analysis has a decisive political import. From the beginning, Lacan posited that for psychoanalysis "its ethics are never individualistic."[7] On the contrary, it has effects on our current civilization. Rereading his early texts, I have been struck by the number of virulent remarks Lacan makes about the era, which can still be perfectly applied to the beginning of the twenty-first century. I shall quickly cite a few. From "Aggressiveness in Psychoanalysis": it is a time of "social hell" in which "touching" victims are produced by the "barbarity of the Darwinian century"[8]; from "Function and Field of Speech and Language": the subject "loses his meaning in the objectifications of discourse" within "our scientific civilization"[9]; from the "Remarks on Daniel Lagache's Presentation": the widespread ethics of the superego and of dread[10]; from "La troisième": we are all proletarians, insofar as we no longer have anything from which we can make a social bond.[11]

Corresponding to each of these diagnoses, the mission of psychoanalysis is redefined: with the touching victim, "we clear anew the path to his meaning in a discrete fraternity"[12]; despite his or her lost meaning "the subject's satisfaction is achievable in the satisfaction of all"[13]; getting out of the ethic of the superego is achieved by the silence of desire. In "Subversion of the Subject and the Dialectic of Desire," it is making one's castration serve as the regulation of desire; in *Television*, it is getting out of the capitalist discourse; and finally, in "La troisième," there is a countering of the real, that is, the real of the proletarian social symptom.

It would be necessary to follow this progression in greater detail, but we can already observe, in every case, that the objective that Lacan prescribes goes in the direction of restoring to subjects a place in the social bond that passes through disalienation.

On this point, what can be said of the identification with the symptom? Does it not add to the modern proletarian's forced individualism and dereliction? Some colleagues have asked, with today's subjects prey to the values of capitalism, how can we still recommend that each "meet at its horizon the subjectivity of his time," as Lacan recommended for the analyst at the end of "The Function and Field of Speech and Language."[14] Perhaps these colleagues have imagined that the identification with the symptom was homogeneous to what I have called the regime of "general narcynicism" that capitalism produces.

This, I think, is the error. The social symptom of all proletarians, which globalizes and standardizes each subject's relation with the products of the market, effectively disrupts the social bond. In its wake, this symptom establishes merely a single—and not very social—bond for each subject to a prescribed surplus *jouissance*. This is not necessarily the case for the Borromean symptom at the end of analysis, which knots desire and *jouissance* for each subject in a singular—never global—way, without at the same time excluding the social bond. Quite to the contrary, the Borromean symptom alone can ensure what Lacan called a more-worthy love, and even "the exit from the herd."

Confronted with the globalization of merchandized *jouissance*, and thus with standardized surplus *jouissance*, identification with the symptom highlights a singularity of *jouissance* without any nostalgic resort to values from the past that have become powerless. It is thus linked to the subjectivity of the age, or at least to what remains of it in a discourse that tries to master desires. Lacan is up to date now more than ever.

Does it not remain the case, however, that the solution to neurosis by identifying with the symptom still is not a way out of an individualistic ethic? This is why, I think, Lacan could say this approach fell short. But it is also the reason why he added the necessity of making a number, and also that of a complement, for analysts; that is, the solution by means of the school.

Notes

1. This text resumes a number of developments begun in 1987, in a text devoted to the aim of the analytic act, and continued until 1994 at the meetings of *L'international des forums-l'Ecole de psychanalyse du Champ Lacanien.*
2. Colette Soler, "Le second retour à Freud," *Boletin del circulo psicanalitico de Vigo* (1986).
3. Jacques Lacan, *The Seminar of Jacques Lacan, Book XX: Encore: On Feminine Sexuality, The Limits of Love and Knowledge*, 1972-1973, ed. Jacques-Alain Miller, trans. Bruce Fink (New York: Norton, 1998), 131.
4. Lacan, *RSI* (1974-1975), unpublished seminar, 18 February 1975.
5. Lacan, *The Seminar of Jacques Lacan, Book XI, The Four Fundamental Concepts of Psychoanalysis*, ed. Jacques-Alain Miller, trans. Alan Sheridan (New York: Norton, 1981), ix.
6. Colette Soler, "Les invariants de l'analyse finie," *Hétérté* 5 (June 2005).
7. Lacan, "The Freudian Thing," in *Écrits*, trans. Bruce Fink in collaboration with Héloïse Fink and Russell Grigg (New York: Norton, 2006), 346.
8. Lacan, "Aggressiveness in Psychoanalysis," *Écrits*, 101, 99.
9. Lacan, "The Function and Field of Speech and Language in Psychoanalysis," *Écrits*, 232-233.
10. Lacan, "Remarks on Daniel Lagache's Presentation," *Écrits*, 543-574.
11. Lacan, "La troisième," *Lettres de l'Ecole freudienne* 16 (1975): 177-203.
12. Lacan, "Aggressiveness in Psychoanalysis," 101.
13. Lacan, "The Function and Field of Speech and Language in Psychoanalysis," 264.
14. Ibid.

13

On the Path of the Semblant

Jelica Šumič

The real is what does not depend on my idea of it.
—Jacques Lacan[1]

HEADING FOR THE REAL

What is the peculiar evocative force of the notion of the real? In the "passion for the real" which, according to Badiou,[2] animated all the subversive inventions of the 20th century—from psychoanalysis to revolutionary politics—is there a mystification at work that merits our critical scrutiny before we so quickly subscribe to its seductive appeal?

Rather than succumbing to the temptation of forcing appearance in order to accede to the real supposed to be lurking behind it—an endeavour which can only engender devastating consequences, as Badiou never tires of repeating[3]—for Lacanian psychoanalysis, the path of access to the real is none other than that of the semblant. Indeed, for psychoanalysis, the question of the real is inseparable from the interrogation of the semblant. This is why, although the semblant is relevant to numerous contemporary discourses, it is only in psychoanalysis that this term was elevated to the level of concept.

The semblant is a term forged by Lacan in the last period of his teaching in order to rework the relation between the symbolic and the real. The introduction of this notion charts a momentous shift in Lacan's teaching from the symbolic to the real as a focal point of psychoanalysis. Thus, to a certain extent, the semblant is a problem specific to psychoanalysis. Omnipresent, unsettling, yet unresolved, the problem of the semblant comes to the fore at critical moments in the history of psychoanalysis, thereby marking turning points at which the orientation of psychoanalysis is at stake. Freud himself already tried to circumscribe the problem of the semblant by claiming that "there are no indications of reality in the unconscious, so that one cannot distinguish between the truth and fiction cathected with affect."[4] Stumbling across what could be termed a primordial deceitfulness at the level of the unconscious, Freud nevertheless refused to consider the distinction between truth and fiction as an operational conceptual opposition in psychoanalysis. He thereby indicates that another dimension, that of the libido and the satisfaction of the drives, is to be taken as a compass for orienting oneself in an unconscious swarming with lures and deceptions.

Lacan, likewise, encounters the problem of the semblant at a crucial moment of his teaching, in particular in his seminar on *The Ethics of Psychoanalysis,* in which he sets out to forge new conceptual tools to treat the real at stake in the analytic experience. More particularly, Lacan broaches the question of semblants at a point in his teaching at which he seems to be turning away from the problematic of truth, that is to say, from that which previously constituted the focal point of psychoanalysis and its specificity in relation to the discourse of science. Indeed, it is under the guise of fiction, a concept borrowed from Bentham, that Lacan first tackles the question of the semblant. What Lacan emphasises here is a conceptual knotting between the Benthamite fictions and his notion of the symbolic. Crucially, he insists that what he means by fiction is not to be confused with its commonly accepted sense: illusion. "Fictitious is not," he claims, "in effect, in its essence that which deceives, but is precisely what I call the symbolic."[5] Moreover, the very fact that Lacan situates fiction in the symbolic order involves the displacement of the notion of truth: it is not enough to state with Freud that the opposition between fiction and truth is untenable since truth itself has the structure of fiction.[6]

One might say that, from the outset, the semblant is conceived by Lacan as a paradox of the relation between the symbolic and the real. In this respect, it is interesting to note that although both French terms, "*semblant*" ("semblance") and "*semblable*" ("similar"), have the same root, the Latin word *similes,* Lacan's category of semblance is not a new name for the imaginary. On the contrary, semblance, as conceived by Lacan, is intended to designate that which, coming from the symbolic, is directed towards the real. This is precisely what characterizes Bentham's fictions. Indeed, as a fact of language, made of nothing but the signifier, Bentham's legal fictions are nonetheless capable of distributing and modifying pleasures and pains, thereby affecting the body. What held Lacan's attention in reading Bentham's *Theory of Fictions* was precisely that something which is ultimately an apparatus of language—Bentham defines fictions as owing their existence to language alone—is capable of inflicting pain or provoking satisfaction that can only be experienced in the body. It appears as if with Bentham's fictions Lacan found at last a missing link, a quilting point between the signifier and *jouissance.* This is why in *Seminar XX*, in a period of his teaching in which the notion of the semblant is well established, he can still remark, in referring expressly to the Benthamite fictions, that the whole purpose of using "old words" is their ability to capture *jouissance.*[7]

There is yet another aspect to the Benthamite fiction that Lacan brought to light, although rather late in the day, in his seminar *D'un Autre à l'autre.* In Lacan's reading, what sets apart Bentham's approach to fictions from the usual understanding of this term is that, with remarkable lucidity, Bentham reveals how all human institutions have as their ultimate aim *jouissance.* Hence by openly stating that fictions are nothing but an artificial device, "a contrivance," to use Bentham's proper term, designed to provoke either pain or pleasure, Bentham brings into question all human institutions insofar as they are an apparatus destined to regulate the modes of *jouissance* by dressing them up in the virtues of the useful and the good.[8] Bentham's concept of fictions can be seen as an effective manner of denouncing the moral and social ideals of the epoch, of exposing them as being nothing but a semblance, a make-believe, precisely to the extent that the human institutions are nothing but semblants, i.e., the means and the modes of *jouissance.* This hardly concealed cynicism, reminding us of the primacy of *jouissance*, is precisely what is scandalous about the Benthamite conception of fictions; and it is from this perspective of the cynicism of *jouissance* that a crucial feature of semblants can be brought to light: the constitutive role of belief. Destined to cover up the economy of *jouissance*, semblants can only succeed in their task inasmuch as we believe in them, that is to say, take their make-believe at face value.

With Bentham's fictions, by contrast, we are dealing with a semblance which openly declares that it is nothing but make-believe. Indeed, in order to be operational, Bentham's fictions, unlike the rest of human institutions, can do without the masquerade or, more precisely, without the belief in moral or cultural ideals. Bentham's fiction—in itself a fallacy, a make-believe, a semblance, yet a semblance which presents itself as semblance, a reflexive semblance, as it were—thus presents us with the paradox of lying truly. As semblant hostile to semblants, the fiction contributes to the unmasking of moral virtues as semblants in the service of *jouissance*, while still touching the real. The lesson to be drawn from Bentham's cynical use of fictions is therefore the following: it is possible to use fictions in order to attain the real without believing in them. It is precisely in view of this double capacity of the Benthamite fiction—as a means both of denouncing, exposing semblants and of attaining the real—that the question of the semblant is posed to Lacan above all as the question of how to put semblants to good use.

The question of know-how with fictions is, indeed, of paramount importance to Lacan once it is admitted that fictions can be considered as a symbolic apparatus destined to intervene in the real of the body. Hence, from the moment fictions are conceived by Lacan as the very means with which to modify the subject's relation to *jouissance*, his whole elaboration of the analytic practice changes. But this emphasis on *jouissance* also demands a radical reorientation of psychoanalysis in which the role of the structuring principle is attributed to the opposition between the real and semblants. In fact, it is

Lacan's redeployment of Bentham's concept of fiction that made it possible for the real at issue in psychoanalysis, the real of *jouissance*, to emerge as such.

In view of this shift in Lacan's teaching, which defines psychoanalysis not in its relation to truth but in its relation to the real, it may appear odd that the notion of the semblant did not find what might be called its proper place until the seventies. There is one further consideration about the Lacanian concept of the semblant that should be mentioned. The fact that this notion, which could truly serve us as a key to Lacan's later teaching, did not receive the attention it deserves until recently, can be attributed in large part to the fact that the seminar which was specifically intended to address the issue of the semblant, *D'un discours qui ne serait pas du semblant* (Of a Discourse Which Would Not Be of the Semblant), occupies a transitional place between *Seminar XVII*, *The Other Side of Psychoanalysis*, and *Seminar XX*, *Encore*. Unlike these two landmark seminars which, because they discuss two issues of general interest—power and sexual difference—have taken up a prominent place in contemporary debate across an impressive range of disciplines, *Seminar XVIII* and, consequently, its key concept have passed largely unnoticed.

It should be noted that although "semblant" as a term may well have been a late entry into Lacan's vocabulary,[9] that which appears to be essential in the question of the semblant—the articulation between two radically heterogeneous if not antinomic registers, the symbolic and the real—is, on the contrary, a persistent problem throughout his teaching. As a matter of fact, Lacan never stopped inventing new terms destined to hold together that which does not hold together: *jouissance* and the signifier. In the course of his teaching, he explored the different ways of capturing *jouissance* via the signifier. Starting with the phallus, also designated as the signifier of *jouissance*, Lacan inaugurates an extraordinary series of terms that replace one another as the anchoring point, the nodal linkage between the symbolic and the real: the phallus, the Name-of-the-Father, the master signifier and, finally, the object *a*. Each of these terms will come, in the course of Lacan's teaching, to fulfil the quilting function, provided that it responds to the structurally necessary demand of building a bridge between two antinomic registers: language and the real. But how exactly, one might wish to ask, do these operators of quilting respond to the notion of the semblant?

One could risk the following thesis in order to link the semblant to the quilting function of these terms. As a matter of fact, each of these terms can be considered a "detached piece," to borrow Jacques-Alain Miller's formulation,[10] an element of the real which, through the operation of significatization, is elevated to the dignity of the signifier, acts as a signifier, in order to stitch together that which does not hold together. Perhaps it would be more appropriate to say that the operation of significatization makes an element of the real ex-sist as a signifier. Not of course as an ordinary signifier but precisely as a signifier that is at odds with all the others, since it is only as such an exception among signifiers, a signifier that marks an exception, that it can assume the function for which it was designed: to be the place-holder of the real within the symbolic. However, it is important to properly situate this place-holder of the real in relation to the real itself. Strictly speaking, what we are dealing with here is a paradoxical movement that goes from the real to the real via the symbolic. Indeed, it is only insofar as these "detached pieces" are converted into signifiers that they can be operational. Thus one could say that Lacan remains within Bentham's paradigm as long as he can conceive of the real solely in terms of the symbolic.

However, the very fact that Lacan invented a new category, that of the semblant, and introduced it into psychoanalysis, along with his major categories of the real, the symbolic and the imaginary, testifies to the fact that all these various attempts at solving the problem of the disharmonic relation between the real and the symbolic—in the final analysis, the relation of the subject of the signifier and the real of *jouissance*—proved to be unsatisfactory. They are unsatisfactory precisely to the extent that the only real with which Lacan was preoccupied before *Seminar XVIII* is the symbolic real or, more precisely, the symbolic as the real.

Yet it is precisely in the context of Lacan's preoccupation with the question of the proper use of some artful devices as a means for handling the real in the analytic experience that, in the seventies, the question of the semblant as the opposite of the real posed itself so acutely. This is also why one finds only then a shift in Lacan's theory of the semblant and a break with the Benthamite paradigm. While one of our aims is to briefly outline the development of the Lacanain concept of the semblant and to draw attention to some difficulties that highlight the ambiguous status that the semblant has in psychoanalysis, we also wish to emphasize the relation between the real and the semblant as being the crux of Lacan's later teaching.

It should be noted that, for Lacan, these two terms, semblant and real, constitute a couple—an odd couple to be sure, since, in order to make it possible for the real to appear in the analytic experience, it is necessary to vacillate the semblant. The very expression, "vacillation of semblants," such as it was elaborated in Lacan's last teaching, is clearly governed by a dichotomy between the real and the semblant.

But does this not amount to saying that, by advancing the orientation towards the real, an orientation that implies both the traversal of the imaginary and the vacillation of semblants, Lacan simply translates, for the proper ends of psychoanalysis, the classic Platonic opposition between appearances and reality? In accordance with this thesis, Freud, in one of his last texts, "Analysis Terminable and Interminable," marked out the aim of the psychoanalytic treatment exactly from the perspective of this opposition. Defined in terms of a pursuit of truth, psychoanalysis is from the outset situated beyond the zone of the "*Schein und Trug*," appearance and deception, which are precisely Freud's names for semblants.[11] That is to say, the analyst must follow the trace of the real in the unconscious, although the latter is swarming with semblants, i.e., delusions, lures, etc., which are but *ersatz* satisfactions according to Freud, thus making it difficult if not impossible to attain the real. Lacan seems to be subscribing to this program because, in his seminar, *D'un discourse qui ne serait pas du semblant,* he recommends the rejection of "all sham (*faux-semblant*) and deception."[12]

Without being entirely unfounded, this alliance between philosophy and psychoanalysis is nevertheless misleading. Here it will suffice to say that, far from being unanimous, the condemnation of appearances has from the outset caused great controversies in philosophy itself—from Plato's adversaries, the sophists, to Nietzsche, who never tired of exposing the real that is operative in philosophical discourse, thus showing the fictional status of truth—there have constantly been attempts to rehabilitate appearance. Lacan's subversion, on the other hand, goes beyond the simple binary of appearance and reality. Just as the real, according to Lacan, is irreducible to the true, the semblant is not to be confused with the false. Furthermore, the traditional philosophical hierarchy is radically displaced by Lacan, since two terms that at first glance seemed to constitute a radical opposition in fact present a continuity. To cite a few typical Lacanian inversions and paradoxes: "the fantasy is the principle of reality," "truth is a semblance," and last but not least, *jouissance,* which may well be situated in the register of the real, "is questioned, evoked, tracked, and elaborated only on the basis of a semblance."[13]

Oddly enough, these paradoxes are in accordance with the structure of the Freudian libido insofar as the drive's satisfaction itself depends on lures and deceptions. The precious indications of the intimate relation between the mode of *jouissance* and the semblants of the social Other can thus be found in Freud's article, "'Civilised' Sexual Morality," in which he brings to light a zone that is beyond the obvious antagonism between the "demands of civilization" and the real of the drive.

Freud was indeed the first to situate the symptomatic dimension of the modes of enjoyment as a mark of civilization's malaise. While criticising the ruthlessness of the cultural demand, which involves a repression of drive-*jouissance*, Freud points out that the growing difficulties of the sexual relation resulting from "the domination of a civilised sexual morality" can lead only to a promotion of "other modalities" of sexual practice. As a matter of fact, according to Freud, "it is not difficult to suppose that under the domination of a civilised sexual morality the health and efficiency of single individuals may be liable to impairment and that ultimately this injury to them, caused by the sacrifices imposed on them, may reach such a point that, by this indirect path, the cultural aim in view will be endangered as well."[14]

Hence it is possible to say that the relation between semblants and psychoanalysis was from the outset marked by a profound ambiguity. The advent of psychoanalysis, by revealing behind moral and social ideals the presence of the libido—thus showing that the moral of castration is in itself a mode of *jouissance*, since the drive attains its satisfaction not despite its renunciation but because of it—provoked a tremendous shake up of the moral and social ideals of the epoch. Lacan in his later teaching qualified these ideals precisely as semblants in order to highlight their fictitious character in relation to what really matters to the subject: the real of *jouissance* and its grappling with it.

Lacan continues in this vein, taking up Freud's idea of the social dimension of the symptom since, in Chapter V of his *Encore* seminar, "Aristotle and Freud: the other satisfaction," he insists that "reality is approached with apparatuses of *jouissance*" since "there's no other apparatus than language"; indeed, it is in this way, Lacan continues, that "language is fitted out in speaking beings."[15] In saying that, for a speaking being, language is an apparatus of *jouissance* through which reality is approached, Lacan clearly rejects as utterly erroneous the idea of a *jouissance* that would be prior to reality. How is, then, this enigmatic thesis, according to which language itself is identified with the apparatus of *jouissance* to be understood?

Miller provides us with the following interpretation based on the notion of the apparatus, which puts emphasis on the instrumental use of language: "When one says that reality is approached by apparatuses, this means that there is an instrumental aspect to it. On the one hand, in the approach to reality through apparatuses of *jouissance* there is the idea of the construction of a fiction, and on the other hand the idea that this fiction is operational, that this fiction is an instrument which is used. What is it used for? Well, I think that it serves to constitute the fantasy."[16] That is to say, if the reality of the speaking being is ultimately fantasmatic, this is because language as such is an apparatus of *jouissance*. There is no other access to reality but through language which is in itself instrumentalized, finalized in view of a special goal: to serve *jouissance*. In other words, the perspective of language as an apparatus is precisely the perspective of the "semblant making" of the symbolic. It is from the perspective of the apparatus of *jouissance* that the status of language—indeed, the symbolic as such—is radically modified: situated within the category of the apparatus, language instead of being perceived as a means to secure access to the real, is envisaged instead in terms of the semblant slaving in the service of *jouissance*.

However, for Freud, as well as for Lacan, there are two apparently contradictory faces of the semblant that are nonetheless bound together. That is what Lacan in particular insists on: as an artful device the semblant can be considered both as a path to accede to the real, as well as a defence against the real. Not surprisingly, this duplicity of the semblant lends itself to two opposing interpretations. According to the first, the semblant is primarily an artifice useful for triggering a misrecognition or for erecting a barrier against the real of *jouissance*; according to the second, however, the semblant is nothing but a suppletory device, be it imaginary or sublimatory, destined to support the drive's satisfaction.

Taking its cue from these two contradictory readings of the semblant, Lacanian psychoanalysis seeks to rethink the real proper to the analytic experience. This would seem to require a new concept of the real which would allow it to come up with a more precise definition of that which is both the proper target and the main tool in psychoanalysis: the symptom. What is called the symptom in psychoanalysis is namely the way the subject invents its relation to the real of *jouissance*. Hence, there is no subject without a symptom since everyone has his or her own symptomatic way of complying with the demands of civilization, i.e., through the impossible.

THE REAL, PLAGUED BY SEMBLANTS

The re-examination of the concept of the real is urgent for a psychoanalysis that is oriented towards it yet proposes to approach it from the perspective of the semblant. It is urgent in terms of creating the concepts it cannot do without in order to situate and circumscribe the real such as it is encountered in the analytic experience but also in redefining the aims of psychoanalysis.

Following Freud, Lacan takes up his idea of the role of psychoanalysis in guiding the subject through the evolution of the semblants of civilization since the mutation of the Other of civilization leads to a modification of the form and usages of *jouissance*: "Psychoanalysis has played a role in the guidance of modern subjectivity, and it would not know how to support it without organising it in accordance with the movement in science that elucidates it."[17]

Clearly, what justifies this guiding role assigned to psychoanalysis is nothing other than the aspiration, shared by Freud and Lacan, that psychoanalysis, just like science, would be a discourse which is not founded on the semblant but on the real. There is, however, a price to pay for this special alliance between science and psychoanalysis. It is in the name of the real that psychoanalysis made it its business to shake the social Other. But once the Other is degraded, downgraded to a mere semblant, the real itself becomes a question to which only uncertain, contradictory, and inconsistent answers can be given. As we can witness today, the inexistence of the Other implies that everything is a semblant, thus entailing a loss of fundamental references and, moreover, the refusal of the real itself.[18]

In his seminar purposively entitled *L'Autre qui n'existe pas et ses comités d'éthique* (The Other Which does not Exist and its Ethical Committees), Miller characterises our world as a world of semblants in which the meaning of the real itself has become a problem. The contemporary subject is immersed in the world of semblants produced by none other than the discourse destined to fix the real for us: the discourse of science. With the concept of the inexistent Other, Miller throws precisely the crisis of the real into relief; in other words, he draws the real with which science is concerned ever closer to the status of the semblant. Ironically, the progress of science has "succeded" in plaguing the real with its semblants, blurring in this way the distinction between the real and the semblant and, ultimately, shattering the real itself as the fixed reference.[19] Suffice it to recall all the gadgets which seem to have taken control of our lives and which are, in effect, a materialization of science's hallucinations. There are two structural consequences to be drawn from this generalised "semblantization" which results from the progress of science: by increasing the possibility of limitless semblant-making, contemporary science has destroyed the fixation of the real. But the discourse of science is equally responsible for the decline of the social Other: insofar as science is, by structural necessity as it were, limitless, it cannot but erode the previous limitations and obstacles set in its way by the ideals of civilization.

In bringing to light the necessary correlation of the inexistence of the Other and the problematization of the real, Miller also points out that the question of the use of semblants appears to have no *raison d'être* and is actually in vain, inoperative, once the real vacillates. This is precisely the reason why Lacan, in his later teaching, strives to show that, at least from the perspective of psychoanalysis, the inexistence of the Other and the real are not mutually exclusive but, on the contrary, correlative. Given the importance of this re-elaboration of the concept of the real for the very existence of psychoanalysis, it becomes imperative for Lacan to break with the scientific paradigm and its concept of the real. The very logic of Lacan's gesture—to tie psychoanalysis to the real as its point of reference, as its compass—requires that he make a sacrifice of that concept of the real which has inspired him throughout all of his teaching: the real as that which always returns to the same place, reliable, law-like, law-abiding, as it were. Yet there still remains the problem of elaborating a new conception of the real proper to psychoanalysis, a radical, unheard-of conception, insofar as the real is now considered to be that which ignores all the rules of the game, an utterly erratic, deceiving, "lawless real," in short, a caprice incarnate.[20]

It is in view of this final elaboration of the real that we propose to reread the precious indications given by Lacan in *Television* regarding the question of *jouissance* in the context of the absence of the Other. Here we witness the emergence of a central distinction, on the basis of *jouissance*, between the object *a* and the Ideal: thus, whereas Ideals always have something of a delusion about them, the object *a* brings out the real of *jouissance*, its irresolvable impasse. Here Lacan puts the accent on the fact that, with the decline of the Other, there is nothing to prevent "our *jouissance* going off track," as he puts it. "The Other does not exist" implies, as Lacan underlines it, that "our mode of *jouissance*" takes "from now on [...] its bearings from the 'surplus-*jouissance*.'"[21] This shows not only a pluralization of modes of *jouissance* but also that there is no defence against the real here as there is no Other to lead the subject through the maze of *jouissance*.

However, by linking the contemporary impasse of *jouissance* to the inexistence of the Other, Lacan also casts a new light on what is meant by a role that he previously attributed to psychoanalysis, namely, to be "the guidance of modern subjectivity." Indeed, what place falls to psychoanalysis when the social Other itself strives to inscribe modes of *jouissance*—which Freud already considered to be symptoms of civilization—while assuring them a wholly new legitimacy and promoting the rules instituting the norms of their integration?

To inscribe contemporary modes of *jouissance* in the current context of the social bond, that is to say in an epoch in which the figure of the Other and its Ideals are declining, it is necessary to account for the substitution that has occurred at the level of that which situates *jouissance* within the social bond. There are two ways in which *jouissance* can be situated: first, by setting up the agent of castration; second, on the contrary, through the investment of the remainder, the plug of castration, what Lacan termed surplus-*jouissance*, *plus-de-jouir*. It is precisely at this level that Lacan's remark that "our *jouissance* [...] takes its bearings from the 'surplus-*jouissance*'" [22] takes on its full value. What Lacan calls "our *jouissance*" is exactly the contemporary mode of *jouissance* in an epoch in which the Other does not exist, a *jouissance* which cannot therefore be situated by means of the Ideal. *Jouissance* today is not situated by means of the master signifier; it is not located on the side of the annulment of *jouissance*, but rather is situated on the side of surplus-*jouissance* as a stopper of castration.

What is new is that today, instead of being forbidden by the Ideal, *jouissance* is on the contrary commanded. What has changed is the way in which mass production, through its imperative "Consume!" proposes *jouissance* as a semblance for everybody. This phenomenon, which Miller describes as "haunting the surplus-*jouissance*," creates the illusion that through the good use of the object *a*, surplus-*jouissance*, we could achieve complete drive-satisfaction. We can thus talk today of the primacy of the object *a* over the Ideal which, in turn, is denounced as a mere semblant. The epoch of the inexistent Other is at the same time the epoch of the limitless production of semblants. Thus, it could be argued that the primacy of surplus-*jouissance* goes hand-in-hand with the generalized "semblantification" where there is nothing to keep *jouissance* in check.

Hence, new practices of perversion, in Freud's time considered to be scandalous, are today considered to be an opportunity for the innovation of new semblants in order to inscribe all these various new modes of *jouissance*. Indeed, it is these new modes of *jouissance* that present themselves today as a condition for inventing new modes of the social bond, new fictions in Bentham's sense of the word, destined to secure the individual's right to his or her particular mode of *jouissance*.

Paradoxically enough, psychoanalysis is not without responsibility for this disorientation of the contemporary subject in relation to *jouissance* since psychoanalysis has itself contributed to the undermining of ideals. Freud, like Bentham, detected behind the ideals of civilization the presence of the libido, i.e., the modes and the forms of *jouissance* since, for him, the superego testifies to a paradoxical satisfaction of the drive disguised as renouncement of satisfaction.

Yet something has radically changed insofar as today psychoanalysis seems to be oddly incapable of effecting a cut in the dominant discourse and of thereby undermining contemporary moral and social semblants. On the contrary, it seems to be a prolongation of this discourse; and it is precisely today, when psychoanalysis seems to be unable to disturb contemporary semblants and to fracture the dominant ideological discourse, that the antinomic relation between the semblant and the real is the decisive issue for psychoanalysis.

This is why, despite the fact that nothing appears to stop the expansion of the empire of semblants, psychoanalysis has to maintain the real as its compass. But in order to succeed, psychoanalysis has to rediscover once more as its proper place the interval between the real and the semblant. Thus, the present interrogation of the semblant stems from the urgency of advancing a new, i.e., "realist" orientation for psychoanalysis in an era in which the Other does not exist. Indeed, in an epoch in which the figure of the Other and its Ideals are declining, the question of the nature and the use of semblants in psychoanalysis looms larger than ever in the history of psychoanalysis.

At the beginning of the 21st century, when practices in which speech is used as a tool for absorbing the traumatism of the real have invaded contemporary utilitarian civilization, psychoanalysis is expected to radically distinguish itself from these practices. Whereas various psychotherapeutic practices set as their goal the patient's well-being, psychoanalysis, on the contrary, aims at a radical subjective mutation which involves the subject's separation from its identifications in order to become a response to the real.

Certainly, this orientation to the real is an extreme position. This is why taking the real seriously as a compass for psychoanalysis entails at the same time pushing psychoanalysis to its limits: not only beyond the Name-of-the-Father, that semblant which, according to Freud, represents the unsurpassable horizon for psychoanalysis, but even further: beyond the Freudian unconscious itself. One is almost tempted to say that the price to be paid for the orientation of psychoanalysis toward the real is the downgrading of the concept of the unconscious.

However, if Lacan is driven so far as to break, at least at certain points, with the Freudian tradition, this is precisely in order to define psychoanalysis according to its proper logic, that is, beyond semblants. This break with Freud concerns first and foremost the status of the real in psychoanalysis. If the Name-of-the-Father, for Freud, is not a mere semblant, this is because it is but another name for the prohibition of *jouissance*. Like Freud, Lacan also draws the genealogy of the father from *jouissance*, but unlike Freud, he considers the prohibition as being but a retroactive rationalization of the sexual non-rapport. Hence, for Lacan, the father is not the name of the obstacle in the way of *jouissance*, but rather a semblance masking an irreducible gap in the very structure of *jouissance*. Indeed, today the Name-of-the-Father proves to be incapable of mastering, dominating the real at stake: the real of *jouissance*. This is because, as Lacan's later teaching is destined to show, the fact that the interdiction of *jouissance* is today replaced by its permission has no bearing on the inherent impasse of *jouissance*.

But the price to be paid for the radical orientation toward the real also implies, as has been underlined by Jacques-Alain Miller, a downgrading of the unconscious to the extent that "the unconscious itself appears as a response made to the real, at the level of the semblant, a response to the hole in the real [due to the fact that there is no sexual relation], a response which has to do with the vain effort to make the absence of sexual programming signify at the level of the real." [23]

One of the unexpected, indeed, paradoxical consequences of such a radical position was that this reference to the real appears as a problematic as well as a problematizing reference in Lacan. At the end of his teaching, Lacan even suggests that the status of the real is that of the symptom, a deduction made from the unconscious: that is to say, the notion of the real, in the last analysis, is nothing more than his invention.

However, if the question of the real poses itself to Lacan so persistently in the final period of his teaching, this is precisely because the real proper to the analytic experience is now considered to be resisting signifierization, i.e., conversion into the symbolic. In view of such a radicalized conception of the real, both the imaginary and the symbolic appear as mere make-believe. Yet it is precisely this question of the real as being both outside the imaginary and the symbolic that prompts Lacan to entertain the hope of a psychoanalysis which would not be founded on the semblant. By naming his seminar consecrated to the question of the semblant, "*Of a Discourse Which Would Not Be of the Semblant,*" Lacan seems to be nourishing and encouraging the mere hope of the possible elaboration of a discourse that would not be reducible, unlike the rest of them, to a mere semblant but would rather be a discourse of the real. To the extent that the symbolic is now seen to be downgraded to the order of the semblant this seminar, which evokes the possibility of a discourse that would take its departure point from the real, thus signals a turning point and a perspective shift in Lacan's teaching insofar as, at the outset, Lacan proposed to ground psychoanalysis as a discourse on the symbolic. It is at this point in Lacan's later teaching, when psychoanalysis is ordered by the relations of the semblant and the real, that a large part of Lacan's theorization, which had been deployed in the register of the symbolic, appears to be reduced to the mere status of semblance: *sicut palea*.

The opposition of the real and semblance is therefore a crucial step in the development of Lacan's teaching: it is a radicalization of the opposition, introduced in his seminar on *The Ethics of Psychoanalysis*, between the real on one hand and the symbolic, and the imaginary on the other. It could be said that, from the point of view of the real, the symbolic and the imaginary appear to be equivalent. Yet this opposition between the real and the semblant became a structuring opposition only when Lacan had constructed the four discourses.

In a sense, it is only from the perspective of the semblant that one can realize that what creates an impasse here is that, actually, the cleavage between the signifier and *jouissance* was surreptitiously created by Lacan's proper definition of the subject. Conceived in terms of the signifier—the subject is what one signifier represents for another signifier—the Lacanian subject is essentially empty, dead, devoid of "enjoying substance," severed from *jouissance.* The outcome of this irreducible disjunction between the subject of the signifier and the real of *jouissance* entails the coupling of the empty subject with the remainder of *jouissance*: the object *a*. With the object *a* as an answer to the lack of the signifier, Lacan inscribed in what he called the four discourses a real that is within the reach of the subject of the signifier

A DISCOURSE WHICH WOULD NOT BE OF THE SEMBLANT

Psychoanalysis is based on the assumption that the treatment of the real, more specifically the real of *jouissance*, by the signifier is only possible within the framework of discourse—not just any discourse, of course, but that which is able, like Freud's, to be "maintained as close as possible to what is related to *jouissance*"[24]—one whose pivotal point is the relation between the signifier and *jouissance.* Indeed, from the perspective of the relation between the signifier and *jouissance*, the task of the analyst's discourse is to expose the surreptitious alliance between the signifier and *jouissance* as constitutive of any social bond. Lacan's definition of discourse as a social bond can thus be understood also in the sense that it is a bond between the signifier and *jouissance.*

The elaboration of the four discourses is for Lacan an opportunity to revisit his initial departure point, the disjunction between the signifier and *jouissance*, in such a way that, behind the overt antithesis between signifier and *jouissance*, their clandestine solidarity is revealed. Before the signifier could be situated in the order of the semblant, it was therefore necessary for Lacan to expose the duplicity of the signifier: the signifier which was initially defined by Lacan through the exclusion of *jouissance*, as a barrier against *jouissance*, is revealed to be an apparatus of *jouissance.*[25] Indeed, there is a dialectic of lack and supplement at work in the relation between the signifier and *jouissance.* On the one hand, the signifier involves the loss of *jouissance*, its annulment; on the other, this very loss, as an effect of the signifier, responds to the supplement of *jouissance* termed by Lacan the object *a*, surplus-*jouissance.* Thus it could be said that the loss of *jouissance* produced through the signifier is the condition of possibility for repetition, *encore*, once more, again and again, and it is precisely through this repetition that a surplus is produced. Hence, the lesson to be drawn from the seminar *The Other Side of Psychoanalysis* is that the loss of *jouissance* and surplus-*jouissance*, *plus-de-jouir*, are both produced through the functioning of the signifier; and it is in view of this dialectic of loss and surplus that the signifier appears as a semblance, that is to say, as a defensive device masking the real of the drive while at the same time supporting the *jouissance* of castration.

However, if the signifier is downgraded to the status of the semblant, then the question arises of whether psychoanalysis can have any bearing on the real of *jouissance*. Indeed, how can it touch on drive-satisfaction if it deals with drives only to the extent that they are present in words? Taking on board the impossibility of an immediate relation to the real, Lacan goes a step further. He claims that the experience of analysis proves that "there is something in the signifier that resonates," that "the drives are the echo in the body of the fact that there is saying,"[26] and that "for this saying to resonate, to be consonant, the body has to be sensitive to it."[27]

In psychoanalysis, the real of *jouissance* is broached from the mark of saying, from the effect produced on the body by saying, a mark which is invisible yet which proves to be legible. This is precisely what the master's discourse reveals: in the master's discourse, the dominant or commanding position is filled by S1, also called the master signifier. As such, it embodies the alienating function of the signifier to which the speaking being is subject. If the analyst's discourse is the other side, the inverse of the master's discourse, this is because the discourse of the unconscious, just like the discourse of the master, is governed by a master signifier. In the master's discourse, the subject finds its identification within the Other. There is always a master signifier there that hooks him up.

Thus, the matrix of the discourse which borrows its name from the place of the agent or the master signifier, S1, discloses how this mark of saying dominates the subject. As has been pointed out by Miller, this mark of saying, S1, is able to "confiscate the representation of the subject"[28] to the extent that it seems to absorb the subject. As a result, the subject appears to be indistinguishable from the mark.

In the analyst's discourse, the place in the upper left-hand corner of Lacan's quadripartite structure, the place of the agent, is attributed to the psychoanalyst in so far as s/he assumes the function of the object *a*, i.e., the place of the *plus-de-jouir*, surplus-*jouissance*. This particular property of the analyst's discourse singles out the place of the agent as equivalent to the semblant. Indeed, semblant is the name by which Lacan designates this place of the agent or "dominant" place, as he calls it, in all four discourses. On this point, the following quotation from his seminar *Encore* is decisive:

> Before the semblance, on which, in effect, everything is based and springs back in fantasy, a strict distinction must be made between the imaginary and the real. It must not be thought that we ourselves in any way serve as a basis for the semblance. We are not even semblance. We are, on occasion, that which can occupy that place, and allow what to reign there? Object *a*. Indeed, the analyst, of all [those whose] orders of discourse are sustained currently [...] is the one who, by putting object *a* in the place of semblance, is in the best position to do what should rightfully be done, namely to investigate the status of truth as knowledge. [...] Analysis came to announce to us that there is knowledge that is not known, knowledge that is based on the signifier as such. [...] The status of knowledge implies as such that there already is knowledge, that it is in the Other, and that it is to be acquired. [...] the subject results from the fact that this knowledge must be learned, and even have a price put on it [...] Knowledge is worth just as much as it costs [...] and that is difficult. Difficult to what? Less to acquire it than to enjoy it. In enjoying, the conquest of this knowledge is renewed every time it is exercised, the power it yields always being directed towards its *jouissance*.[29]

In using its proper apparatus of semblants, that is to say, in showing that the analyst, by positioning himself or herself as object *a* in the place of the agent, occupies the place of semblance, the analyst's discourse kills two birds with one stone. As "a specialist in the S1,"[30] to borrow Miller's formula which captures very well the gist of the matter, the analyst makes it possible for the subject to "cough up" this mark that has absorbed it until now. It is from the position of the object *a* that the analyst sets the subject at work and thus makes it possible for a transmutation—of the invisible yet legible mark that dominates the subject into a new master signifier—to occur.

What is at stake in psychoanalysis is to make the identifying signifier, the master signifier, vacillate and to displace it. But what can make the identifying semblants vacillate if not another master signifier, an S1, produced by the analyst's discourse itself? In the matheme of the analyst's discourse, the S1, produced in the very analytic experience, is situated in the place of the real, in the place of the product. Although this new S1 occupies the place of the real, it is but a false real. As a matter of fact, what the analyst's discourse brings to light at the end of the analysis is precisely that the real cannot be situated in any of the places provided by the structure of the discourse. It is in this sense that one can say that discourse as such, even the analyst's discourse, is an apparatus of the semblant specifically designed to avoid the real.

At the same time, by situating the analyst in the place of the agent, the analyst's discourse thus shows its true character as semblant. Far from being the master of discourse, the term occupying the place of the agent, as its appointed "functionary," suffers truth effects rather than provoking them. This place seems only to be one of an acting subject; indeed, it is but a semblance brought in by the discourse structure as such.

It is for that reason that, according to Lacan, the discourse that brings the other three to light is the analyst's discourse. That is to say, by exposing as a semblant, as a deceitful fiction, that term which, by occupying the dominant place, commands all the relations between the terms of any discourse structure, the analyst's discourse is for that reason able to subvert the make-believe of the social bond that is present in the other three discourses. From such a perspective, the analytic discourse can then be seen as a specific apparatus which, by being situated at a paradoxical Archimedean position of extimacy in relation to any discourse, brings to light the functioning of the semblant in all other discourses.

While strictly speaking, the analyst's discourse cannot be considered to be a discourse that is not of the semblant, its privilege consists nevertheless in its ability to perceive the semblant for what it is: precisely a semblant. The very fact that in the analyst's discourse the analyst is situated in the place of the agent permits it, by using the very mechanism of the production of the social bond—i.e., this peculiar mode of mimicking the structure of the social bond which is sustained only by virtue of the make-believe situated in the place of the agent—to reveal the semblant itself.

It is from such a perspective that Lacan himself underlined the fictional foundation of psychoanalysis: paradoxically one should pay respect to the psychoanalysis of our time, he said, insofar as it "is a discipline which produces itself only through the semblant. The latter is denuded to the point that it unsettles the semblants which support religion, magic, piety, all that which conceals the economy of *jouissance*."[31] This remark assumes its full value on the condition that one treats the semblant through the psychoanalytic discourse.[32]

The opposition between the real and the semblant therefore remains essential for Lacan's elaboration of the four discourses. Even so, there remains the problem of knowing not only how the relation between the real and the semblant is located within each discourse but, more importantly, whether among the four discourses there is one which is also of the real and not only of the semblant.

In this seminar Lacan argues that discourse, namely, is a structure which is able to subsist without words due to certain fundamental relations that would not be able to be maintained without language.[33] The distinction between discourse and speech, the latter being always more or less occasional, is crucial here insofar as it translates, at the level of language, the distinction between variable and invariable. Indeed, by opposing discourse and speech, Lacan clearly aims at situating discourse on the side of that which remains invariable, that which remains the same, untouched by what is meant or said of it. One is almost tempted to say that discourse, to the extent that it is defined as a structure, is an instance of the real in language.

Indeed, Lacan's theory of the four discourses is grounded in an idea which traverses the whole of his teaching, namely, that for psychoanalysis, as for science, there should be some symbolic in the real. If psychoanalytic theory has for its object the unconscious, then it has as its charge the task of demonstrating that this peculiar kind of knowledge which cannot be assigned to an "I" keeps returning to the same place, i.e., is situated in the real. Clearly, mathematical writing provides a model in this regard insofar as Lacan indicates that there is discourse in the real, that there are formulas which the subject obeys without knowing it.

The very promotion of the social bond implies for Lacan the radicalization of the antinomic relation between the real and the semblant. Indeed, the point of departure of the Lacanian concept of discourse is the steady erosion of the Other and its Ideals. If the question of the real was so acute in *Seminar XVII* it is because from the perspective of the inexistence of the Other, from a perspective in which the Other with its Ideals is downgraded to the status of the semblant, the real itself seems to vacillate. Indeed, what remains of the real if the Other is not real, if it has the structure of a fiction?

Actually, the very idea of the four discourses, four mathemes, four discursive structures, is inspired by the knowledge in the real that the discourse of science transcribes in mathematical formulae. In a way, the four discourses are Lacan's desperate attempt at restoring the Other—under the guise of discourse structures. Just as for science there is knowledge in the real, there are discourse structures in the real for psychoanalysis. Lacan's concept of discourse could then be considered a new edition of the Other as a structure in the real.

Of course, the Other in this new edition is not to be confused with the master signifier. The Other may well be concentrated in the place of the master signifier, but it could also be situated in the place of knowledge, of product; in short, it would be more appropriate to situate knowledge at the level of discourse as such. It is the structure of discourse which can now be identified with the Other. Only in this sense can Lacan maintain in his seminar *Encore* that "the notion of discourse should be taken as a social link, founded on language."[34] In other words the Other, from the perspective of the four discourses, cannot be isolated; rather, it is the very knot of all four discourses. It is an attempt at maintaining the function of the quilting point without it being assigned to a particular discourse. In this sense, the four discourses as a figure of the Other already announce the Borromean knot insofar as the knot is a solution proposed by Lacan to show how three heterogeneous orders—the imaginary order of meaning, the symbolic order of knowledge and the real order of *jouissance*—hold together.

The four discourses can then be perceived as the last desperate attempt to elevate psychoanalysis to the level of science. The idea according to which the structures of discourse are inscribed in the real is an ingenious invention which permits psychoanalysis to determine the specificity of the real that is at the core of its experience and at the same time to avoid the snares of contemporary nominalism according to which everything is a semblant. The construction of the four discourses is an operation comparable to Galileo's and Newton's founding gesture of science, a gesture which consists in the strict separation of the real from the semblant. In other words, the four discourses are Lacan's attempt at circumscribing the place of the real in psychoanalysis while limiting the imperialism of semblants; and just like the discourse of science that not only "reads," determines, deciphers the knowledge in the real, but writes it down in mathematical formulae in order to transform it, psychoanalysis also presumes to be able to determine the real it deals with and to find a way to transform it.

Thus, considered in retrospect, it is perhaps no accident that Lacan raised the thorny question of the semblant in the wake of his seminar *The Other Side of Psychoanalysis.* Contrary to what one might believe according solely to the title, which is rather equivocal since it evokes the possibility of a discourse that would not be a semblant, the central issue in the seminar *D'un discours qui ne serait pas du semblant* is not the elaboration of a discourse that would not be a semblant, with the surreptitious implication that psychoanalysis might be, together with science, this discourse. On the contrary, from the beginning of this seminar, Lacan states in no uncertain terms that insofar as the signifier itself is the semblant, all that belongs to the discursive order necessarily falls under the rubric of the semblant.[35] In other words, the semblant is a category inherent to discourse as such.

Having established that in discourse the semblant is irreducible and that, consequently, there is no discourse that is not of the semblant—the discourse of psychoanalysis being no exception—Lacan moves on to broach the question which is undoubtedly the crucial issue around which the major part of *Seminar XVIII* revolves: once the constitutive lack of the discourse of the real is admitted, how to solve the problem of holding together the symbolic and the real, two heterogeneous registers, while maintaining their irreducible heterogeneity? This constitutive lack of the discourse of the real is what leads Lacan to deploy a new category and to pose the question of knowing what is the real from a new perspective.

In *Seminar XVIII* Lacan started to bring into question the union of the symbolic and the real and, by so doing, he proposed at the same time to reconsider psychoanalysis and its practice from a different perspective: from the disjunction of the symbolic and the real, from the rapport of the exteriority between the two and, ultimately, from their non-rapport.

From this perspective of non-rapport, Lacan's seminar *D'un discourse qui ne serait pas du semblant* marks a crucial turning point in which the future orientation of psychoanalysis is at stake. Hence, despite Lacan's usual style of self-assurance and confidence, in this seminar he nevertheless hesitates as regards the possible ways of overcoming the impasse implied in the non-rapport between the signifier and *jouissance*. In fact, the question of a new departure point involving a radical inversion of perspectives plays across the whole surface of this seminar. Throughout this seminar, the deployment of the notion of the semblant allows it to gather its consistency, while at the same time providing the points of vacillation and resistance necessary for it to establish the themes that Lacan pursues in the final period of his teaching. Lacan tentatively proposes various solutions to the problem posed by the articulation of absolutely heterogeneous registers, while at the same time avoiding the previously privileged device: the quilting point.

Lacan's theory of the semblant clearly follows a certain dynamic, a logic of its own. In *Seminar XVIII*, we can witness the displacement of this concept in relation to the quilting point. With his elaboration of the notion of the semblant, Lacan throws precisely the quilting function of the signifier into relief. And it is by redefining what is at stake in this function that Lacan comes to effect, by replacing the term "fiction" with that of "semblant," a singular devaluation, the downgrading of the term whose role is precisely to pin the real to the symbolic.

Lacan initially introduced the notion of the semblant into pyschoanalysis, under the guise of the fiction, in order to situate the real in the symbolic (which is to say, to make the real obey the rules of the signifier). In his later teaching, the same terms that were previously considered to secure access to the real (the phallus, the master signifier, the Name-of-the-Father, the Other, the object *a*) and were as such valorised now, under a new light, appeared to be the very obstacle on the path to the real and were consequently downgraded to the status of semblance. In fact, as has been pointed out, the substitution of the term "fiction" by "semblant," to the extent that it implies a certain downgrading of the terms designated as semblant, involves at the same time a paradigm shift.

In this regard, it is perhaps not without reason that Lacan, starting with *Seminar XVIII*, preferred the term "semblant" to that of "fiction." However, this final choice cannot be justified by saying that the semblant, as a concept, is broader and can include fiction; nor is it enough to insist on a distinction between discursive and non-discursive semblants, semblants in nature, since Lacan is primarily interested in discursive semblants. On the contrary, what justifies the substitution is Lacan's re-examination of the nature of the semblant and the function attributed to it. Thus one could say that it is the inversion of perspective that makes Lacan downgrade the semblant. More particularly, a term is denounced as semblant insofar as it responds to the function of the quilting point. What downgrades the semblant is precisely its function. From this inverted perspective, which takes as its departure point the non-rapport of the symbolic and the real, all these instances of the quilting point are seen now as being but a mere make-believe, a cover-up.

Indeed, the semblant is essentially make-believe: by pinning down the imaginary, the quilting signifier makes us believe that it is the thing itself. In other words, the semblant is a symbolic construct which, by quilting, makes us believe that it is the other of the symbolic, namely, the real. This is why, for Lacan, the father is by definition a semblance. The father only exists in the form of the signifier and he exists as long as this signifier, the Name-of-the-Father, produces certain effects. The phallus, from this point of view, is also seen as a semblant since, strictly speaking, it is but a supporting piece of evidence for the semblance of the father. And there is yet another, third figure of the semblant, more delicate than the other two, the object *a*, invented by Lacan to designate the remainder of *jouissance* which is not converted into the signifier and which remains outside the signifier's quilting function. If the object *a*, from this perspective, is yet another name for the semblant alongside the father and the phallus, this is because it is strategically positioned at a place where, instead of the expected *jouissance*, one only encounters its loss. The object *a* is the semblant which effects the conversion of the loss of *jouissance* into a surplus, one which curiously is not to be found on the side of the real *jouissance* but on the side of the symbolic. Hence the equivalence, established by Lacan, between *jouissance* under the guise of *plus-de-jouir*, and *sens-joui* [enjoy-meant]—the only *jouissance* that a speaking being can attain is precisely *sens-joui*.

In fact, we might say that with the quilting point thus exposed, the affinity of the semblant to the hole, the void, is also brought to light. From such a perspective, all these various names of the quilting point have something in common: their only function is to veil, to cover up with their flimsy materiality, a hole, a void in the structure. Indeed, we would argue that there is a structural, constitutive relation between the semblant and the hole. The question of the semblant is essentially the question of the relation between void and veil. By following Miller, we could propose the following succinct definition of the semblant: the semblant is a mask of nothing.[36] As a matter of fact, the semblant is only encountered where something is expected but one only encounters a hole, a void, an emptiness, an absence. The function of the semblant is solely to cover up, by its very presence, the empty place of a term which is constitutively lacking; but in so doing, the semblant at the same time reveals that this term ex-sists only through this empty place.

In this regard, psychoanalysis seems to be inverting Leibniz's famous question: instead of asking why there is something rather than nothing, the question with which psychoanalysis is preoccupied is rather: why is only a void, an absence, an emptiness encountered where something is expected? All semblants deployed by Lacan (from the phallus to the Other and Woman) are as many deceitful answers to this question. Semblants, in the final period of Lacan's teaching, are therefore all designed to veil, to mask the nothing: the phallus covers up castration, the Name-of-the-Father is a mask concealing the hole in the Other of language and, finally, Woman is nothing but a veil which disguises that there is no such thing as a sexual relation. The semblant can then be understood as an envelope of nothing, one which conceals precisely that, behind the semblant, there is nothing but the void.

Indeed, it is precisely in throwing into relief the dialectics of void and veil that the concept of the quilting point comes undone. This conveys a profound switch in the line of Lacan's elaboration of the relation between the symbolic and the real, one which implies a renouncement of any kind of quilting point. In fact, this question of the articulation between the symbolic and the real, while giving up the quilting of these two orders, offers a guiding thread through Lacan's seminar *D'un discourse qui ne serait pas du semblant.* Indeed, we would argue that he poses this question precisely in order to overcome the impasse left over at the end of his seminar on the four discourses, in which the revolving circle of the four discourses leads to a somewhat unexpected and certainly unwanted conclusion: if there is no discourse which is not of the semblant, this only means that any attempt at converting the real into the signifier brings about the emergence of the semblant. By paraphrasing Miller, one could thus say: what is signifierized is by the same token "semblantified."

This is why Lacan in "Lituraterre," the published part of *Seminar XVIII,* proposes as a possible solution for holding together that which does not hold together a new concept, that of the letter insofar as it is itself identified with the litoral: "Is the letter not [...] more properly *littorale* [coast-line], figuring that one domain in its entirety makes for the other a frontier, because of their being foreign to each other, to the extent of not falling into a reciprocal relation. Is the edge of the hole in knowledge not what it traces?"[37] To propose the littoral as a solution consists in nothing other than to propose the void itself as the mediator, the "void-median," as Lacan calls it. The operation involving the littoral is the inverse of the quilting operation since, with the littoral, the void holds together by keeping the heterogeneous instances apart: "between knowledge and *jouissance,* there is a littoral that only turns towards the literal on condition that this turn may be taken likewise at any instance."[38] Littoral, by activating the void itself as a mediator, is certainly a way of relating to *jouissance*, which can do without the semblant. On the other hand, when Lacan posed a rhetorical question—"Is it possible for the littoral to constitute such a discourse that is characterised by not being issued form the semblant?"[39]—his answer is clearly no. The littoral can only testify to the fracture of that which it is itself an effect. But it is unable to effect the cut. Only a discourse can produce a cut. One can see in what sense the theory of semblants constitutes a clearing gesture: indeed, it is only after bringing into question any instance of quilting that something like a littoral can be established, an empty plane in which something new can be inscribed. In the seminar *D'un discourse qui ne serait pas du semblant,* Lacan still seems to be harboring the hope of writing the formula of the sexual relation, a hope quelled with the seminar *Encore.* But just as the formula "there is no sexual relation" does not abolish the contingency of the encounter, the littoral proposes itself as a virgin canvas on which new combinations of knotting the real, the imaginary, and the symbolic can be inscribed.

By taking up the question of the semblant in its relation to the real, Lacan's *Seminar XVIII* is therefore, from the beginning, quite radically a question of defining a new type of articulation separating *jouissance* and the signifying articulation. In the context of Lacan's project thus outlined, the theory of semblants, insofar as it breaks with his previous assertion of the primacy of the symbolic, can be perceived as a "vanishing mediator," a necessary step on the path to the final solution: the Borromean knot, this being exactly the perspective in which all three registers—the symbolic, the imaginary and the real—are considered to be independent and autonomous registers, absolutely equivalent at the level of the knot. Lacan's project thus becomes that of separating the three orders, while at the same time exploring the many different ways in which it is possible to produce a new kind of knotting at the level of *jouissance.* The issue here is of course that of *jouissance* and the different ways in which it is elaborated at the level of the knot. In fact, we would argue that it is above all in order to explore this transformative aspect of knotting that Lacan explores *jouissance* as an enigma that drills a hole in sense. It is obvious that such a project has many consequences for the way in which psychoanalysis tries to situate the real from the perspective of the outside-sense. But it is also from this perspective that the notion of the semblant assumes its full value.

Notes

1. Jacques Lacan, *Les non-dupes errent* (1974), unpublished seminar, 23 April 1974.
2. Alain Badiou, *The Century, trans. Alberto Toscano* (Cambridge: Polity Press, 2007), 48-57.
3. Alain Badiou, *Ethics. An Essay on the Understanding of Evil,* trans. Peter Hallward (London and New York: Verso, 2001), 69-71.
4. Sigmund Freud, "Letter to Fliess #69, 21 September 1897," *The Standard Edition of the Complete Psychological Works of Sigmund Freud* (hereafter *SE*) ed. and trans. James Strachey et al. (London: Hogarth Press, 1953-1974), 1: 260.
5. Lacan, *The Seminar of Jacques Lacan. Book VII: The Ethics of Psychoanalysis (1959-1960),* ed. Jacques-Alain Miller, trans. Dennis Porter (London: W.W. Norton, 1992), 12.
6. "'Fictitious' means 'fictive' but, as I have already explained to you, in the sense that every truth has the structure of fiction." Ibid.
7. Lacan, *The Seminar of Jacques Lacan. Book XX: Encore, On Feminine Sexuality,*

The Limits of Love and Knowledge (1972-1973), ed. Jacques-Alain Miller, trans. Bruce Fink (New York: W.W. Norton, 1998), 58.

8. Lacan, *Le séminaire, livre XVI: D'un Autre à l'autre* (Paris: Seuil, 2006), 190.

9. The genesis of Lacan's notion of the semblant has been outlined by Pierre-Gilles Gueguen in the 17 December 1997 session of Jacques-Alain Miller's course "Le partenaire-symptôme," 1997-98. He also pointed out that, at the beginning, Lacan used both terms, "semblant" and "fiction," practically as synonymous. To account for this equivalence of both terms, Gueguen proposes the following hypothesis: if "semblant" and "fiction" are in Lacan's view interchangeable, this is because both concepts were perfectly capable of effecting the knot between the symbolic and the real and therefore of accounting for the manner in which a mere signifying device is able to distribute *jouissance*. Nevertheless, in the seventies, the term "fiction" practically disappears from Lacan's vocabulary. One reason why he finally gives up the notion of the fiction is no doubt that the concept of the fiction is too restrictive: whereas the fiction is strictly speaking language dependent, the semblant, insofar as it exists in nature, does not owe its existence to language. Actually, all the examples used by Lacan to illustrate the notion of the semblant in his seminar *D'un discours qui ne serait pas du semblant*, are exactly non-discursive semblants, semblants in nature, such as rainbow, thunder, and meteors. This very fact indicates that the concept of the semblant, while partly overlapping with that of the fiction, is nonetheless irreducible to it. There is yet another aspect of this substitution that should be noted here. In fact, this replacement coincides with the change in value of the term concerned: while the status of the Benthamite fiction was undoubtedly valorised, that of the semblant was on the contrary downgraded.

10. Consider the title of one of Miller's recent courses: *Pièces détachées* (2004-2005), unpublished seminar.

11. See Freud, "Analysis Terminable and Interminable," *SE* 23: 216-253.

12. Lacan, *Le séminaire, livre XVIII : D'un discours qui ne serait pas du semblant* (1970-71) (Paris: Seuil, 2006).

13. Lacan, *Encore*, 92.

14. Freud, "'Civilised' Sexual Morality and Modern Nervous Illness" (1908), *SE* 9: 181.

15. Lacan, *Encore*, 55.

16. Jacques-Alain Miller, *La fuite du sens* (1995-1996), unpublished, 31 January 1996.

17. Lacan, "The Function and Field of Speech and Language in Psychoanalysis," *Ecrits: A Selection*, trans. Alan Sheridan (London:

Routledge, 1977), 72.

18. Paradoxically, the collapse of the Other, in particular that of its emblem, the Name-of-the-Father, has made it possible for an unlikely alliance such as that between deconstruction and utilitarianism. Indeed, what deconstruction and utilitarianism have in common is the consideration of the social bond, and the sexual relationship with it, simply in terms of semblants. To the extent that, from such a perspective, the subject is ultimately $\$$, an empty set condemned to an ever changing series of identifications, all identity, sexual identity included, can only be a provisory stopper of a process of identification that knows no limit. Consequently, all identity is a semblant destined to be deconstructed. Characteristic in this respect is Judith Butler's radical critique of any politics of identity. See Butler, "Competing Universalities," *Contingency, Hegemony, Universality: Contemporary Dialogues on the Left* (London: Verso, 2000), 136-183. Indeed, for her, the path opening new political possibilities is that of a radical critique of the category of identity as such, insofar as no name, no identity, man or woman notwithstanding, is capable of adequately capturing the particular experience of *jouissance*. However, such a position, which may appear at first sight to be a radical one, is only possible on the basis of the identification of the subject with a radical nothingness since it is only as such a nothingness that the subject can experience the giddy freedom in relation to all identities and to all modes of enjoyment that characterizes the Butlerian subject. This is a subject that is, in the last analysis, nothing but an endless process of identifications. Butler insists that, inasmuch as it is not possible to designate the proper place of the subject from *jouissance*, the mode of enjoyment being always singular, the subject is nothing other than an incessant process of rejections of the proposed identities. The Butlerian subject is thus torn between its ever-changing particular *jouissance* on the one hand, and the endless process of identification desperately trying to keep pace with the breathtaking pluralization of the practices of *jouissance* on the other. Indeed, with Butler, we are dealing with a process in which only imaginary identity and symbolic identification, *automaton*, are involved, while the driving force of this dialectic between identity and identification—the impasse of *jouissance* itself as the category of the real—is evacuated. As a consequence, identity and identification remain polarized according to the opposition between imaginary construction and symbolic deconstruction. What is problematic here is that such a project of politicizing *jouissance* is, ultimately, grounded in the rejection of the real. In other words, what is lacking in such a project is precisely the third instance, that which would tie the subject to its mode of *jouissance*: the inexistence of the sexual relation as a hole in the real. Thus, instead of reproaching psychoanalysis for maintaining the Name-of-the-Father as a norm according

to which sexual identities are distributed—indeed, as a guarantor of the consistency of the social Other—it would be more appropriate to consider it, from a Lacanian perspective, as a term that marks a radical limit, an impossibility: that of the sexual relation. Indeed, it is only from such a perspective that takes into account the impossible that any attempt at invention, at creation, can even be envisaged; it is only against the background of such a hole in the real that an attempt can be made of writing the impossible, that is, an attempt at "possibilizing" the impossible.

19. Eric Laurent and Jacques-Alain Miller, "L'Autre qui n'existe pas et ses comités d'éthique. Introduction," *La Cause freudienne* 35 (1997): 7-14.

20. If Lacan defines the real as that which is impossible, this is, as he emphasizes himself, because "the real—well, *I believe*, if this is my symptom, tell me—the real is [...] without law. The true real implies the absence of the law. The real has no order. " Lacan, *Le séminaire, livre XXIII: Le sinthome* (Paris: Seuil, 2005), 137-138.

21. Lacan, *Television. A Challenge to the Psychoanalytic Establishment*, trans. Dennis Hollier, Rosalind Krauss, and Annette Michelson (New York: W.W. Norton, 1990), 32.

22. Ibid.

23. Miller, *L'exprérience du réel dans la cure analytique* (1998), unpublished seminar, 25 November 1998.

24. Ibid., 81.

25. See Miller, "Equivalence Between the Other and the Symptom," *Psychoanalytical Notebooks* 12 (2004): 9-31.

26. Lacan, *Le sinthome*, 17.

27. Ibid.

28. Miller, "The Sinthome, a Mixture of Symptom and Fantasy," *Psychoanalytical Notebooks* 5 (2001): 10.

29. Lacan, *Encore*, 95-97.

30. Miller, *Pièces détachées*, 26 January 2005.

31. Lacan, "Discours à l'Ecole Freudienne de Paris," *Autres écrits* (Paris: Seuil, 2001), 280-1.

32. Lacan, "L'Etourdit, " *Autres écrits*, 449-495.

33. Lacan, *The Seminar of Jacques Lacan. Book XVII: The Other Side of Psychoanalysis* (New York: W.W. Norton, 2006).

34. Lacan, *Encore*, 17.

35. Lacan, *Le séminaire, livre XVIII: D'un discours qui ne serait pas du semblant* (1970-71), 14.

36. Miller, "Of Semblants in the Relation Between Sexes," *Psychoanalytical*

Notebooks 3 (1999): 10.

37. Lacan, "Lituraterre," *Autres écrits*, 14.

38. Ibid., 16.

39. Ibid., 18.

14

Nowhere Else: On Utopia

Juliet Flower MacCannell

> Then at last my soul broke forth, and wisely did she cry,
> "No matter where, no matter where, so long as it is out of the world!"
> —Charles Baudelaire

Utopias do not ordinarily inspire me—except perhaps to want to break open their artificial perfection. Like any thinking person, I naturally feel an obligation to imagine how our condition might be better than it now is, but I am unable to do so without making an analysis of things as they are (including their unconscious aspects). If the implicit claim of a utopia is that it offers a cure for the discontent with civilization that Freud discovered as being endemic to it, this strikes me as at the very least, premature, and possibly dangerously naïve. Thus, I have always preferred Rousseau's stance in the *Social Contract* over full-blown utopias: while trying to frame a new relation to the law, Rousseau took men "as they are and the laws as they might be." His attack on the dream of "perfectibility," which was driving the cultural developments of his era (in the wrong direction), is still relevant today: witness the many planned-to-be-perfect communities now dotting the globe (such as Disney's town of Celebration, Seaside in Florida, Orange County China).[2] His complaint that we lack sufficient imagination to place ourselves in a different "situation from the one we find ourselves in" should still strike a chord in us.

Rousseau's urging us toward "an other situation than the one we are in" could be characterized as *utopian*, even though it does not call for a complete escape from civilization—a wish that clearly underlies some utopian impulses.[3] His call is more akin to Walter Benjamin's "destructive character," who does not know *why* but nevertheless knows *that* s/he must break out of the stifling situation s/he is in—to make a "way through."[4] Into *"what else?"*

remains unspecified, and necessarily so if the future is to be granted the freedom to be defined as indefiniteness, as openness to change.

EVERYWHERE: UTOPIA AT THE "END OF HISTORY"

Today, the sort of utopian drive I see in Rousseau's critical fictions and Benjamin's "destructive character" seems "quaint," even antiquated—lost to the charms of the "utopia" that, it is claimed, has emerged at (and as) the "end of history" (a utopia many of us experience as suffocating, to be sure). Neo-liberals, neo-conservatives, the "beltway" Hegelians, all have represented this utopia as a post-scarcity economy of plenty, as the end to all serious war (since conflict is no longer the driving force behind history), and as a universal, "global" inclusiveness—an "everywhere" utopia—in which no one need be left out or behind. Not only are we supposedly immersed in this plenty, which has oozed out to coat the entire world like the waste/excess on which it is based (oil), but we are also said to have at last managed to stop time at a particularly propitious, which is to say *faultless*, utopian moment. It is no accident that utopia today presents itself more directly as instituting the "end of history."

The facts on the ground are not reassuring, as the horrifying and deadly wars which have emerged from this golden age of peace make plain. The articulation of this set of utopian ideals offers, however, an opportunity to reconsider utopia. What is its enduring appeal? Is it the appeal *of* destructiveness (that is, the success of that primal "hostility" to civilization first noted by Freud)? Or is it the selfish appeal to the notion that we can finally rid ourselves of any obligation to other generations? After all, one precondition of utopia is its timelessness, its break with any real commitment to the *past* or to the *future*. Benjamin already perceived this in his "Theses on the Philosophy of History," where he quotes Lotze's comment that the present is remarkably free of envy toward the future.[5] Our unconcern for what comes "after" is rooted in our wish to believe ours is an already perfected present with no need of a future that would consist of anything other than its own repetition. The promise of a permanent Eden or Nirvana quickly puts us in the region of Freud's pleasure-principled death drive, aimed at eternalizing a moment that will never transform or change; an atemporal state of being, assembled out of bits of mythic pre-history and forged into a controlled, tightly designed post-history with no room for accident, discovery, or chance.[6] A nowhereness, then, that is everywhere; a timelessness that contains all time.

We have cause for suspicion regarding the universality of these claims, since no dreamed-of utopia has ever failed to require crucial sacrifices later considered unnecessary. Most often these go well beyond the original sacrifice of *libido* (Freud's conception of the problematic insertion of the natural into the cultural); instead, they almost always take the form of a total ban on some particular element (a person or a passion, a class or a race) which, deemed inimical to a projected harmony, must therefore be radically excised.

By contrast, *dystopias* are largely constructed out of the opposite impulse towards a future they view with deep consternation. They precipitate out a specific weakness in culture's here and now and extrapolate this often apparently minor flaw to its catastrophic logical conclusion in a proximal (and not entirely improbable) future. Dystopias are constructed along the faultline they discover underlying a taken-for-granted feature of current culture, a faultline that is then forced open until its extreme expression emerges full-blown in a vile future created by this magnified flaw. Dystopias are intended as a corrective to the distortedly positive view of a culture's own present. Huxley's *Brave New World*, Orwell's *1984*, Atwood's *The Handmaid's Tale*, Ridley Scott's *Blade Runner*, and Michael Bay's *The Island* all try to find *the* flaw in their culture's pretense to perfection. For Orwell, this feature is the debasing of everyday language in the service of power, resulting in unimaginable totalitarianism. For Atwood, it is our do-good desire (even on the part of the best-intentioned feminism) to rationalize and regulate our disordered, conflictual sexual arrangements, resulting in a theocratic "solution" that assigns women specific functionalities such that the roles of wife, mother, mistress can no longer overlap. For *Blade Runner*, it is the increasingly vertical structure of our economic arrangements that progressively distance wealthy whites (in high towers or gated communities) from their ethnic and poorer brethren (who are nonetheless the source of their wealth). On the ground, these "others" tear at each other just to get by.

The Island (a minor film, but with outstanding car-motorbike-helicopter chases) shows the dystopian future of today's worship of wealth. Thousands of young adults work at bio-medical tasks in a secluded research institute where they must also live in order to remain sheltered from an outside world that has suffered global "contamination." If a person is lucky enough to win the nightly lottery, however, s/he wins a place on "the Island," a paradise that miraculously escaped the contamination and is located outside the institute's hermetic walls. The trick is that there never was any contamination; each inhabitant/worker is unaware that s/he is the clone of a wealthy person created by the institute from the wealthy donor's DNA. The clones are "born" full-grown from pods where they have been implanted with artificial childhood memories and sufficient education to perform the institute's tasks. For the client, their clone is an "insurance policy": the institute will harvest the clone's mature organs should the client ever suffer an accident or a fatal disease. The problem begins when the clones start to wonder, to think for themselves, even in very small measure. One clone tries to map the probabilities of who will win the lottery based on the letters of their names. Another finds a flying insect, which must have come from the outside, and is curious about how it could have survived the contamination. The desire to know—"What if?"—is the one urge the scientists have concentrated on eliminating from the clones' mental apparatus.[7]

Classical utopias deny such incipient faults could lead to their ruination from within and gird themselves against dangerous exposure to competing social orders (they are often sealed off spatially and temporally from other communities; think, for example, of the trench that protects More's Utopia from other societies, or the mountains that mark the uncrossable boundary of Hilton's Shangri-La).[8] It could even be said that, as a rule, no utopia can entertain any intercourse with other communities if it hopes to persist in its being. Witness the travails of Bill Paxton's character (Bill) in the HBO series *Big Love*, who perpetually tries to immunize his personal utopia (consisting of a three-wife, three-house family faithful to the Principle of righteous polygamy) from attacks by the radical polygamous outlaw "Compound," presided over by the totalitarian leader Roman Grant. Bill was born at the Compound, but exiled from it as a potential troublemaker when he was a teenager. He also has to protect his utopian commune-family from potentially damaging censure from the surrounding Mormon culture, should his "lifestyle" become known (the Mormons gave up polygamy a century ago so that Utah could become a state). Bill juggles his life by becoming a successful Salt Lake City entrepreneur, which places him in constant jeopardy of exposure because it earns him a precarious prominence in the business community. On the other front, he intervenes in the internal power politics of the Compound, and attempts at the same time to outmaneuver its members by snatching profitable investments from their large portfolio, thus incurring their wrath. It is because Bill struggles on all these fronts that his utopian home front comes near to ruin.

NOWHERE

> When There's Nowhere You Have To Be,
> Where Do You Go?[9]

Can a case be made *for* utopia today? In its very "nowhereness" is there not something to be said for the utopian urge that might still manifest itself *against* our own presumptive plenitude, the saturation of satisfaction, or what I am calling the Utopia of Everywhere?[10] Could a different utopian impulse and a more fertile imagination conceive of new satisfactions and other forms of enjoyment not (death) driven by a pleasure principle that inevitably joins the reality principle in a lethal finale?[11]

Despite the resistance I have to utopianism, I must admit that most famous literary and philosophical utopias, from Plato's *Republic* to Thomas More's *Utopia*, actually can and possibly should be read completely upside down, ironically, if only because they are composed by language (which always has a repressed, unconscious, and therefore metaphoric side). In stating their claims, utopian works inevitably lead us to question the situation surrounding their enunciation. Reading utopias crosswise to their self-representation is possible and possibly necessary. And this possibility is even built into works such as More's, where the narrator explains that Utopia bears a name, Hythloday, whose Greek root points to a triviality that undercuts his reports. Moreover, theoretical utopias often go so far in their proscriptions that they edge toward self-satire: when they insist on banning, say, poets from the Republic, readers feel compelled to question why—and they often side with the excluded, not with the utopians: *with* the poets; *with* the lying (and hence the possibilities of metaphor and fiction) that are banished from Swift's Land of the Houyhnhnms in which no one can "say the thing that is not;" *with* the theater outlawed by Rousseau's idyllic "Geneva" in his *Lettre à D'Alembert sur les Spectacles* (a Geneva whose isolation and self-satisfied smugness he could hardly wait to flee as a boy). Fictional and theoretical Utopias can be ironically reversed because they are composed of the ambivalent form called language, language being the central formative force of civilization and thus the ultimate source of our discontent with it. Language is also our primary, if not only, means of dealing with that discontent. Plato, More, Swift, Rousseau (who first made the case that "perfectibility" was the source of a great human misery) wrote their "utopias" to maximize the potential to read them satirically while at the same time taking them seriously.

Taking perfectibility "seriously" leads to nightmarish outcomes. Efforts to institute actual utopias (and not only by the neo-cons today, but also by the myriad others who preceded them from the phalansteries of Fourier to the often religious utopian communities of upstate New York, to Jonestown, Waco, and the Kampuchea of the Khmer Rouge) have had decidedly mixed and often extremely negative results. When the Khmer Rouge dreamt of extracting a truer, purer, more original authentic Kampuchea out of the Cambodia it had become under various colonialisms, they banned many things, among them those with weak eyesight and less-than-ideal body shapes. These, along with the artists, they killed.

While the excisions that found a fictional utopia as a *nowhere* are intended to preserve the community's serene detachment, the violent cuts required to establish de facto utopias are always lethal—for some.

ANYWHERE: UTOPIA, SUBURBIA, & THE UNCONSCIOUS

> The processes of the system Ucs are timeless; i.e., they are not ordered temporally, are not altered by the passage of time; they have no reference to time at all.... Disregard of the characteristic of time is no doubt an essential distinction between the activity of the Pcs. and the Ucs.
>
> —Sigmund Freud[12]

This leads me to my longstanding criticism of the idea that we are at the "end of history." This idea has opened the door to a belief in an actually utopian world of plenty or full satisfaction,[13] one that has materially shaped and also fundamentally distorted communal life. Contemporary culture and its economy have not failed to present themselves as *global* in character, as a comprehensive single system encircling the entire world,[14] a world of wealth gained peacefully, without exploitation.[15] If wealth, as Freud defined it, represents the "amount of instinctual satisfaction" obtainable by its means, and if civilization formerly required that certain instinctual satisfactions be sacrificed for the good of the human group, today's "immense accumulation of commodities" (Marx's phrase) renders such sacrifice unnecessary—or so the argument goes.[16] A culture of satisfaction, of *jouissance* aplenty (even if Lacan revealed the fakeness of such *jouissance*) is the center of today's representations of the world as a utopia of timeless, universal enjoyment. But *in refusing to acknowledge any possible other side, its global character must be called into question.* What is the drive to install ours as a one-dimensional universe free of the internal and external contradictions that might propel it in unpredictable ways?

The reader may by now have seen that I have been building a picture of this everywhere/anywhere utopia on the model of the Freudian unconscious: timeless, without contradiction, inalterable. Neoconservative/neo-liberal theory frames its utopia as a space(less)-time(less) that fully saturates the drives once consigned or confined to the unconscious. The pre-eminent concrete expression of its ideal global state (concrete, literally and figuratively), that which anchors its vision, is suburbia-as-utopia. The suburb, whose architecture and installation over tracts of land cleared of all historical reference and distinctive natural features, also happens to be the site where the plethora of ready-to-wear satisfactions are supposedly freely enjoyed.[17]

In contemporary cultural images, suburbia is depicted as that special non-place where incest and murder are no longer punishable transgressions, and where the drives that fuel them need no longer be repressed or even symbolically sacrificed. See the infamous show, *Desperate Housewives*, where murder, child abuse, pederasty and incest flourish on the Wisteria Lane of suburban Fairview. Or take the BBC's *Murder in Suburbia,* which uncovers the wild sexual lives led by murder victims, lives that often shock the two young women detectives, but not the victims' blasé neighbors, who are not only fully cognizant of these sexual aberrations but often their cheerful co-participants. Or consider Showtime's *Weeds*, which features a widowed housewife in a San Fernando Valley suburb of Los Angeles, who also happens to be a dope dealer. She has soccer mom values, yet in one episode she will casually have sex with a rival dealer (a Latino) on the hood of a car, in an urban alley, in broad daylight. (This is to keep him away from her ideal neighborhood, where pedophile millionaires prey on teenage boys and everyone engages in all manner of what were once considered deviant sexual practices.) Advertised, then, by and as our new utopia: "An orgy of sexual transgression now available in your nearest neighborhood suburb."

Suburbia is not, of course, *the* unconscious: it simply denies that limits are necessarily placed on absolute enjoyment. It is a will-to-*jouissance*, an effort to control this unruly and unmanageable excess. As such it is only *modeled* on the unconscious—on that no-place where antipathy to civilization reigns supreme. This may be the key to comprehending why suburbia must be a bland sameness—it must be an "anywhere." If it had a specific spatiality and a genuine historicity it could not aspire to the utopian nowhere of the unconscious unleashed.

The problem is obviously that where this "repressive desublimation" masquerades as the unconscious unbound, all it actually realizes is a sadistic pseudo-utopia where "unfettered" enjoyment is tied up—in bondage, chains, forced confinement; in sequestered bedchambers, fortified enclosures, prisons. Spaces self-declared to be exempt from the Law (in the Lacanian, symbolic and linguistic sense, not in the sense of positive law). We now translate these into the forms of gated communities, of the "entourages" who guard the privacy of the billionaire, of the infamous "bubbles" enveloping our political leaders where they enjoy the bliss of ignorance and irresponsibility.

Is consumer capitalism's pretension to full "satisfaction" (that one that de Sade dreamed up for his own utopias) really a final conquest of the repressions that drive the Freudian unconscious? Has it achieved the universal "right to *jouissance*" that Lacan once claimed would alone be truly revolutionary?[18] Here I cannot help but recall Freud's remark (re-emphasized by Lacan) that the damming up of libido is a hallmark of the *impotent* subject, the one unable to partake of "good old fashioned enjoyment." This impotence, Lacan adds, is the psychical foundation of capitalism. The dream of stockpiling *jouissance* is the act of someone lacking actual political or social power.[19]

I have argued that the "reality" of late capitalist life is shaped *as if* it were a realization of our deepest fantasies, so fully satisfying that we need be tempted by no elsewhere and by no other moment. If this is utopia, it may be high time to find a new way out. For, after all, as Lacan wryly remarks in *Seminar VII*, "we haven't even been able to create a single new perversion."[20] If not that, then what is at stake in touting utopia's long-awaited arrival?

ELSEWHERE

> *La vie est ailleurs*[21]
>
> In these any-spaces-whatever a new race of characters
> was stirring, a kind of mutant ... they were *seers*.
>
> —Gilles Deleuze[22]

At this point, I will be mercifully brief. We stand in the greatest need of imagination to pursue (as Ambasz says) "alternative futures." It is indeed *seers* we need now, seers who will dream utopia for us neither as a "nowhere-and-everywhere," nor as a "never-and-forever," but simply as *elsewhere.* The "utopian" turn of the post-war mid-century has now reached a *dénouement* that turns out to be only the bland, blank anywhereness of global sadism-as-suburbia. In other words, it has arrived at no utopia at all. Its subjective commandment—superegoic in form—to enjoy by respecting none of the laws of "civilization" shows itself as nothing more than the age-old game of exploiting us by extracting our wealth and adding it to the stores of the already wealthy.

What is to be done? If utopias have been the chief mode of attempting to solve the insoluble puzzle of what to do with the surplus that comes from/with the sacrifices (of enjoyment) imposed on us in the name of civilization, they have never yet come up with anything more than a series of proposals for *administering* this excess—which is also its waste. None has yet devised anything like a perfect solution. Recall Freud's late thesis has civilization spontaneously generating three ways to treat the problem of surplus enjoyment: *identification* (with cultural ideals);[23] *art* (defined as the sublimated substitute for vicariously satisfying forbidden drives); and *religion* (which orders society around a non-negotiable demand to keep the basis for its authority closed to inspection).[24] Freud found all three of these "illusions" wanting; they have become increasingly ineffectual the more civilization "perfects" itself. The only hope he held out was that human curiosity, the desire to *know*, science (for example, psychoanalysis), would ultimately trump the all-pervasive illusions civilization has devised as palliatives for the malaise it creates in all of us.

When I was a child, Freud's utopian dream of endless learning was mine, too: I imagined always being able to live in the land of the free(thinking). But this utopia now seems as impossible to me as continuing to believe we could live forever in the land of the free. A passion for ignorance and confinement washes over global culture as it reaches the "end of history."

But should we not rethink at least one of Freud's premises about the illusions that falsely reconcile us to a civilization to which we can never really be reconciled? At least in the domain of art, I think we should entertain some new hypotheses. The value of art, according to Freud, lies in its sublimation, its illusion of satisfying our necessarily repressed drives.[25]

But what if we were to consider art differently: as a unique undertaking to confront the Real (with its unknowable, terrifying *jouissance*) and to transmute the experience of that confrontation into something that not only places it at a protective distance (sublimation) but also brings it unimaginably *closer* than we could ever dream possible? By making it into an entirely new, transmissible experience of the Thing, without deceiving ourselves as to its horror and its pleasure.

At the end of his life, Lacan set off along this other pathway and wondered if we could not, indeed, get out from under the burdens civilization forcibly imposes on speaking beings while yet retaining the crucial generative value of the language that is its instrument of choice. He turned to James Joyce who, Lacan thought, had contrived a way to convey *jouissance* (which the signifier carves off) in language. To read Joyce, Lacan notes, is not necessarily to experience the promise of meaning inherent to the structure of language, but to feel instead the reality of the author's *jouissance*. To accomplish this impossible task, Lacan says, Joyce had to destroy the English language as we know it. Joyce's personal malaise in his own (Irish) civilization was that of a double encirclement by the hell of an English language that had been forcibly imposed on his culture and that had remained fixed at the moment of its imposition. It had no freedom to change or evolve. Like the language of conquerors forced upon their new subjects, it brooked none of the playful, metaphoric outlets for the *jouissance* language represses—outlets open to any "native" speaker. English stagnated in its Irish iteration. (See the passage in *A Portrait of the Artist as a Young Man*, where young Stephen discovers that only he knows that the English priest laughs at the old-fashioned word for candle-snuffer, *tundish*, one no longer current in English usage.) The upshot was that Joyce was oppressed not simply by *language*, but that his oppression was aggravated by the fact that this language was deeply foreign to his culture; it was the language of his imperial oppressor.

Lacan saw that Joyce's solution to the double impasse he encountered in language was his breaking out of (while not altogether breaking with) language. For Lacan, Joyce was the sinthome, the one who forged unimaginable signifiers that *bear jouissance*.[26]

What can we draw from Lacan's appreciation of Joyce? Perhaps this: that art can now be charged with the singular burden of absorbing the slings and arrows of our permanent cultural misfortune in order to turn them into a new experience of *jouissance*. Not just for the sake (as in Joyce's case) of the artist's treating her own impossible condition, but rather to transmit her own transmuting of that experience, a transmutation that has allowed her to bear it, and to bear witness to it, and to *share* it with others. This would be an art that follows an alternative path, then, from the consumer path along which art is currently racing.

Notes

1. Charles Baudelaire, "XLVIII: Anywhere, Anywhere Out of the World" in *Little Poems in Prose*, ed. Martin P. Starr, trans. Aleister Crowley (Chicago: The Teitan Press, 1995), 117-119.
2. See Dean MacCanell, "New Urbanism and its Discontents" in *Giving Ground: The Politics of Propinquity*, ed. Joan Copjec and Michael Sorkin

(London and New York: Verso, 1999), 106-128.

3. Rousseau is, of course, charged with just that; but I have argued that he actually takes the reverse position, seeing the "state of nature" as *the* utopian dream of a culture formed around an ego center, which he deplores. He intended to recast culture from egocentricity into a new form of sociality. See Juliet Flower MacCannell, "Rousseau and Law: Monstrous Logic" in *Law, Justice, Power*, ed. S. Cheng (Stanford: Stanford University Press, 2004), 240-258; and "The City, Year Zero: Memory and the Spatial Unconscious," in *The Journal of Romance Studies*, 7:2 (2007): 1-18.
4. Walter Benjamin, "The Destructive Character" in *Reflections*, ed. Peter Demetz (New York: Schocken Books, 1986), 301-303.
5. "'One of the most remarkable characteristics of human nature', writes Lotze, 'is, alongside so much selfishness in specific instances, the freedom from envy which the present displays toward the future.' Reflection shows us that our image of happiness is thoroughly colored by the time to which the course of our own existence has assigned us. The kind of happiness that could arouse envy in us exists only in the air we have breathed, among people we could have talked to, women who could have given themselves to us. In other words, our image of happiness is indissolubly bound up with the image of redemption." Benjamin, "Theses on the Philosophy of History" in *Illuminations*, ed. Hannah Arendt (New York: Schocken Books, 1969), 253-254.
6. "The same applies to our view of the past, which is the concern of history. The past carries with it a temporal index by which it is referred to redemption. There is a secret agreement between past generations and the present one. Our coming was expected on earth. Like every generation that preceded us, we have been endowed with a *weak* Messianic power, a power to which the past has a claim. That claim cannot be settled cheaply." Ibid., 254.
7. Freud believed that the only "way out" for a civilization increasingly trapped by its own conflicting desires to exploit and stifle it was the unquenchable *desire to know*. We can no longer be so certain of this hope as Freud was. But I suggest other possibilities at the end of this essay. Sigmund Freud, *The Future of an Illusion*, in *The Standard Edition of the Complete Psychological Works of Sigmund Freud* (hereafter *SE*), ed. and trans. James Strachey et al. (London: Hogarth Press, 1953-1974), 21: 53.
8. The excisions required to manufacture a utopia also extend to its need to cut itself off. More's Utopia enters into relations with other non-utopian societies mainly to recruit the mercenaries they need to protect them (Utopians themselves are pacifists). As the mercenaries are naturally killed in the course of their service, the Utopians justify these deaths with

Panglossian logic: eliminating the violence-prone from other societies will help advance those societies along the path to perfection.

9. The caption of an advertisement for a luxury hotel (Hyatt Corporation), *The New Yorker*, 28 December 1998/9 January 1999 double issue, inside back cover.

10. The Google Corporation could stand as the utopian emblem of this. It not only seems to generate endless profits, its campus swathes its knowledge-workers with every creature comfort and every amenity, including gourmet lunches and personal on-demand massages. One masseuse, brought in to service the workers, has recently retired, as a multimillionaire, on the stock options granted her when she was first hired. At the same time, the dialectical opposition to this plenitude is already emerging, as we look towards an ecotopia whose hallmark would be the cut: in energy consumption, greenhouse gases, waste. See also the various abstinence movements (in eating and in sex) now becoming common. The quest for the solution to the problem of surplus enjoyment seems increasingly desperate.

11. I am thinking of someone like Emilio Ambasz, who, in *Analyzing Ambasz*, describes his architecture as the "pursuit of alternative futures." *Analyzing Ambasz*, ed. Michael Sorkin (New York: Monacelli, 2004), 108.

12. Freud, "The Unconscious," *SE* 14:187.

13. This is, at least, how it is described by the neo-conservatives and "Kojevian/Beltway" Hegelians, whose theses achieved their apogee under the regime of the second Bush administration.

14. Already in 1969, Lacan speaks of an alethosphere girdling the world, filled with intangible messages and messengers of *jouissance* that he calls lathouses (gadgets). See Jacques Lacan, *The Seminar of Jacques Lacan. Book XVII: The Other Side of Psychoanalysis (1969-1970)*, ed. Jacques-Alain Miller, trans. Russell Grigg (New York and London: W.W. Norton & Company, 2007), 150-163.

15. The neo-conservative argument refuses to be belied by empirical experience. Indeed, disasters are now considered opportunities: witness Condoleezza Rice's slip of the tongue regarding the South Asian tsunami of 2006. See also Naomi Klein, *The Shock Doctrine: The Rise of Disaster Capitalism* (Metropolitan Books/Henry Holt and Company, 2007) and "The Rise of Disaster Capitalism," *The Nation*, 2 May 2005, 9-11.

16. Freud, in *The Future of an Illusion*, had said that individuals must band together "to control the forces of nature, and extract its wealth for the satisfaction of human needs." Yet, he notes that men have remained unconsciously hostile to the ban on satisfying their animal body by the demand for social coexistence. On the other hand, even though communal or common wealth is its byproduct, Freud notes, the result is that its

use becomes the subject of regulation, made "necessary in order to adjust the relations of men to one another… especially in the distribution of the available wealth" (Freud, *The Future of an Illusion*, *SE* 21:6).

17. *Desperate Housewives* is broadcast on Disney-owned ABC.

18. Lacan, "Kant with Sade" in *Écrits: The First Complete Edition in English*, trans. Bruce Fink (New York and London: W.W. Norton & Company, 2006), 645-668.

19. See Lacan, *The Seminar of Jacques Lacan. Book XVII: The Other Side of Psychoanalysis*. See also Juliet Flower MacCannell, "More Thoughts for the Times on War and Death: The Discourse of Capitalism in *Seminar XVII*" in *Jacques Lacan and the Other Side of Psychoanalysis: Reflections on Seminar XVII*, ed. Justin Clemens and Russell Grigg (Durham: Duke University Press, 2006), 195-215.

20. Lacan, *The Seminar of Jacques Lacan. Book VII: The Ethics of Psychoanalysis, 1959-1960*, ed. Jacques-Alain Miller, trans. Dennis Porter (New York and London: W.W. Norton & Company, 1992), 15.

21. Wall graffiti, Paris, 1968.

22. Gilles Deleuze, *Cinema II: The Time-Image*, trans. Hugh Tomlinson and Robert Galeta (Minneapolis: The University of Minnesota Press, 1989), xi.

23. "No doubt one is a wretched plebeian, harassed by debts and military service; but to make up for it, one is a Roman citizen, one has one's share in the task of ruling other nations and dictating their laws" (Freud, *The Future of an Illusion*, *SE* 21:13).

24. Ibid., 54-55.

25. "Art offers substitutive satisfactions for the oldest and still most deeply felt renunciations, and for that reason it serves as nothing else to reconcile man to the sacrifices he has made on behalf of civilization." Freud goes on to say it heightens our feeling of identification, and as a product of our own particular culture, it is also a "narcissistic satisfaction" (Ibid., 14).

26. Lacan, *Le Séminaire de Jacques Lacan. Livre XXIII, Le Sinthome*, 1975-1976 (Paris: Seuil, 2005). A more contemporary example is the comic genius of Denis Leary, who laces his brilliant language with profanities that are not meant simply to be rude and transgressive; instead, they convey to his listeners an unnameable passion and intensity. Another device, dreamt up by some unknown genius, is that series of symbols inserted into cartoons to indicate the strongest emotions, expressing profanity without saying a word: !!$#@%!!

15

The Censorship of Interiority

Joan Copjec

Iranian films are an exotic experience for audiences accustomed to Hollywood-dominated cinema. Not just for obvious reasons, but because the obvious—the foreign locations, customs, and people, everything we actually see on screen—is produced by a different distribution of the visible and the invisible and an alien logic of the look.

One of the most spectacular heralds of Iran's 1978-1979 Islamic Revolution was the torching of spectacle. Movie theaters—in one horrific case, with the audience still in it—were set on fire and incinerated by fundamentalists. Fittingly, in this respect, Khomeini spoke, in his first public appearance as Iran's new leader, not only of his intent to restore the authority of the mullahs and to purge the country of all foreign influences, Eastern as well as Western; he also broached the question of cinema directly. As might be expected, he vehemently denounced the cinema of that "vile traitor," the ousted Shah, as "a center of vice," but he refrained from banning cinema outright as a wicked modern invention.[1] For, Khomeini recognized immediately the value of cinema, the possibilities for mobilizing it in the service of his grand scheme to reeducate the people in the ways of Islam. Post-revolutionary Iran witnessed, then, not the tabooing, but the flourishing of a heavily subsidized and officially promoted cinema, though one strictly regulated by the Ministry of Culture and Islamic Guidance, which explicitly forbade the smallest signs of foreign influence—such as the wearing of ties, the smoking of cigarettes, and the drinking of alcohol, and so on—and, more importantly and more globally, any infraction of the Islamic system of *hejab*. In its strictest sense, *hejab* is a veil or cloth covering used to obscure women from the sight of men to whom they are not related; in the widest sense, it is the entire "system of modesty" that demands the concealment of even the contour of a woman's body, which is always in danger of being revealed by her gestures and movements. Indeed, *hejab* seems to be motivated by the belief that there is something about women that can never be covered up enough, that surreptitiously bares itself even beneath her clothing. Thus, the precautionary task of veiling is buttressed by architectural design and rigid social protocols that further protect women from exposing themselves and men from being exposed to the sight of them.

The impact of *hejab* regulations on cinema was massive.[2] For, it was not just the figure and movement of the woman that required veiling, but also the look directed at her. Strictures against the eros of the unrelated meant that not even religiously sanctioned forms of erotic engagement between men and women could be represented, since filming made women vulnerable to the extradiegetic look of the director, crew, and, of course, the audience. Thus, the look of desire around which Hollywood-dominated cinema is plotted had to be forsaken, along with the well-established system of relaying that look through an alternating pattern of shots and counter-shots and the telling insertion of psychologically motivated close-ups. Besides restricting narrative situations and tabooing the most common style of editing, the system of modesty also obliged any filmmaker committed to maintaining a modicum of realism to shoot outdoors. Although, in real life, Iranian women need not and do not wear headscarves at home, in cinematic interiors they were forced to don them because of the presence, once again, of the extradiegetic look which exposed them to the view of unrelated men. But incongruous images of headscarves in scenes of family intimacy were more than unrealistic; they were oftentimes risible, and filmmakers thus tended to avoid domestic scenes as much as possible. Ultimately, then, it was interiority that was the most significant cinematic casualty of *hejab*. Iranian cinema came to be composed *only* of exterior shots, whether in the form of actual spatial exteriors—the improbable abundance of rural landscapes and city streets, hallmarks of Iranian cinema—or in the form of virtual exteriors—interior domestic spaces in which women remained veiled and secluded from desire, outside the reach of any affectionate or passionate caress. The challenge facing all Iranian filmmakers, then, is to make credible and compelling films under this condition, namely: *the censorship of interiority, the taboo of intimacy*.

Revelations of American torture of Iraqi prisoners at Abu Ghraib brought to light an abusive reaction to the Islamic system of modesty. It turns out that *The Arab Mind*, a book first published in 1973 and reprinted only a few months prior to the U.S. invasion of Iraq, got into the hands of pro-war Washington conservatives and became, in the words of one academic, "the Bible of the neo-cons on Arab behavior." Of special interest to these conservatives was a chapter on "Arabs and Sex," which argued that "the segregation of the sexes, the veiling of women…and all the other minute rules that govern and restrict contact between men and women, have the effect of making sex a prime mental preoccupation in the Arab world."[3] It was this sort of speculation that was responsible for planting in the heads of calculating conservatives the idea that shame would be the most effective device for breaking down Iraqi prisoners psychologically. According to a report in *The New Yorker*, two themes emerged as "talking points" in the discussions of the strategists: (1) "Arabs only understand force," and (2) "the biggest weakness of Arabs is shame and humiliation." In brief, shaming was chosen as the method of torture precisely because the torturers believed that Arab culture made the prisoners particularly vulnerable to it.

This belief was nourished on the banquet of that crude and—one would have thought—thoroughly discredited sociological division of the world into "guilt cultures" and "shame cultures." The distinction classifies guilt as an affect characteristic of advanced cultures, whose members have graduated to the stage where they possess an internal principle of morality, and shame as a "primitive" affect characteristic of cultures forced to rely, for want of such a principle, on the approving or disapproving gaze of other people to monitor morality. I will focalize my criticisms by offering my own curt and contrary thesis: *The affects of shame and guilt are improperly used to define kinds of cultures; what they define, rather, are different relations to one's culture.* I use *culture* here to refer to the form of life we inherit at birth (not our biological birth, but our birth into language), all those things—family, race, ethnicity, sex—we do not choose, but which choose us, the entire past that precedes us and marks our belatedness. The manner in which we assume this inheritance, and the way we understand what it means to keep faith with it, are, I will argue, what distinguish shame from guilt.

Distancing herself from the dubious correlation of affects with stages of cultural and moral development, Eve Sedgwick offers an alternative to the neoconservative view of shame as she reflects on her own experience of it in the aftermath of another violent confrontation between America and Islam, the attack of September 11. Sedgwick tells us that she was suddenly overcome by shame whenever she happened, post-9/11, to catch a glimpse of the void that occupied the site where the Twin Towers once stood.[4] This example is striking in its uncommonness, for the circumstances that give rise to her shame are not the sort one usually associates with it. This is, however, Sedgwick's point: shame is *not* occasioned, as is usually thought, by prohibition or repression, by a look of condemnation or disapproval. It is a response, rather, to a rupturing of the comforting circuit of recognition and social exchange that ordinarily defines us. The absence of the Towers—the demolition of the edifices that stood as icons of the reinforced invulnerability of the U.S. and as landmarks by which New Yorkers used to orient themselves in the city—signal the point of a rupture. Witnessing their absence, Sedgwick experiences a loss of familiar coordinates, a fundamental disorientation. It is in this context that she describes the blush of shame as the "betraying blazon of a ruptured narcissistic circuit."[5] Shame always results from a sneak attack, an upsetting of expectations that wounds ego identity. Yet what is odd is that this wound is not accompanied by a simple feeling of isolation, of being separated from society. This is the second important point. Sedgwick describes the paradox of shame as a simultaneous movement "toward [...] individuation" *and* "toward uncontrollable relationality," or social contagion.[6] That is, alongside the feeling of a disconcerting and often searing self-awareness, shame is marked by a kind of group sentiment, a feeling of solidarity with others.

In an effort to interpret this often-remarked paradox, Sedgwick insists that the shame she felt after 9/11 was not for herself, but for the missing Towers. That is, she interprets her social sentiment as a feeling of shame for or on behalf of something other than herself. But this is a mistake, for it gives shame an object, here: the destroyed Towers. Strictly speaking, however, the syntagm "shame for" is a solecism; one feels shame neither for oneself nor for others. Shame is intransitive; it has no object in the ordinary sense. To experience it is to experience oneself as subject, not as a degraded or despised object. I am not ashamed of myself, I am the shame I feel. Giorgio Agamben makes this point clearly when he designates shame as the "proper emotive tonality of subjectivity" and as "the fundamental sentiment of being *a subject*."[7] And, indeed, Sedgwick herself points in this direction when she describes shame as the sentiment that "attaches to and sharpens the sense of who one is," noting—and this is a crucial qualifier—that this sentiment of self also consists of a feeling of not being "integrated" with who we are.[8] In shame one encounters one's self outside the self, engaged in society.

Let us put aside for the moment this inquiry into how we in the U.S. understand or misunderstand shame and look at it from the other side. Turning back to the Islamic system of modesty, let us take a closer look at the films of Abbas Kiarostami, one of the most important and best known directors to make films under this system. What gives the neoconservative association of shame and *hejab* its legs, of course, is the fact that both involve veiling. In the modesty system, as with shame, a curtain is always drawn, looks averted, heads bowed. On first approach, it would seem that no director is more in tune with the *hejab* system than Kiarostami, for his is a cinema of respectful reserve and restraint. This reserve is expressed most emblematically in his preference for what can be described as "discreet" long-shots. Especially in moments of dramatic intimacy—a skittish suitor's approach to the girl he loves, the meeting between a man who impersonates another and the man he impersonates—Kiarostami's camera tends to hold back, to separate itself from the action by inserting a distance between itself and the scene and refusing to venture forward into the private space of the characters. So marked is the tactfulness of his camera that Kiarostami sometimes seems a reluctant filmmaker.

In light of this overall filming strategy, one sequence from *The Wind Will Carry Us* (1999) stands out as an aberration. Its protagonist, Behzad, a documentary filmmaker, has traveled to the Kurdish village of Siah Darreh with his crew to film the ceremony of scarification still practiced by mourning villagers after someone from the village dies. In the sequence in question, Behzad, biding his time as he awaits the imminent death of Mrs. Malek, the village's oldest inhabitant, amuses himself by attempting to purchase some fresh milk from Zeynab, a young village girl and the fiancée of a gravedigger he has befriended. Hamid Dabashi, author of a book on Iranian cinema and normally a great admirer of Kiarostami, excoriates the director for the utter shamelessness of this sequence in which, in Dabashi's view, an Iranian woman's privacy and dignity are raped by a boorish Iranian man, whose crime is all the more offensive for being paraded before the eyes of the world.[9] This is what Dabashi sees: Behzad descending into a hidden, underground space, penetrating the darkness that protects a shy, unsophisticated village girl from violation, and aggressively trying to expose her, despite her obvious resistance, to the light of his lamp, his incautious look, his lies, and his sexual seduction.

ANXIETY & THE "INEXPRESSIBLE FLAVOR OF THE ABSOLUTE"

Dabashi's disdain for Behzad is heavily informed by his assessment of the protagonist as merely a Tehrani interloper adrift in rural Iran. This reading of Behzad's puzzled and sometimes combative disorientation—a disorientation he shares with many of Kiarostami's protagonists, who are almost all screen doubles of the director—is a common one: geographically and culturally displaced, the modern urban sophisticate finds himself at a loss amidst rural peoples and traditions. One is obliged to note, however, that it is as much the peri-urban character of these rural areas as their pristine primitiveness, notably in decline, which catches Kiarostami's eye. Cell phone reception may not always be good in the villages, but new telecommunications systems are already being installed and the sight of random television antennae and satellite dishes atop thatched roofs assure us that no one in this part of the world need miss a simulcast soccer game. Regarding the traditional ceremony of scarification, for example, we learn in the film that it has been retrofitted, turned some time ago into a means of advancing oneself on the professional ladder. Whenever a relative of one of the bosses dies, the workers compete for the distinction of being the most loyal mourner, exhibiting their self-scarred faces and bodies in hopes of impressing their bosses and being rewarded with a raise or promotion. Incipient capitalism is here in bed with traditional culture, exploiting rather than eliminating it.

This abbreviation of the distance between Behzad and the villagers does not exonerate his insensitive behavior, but it does suggest that we need to look elsewhere for a more accurate explanation of his disorientation, which goes deeper than the narrative alibi implies. Like other Kiarostami protagonists,

Behzad behaves, I will argue, less like a rootless or deterritorialized modern man than like one who has been uprooted from his modern unrootedness to experience himself as *riveted* to a culture, a land, an ethnicity that remains inscrutable and that he tries to understand, without much success, by engaging in a quasi-ethnographic exploration of them. That modernity melted everything solid into air is an exaggerated claim, but it was expected that it would at least soften all that had once been solid to the consistency of clay, to render everything, including the subject, infinitely pliable. Contrary to expectations, however, supposedly malleable modern man found himself *stuck* to something; something tore him away from the free-flowing current of modern life. It is as if a drain hole were inexplicably opened in the modern world, lending our fleeting "temporal existence [...] the inexpressible flavor of the absolute" and giving rise to "an acute feeling of being held fast."[10] That this riveting or reterritorialization is a confounding fact of modern life and no mere theoretical abstraction is evidenced most emphatically in all the stubborn outbreaks of national, ethnic, racial, and religious loyalties at a moment when such loyalties were expected to be dissolved by the deterritorializing thrust of global capitalism.

We know that modernity was founded on a definitive break with the authority of our ancestors, who were no longer conceived as the ground for our actions or beliefs. Yet the undermining of their authority confronted us with another difficulty; it is as if in rendering our ancestors fallible we had transformed the past from the repository of their already accomplished deeds and discovered truths into a kind of holding cell of all that was unactualized and unthought. Suddenly it was the *desire* of our ancestors and thus the virtual past, the past that had never come to pass or had not yet been completed, that weighed disturbingly on us. The theorization of this unfinished past was focused in the West around the concept of anxiety.[11] If it seemed necessary to come to terms theoretically with anxiety—as it did to Kierkegaard, Freud, and Heidegger, among others—this is because this affect bore witness to an altered relation to a past now conceived as incompletely actualized. The assumption that modern man would become pliable (to market forces or even the force of his own will) rested on the belief that the break with the authoritative past placed a zero in the denominator of our foundations, rooted us in, or attached us to—precisely nothing. But anxiety, the affect that arises in moments when radical breaks in the continuity of existence occur, belies this assumption; subjects find themselves, rather, to be "not without roots," which is significantly different from feeling rooted in the past, to a race or ethnicity that is transparent to us. For what is affirmed in the experience of being riveted is nothing that can be objectified or personalized as one's own.[12] It is, rather, the experience of being attached to a "prehistoric Other that it is impossible to forget," even if—in being without attributes—it offers us nothing to remember.[13]

It has been observed that anxiety often overtakes revolutionaries immediately after revolutions, and seems not to free but to paralyze the hand that would draft a new constitution. What accounts for this curious phenomenon? While many psychoanalysts were insisting that anxiety was an affective response to loss or abandonment, Freud reasoned that this could not be so, since the proper response to loss would be mourning, not anxiety. Like Freud, the philosophers mentioned maintained that anxiety is not dependent on any actual condition, albeit one of loss, but rather on "a condition that is not." Kierkegaard offers a clarifying illustration of the difference: The feeling of anxiety is not captured, he says, by the complaint, "My God, my God, why hast thou forsaken me?" but rather by the entreaty, "What you are going to do, do quickly!"[14] Anxiety is not the experience of a loss that has taken place; it is the experience of some impending event, the anticipation of something that, while connected to what precedes us, has not yet happened. It is the looming of the unknown, the awakening of a possibility whose contours are indiscernible.

In other words, the break instituted by modernity did not render the past totally dead to us. It did not abandon us to a solitary present divorced from the past, but handed us over to a present that felt overpopulated—not, as is usually said, because of the increasing density of cities or our bombardment by an increasing number of new stimuli, but because we seemed to be parasitized by an excess that refused to disclose itself to us. Anxiety is the feeling of being stuck to an excess that we can neither separate ourselves from nor lay claim to, of being tied to a past that, not having happened, cannot be shed. Our implication in the past thus took on a different complexion. For, while formerly a subject's ties to her past were rigidly binding, they were experienced as external, as of the order of simple constraint. One had to submit to a destiny one did not elect and often experienced as unjust. But one could—like Job or the heroes and heroines of classical tragedies—rail against one's destiny, curse one's fate. With modernity this is no longer possible. The "God of destiny" is now dead and we no longer inherit the debts of our ancestors, but become that debt. We are unable to distance ourselves sufficiently from the desire of our ancestors to curse the fate it hands us, but must, as Lacan put it, "bear as *jouissance* the injustice that horrifies us."[15] *Jouissance*—roughly equivalent to Freud's libido—names our capacity to put ourselves forward and determine our destiny. Yet unlike libido, it characterizes this capacity as something we cannot possess and thus as horrifying: a monstrous otherness that is not at our disposal, but must rather be suffered.

If we think once more of the revolutionary whose hand is paralyzed by anxiety, we will see how closely Lacan's account hews to Freud's account of anxiety. If, stricken by anxiety, my hand goes on strike, refuses to write, this is because it has become saturated with libido, gripped by *jouissance*. My hand behaves, Freud explains, like a maid who, having begun a love affair with her master, refuses to continue doing her household chores.[16] In the moment of anxiety, one loses one's taste for ordinary, routinized life; cooking, cleaning, all practical interests; it is this automatic way of life that is paralyzed by anxiety. This analogy is, however, as Freud himself says, "rather absurd," insofar as it fails to account for the real situation of the maid, who, while torn away from her mundane duties, is now bound to a terrible, inscrutable master: her own libido, or potentiality. Elsewhere, Freud will dispense with the analogy and define anxiety more straightforwardly as *fear of one's own libido.*[17] As with Melville's Bartleby—the scrivener who goes on strike, refuses to write—we are struck by the involuted refusal, "I would prefer not to," the preference or *clinamen*, the flash of potentiality that will not unfold itself, but that manifests itself only as a tension-filled paralysis.

Kiarostami's protagonists exhibit a paralysis of this kind, one occasioned by their inability to comprehend the desire of their ancestors and thus their own place in the very culture to which they nevertheless maintain a feeling of anonymous belonging. One of the primary locations in *The Wind Will Carry Us* is a cemetery to which Behzad continuously repairs to pick up a stronger cell phone signal and where Youssef, a gravedigger, continuously digs, remaining thus underground and invisible throughout most of the film. We surmise that the purpose of his efforts is ultimately the installation of a telecommunications tower, but since Mrs. Malek is on the verge of death, the digging simultaneously hints at preparations for her funeral. That a burial ground would become the site of telecommunications efforts bespeaks an anxiety attendant upon the loss of any clear signals issuing from a past that remains inscrutable. Eventually, the earth beneath which he digs caves in on Youssef, who has to be dug out. But the unsteadiness of the ground is not unique to this film; it is a constant in Kiarostami's work, where the salient characteristic of the earth is its unsteadiness: it is always caving in, buckling, quaking.[18] The ground in all his films seems ungrounded, hollowed out—or more precisely, *catacombed.* While earthquakes are a difficult geographical fact of life in Iran, Kiarostami's continuous reference to this datum in his films turns it into a fact of another order; no longer just an uncompromising truth of the terrain, it becomes a cultural fact the meaning of which cannot be unearthed. Like the past buried in it, the ground turns out in Kiarostami's world to be active and shifting, an unsettled affair. It is as if the past itself were under construction in his films.

In *The Wind Will Carry Us*, it is not only Youssef who remains invisible to us throughout the film; several characters—eleven by Kiarostami's count—remain out of frame and thus unseen. Asked by an interviewer what these curiously insistent visual absences signified, Kiarostami replied that the film is about "beings without being."[19] In *Where Is the Friend's House?* (1986), "being without being"—that is, being that *is* not, but which, remaining unrealized, perplexes characters by affixing itself to them—assumes the form of a notebook which a young schoolboy is certain is not his own, though it appears in all particulars exactly like his. He spends the majority of the film trying unsuccessfully to return it, mysteriously deciding in the end not to give it back to its ostensible owner. Effectively, the notebook has no exclusive owner but becomes the bond between the two students. In *Taste of Cherry* (1997), the anxiety-provoking element fails to take the form of a putative object and instead infuses the film with a perplexing textual opacity. The film follows a middle-aged man, Mr. Badii, who has no discernible reason for discontent (far from it) and yet spends the entire film trying to find an accomplice to his suicide, one who will promise to cover him with twenty shovels-full of dirt and double-check to make sure he is really and truly dead. From this we suspect that Mr. Badii is bothered by a fear of being buried alive. It is as if he were trying not simply to kill himself, but to extinguish some surplus of self that does not respond to his wishes and thus impresses him as capable of surviving even his death.

Speaking in an interview about *Taste of Cherry*, Kiarostami offered this comment: "The choice of death is the only prerogative possible [...] because everything in our lives has been imposed by birth [...] our parents, our home, our nationality, our build, the color of our skin, our culture."[20] Though Mr. Badii has no personal complaint, the thick presence of militia, the oppressive evidence of poverty, and the dust of industrialization visible in the urban perimeter through which he drives suggest choking. His suicide is thus readable as an attempt to escape the suffocation brought on by a world where one's identity is laid down by authorities who leave no room for freedom, no chance to choose what form one's life will take. And yet, if that which is imposed on us by birth is as enigmatic as Kiarostami's films tell us it is, then the rigidity of a life laid out by law must be read as a means of *dodging* a more primary experience, that of anxiety, which is stirred in us by an encounter with our capacity to break from this rigidity.[21] What Mr. Badii cannot abide is being riveted to the inscrutable desire of his ancestors, imposed on him by his birth into a culture that appears radically heteroclite. It is the incomprehensibility of "unrealized being," of his own potentiality, which suffocates him. He seeks through suicide to escape not the actual restrictions his culture imposes, but the overcrowded space in which he finds himself bound to its unreadable imperative.

THE AFFECTIVE TONALITY OF CAPITALISM

My reason for lingering so long on anxiety is this: shame only becomes comprehensible in relation to anxiety. Fundamental to both shame and anxiety is the sense of being able neither to integrate nor to divorce oneself from a strangeness that is "closer to [oneself] than [one's] jugular vein."[22] So similar are these affects that Levinas, in his early work *On Escape*, differentiates them only by the tiny hiccup of hope that is present in anxiety and dashed in shame. Like others, including Freud and Lacan, Levinas characterizes anxiety as a kind of state of emergency, a signal or imperative to flee, to escape the alarming strangeness that grips us. It is only when this imperative faces the impossibility of success that anxiety turns dejectedly to shame. But where Levinas takes it for granted that it is the *hope* of flight that fades in shame, I will argue that what disappears is the *imperative* of flight.

While many Lacanians claim that anxiety is an *exceptional* affect (much like respect for the moral law in Kant), Lacan himself called it the *only* affect. I prefer to merge the two by approaching anxiety as the *stem cell of affects*, which is transformed *in situ*, in different social theaters, to produce guilt and shame. The society of others serves a civilizing function not, as is usually said, because it tames primitive animal instincts, but because it colonizes our savage, inhuman *jouissance*. Unable to tolerate being alone with this inhuman partner, we find in the company of others, in society, some means of mollifying the anxious sense of our estrangement from ourselves. This point prepares us to approach again the distinction I made at the outset between shame and guilt as two different relations to our culture, or as we can now say, two ways of distancing ourselves from the stifling sense of foreignness imparted to us by our own culture.

The unctuous aggressiveness exhibited by Behzad toward Zeynab is only one episode of his generally insensitive behavior. As he hangs around Siah Darreh waiting for Mrs. Malek to die, he occupies himself not only with bothering Zeynab, but also with trying to take photographs of villagers who cover their faces and command him to put his camera away. The film clearly indicts him for his rudeness and indiscretion, but in what precisely do his crimes consist, and why do the villagers not want their pictures taken? If every subject as alien to herself lacks a proper image of who she is, why is Behzad's attempt to offer the villagers photographs of themselves counted as an act of rudeness or malice, rather than one of kindness? One of the villagers in *Life and Nothing More* seems to respond directly to this question when he complains to Farhad, the film-director protagonist of that film, that the images of the villagers captured by his camera make the villagers appear "*worse than they are*."

It is not the taking of photographs per se, but these particular photographs that are the problem. Behzad and Farhad travel to the villages to document, to archive phenomena on the verge of disappearing. Their mission is to capture a world in the process of being lost, people about to die or presumed to be buried in rubble, ritual practices and ways of life on the edge of extinction. The imminence of loss, of death, licenses the rudeness of the photographers, justifying in their minds their indiscreet attempts to snatch from loss—from transitory, fleeting life—something lasting, images that can be stored in the memory banks of their culture. But it is not merely the race against time that powers their rudeness, for these nosy archivists believe they confront an additional obstacle in the villagers themselves, who refuse, they assume, to disclose to them the information they seek to record. In other words, what these diegetic film directors disregard while making their images is the *jouissance* of the villagers that renders them incomprehensible to themselves. These colonizing directors want to pry from the villagers secrets that are not theirs to disclose and thus to claim for the light, for the order of the visible, every dark, hidden thing.

Is Behzad's obscene rudeness not of the same sort as that made scandalously evident in the Abu Ghraib photographs? The problem is not simply that the photographers in each case invaded the privacy of those whom they photographed; it consists, rather, in the same obscene denial that there is any obscene, any off-screen, that cannot be exposed to a persistent, prying eye. The ultimate crime of both series of photographs, the source of their malicious abjuration of respect, is their assumption that the photographed subjects *have no privacy to invade.* This is the bottom line, the point on which I am insisting: privacy cannot be invaded, cannot be penetrated, either by the subject or by others.

At the dawn of the twentieth century, Nietzsche expressed his scorn for that century's characteristic and misguided belief that it was possible to see *through* everything.[23] He protested the lack of reverence and discretion that fueled his contemporaries' tactless preoccupation with disclosing and unmasking everything. "Nothing is so nauseating in [...] the believers in 'modern ideas,'" he scoffed, "as their lack of shame, their complaisant impudence of eye and hand with which they touch, lick, and finger everything."[24] This frenzied desire to cast aside every veil, penetrate every surface, transgress every barrier standing between us and the real thing lying behind it installed in the modern world a new sort of "beyondness," a new untouchable, one that is in principle there for the grasping, even if in actuality it is always out of reach. This secularized sacred, which inspires a new, modern desire for transgression, does not originate in a belief in the existence of another world, but in the belief that what we want in this world always lies just behind some roadblock preventing our access to it.

This new "beyondness" is held in place by a definable structure, that of guilt, which must be understood not in its limited, psychological sense, but in the sense I proposed above: a specific form of relation to one's own culture. Agamben offers in passing a broader definition of guilt in line with our own; in *Homo Sacer*, he defines "the cipher of this capture of life in law" (that is, the cipher of biopolitics) as "guilt (not in the technical sense [...] but in the originary sense that indicates a being-in-debt: *in culpa esse*), which is to say, precisely the condition of being included through an exclusion, of being in relation to something from which one is excluded or which one cannot fully assume."[25] It is the phrase "being in relation to something one cannot [...] assume" that first catches our attention, because it happens to be the one

Levinas uses to describe anxiety and shame, the complex feeling of being riveted to an inalienable and opaque surplus of being. Agamben sets Levinas's phrase alongside an apposite one of his own, "being in relation to something from which one is excluded." The latter phrase absorbs and slightly alters the former and thereby defines guilt as a transformation of anxiety. Like anxiety, the feeling of guilt consists in a feeling of being unable to coincide with oneself by integrating the troubling surplus of being; in guilt, however, this inability is no longer experienced as being stuck to an inalienable alienness, but as an inability to close the distance that separates us from something that excludes us. How does this transformation come about? How does one become *excluded* from a part of oneself with which one cannot quite catch up, rather than attached to what one cannot assume?

We find our answer in the Freudian theory of guilt, in the paradox of the superego (which punishes obedience with guilt) that is inextricable from the paradox of ego and cultural ideals (which we are simultaneously enjoined to live up to and forbidden to attain). Faced with the unbearable opaqueness we are to ourselves, with the unassumable excess that sticks to us, we unburden ourselves by allowing the ideals set up by society to become blueprints for our identity and action and to thereby provide us with some clarity. Through cultural ideals, the question of what it means to belong to a culture is silenced and replaced by mesmerizing cultural goals that gather awestruck subjects. But because every ideal is sustained by a prohibition against attaining it, we are always in debt to them, always in arrears to our ego and cultural ideals, which insert us into our culture precisely by excluding us from its inner sanctum. The very prohibition/exclusion that binds us to these ideals also invites transgression. What is forbidden lures us with its unattainability—if only we could summon the courage to disobey, the fortitude to step over the line. In short, ideals are the source of that secularized sacred deplored by Nietzsche, the just-beyond-reach that ignores the impenetrability of one's own as well as others' self-opacity. What was hidden and paralyzing is now tantalizingly close and urges transgression.

The Ego and the Id presents an argument about guilt profoundly tributary to this one. There, Freud writes that "reflection [...] shows us that no external vicissitudes can be experienced or undergone by the id, except by way of the ego, which is the representative of the external world to the id. Nevertheless *it is not possible to speak of direct inheritance in the ego*. It is here that *the gulf between an actual individual and the concept of a species becomes evident*."[26] I understand this "no direct inheritance in the ego" as sanction to treat cultural inheritance *as* libido or *jouissance* excited by the brush with ancestral desire. This inheritance can only lead to anxiety, however, and so must go through the external world, through society, if it is to be accessed or unfolded in some way. The meandering route of inheritance leaves its mark in the fact that the subject is never completely absorbed into her culture, but is always slightly misaligned with it.

We have yet to see what this means for shame, but for guilt we can now see that it entails a drive to attain what can never be fully acquired and a sense of exclusion from some sacred core of being. With regard to the question of photographic images that is raised in Kiarostami's films, we can now add the following: if these images make their subjects look worse than they are, this is because the photographs taken by these diegetic filmmakers hold the order of appearances in disdain. For them, appearances are always only a nuisance standing in the way of truth; they lack the dignity of the true. In *The Wind Will Carry Us*, the fault lies not only with Behzad, but also with the villagers who scar themselves to attract the attention of their bosses. These villagers seem to have bought into the capitalist belief that there is nothing that is not ripe for exposure. They, too, have begun to acquire that immodest, capitalist taste for what C.S. Lewis referred to as a "very cheap [form of] frankness."[27]

In this light, the Islamic system of modesty—with its volatile disdain for the modern passion for exposing everything, its loud protestations and rigid protections against the "touching, licking, and fingering" of everything—would seem to offer an important antidote to the global immodesty fashioned by Western capitalism. The system of modesty undeniably targets a worthy enemy, but the question before us is whether it adopts effective measures against its target, whether it succeeds or fails to protect the subject's modesty. With this question in mind, we return to the fresh milk sequence in *The Wind Will Carry Us* to determine if it deserves the tongue lashing Dabashi gives it.

SCENES OF SHAME

As Behzad descends into the subterranean chamber, the catacomb, where he will catch up with Zeynab, we are invited to wonder, "What sort of place is this?" One need not know anything about villages in Northern Iran to know that not even here do people milk cows in pitch black underground caves. This is no ordinary or actual location, no touristic glimpse of some of Iran's exotic landscape; it is rather an example of "visionary geography," a liminal space defined in Islamic philosophy as the place from which new forms emerge.[28] After Behzad crosses the threshold, the screen goes black for several long seconds, as if to mark the absolute separation of this from the other spaces in the film. Holding on the black screen for an uncomfortably long time, Kiarostami also allows the depth of the blinding darkness in which Zeynab remains enshrouded to sink in. From the bright sunlight outside, we pass into a place so luminous that nothing stands out against it; a place filled with a light so intense that nothing in it is distinguishable from anything else, a place of pure exposure, of dazzling blackness. While the screen is still black, the voice of Behzad inquires, "Is there anyone here?" Answerable in the negative, this question is more profound than it might first seem. For there is in fact no one here in this darkness, no "I," only the milking of a cow, the gerundive form of the action Zeynab is performing substantivized, lacking any subjective support.

In *Being and Nothingness*, Sartre describes a scene that is in many points similar to this one in *The Wind Will Carry Us.* A voyeur, crouched before a keyhole, peers through it intently. At this point, there is nothing but this pure act of looking, peering through a keyhole, the act that totally absorbs the voyeur.[29] The voyeur himself is not present. He is precipitated out from his act as a subject only at the point when a sudden rustling of leaves startles him and fills him with shame. The voyeur appears only *as* the experience of shame, as shame-full in the precise sense. It is only when he senses his being looked at by the "gaze" of an indeterminate other that the voyeur acquires a sentiment of self. The sentiment of self and the experience of shame are synonymous. The scenes from Kiarostami and Sartre are similar, then, in that in each the gerundive form of an act—milking a cow, peering through a keyhole—indicates the absence of a subject, whose emergence will be marked only later by the arousal of shame.

The apparent dissimilarity between the two acts may make my analogy sound tenuous, however, and so I will address this difficulty by focusing first on the scene of peering through a keyhole. What does Sartre say about it? Surprisingly little. In fact, he seems remarkably intent on refraining from drawing too much attention to the act in which his Peeping Tom is engaged when interrupted by the gaze. This polite inattention is partly explained by the fact that Sartre does not want to distract from his point that he is not speaking of shame in the "civic" sense, as he says. By this he seems to mean that sense in which, having already entered polite society and learned its rules, one is disgraced by being caught breaking one of them. Sartre is concerned, rather, with a more fundamental sense of shame as that feeling that attends the insertion of the subject into society, his sudden immersion in a world of others. This insertion into the social precedes all measure and every rule by which a subject might find himself judged. It is not, therefore, the nature of his act, the fact that it is one of *lascivious* looking, that causes the voyeur shame, but the fact that the gaze makes him suddenly aware of the presence of others as such.

There can be no denying, however, that there is something more going on in Sartre's refusal to utter a peep about this peeping. Plainly, he is sanitizing the scene, scrubbing it clean of sex. Less discreet, Lacan returns to the scene precisely to highlight the presence of sex in it. It is not by chance, he unblinkingly observes, that shame catches the voyeur in a moment of desire. He does not reject Sartre's argument that the gaze of the Other does not judge the act of the voyeur as socially unacceptable, nor try to stop it by prohibiting it. But to deny the censoriousness of the gaze is not to deny any relation between it and desire. Lacan's point is just that: rather than condemn or prohibit, the gaze *enflames* desire; shame *is* a sexual "conflagration."[30]

Excising sex, Sartre produces a chaste reading of the shame scenario, which he turns into a bathetic drama wherein an abstract and sovereign act of looking is forced to confront its anchorage in the vulnerability of its bodily foundations. The rustling of leaves functions as a kind of index finger that picks out the voyeur, rendering him painfully conspicuous, a body too much in a scene where he thought himself bodiless and unobserved. The emperor of seeing is suddenly brought down, reduced to the dead weight of his body, his body as object. Sartre trades the censoring function that is usually ascribed to the gaze for an alternative function: limitation. In his interpretation, what the gaze exposes is the subject's finitude; it reminds us that others as such set limits on our freedom, impede our actions and get in the way of our plans. The body exposed by shame is thus nothing more than a figure for this limitation of my freedom; it is a body that can be hurt by others, that remains ever vulnerable to all that is external to and opposes it.

From this point we can begin to measure the consequences of Lacan's opposition to Sartre's sanitization of the scene, which is stated in the following counter insistence: "It is *not* the annihilating subject, correlative of the world of objectivity, who feels himself surprised, but the subject sustaining himself in a function of desire."[31] If it is not the subject who experiences his freedom as limited by others who experiences shame, then neither is the body at stake in this experience the stupid, delimited object Sartre imagines. One problem with the latter's reading is that it fails to capture the squirminess of shame, which is more clearly evoked in Kiarostami's sequence by the camera's exposure of the cow's udders as they are being milked by Zeynab. It is not the body as figure of limitation, but the body as figure of one's nakedness that is exposed by shame. The nakedness of the body is not, however, a simple function of its being unclothed. As is attested in Kiarostami's scene and by the obsessive fears that, at its extreme, haunt the *hejab* system—which visualizes in the clicking of a woman's heels the place where her legs join her body, and in the cadences of her voice the softness of her skin—one can remain naked beneath yards of clothing. As we will see, the dialectic of shame eschews simple opposition (naked/clothed or exposed/concealed). For now, we can say that the body's nakedness is a function of its sexualization. Sexualized, the body is vulnerable not, as in Sartre's version of the story, to other subjects, but to the savage otherness of its own libido. The sexualized body is one whose boundaries have already been breached, one that has suffered an irreparable and constitutive hurt.

Lacan's reintroduction of sexuality into the Sartrean account of shame paves the way for us to reconnect shame to anxiety, while reexamining Levinas's argument about their relation and the question of cultural inheritance they raise. Although Levinas does not explicitly conceive the surplus that rivets the subject as *libido*, his argument does broach the question of racial inheritance, and sexual pleasure does emerge in his discussion at the point at which shame is introduced.[32] Levinas' argument is that, while pleasure promises escape from anxiety, shame testifies to the inadequacy of sexual pleasure, which proves incapable of delivering on this promise. Earlier I left hanging the question of the validity of this argument about shame's disappointment. I return to it now by taking a look at one more scene of shame made famous by its theorization: I refer to the scene Agamben introduces in *Remnants of Auschwitz* to flesh out Levinas' theory of shame.

Originally recounted by Robert Antelme, the scene concerns a student from Bologna who is arbitrarily picked out of a line of students by an S.S. officer and thereby marked for execution.[33] Remarkably, the unfortunate student does not question his selection nor persist in looking over his shoulder in hopes of discovering that it was someone other than he who had been selected. No, the pink flush of his cheeks signs his recognition that it is he who has been designated and that he will not try to escape this fact. The dead certainty that accompanies anxiety sticks, too, we see, to shame. This common sense of certainty may in part be what leads Levinas to nearly conflate the two affects, with the small distinction that shame is certainty more emphatic because more fatalistic. Not only do I know beyond doubt that *I am that*, that which rivets me; I also know that there is no escape from *that. That is that.* The reddening of the Italian student's face would seem to blurt out an "I am here," a resigned surrender to the fate handed him by the S.S. officer. But is that really the end of it? Does the sudden surging up of the question of pleasure in Levinas's discussion of shame not betray a disavowed recognition that some difference is being overlooked? Is Levinas not guilty, in short, of the same error as Sartre, of de-eroticizing shame? The heat and glow that suffuses the face of the one shamed telegraphs this eroticization and their error.

On the elementary level of description there is a common distinction between anxiety and shame that we must now consider. While anxiety manifests itself in an impulse to flee, shame is manifested in an impulse to hide. Levinas's argument depends on our reading this transformation of the impulse as necessitated by the *defeat* of its first manifestation: because flight is hopeless, all I can do is try to hide. But this is not the proper way to read this transformation, which depends, rather, on an alteration of my relation to that which anxiety desires to escape. To test this hypothesis, we need to take a closer look at the relation between exposure and concealment, which may be said to substitute for the anxious relation between paralysis and flight. Although the relation is usually assumed to be sequential—exposure coming first, followed by the defensive attempt to conceal—the pink cheeks of the student from Bologna raise questions about this assumption. As much as his blush broadcasts his presence, it also seems like the lowering of a shade to shutter or shield him from view. It is as if in his very exposure, his very visibility, he were announcing his disappearance from view, his retreat.

If blushing, the most common visual manifestation of shame, is critical to understanding it, this is because this affect has a special relation to sight, to the gaze, in contrast to guilt, in which the relation to the voice is what matters. Even when it is a sound that occasions shame, the experience of it is one of being looked at, submitted to a gaze. This is how it happens that the question of shame intersects the question of the image in Kiarostami's cinema. What shame seeks is the same thing Kiarostami, as filmmaker, wants to create: an image that is capable of capturing the reflection of what has no image. Be attentive, for here is where the detour through anxiety repays its costs. Those who dispense with this detour are precisely those who end up regarding shame as a passive suffering of exposure to a look against which only a pathetic defense is available: cowering beneath covers. Exactly what does the gaze expose? This is a question about which there is far too little reflection. It is easy to accept the description offered above—shame erupts in response to a rupturing of the circuit of communication-recognition—as supplying the following answer: the gaze exposes a different, less flattering image of ourselves than we previously held. But this is clearly a mistake, for what the gaze makes visible is that very thing that *has no image*, that unassumable, opaque surplus of self that anxiety wants to be rid of. In shame, however, the inalienable alienness that attaches itself to me no longer threatens me with its suffocating over-presence, but comes to define the *intimate distance* that constitutes my sense of interiority, my sense of myself as subject.

I have from the start been trying to define shame as a sense of self. It might be helpful at this point to turn this strategy around by defining the experience of self through shame. Philosophers have taught us that the self, or subject, can never be experienced as a coincidence of the self with itself, but is experienced rather as the gap or void that forever separates me from myself. The void left by the destruction of the Twin Towers would thus conveniently serve to represent Sedgwick's feeling of shame as a feeling of self. But while this account is not altogether incorrect, it is anemic. We look to psychoanalysis, then, for a more robust account of the same experience, and begin to locate it in the proposition that the subject's inability to coincide with herself stems from the fact that (her) libido or *jouissance* appears more like something that attaches itself to her than something she is. The various affects of anxiety, guilt, and shame make plain a further inadequacy of the bald philosophical assertion that the subject experiences herself as void. For not every—but only one particular—experience of the gap separating me from myself offers an experience of self. In anxiety, the gap is felt as an overwhelming and paralyzing opacity; in guilt, as an exclusion from myself. How can the experience of my non-transparency to myself be anything but a negative one, as these two—of pending annihilation or continuous failure—are? How can the gaze that causes shame expose, make visible, the *jouissance* I cannot assume without making me transparent to myself? What is the experience of self to which shame holds the key?

Imagine a young girl sitting contentedly at a soda fountain with her polite, well-to-do friends, sipping a milkshake as she looks distractedly into the mirror behind the counter. Suddenly the image of her mother, who has just ambled into the drugstore, appears in the mirror. It is a ridiculous image of a preposterously festooned mother; seeing it, the daughter burns with shame.[34] If shame is the experience not of some object (and the girl does not therefore feel shame for her mother or for herself), but is rather the feeling of self, how is this truth exemplified in the scene? Why does the appearance of the mother's image cause shame? It is unlikely that the reflection in the mirror would have caused shame if it had been that of a stranger or an acquaintance to whom the girl was indifferent. It matters that there is a strong bond of love connecting the daughter to the mother; without this there would be no shame. Something about the daughter that is normally hidden is exposed in the scene, but it is not that this silly woman *is* her mother, nor is it that she is more like her mother than her fine manners and tastes have so far let on.

What shame exposes is her love for her mother—though to state it this way is not yet to capture the feeling precisely. The daughter's love for her mother has been fully evident before this event, to others and to the daughter herself, just as the interest of Sartre's voyeur in what is happening on the other side of the keyhole is evident. But these experiences of love and intense curiosity are, up to the moment the gaze appears, consumed by the objects on which they are lavished and the actions they entail. The moment of shame arrives when the subject who loves or peers intently through the keyhole makes herself visible to herself and others as a subject, as the one who loves, is curious, desires. The subject sees herself *as desiring, as actively submitting to the passion of her attachments*. It matters less what incident occasions the feeling or what else the subject is doing at the time; what matters is that, at the moment the gaze appears, the subject experiences herself as engaged in active submission to some passion.

To put this in terms of the proposal I made regarding the psychoanalytic invigoration of philosophy, this experience of self as subject *is the same one* philosophy describes, an experience of the void that prevents me from coinciding with myself, understood now as an encounter with *jouissance*. In contrast to the feeling of being parasited by a crushing presence or punishing superego, however, this feeling is one of *enjoying one's jouissance*. It may at first seem surprising that the experience of oneself as subject is not one of "pure activity," but one of "passivity," or the assumption of a "feminine attitude" (to use Freud's terms), but this is the description of the experience of self that shame makes available.

One of the finest illustrations of this psycho-philosophical point is found in Joan Riviere's justly famous case study.[35] The unnamed patient is a woman who constantly battles anxiety. Curiously, this does not manifest itself as performance anxiety; a political activist with a strong intellect and oratorical skills, she frequently delivers public lectures. Her problem is a post-performance anxiety that befalls her *after* these speeches, which she deals with through "compulsive ogling" and flirting with men from the audience and through the fantasmatic production of scenarios in which she submits herself sexually to black men while plotting against them. Riviere contends that the woman's anxiety is aroused by a fear that she will be caught in possession of something (the phallus) that is not rightly hers (but has been stolen from her father) and that her defense strategy is to pretend *not* to have it by concealing her possession of it. We know that anxiety is caused by a surplus that one feels is not rightly one's own; but that surplus possesses the subject, not the other way around. It is obvious that this woman wants desperately to make an appearance, to exhibit herself on the public stage in order to escape the oblivion anxiety threatens, but her public speech-making seems inadequate to the task. The reason? Alienating herself in her professional role, she disappears into it; there is no remainder, no subject left over. She thus resorts to a different strategy: making herself visible in shameful scenes of degradation or the performance of demeaning tasks. That these are not scenes of simple passivity is evident in her plots to turn these men over to justice or to escape them. It is quite apparent that she is pulling the strings in these scenarios, actively passive within them.

A number of other questions spring from this; let us return to the fresh milk sequence (readable alongside the other scenes of shame we have looked at) and approach them from there. A simple village girl and a minor character in the narrative, Zeynab moves about her world without any particular self-awareness, absorbed by everyday chores. In the intimate grotto-like space in which the scene is set, however—a space associated with burial, unforgettable ancestors, and the pressure of their desire on her—she is foregrounded, drawn out of herself. It is not Behzad's impertinent look that disturbs her; she is relatively indifferent to him and his bad manners. What interrupts her complacency, her full absorption in the world, is the erotic poem by Forugh Farrokhzad that Behzad reads to her as part of his bungled attempt at seduction. From the interior of the poem, the gaze emerges and is even explicitly mentioned: "the earth/ screeching to a halt,/ something unknown watching you and me/ beyond this window."[36] Visibly fascinated by this poem, the red-robed Zeynab is not *entirely* exposed (for this would render her simply passive), but rather exposes herself (an active passivity) as desiring. It is important to reemphasize this distinction to prevent shame from being reduced, as it too often is, to a retiring shyness, even though some have correctly observed that this affect often manifests itself as a "bold [...]

candor," in candid acknowledgments of the libidinal investments that ravish and surprise.[37] Another point not to be missed, once again, is that this feeling of submission to one's own *jouissance* (which appears to us as something that attaches itself to us) is not a solipsistic experience, but only arises in connection with an investment of one's *jouissance* (its attachment to objects) in a way that allows Zeynab to appear without losing herself in her appearance.

How to appear without disappearing into our appearance? This is finally the question we must answer. Think of the extreme poles of shame scenarios. On the one hand, the first horrified sight of the death camps by liberating armies, which was said to have aroused shame and thus to have forced witnesses to look away. On the other, "actions of love and extravagant generosity," in response to which Nietzsche once said, "nothing is more advisable than to take a stick and give any eyewitnesses a sound thrashing."[38] Why do we avert our gaze and feel shame in response to the inhumanly awful and the exquisitely beautiful? The first answer likely to be offered must be discarded, for shame involves no taboo against looking or touching. To distinguish this affect from guilt requires us to refuse taboo—which is uttered from a beyond in order to protect a beyond—any say in the matter. Declaring something untouchable, out of bounds, taboo not only creates a beyond, a sacred zone set apart from us; it also incites, as we noted, a counter-imperative to transgress the boundaries excluding us from that sacred place, to touch, finger, penetrate with our look all it would withhold from us. Still, we cannot deny that shame often betrays itself in an *averted look.* The averted look is not, however, a sign of obedience to a stricture against looking, but of the appearance of a new opportunity to look: inward. It is as if our attention were directed not to a parallel, transcendent space, but to an *oblique* one slightly detached from visibility—the space of a self into which we could withdraw from the scene that engages us. This simultaneous relation between exposure and concealment now needs to be formulated.

In contrast to guilt, which introduces through prohibition a division between the sensible world and an ideal one that transcends it, shame operates without recourse to prohibition, ideals, or a heterogeneous realm outside the sensible; it operates, in other words, entirely within the sensible realm of vision, introducing there—within the visible—a division or slight separation of the visible and invisible. One could describe the experience of shame, in sum, as that of witnessing oneself hiding, as the sense that one has ducked behind one's appearance. Between the appearance and what remains invisible no interdiction intervenes; nothing is prohibited from appearing. It is a question, rather, of an appearance that *permits* something to disappear.

What is it that thus permits me to disappear? What allows me to camouflage myself behind my visibility? That very thing that has dominated the scene while avoiding analysis up until now: the gaze. Sartre brings it into focus and makes a breakthrough in conceptualizing it. The gaze, he says, cannot be matched to an actual pair of eyes; it is not locatable in a person. The gaze has no bearer, belongs to no one. If, feeling a gaze rest upon me, I scan the subway car to try to pin it on some suspicious-looking person, the experience of the gaze will evaporate at each point on which my accusation alights. There is a fantasmatic dimension of the gaze that suggests it cannot be contained within an intersubjective dialectic. But, in the end, Sartre does not follow up on this suggestion and thus the a-personal dimension of the gaze serves in his account merely to enhance the power of the Other by effacing his limits. The fact that I cannot attach it to the actual eyes of an objectified other gives the gaze all the more power to objectify and limit me. This is a point Val Lewton, the legendary producer of horror films, well understood: do not show the horrible thing directly embodied in a person, for this will only have the effect of attenuating the threat.

Lacan reads the fantasmatic dimension of the gaze differently. There is no warrant, he argues, for Sartre's placement of the gaze exclusively on the side of an adversarial other. Detached from every observer, it is detached, too, from the voyeur and not only from the Other. It is as if, through participation in the social or public field, the voyeur were lent a gaze by which he is permitted to see himself appear. The gaze lends the subject the exteriority or detachment necessary to look back and see the one thing he was unable to see: his own appearance. What this recurvant gaze sees, however, is not merely the subject's emergent image, but the detachment that permits it to emerge. My image is my disguise, my veil; it enables me to appear in public while preserving my privacy. In a gesture of sleazy flattery, Behzad tries to establish some silly points of coincidence between Zeynab and Forugh, the leading Persian poet of the twentieth century. There is absolutely no sign, however, that Zeynab is interested in *being like* the poet. What interests Zeynab is *dissimulation* (the possibility of which is opened by the poem), the possibility of being able to present herself in public while remaining concealed.

Unlike anxiety, shame is not a signal to take action; it does not cry out for cover. It accompanies an action taken; it is the feeling of having found cover in the folds of one's appearance. Not "I am here," but "I lie here disguised." An S.S. officer may order me to step forward and I may obey by presenting myself before him. But to experience shame in doing so is to stand a little to the side of one's appearance and to remain there, undetected. Make no mistake: I can have no shame or shield *apart from* my appearance, for my interiority or self-intimacy is not a primitive condition but the recurvant effect of a certain form of publicity. If one takes anxiety as the subject's primitive condition, one sees that the "gaze of the Other"—the gaze I *borrow* from the Other, from the space of the Other—does serve to limit, not my freedom, but my devouring, limitless libido.

This is not inconsistent with my earlier point that the gaze *enflames desire*. The paradox of libido uncovered by Freud is that some limitation or obstacle is necessary, not to prevent it from spilling over into public space, but to "raise its tide," to reduce it to the measure of desire. Limitless, libido can only be felt as a danger to *my publicity*, to my emergence into appearance. The gaze is, however, a factor of limitation, it frames libido by objectifying it slightly, setting it at a minimum distance from me. Through contact with the external world, I meet with an obstacle. The gaze registers this obstacle by sending my look, like a shuttlecock, back toward me; it sees me as part of the world, *but does not censor or judge.* In fact it acts as a prophylactic to protect us against any all-seeing Censor.

The point is often made that censorship does not merely negate but is also productive. Without the Hays code, for example, no one would ever have known the "Lubitsch Touch," just as without *hejab* regulations, Iranian cinema might not have blossomed as it did. This flat dictum has never seemed satisfying to me. It is not simply censorship that produces great works of art, just as it is not every obstacle that raises the tide of libido. We know from our discussion of ego and social ideals that that there are some obstacles that can never be overcome because acts of transgression only fortify them. For censorship to be productive there must be some recognition that the Censor has a blind spot and thus some positive belief that the order of appearances is neither fully transparent to the Censor's or any other look, nor simply a realm of illusion and distortion and thus an inappropriate vehicle for the truth. The gaze looks back at me not only at that point where my look encounters its limit, but also where it encounters a fissure in the world or in the Censor's eyeball. I look at the place where the Twin Towers once stood or into the eyes of an S.S. officer and I encounter not just an obstacle to my look, but this fissure, this blind spot of the Other, from which point no destiny can be foreseen, not mine, not anyone's. For even if this moment marks the hour of my death, it is the accident of this death that shame highlights. My destiny finds harbor in my appearance and remains undisclosed, even to me.

A final point about the fresh milk sequence in Kiarostami's film. While I have attended only to the diegetic unfolding of shame in it, it is clear that a sense of shame pervades not only the diegetic situation, but also the audience's relation to this situation. Extremely discomfiting, the scene does not allow us to sit unobserved in the darkness of the auditorium, but forces us to experience our own uneasy, hidden presence *on the scene.* A gaze looks out from the screen and invites us to feel shame. The final quarrel I have with Dabashi's outraged response to the sequence is that it declines Kiarostami's invitation; it refuses shame by instead expressing shame for or on behalf of Zeynab, as if to distance Dabashi from the experience itself. I repeat my initial proposition: there is no such thing as "shame for." There is only shame, the experience of submitting to the gaze *oneself.* There are no spectators or witnesses to shame; one is always interior to the experience of it. Yet there is no denying that the gaze wounds; it severs the subject from herself and causes her to submit to an experience whose disturbing complexity is not adequately captured by the terms "pleasure" or "enjoyment." What happens, however, when one resists and tries through an alternative view of shame to defend oneself against the experience of it? In this case the gaze will be perceived, as in Sartre, as coming from without, from an annihilating other, and as falling on some poor others who are made to feel shame. From a safe distance, unaffected by its wounding, I will experience shame only secondhand, on behalf of these others. This is not, I would argue, a scenario of contagious sociality, but of a false, self-protective chivalry.

I have placed this discussion of shame *as a provocation* at the point of conflict between Islam and the West. One of the most heated and defining debates of that conflict centers on the forced wearing of the veil and the *hejab* system generally, which are met with violent condemnation in the West. The debate has thus far been too narrowly framed and ought to be broadened, I suggest, on the basis of a proper ontological understanding of shame. This understanding will raise serious challenges to both sides of the argument. The recurrent image in *The Wind Will Carry Us* of Behzad running about, trying to pick up a better signal for his mobile phone, brings to mind the historic debates over wiretapping in the U.S. During these debates, it was argued that privacy was not localizable in a delimited *space* that might then be ruled out of reach to the State, but was rather attached to the *subject* and remained inviolable no matter where a citizen might be, in public or in private space. This argument exemplifies the ideology of freedom on the basis of which the West opposes the *hejab* system and regards itself as superior to the Islamic world and its doctrine of submission. Yet the belief that the subject has property in the self, property privately held, is clearly untenable in the face of shame, which counts on publicity to dispossess the subject of that which it can never assume as property. On the other hand, the chivalry of the Islamic State can only strike one as a defensive posture, and raises the question whether the State's interpretation of submission is as radical as it needs to be or simply an avoidance of its deepest implications.

In any case, we owe this entire speculation to the modesty system's strict regulation of cinema, which, by obliging filmmakers to film mainly exterior spaces, set Kiarostami the task of demonstrating that interiority is not only compatible with, but dependent upon, the existence of an all-exterior world.

Notes

1. Imam Khomeini, "Address at Bihisht-i Zahra," in *Islam and Revolution: Writings and Declarations of Imam Khomeini*, trans. Hamid Algar (Berkeley: Mizan Press, 1981), 254-60. This speech, delivered on February 2, 1979, at a cemetery outside Tehran where martyrs of the Islamic Revolution were buried, took place the day after Khomeini arrived in Tehran from his ex-

ile in Paris.

2. The regulations aimed at "Islamicizing" Iranian cinema were ratified, and the Ministry of Culture and Islamic Guidance instituted them in February 1983. Hamid Naficy provides the most comprehensive and cogent analysis of the impact of these regulations on Iranian films; I rely heavily on his account. See, in particular, his "Veiled Vision/Powerful Presences: Women in Post-Revolutionary Iranian Cinema," in *Life and Art: The New Iranian Cinema*, ed. Rose Issa and Sheila Whitaker (London: NFT and BFI, 1999).

3. The source of my information about the relation between Raphael Patai's *The Arab Mind* and the strategy of "shaming" adopted by the U.S. at Abu Ghraib is Seymour M. Hersh, "The Gray Zone: How a secret Pentagon program came to Abu Ghraib," *New Yorker*, May 24, 2004, 38. All quotations in this paragraph are from Hersh's essay.

4. Eve Kosofsky Sedgwick, *Touching Feeling: Affect, Pedagogy, Performativity* (Durham: Duke University Press, 2003).

5. Ibid., 41.

6. Ibid., 37. On this paradox, see also Stanley Cavell, *Must We Mean What We Say?: A Book of Essays* (Cambridge: Cambridge University Press, 1976): "Shame [...] is the most isolating of feelings," but also "the most primitive of social responses," the "simultaneous discovery of the isolation of the individual; his presence to himself, but simultaneously to others" (286). References to this paradox are widespread and not limited to these exemplary instances.

7. Giorgio Agamben, *Remnants of Auschwitz: The Witness and the Archive*, trans. Daniel Heller-Roazen (New York: Zone Books, 1999), 110, 107.

8. Sedgwick, *Touching Feeling*, 37.

9. Hamid Dabashi's otherwise highly informative *Close-Up: Iranian Cinema Past, Present and Future* (London: Verso, 2001) explodes in its final chapter into an unfair (to my mind) rant against *The Wind Will Carry Us*.

10. Emmanuel Levinas, *On Escape*, trans. Bettina Bergo (Stanford: Stanford University Press, 2003), 52. For further discussion of Levinas and shame, see my "May '68, the Emotional Month," in *Lacan: The Silent Partners*, ed. Slavoj Žižek (London: Verso, 2006), 90-114.

11. My implication is that we should also look to Islamic philosophy for a theory of the "unfinished past." See, for example, Henry Corbin's "Prologue" to his study of Islamic philosophy in *Spiritual Body and Celestial Earth: From Mazdean Iran to Shi'ite Iran*, trans. Nancy Pearson (Princeton: Princeton University Press, 1977): "Our authors suggest that if our past were really what we believe it to be, that is, completed and closed, it would not be the grounds of such vehement discussions. They suggest that all our *acts*

of understanding are so many recommencements, re-*iterations* of events still unconcluded" (xv).

12. Rudi Visker, in *Truth and Singularity: Taking Foucault into Phenomenology* (Dordrect: Kluwer Academic Publishers, 1999), adopts this same phrase in conformity with Lacan's definition of anxiety as "not without object." Arriving at shame through anxiety, Visker offers a theory of the former similar to my own, even though he does not focus on the question of *jouissance.* The idea of a paradoxical, rootless root can be traced backed to Heidegger's discussion of imagination in his Kantbook.

13. Jacques Lacan, *The Seminar of Jacques Lacan, Book VII: The Ethics of Psychoanalysis, 1959-1960*, ed. Jacques-Alain Miller, trans. Dennis Porter (New York: W.W. Norton & Company, 1992), 71.

14. Søren Kierkegaard, *The Concept of Anxiety: A Simple Psychologically Orienting Deliberation on the Dogmatic Issue of Hereditary Sin* (Princeton: Princeton University Press, 1980), 155.

15. Jacques Lacan, *Le Séminaire de Jacques Lacan, Livre VIII: Le transfert*, ed. Jacques-Alain Miller (Paris: Seuil, 1991), 155.

16. Sigmund Freud, *Inhibitions, Symptoms, and Anxiety*, in *The Standard Edition of the Complete Psychological Works of Sigmund Freud* (hereafter *SE*), ed. and trans. James Strachey et al. (London: Hogarth Press, 1953-1974), 20: 77-174. "Analysis shows that when activities like [...] writing [...] are subjected to neurotic inhibitions it is because [...] the fingers [...] have become too strongly eroticized. It has been discovered as a general fact that the ego-function of an organ is impaired if its erotogenicity—its sexual significance—is increased. It behaves, if I may be allowed a rather absurd analogy, like a maid-servant who refuses to go on cooking because her master has started a love-affair with her" (89-90).

17. Ibid., 84.

18. Jean-Luc Nancy notes the instability of the earth in Kiarostami's films in his excellent study, *The Evidence of Film: Abbas Kiarostami*, trans. Christine Irizarry and Verena Andermatt Conley (Brussels: Yves Gevaert, 2001).

19. David Sterritt, "Taste of Kiarostami" (interview with Abbas Kiarostami), http://archive.sensesofcinema.com/contents/00/9/kiarostami.html.

20. Michel Ciment and Stéphane Goudet, "Une approche existentialiste de la vie" (interview with Abbas Kiarostami), *Positif* 442 (December, 1997), 85; also cited in Stéphane Goudet, "Le Gout de la cerise...et la saveur de la mure," *L'Avant Scene* 471 (April 1998), 1.

21. See Lacan, *Ethics.*

22. Qur'an, 50:16. For a fascinating discussion of the way Ibn 'Arabî interprets this notion, see Henry Corbin, *Alone with the Alone: Creative Imagination*

and the Sufism of Ibn 'Arabî, (Princeton: Princeton University Press, 1969).

23. Friedrich Nietzsche, *Beyond Good and Evil: Prelude to a Philosophy of the Future*, trans. Walter Kaufmann (New York: Vintage Books, 1989), 213.

24. Ibid.

25. Giorgio Agamben, *Homo Sacer: Sovereign Power and Bare Life*, trans. Daniel Heller-Roazen (Stanford: Stanford University Press, 1998), 26-27.

26. Freud, *The Ego and the Id*, *SE* 19:38; my emphasis.

27. Quoted in Carl D. Schneider, *Shame, Exposure, and Privacy* (New York: W.W. Norton & Company, 1977), 38.

28. See Corbin, *Spiritual Body and Celestial Earth* for a discussion of this idea in medieval Islamic philosophy.

29. Jean-Paul Sartre, *Being and Nothingness: An Essay in Phenomenological Ontology*, trans. Hazel E. Barnes (New York: Washington Square Press, 1956), 369.

30. Jacques Lacan, *The Seminar of Jacques Lacan, Book XI: The Four Fundamental Concept of Psycho-Analysis*, ed. Jacques-Alain Miller, trans. Alain Sheridan (New York: W.W. Norton & Company, 1998), 182.

31. Ibid., 84-85; my emphasis.

32. Again, see my "May '68: the Emotional Month."

33. Agamben, *Remnants of Auschwitz*, 103-104.

34. This is obviously a description of a scene from the film *Stella Dallas* (King Vidor, 1937).

35. Joan Riviere, "Womanliness as a Masquerade," in *Formations of Fantasy*, ed. Victor Burgin, James Donald, and Cora Kaplan (London: Routledge, 1986), 37. All subsequent quotations in this paragraph are to be found on page 37 of Riviere's essay.

36. I have used the translation of Forugh's poem by Ahmad Karimi-Hakkak, which is cited in Mehrnaz Saeed-Vafa and Jonathan Rosenbaum, *Abbas Kiarostami* (Urbana: University of Illinois Press, 2003), 33-34.

37. Havelock Ellis, quoted in Schneider, *Shame, Exposure, and Privacy*, 60.

38. Nietzsche, *Beyond Good and Evil*, 50.

16

Signifier and Letter in Kierkegaard and Lacan

Sigi Jöttkandt

> When you scribble and when I too scribble, it is always on a page with lines, and we are thus immediately enmeshed in this business of dimensions.
>
> —Jacques Lacan, *Encore*

In *Seminar XX; Encore*, Lacan offers his famous definition of love as "the displacement of the negation from the "stops not being written" to the "doesn't stop being written."[1] It is to this "point of suspension," he claims, that is, the point between the contingency of the "stops not being written" and the necessity of the "doesn't stop being written" that "all love is attached" (*Encore*, 145). As is well known, the thing whose questionable scriptivity Lacan is referring to in this formula is the sexual relationship. Lacan repeatedly maintains in his later seminars that the sexual relationship cannot be written. A strict impossibility, the sexual relationship is the "sole part of the real that cannot manage to be formed from being" he says (*Encore*, 48). Nevertheless, as is also well-known, something makes up for the sexual relationship's absence (albeit always inadequately, as Lacan also constantly reminds us, *Encore*, 45). This something is writing itself.

Precisely what Lacan means by writing will clearly require further investigation. Closely associated with love in Lacan's later seminars, it transpires that 'writing' will enable a formalization to take place that is not entirely ruled by the phallic signifier. Yet, as we will also see, this is not to say that writing has nothing to do with signifier and its regime of law. On the contrary, the bar between signifier and signified "is precisely the point at which, in every use of language, writing may be produced," Lacan claims (*Encore*, 34).

We can make our initial way in to the problem by recalling how, in *Seminar XX*, Lacan refers to the remarkable leap set theory makes when it posits our ability to group disparate objects together and declare them to be One. More momentous, however, than this declaration of the One, whose creation *ex nihilo* Lacan identifies throughout his teachings with the birth of modern science, is the way that set theory additionally grants us "the right to designate the resulting assemblage by a letter" (*Encore*, 47). In very much the same way that the signifier One comes to stand in for the grouped objects in modern science's discovery, the letter in set theory performs a similar substitutive role. Yet despite a certain synchronism of the two gestures, Lacan cautions in this seminar that the letter is of a different order than the signifier. The written, he says, "is in no way in the same register or made of the same stuff, . . . as the signifier" (*Encore*, 29). This is because, insofar as the letter constitutes an *assemblage*, it necessarily brings into play a second-order formalization or abstraction whose advance on modern science can be put as follows: with the letter comes the ability to deal simultaneously with multiple Ones.

We can understand this better if we pursue the thread Lacan dangles at the close of his lesson of February 20, 1971, when he concludes that "it is no accident that Kierkegaard discovered existence in a seducer's little love affair" (*Encore*, 77). In what follows, I propose to examine not the *Diary of a Seducer* that Lacan is probably referring to, but another, somewhat less well-known text from *Either/Or*, the chapter on Eugene Scribe's comedy, *Les premiers amours*.[2]

THE FIRST LOVE

Little introduction is needed for Kierkegaard's major work, whose conceit is outlined in the opening chapters. *Either/Or* is a collection of essays, supposedly discovered and gathered together by the work's editor, one Victor Eremita. The work is composed of two parts, the initial half authored by the aesthetic figure Eremita calls A, and the second, by an ethical individual, Judge William, whom Eremita designates B. *Either/Or* presents arguments in support of the aesthetic and ethical ways of life. In the sixth chapter of *Either*, the text we will be dealing with here, A reviews Scribe's comedy *Les premiers amours*. In Scribe's play, A finds a superlative expression of his aesthetic theory that he has been developing so far.

As we learn in his preamble to the review, Kierkegaard's aesthete holds *Les premiers amours* in the highest esteem, thereby sharing the general acclaim with which the play was received during its 131 performances in Copenhagen over the later half of the nineteenth century. Calling it "a play without a fault," a play "so perfect that it alone should make Scribe immortal," we soon learn that *Les premiers amours* occupies a unique place in A's own personal history as well, as a play he first watched in the presence of his own former sweetheart, his own "first love."

In the tradition of good French comedy, the plot is by every standard stupid enough: Emmeline, the only daughter of a wealthy iron-founder, is about to be married off to the young man Rinville. Brought up on an unhealthy diet of romantic novels by her Aunt Judith, Emmeline refuses to meet him, claiming she is still in love with her childhood sweetheart, her cousin Charles whom she last saw when she was eight. Intercepting a letter that informs him where Emmeline's heart really lies, Rinville decides to increase his chance of success by passing himself off as the long absent Charles. When Charles unexpectedly arrives home, already secretly married and with debts he hopes his uncle will pay, he agrees to join in the masquerade. Predictably, the comedic change of identity has its desired effect: Emmeline, on first meeting "Charles" again (really Rinville), declares her undying love for him. But once she discovers he no longer has the ring she gave him, she falls rapidly out of love. Emmeline's love mysteriously returns as soon as "Charles" is able to produce the token. After much hilarious confusion, their true identities are finally revealed, upon which Emmeline agrees to marry Rinville. "It was a mistake," she tells him, "I confused the past with the future" (*Either*, 253).

The key to the aesthete's reading of the play—what makes it for him a "masterpiece of dramatic perfection"—lies in this final statement of Emmeline's, which he emphatically does not take as an admission of a mistake, that is, as a sign of a change in Emmeline's outlook. Indeed, it is against this "moralizing" narrative of ethical progress that his entire reading of the play is pitted. For A, there is "not the least thing discernible in the play to indicate that her choice of Rinville might be more reasonable than anything else she has done" (*Either*, 255). For A, "Emmeline's nature is infinite nonsense, she is quite as silly at the end as in the beginning." In A's reading of the play, Emmeline does not marry Rinville because she suddenly realizes that she has loved him all along as the pseudo-Charles and, in so recognizing, discovers the error of her maxim, learned from their Aunt Judith in the course of their literary education, that "the first love is the true love and one only loves once." Quite the contrary, says A. If Emmeline discovers that the real Charles is not her Charles, she soon discovers that Rinville is not her Charles either, leaving open the possibility that "a new figure will appear, who resembles Charles, and so forth" (*Either*, 256). Thus, far from ending, the play continues in an "infinite jest" about Emmeline, and her final speech must be understood in the following way: "Previously," says A, "her illusion lay behind her in the past, now she will seek it in the world and in the future, for she has not renounced the romantic Charles" (*Either*, 257). Emmeline's closing speech thus indicates not a change of heart but "a change of movement," but "whether she travels forward or backward, her expedition in search of the first love is comparable to the journey one undertakes in search of health which, as someone has said, is always one station ahead" (*Either*, 252).

The reader will not find it hard to recognize shades of the Freudian lost object in A's description of first love. The lost object, classically the mother for Freud, is permanently "one station ahead," requiring not to be found but *re*-found—re-found, because as soon as we believe we have reached it, we immediately discover that "that's not it!" which obliges us to begin the search anew. In the conventional reading of this Freudian narrative, the paths we trace in desire represent our attempts recover the original blissful union with this irretrievably lost first love, the mother. I scarcely need add that this attempt is notoriously hopeless, simply because no real object can ever match the mythical maternal ideal which, as psychoanalysis also reminds us, has no more actual existence than Emmeline's Charles. The entire ensuing trajectory of the subject as a subject of desire revolves around this originally missing object that we can subsequently only approach piecemeal, through the exigency of what Lacan calls the object *a*—the little piece of the subject that was cut loose by castration and had to be given up in order to accede to a symbolic identity. Assuming objective form as the *Unheimlich* objects Lacan identifies as the voice, the gaze, the faeces and the breast, the principal feature of the object *a* lies in the way it continually slips from the subject's grasp.[3] The moment this infinitely desired object is reached, it immediately divests itself of its magical qualities which are transferred over onto another, now desired, object *ad infinitum* in what Lacan calls the "metonymy" of desire. Psychoanalytically speaking, we are all Emmelines, "spirits of the ring": held in thrall by some nonsensical little nullity, literally a nothing that we chase after, we obey—that is to say, fall in love with—anyone along the way who is regarded "as hav[ing] the ring in his hand" (*Either*, 269).

The only problem with this Freudian story, of course, is that it isn't true. Like Emmeline's enchanted vision of the love she and Charles shared as eight year olds, the experience of unity with the mother never happened; it is a myth. Yet like the other famous psychoanalytic "myth" (that of the primal "father of enjoyment" from *Totem and Taboo*), the fact that it has no empirical reality does not mean that it has no "truth." For psychoanalysis, which famously distinguishes between truth and knowledge, the lack of a basis in physical reality has never stopped one from claiming that something—an hysterical symptom, say—possesses truth.[4]

So let us take Emmeline's motto as our starting point. On an initial reading, it appears both categorical and irrevocable: "the first love is the true love and one only loves once." You have only one chance in your life, it seems to say, to really love someone, and the first person you love is the only one you will ever really love. Nevertheless, as we learn in the preamble in which A tells the story of his own "first love," in practice the "first" turns out to be a rather slippery category. In his lead-up to his review of Scribe, A tells the story of how, on meeting his former sweetheart again—the same one with whom he had first attended a performance of *Les premieres amours,*—he finds her telling exactly the same story as Emmeline. Seeing A again after many years, his former lover "assured me that she had never loved me, but that her betrothed was her first love, and that 'only the first love is the true love'" (*Either*, 242)

For A's former lover, the first love is apparently a qualitative category, one that allows a certain (convenient) revisionism in one's personal history.

Such a qualitative first, however, is assuredly not what Emmeline has in mind. Nor would it make *Les premieres amours* in A's estimation a play that is "infinitely comic" (*Either*, 253), and Emmeline's character one of "infinite nonsense (*Either*, 255). From A's former lover's "sophistical" approach, Emmeline would on the contrary recoil in horror. As A explains:

> When a widower and a widow join fortunes, and each one brings five children along, then they still assure each other on their wedding day that this love is their first love. Emmeline in her romantic orthodoxy would look upon such a connection with aversion; it would be to her a mendacious abomination, which would be as loathsome to her as a marriage between a monk and a nun was to the Middle Ages. (*Either*, 252)

Emmeline, by contrast, "holds fast to her proposition numerically understood" (*Either*, 252), which A goes on a page later to qualify in the following way: "She loves [Charles] with an objective, *mathematical* love" (*Either*, 253). Clearly, the manner in which we understand this "mathematical" love will decide whether the wit of the Scribe's play stands or falls for, as A puts it, Emmeline "must now acquire experience and the experience refutes her. It appears that she loves Rinville" (*Either*, 253). To determine whether the play is "infinitely comic, or finitely moralizing," the validity of Emmeline's maxim must be put to the test (*Either*, 253).

The irony of the play lies of course in the statement's patent falsity, for not only does Emmeline love more than once (first Charles and then Rinville), at another level she has never loved at all: to the extent that she refuses to give up her "illusion" of Charles, Emmeline's first love is "always one station ahead" (*Either*, 257). How, then, can she claim to love only once? The only meaningful answer is that Emmeline's statement refers not to any actual or imagined loved object but to the manner, the *way* in which Emmeline loves. For psychoanalysis, it is perfectly reasonable to say that one "only loves once," even if one can rattle off a reel of past lovers, each of whom enjoyed the genuine privilege of being the "first" and "true" love. However, the Freudian first love differs markedly from A's former sweetheart's revisionist notion of first love, for the psychoanalytic formula holds just as true even if one has yet to find one's "true love." What psychoanalysis is referring to here, in other words, is an original choice, expressed by the Freudian term *Neurosenwahl*. This is the choice we carry with us throughout all of our loving history that directs which "stage" our subjective drama will be performed on, whether neurotic, perverse or psychotic. In this sense, to say "one loves only once" is to say we are capable of only one desiring scenario, one fundamental fantasy that organizes the multiple encounters (real and imagined) of our love lives and which itself *never changes*. The fantasy is what guarantees that beyond all of their infinite variety or superficial or "small" differences, each of our lovers is at some unconscious level the Same, a partner in a specific pattern of desire that, chosen once and once only, cannot be undone.[5]

This should become clearer if we now look a little more closely at the ways Emmeline and Charles "love only once." Emmeline, as we saw, is perpetually in search of the "first love" as an event that is infinitely to come. No single lover comes up to her vision of the "romantic Charles" which, the aesthete never stops reminding us, is an "illusion." As it turns out, Charles, too, is in the grip of an illusion, insofar as he had the same "romantic training" as Emmeline. However, unlike his cousin, who is "hidden from [her]self" as A puts it, Charles believes he can hide from others. Charles's belief in his own powers of mystification, A tells us, "is just as fantastic as Emmeline's illusion, and one recognizes Judith's schooling in both (*Either*, 249).

Consequently, in these two eager readers of romantic novels, we find a remarkable illustration of two different ways a lover can miss the "first" love. Eternally in search of her One, Emmeline must always begin her quest for Charles anew because each time she finds him he will fail to be "Charles." More acquainted with the "pinch of reality," Charles, on the other hand, has already expended his illusion and, having become "a dissolute fellow" (*Either*, 247), finds himself tricked into marriage by a woman more well-versed in mystification than he. Not one to admit defeat, Charles will employ any number of disguises to obtain his goal—as A puts it, "he knows that there are five or six ways whereby one can move an uncle's heart"—and if the first is unsuccessful, he will try on another, and then another in an infinite display of confidence in his ability "not to be recognized" (*Either*, 248).

While both Emmeline's and Charles's different attempts to obtain the first love thereby inevitably fail, what is of interest is the way each of these failures generates its own unique form of infinity. From a certain perspective, it not hard to see how Emmeline's failure corresponds to the infinity of Zeno's paradox of Achilles and the tortoise. Recall how Achilles permits the tortoise a head-start in the race only to discover he can never catch up with her since, in the time he covers the distance the tortoise has already traveled, the tortoise will have "run" farther ahead. To make up time, Achilles must then cover the new distance, by which point the tortoise will have advanced further still. Like Emmeline, who will always be either behind or ahead of "Charles," Achilles can only "pass or leap-frog" the tortoise, as Lacan puts it in his comment on this paradox in *Seminar XX* (*Encore*, 8).

In Charles's case, on the other hand, we enter the infinity corresponding to Zeno's other paradox—that of the arrow in motion. The paradox here is Zeno's proof of motion's "impossibility": the arrow will never "move" since it can eternally be divided into ever smaller units of measurement. If Emmeline's first love lies forever in the future, Charles's is always already in the past—as a married man, he has already found his "One" (Paméla). Yet, as a master of disguise himself, he can never really be certain of the very "first" One, that is, of whether he is not still being taken in by Paméla or Rinville or indeed even by Emmeline. Like the arrow, Charles's "count" is strictly speaking immobile—he can never get to Two because he can never agree on where the "One" really began.

In a pleasing symmetry, these two forms of failure, and the infinities they correspondingly generate, can be aptly illustrated in the fantasies of the hysterical and obsessional subjects:

Hysterical fantasy: $\frac{a}{-\varphi} \diamond A$

Obsessional fantasy: $\not{A} \diamond \varphi$ (a' a" a'" …)

In the first, we see described the hysteric's strategy of covering her own intrinsic lack ($-\varphi$) by way of an identification with what one believes the Other desires *a*. When this identification fails, as of course it always will for the Emmelines of the world, this is not so much because "Charles" does not match up to her illusion of him—although this is typically regarded as the source of the hysteric's constitutive disappointment in the Master. Rather, as A continually reminds us, Emmeline fundamentally does not *know* Charles. Thus how could she know what to match him against? Hence when Emmeline becomes convinced that "Charles" is not "Charles," we must conclude that her conviction derives not from any change in Charles's real or imagined characteristics, but rather because at some level he has failed to recognize *her*. A explains how Emmeline "does not seek the alteration in the fact that Charles has become a spendthrift or possibly something even worse, but in that he has not confided everything to her, as he was accustomed to do" (*Either*, 268). It is this change in his relation to her, rather than his failure to match up to her ideal, that convinces the hysteric that "Charles" "is not the same anymore" (*Either*, 267). Read this way, Kierkegaard thus offers an intriguing new slant no the hysteric's eternal question to the Master, "what [or who] am I?"[6] For here we see that the hysteric knows very well who *she* is—the question is whether the Master also knows, and when it becomes apparent he does not, she re-embarks on her quest for a new One, a Master who *truly* knows and recognizes who she is.

A different objective drives the obsessional fantasy, which in this case is not propelled by the subject's lack. The obsessional, famously, does not feel he lacks anything. It is, on the contrary, precisely because he feels he satisfies the Other all too well that he is led in his fantasy to emphasize the lack in the Other ($\not{A}$). Accordingly, the obsessional's entire fantasmatic scenario is designed to keep the Other in a state of desire, which he employs as a defense against the threat of being entirely swallowed up by the (m)Other. Thus, like Charles, the obsessional becomes an expert in mystification. The obsessional generates a proliferating series of substitutive objects—the traditional obsessional behaviours or "disguises" that are to keep the Other (in

Charles' case, his uncle and Emmeline) occupied while preserving his real identity (as a married man) beyond the Other's reach. These "disguises" are what is expressed in the formula as the little a-apostrophes, semblances of the semblance that the obsessional, as the Other's *a*, attempts to hide behind. Naturally what the obsessional fails to realize, however, is that, like Charles, it is he who is the most taken in by his disguises. As A puts it, Charles "believes it is he who contrives intrigues, he who mystifies, and yet the spectator sees that the mystification was in operation before Charles appears" (*Either*, 259). Imagining that he is the puppet master generating illusion, the obsessional in fact "give[s] the whole thing away" (*Either*, 260).

One might ask what is the point of these "fantasies"? As is well-known, the fantasy's psychic function is to mitigate an original trauma Freud termed an "internal" arousal, renamed by Lacan as *jouissance*. The various fantasies achieve this by providing this incomprehensible arousal or *jouissance* with some kind of interim representation. This provisional representation acts to reduce and siphon off the anxiety the subject experiences in its confrontation with what it cannot comprehend—the Other's desire[7]—by supplying some kind of form to the nothing, the original "object" of anxiety. One can thus regard the different fantasies—hysteric, obsessional and perverse—as different ways of "dramatizing" this nothing.[8] Like comedy, with which they therefore share an intrinsic kinship, the fantasies put the nothing or "void," *on stage*.

The fantasy's generic "equation" $\$ \diamond a$ can accordingly be put in mathematical terms in the following way:

$$\varnothing \sim (\{\varnothing\} = 1) = 0$$

This expresses how the void or unpresentable point of being, ∅, is made 'equivalent' to the empty set {∅}, which can serve as the first provisional representational placeholder for the void, and accordingly be counted 'as' One in the ordinal counting system. The ordinal count gives this void a name, the empty set or zero, which forms the first and original One from which all subsequent addition springs. The number 2 is accordingly derived from the empty set +1, while the number 3 is derived from the empty set +1 +1, and so on.

In the algebra of the fantasies, the ultimate result of this 'equation' is "inertia"—the ideal state of the subject prior to the eruption of *jouissance*. The empty set, counted here as the first positive One, balances the pure negative (or minus "One") of the void, returning the subject's psychic state to zero. Expressed in words, we get:

Void, equated to the empty set, which can then be counted 'as' One, gives the result "inertia" or zero.

If we now populate this generic formula for fantasy with the specific values of the hysteric's fantasy, we obtain the following:

$$\varnothing \sim (\{\tfrac{a}{-\varphi} \diamond A\} = 1) = 0$$

In this formula, the generic empty set {∅} has been filled in with the specifics of how the hysteric "stages" the appearance of the "nothing" or void. The equation depicts how the hysterical subject positions herself in the fantasy as vertically split between her phallic castration (minus phi) and the object *a* which, as we saw, represents her identification with what she believes the Other (A) wants from her.[9] Like the generic version of the equation, the hysterical fantasy also aims to "count" to One (whose ultimate result, as for all the fantasies, is a return to inertia, or zero). However, we quickly see how the hysteric encounters a difficulty in performing her "addition." The problem lies with the *a*, the semblance of the Other's desire with which the hysteric attempts to cover over her imaginary lack ($-\varphi$). It is this *a* that ensures her count will always, like Achilles, either over- or undershoot its mark.

In Lacan's teaching, the cause of this permanent over- or under-shooting is found in the fact that the field of representation where the fantasy is "staged" is not flat but is topologically distorted by the *a* insofar as it belongs to another register than the symbolic "count." Created in the original nominal act of "making equivalence" that enabled the void to be bracketed as the empty set and counted 'as' the first One, the *a* is that part of the void or Real that was never completely taken up by the provisional presentation (which psychoanalysis calls the phallic signifier). As a result, the *a* guarantees that every fantasmatic "equation's" staging of the impossible sexual relation through the exigencies of a subject-object relation will always be inflected with something of the original traumatic *jouissance* that the fantasies were intended to palliate. This little sliver of *jouissance* that slipped into the symbolic through the back door during the original catastrophic equating of the void ("castration") ensures that the fantasy of a complete or intact One (i.e. an utterly seamless fusion of the subject and object) will never be attained. For it is this *a* that drives the subject's unconscious repetition. The *a* is the source of the continual failure that causes every count to One to always have to begin again. It is for this reason, then, that any "mathematical" equation that contains the *a* will always come up lacking in its final result in a very precise way.[10] As we saw, the One-result of the hysterical fantasy will always necessarily be missing a little bit since the presence of the *a* ensures the Other (A) will never be completely satisfied with her. Despite all the "narcissistic coatings" as Lacan puts it, that subsequently come to envelop and surround it, the *a* never fully covers over the minus phi of the hysteric's castration, and the resultant One of the hysterical fantasy always falls short.[11]

A similar, albeit opposite, thing happens with the obsessional. Although his desiring formula also aims to count to One, the obsessional's One-result will always be a little bit in surfeit, again because it is produced by an object *a* that carries along with it something of the same impossible void. In the obsessional's formula, this surplus is indicated by the little distinguishing supra symbols that mark the substitute *a* objects with which he showers the Other in the fantasy (a', a", a'" ... etc.). These marks give themselves away as the semblances of the *a* that they are:

$$\varnothing \sim (\{\not{A} \diamond \varphi\,(a'\,a''\,a'''\,\ldots)\} = 1) = 0$$

The question is why the obsessional's One-result will always be a tiny bit more than One, while the hysteric's always a little less? It stems from the neurotic structures' original affective response to the traumatic arousal of *jouissance*. In "Heredity and the Aetiology of the Neuroses," Freud locates at the basis of hysteria an original experience of unpleasure, "an event of passive sexuality" that was "submitted to with indifference or with a small degree of annoyance or fright."[12] Accordingly, as a "representative" (*Vorstellung*) of this original experience, the *a* hauls something of this unpleasure along with it into the hysterical desiring fantasy, ensuring that her One-result will always be inflected with a tiny little lacking sign or "minus." For the obsessional, on the other hand, it concerns an event which originally, Freud says, "has given pleasure." The obsessional's *a* will thus ensure that his One-result always suffers from a tiny little surfeit, expressing how the obsessional's "disguises" are just that tiny bit too successful in deceiving the Other. At some point, the Other will inevitably take him too literally and mistake the semblance for the real thing. In this way, the Other will sabotage his fantasy that he can endlessly keep substituting new objects for himself ad infinitum.

CODA

Although Lacan maintains that the sexual relation "doesn't stop not being written," it transpires that if this impossibility undergoes a certain procedure, the sexual relation "stops not being written." As the discussion above helps us to see, the sexual relation evidently "stops not being written" at the moment when the impossible is "mathematized," that is to say, formalized as the "provisional representation" of the phallic signifier. Hence, contrary to the popular idea of the phallus as a form of determination, as a *provisional* representation, the phallus is therefore "contingent." Lacan states that "It is as a mode of the contingent that the phallic function stops not being written."[13] By this I understand him to mean that this formalization of the void of the sexual relation might not have taken place (or might not have fully succeeded, as is the case, for example, for the psychotic and the perverse subjects). If we now follow Lacan's own loving formula to its final step, we go from the contingency implied by the phallus to a necessity that Lacan expresses in the phrase "doesn't stop being written" (*ne pas de s'ecrire*). This step is famously taken by "love." All love, Lacan explains, "subsisting only on the basis of the 'stops not being written' tends to make the negation shift to the 'doesn't stop being written,' doesn't stop, won't stop" (*Encore*, 145). In this formulation, whose seeming nonsense appears worthy of a Kierkegaardian heroine, Lacan appears to be asserting that love is nothing more than a shift of a negation in a sentence about writing: "The displacement of the negation from the 'stops not being written' to the 'doesn't stop being written,' in other words, from contingency to necessity—there lies the point of suspension to which all love is attached."[14]

Despite its apparent nonsensicalness, what Lacan is driving at in this distinctly unromantic sounding statement is the way love's "doesn't stop being written" enables the subject to approach the impossible *jouissance* of the sexual relation in a way that is not entirely governed by (phallic) contingency and its imaginary stagings in the fundamental fantasies. But as it now appears, this is not to say that love somehow by-passes or short-circuits the phallic fantasies. Love, it would seem, "subsists" *only* on the basis of the "stops not being written" or, as we are now comprehending this phrase, on the basis of the formalization of impossible *jouissance* by means of the phallus. However, whereas the phallic formalization succeeded in mathematizing the Real to produce the first signifier (the phallus, or "empty set" in my schema), with their use of letters, the fantasies perform an additional formalization and *write* this Real. Letterating the phallus's (binary) numericization of the void in this way, the fantasies can be said to perform a second-order abstraction of that first suturing act that produced the phallic signifier. In doing so, they enable us to achieve the earlier mentioned breakthrough with which Lacan credits Cantorian set theory

Emmeline and Charles can once more come to our rescue in understanding precisely how writing accomplishes this breakthrough. As we have seen in the above discussion, each of their fantasies are limited in advance by the structural failure of the *a* that ensures that none of their attempts to count to One will succeed, obliging them to begin again in a gesture of infinite repetition. Nevertheless, it seems that if each of their individual unsuccessful attempts are grouped together in a series, a "One" may be reached by means of a different mathematical procedure than that of the (failed) count. The method for obtaining this "supplementary One," as Lacan calls it, relies on the same axiom as proposed by set theory: the power set of x is greater than x.[15]

Rather than taxing ourselves with an explanation of the mathematical basis of this axiom, we can turn to Lacan's discussion of the same problem in *Seminar XIV: the Logic of Fantasy* (1966-67) where he introduces this idea of a supplementary One in the context of a discussion of Bertrand Russell's catalogue of all catalogues that do not contain themselves. In his lesson of 23 November, 1966, Lacan counters Russell's famous catalogue with the idea of a catalogue that lists all the books referred to in a single volume's bibliography.[16] Unlike Russell's catalogue, there is no question of whether the book whose bibliography is being listed should be included (of course it should not). However, another catalogue that lists all the books that a second book's bibliography contains, may well include the title of the first book (although, naturally, not that of the second), and so on. By effectively grouping books into 'sets' in this way, Lacan swiftly demonstrates how a totality may be achieved without falling into Russell's paradox. As Lacan explains, although each bibliographic catalogue will not include the title of the book from which it has been derived, once we group these catalogues together into a *series*, it is not unthinkable that, between them, they will succeed in listing all of the books in the world.[17]

Returning, then, to our first lovers, although the *a*'s structural failure ensures that that Emmeline and Charles will, by a certain inevitability, fail to reach their desired object in the fantasmatic count, if each of these unsuccessful attempts are collated and grouped together in a series, an 'all' may be created that is more than the sum of its individual parts. Inaccessible to the count, this 'all' or supplementary One results from the principle of limitation that is encoded into every fantasy in the form of the letter.

Space constraints here prevent a proper treatment of the precise way that love, through the nonsense it suddenly induces lovers to speak, gives us access to this "supplementary One" that is "not grasped [or counted] in the chain, as Lacan puts it in his seminar, *The Psychoanalytic Act* (Seminar XIV).[18] Let us conclude instead with a final comment. We have seen how, as an "assemblage," the letter by definition keeps the original relations of the subject, Other and *a* that constitute the One intact, even as the letter permits us to go on and manipulate multiple instances of these Ones. Accordingly, one could say that when the letter 'writes' the failure of the phallic count to One in the fantasies, it simultaneously carries with it the history of that signifier's original formation. The letter, as it were, carries some kind of 'memory' of the One's primordial creation *ex nihilo*. I cannot help speculating that it is something of this 'memory' that Lacan is referring to when he states in *Seminar XX* that "Writing is ... a trace in which an effect of language can be read" (Encore, 121). Within it, the letter contains the traces of the original formalization that first enabled a signifier, One, to stand in for a disparate group of objects. Invisibly stamped with the 'memory' of the One's original formation, the letter is thus the carrier of that archaic decision of substitution that Lacan calls an "effect of language."

Notes

1. Jacques Lacan, *The Seminar of Jacques Lacan, Book XX, Encore: On Feminine Sexuality, The Limits of Love and Knowledge (1972-1973)*, ed. Jacques-Alain Miller, trans. Bruce Fink (New York: Norton, 1998), 145.
2. Søren Kierkegaard, *Either/Or*, Vol. 1, trans. David F. Swenson and Lillian Marvin Swenson, rev. and foreword Howard A. Johnson (New York: Anchor Books, 1959).
3. In his seminar devoted to the object *a* , for example, Lacan offers a working definition of the object *a* as what "falls" (chute) from the field of the

symbolic. See, for example, the lesson of 22.12.65, *Le séminaire, livre XIII, L' objet de la psychanalyse* (1965-1966), unpublished seminar.

4. As Lacan puts it in *Encore*, "Something true can still be said about what cannot be demonstrated," 119.
5. Both Freud and Lacan have wavered on this point, with Freud ultimately opting for an original, non-negotiable choice which is "independent of experience." See Freud's discussion of a seeming conversion from anxiety hysteria to obsessional neurosis in "The Disposition to Obsessional Neurosis," (1911-1913), *The Standard Edition of the Complete Psychological Works of Sigmund Freud*, trans. James Strachey, et. al. (London: The Hogarth Press, 1953-1974) 12: 317-26. Hereafter *SE*. But even if the choice itself can never be undone, this is not to say that the *way* it was made cannot be revised as Paul Verhaeghe explains in his elaboration of psychoanalysis' various "therapeutic effects." See Paul Verhaeghe, *On Being Normal and Other Disorders*, trans. Sigi Jöttkandt (New York: Other Press, 2004).
6. See Lacan's lesson of 19 April, 1961, *Le séminaire, livre VIII, Le transfert (1960-1961)*, ed. Jacques-Alain Miller (Paris: Seuil, 2001) 297-331.
7. In *Seminar IX*, Lacan defines anxiety as "the sensation of the desire of the Other." Lesson of 4 April, 1962, *Le séminaire, livre IX, L'identification* (1961-1962), unpublished seminar.
8. Psychosis has no fantasy but is instead described by Lacan as "delusion."
9. See Lacan's discussion of the hysteric's fantasy in *Seminar VIII*, lesson of 19 April, 1961. For a refreshingly lucid explanation of this formula, see Verhaeghe, 373-81.
10. For a mathematical explanation of the derivation of the *a*, see Lacan's discussion in *Seminar XIV*, lessons of 22 and 29 January, 1969. Briefly, the a is not "equal" to 1, but holds the value of the relation of one term in a Fibonacci series to the next. Thus, if 1+1+2, 1+2+3, in the converging series (hysteria) or, in reverse, the diverging series (obsession) 1-a, 2a-1, 2-3a, etc. the "value" of *a* will always be the proportional difference between one term and the next in the Fibonacci series, a difference which is computed as 0.618. Lacan's use of the Fibonacci series here and elsewhere is designed to model the relationship of the speaking subject to the signifier which represents the subject for another signifier. As Lacan explains, "here it is the relationship not of 1 to 1 but of 1 to 2 that is at stake." See his discussion on 29 January, 1969.
11. *Le séminaire, livre XV, L'acte psychanalytique (1967-68)*, unpublished seminar (lesson of 21 February, 1968).
12. Sigmund Freud, "Heredity and the Aetiology of the Neuroses," (1893-1899), *SE* 3, trans. James Strachey (London: Hogarth, 1955) 141-56.

13. Lacan, *Seminar XX*, 94. The English translation is a little ambiguous here. To clarify, it is not the "phallic function" that "stops not being written." It is rather the unwritable *jouissance* that stops not being written (in the form of the phallic function).

14. Lacan, *Seminar XX*, 145.

15. See Mary Tiles, *The Philosophy of Set Theory: An Introduction to Cantor's Paradise* (Oxford: Blackwell, 1999), 104-5.

16. Lacan, *Le séminaire, livre XIV, La logique du fantasme (1966-67)*, unpublished seminar (lesson of 23 November, 1966).

17. This can be expressed in digrammatic form, where each letter outside each set represents the title of the 'book' whose bibliography is being catalogued:
A (B, C, D)
B (A, C, D)
C (A, B, D)
D (A, B, C)
Between them, every 'book' has thus been catalogued (represented), even though there is no single catalogue that contains them all. For further discussion, see *Seminar XIV* (1966-67), lessons of 16 and 23 November, 1966.

18. '. . . by simply closing the chain, there results that each group of four [catalogues in the example Lacan is using] can easily leave outside itself the extraneous signifier, which can serve to designate the group, for the simple reason that it is not represented in it, and that nevertheless the whole chain will be found to constitute the totality of all these signifiers, giving rise to this additional unit, uncountable as such, which is essential for a whole series of structures, which are precisely the ones on which I founded, since the year 1960, my whole operation of identification,' *Seminar XIV* (lesson of 23.11.66).

17

(Marxian-Psychoanalytic) Biopolitics and Bioracism

A. Kiarina Kordela

(PSYCHOANALYTIC) BIOPOLITICS

According to Michel Foucault, the thinker who introduced the concept, biopolitics is a form of power that emerged with and continues to accompany capitalist modernity; according to others, notably Giorgio Agamben, it has existed since antiquity's linkages of *nomos* (the law) and *physis* (the state of nature).[1] Though I could argue that, in a sense (and a very psychoanalytic one), biopolitics has actually existed since the very tribal beginnings of any social formation, I would also acknowledge that the two positions do not really contradict each other. Rather, their apparent discord is indicative of the fact that biopolitics, like any political concept, undergoes fundamental mutations, adjusting and developing according to the historical formations in which it is exercised. Here I want to focus on the specificities of biopolitics within the particular historical era of capitalist secular modernity.

Value is something that existed in the most primitive societies, given that, as Aristotle noted, "the technique of exchange [...] has its origin in a state of affairs often to be found in nature, namely, men having too much of this and not enough of that."[2] Yet, Aristotle was, by historical necessity, incapable of grasping the value form as it is required for the development of capitalism. It is for this reason, as Karl Marx comments, that when faced with the possibility that the equation "'5 beds = 1 house' [...] is indistinguishable from '5 beds = a certain amount of money,'" Aristotle could only feel indignation and declare that it is "in reality, impossible [...] that such unlike things can be commensurable."[3] For Aristotle, Marx continues, this equivalence means "that the house should be qualitatively equated with the bed, and that these things, being distinct to the senses could not be compared with each other as commensurable magnitudes" (151). Aristotle therefore "abandons [...] the further analysis of the form of value," concluding that this "form of equation can only be something foreign to the true nature of the things," reduced only to "a makeshift for practical purposes" (151).

Aristotle cannot conceive that what is "really equal, both in the bed and in the house," the "common substance" shared by both, is "human labour," and that it is not the sensuous bed and house that are actually compared in exchange but sheer quantities of abstract human labor-time (151). It is *only* "in the form of the commodity-values [that] all labour is expressed as...labour of equal quality" (152). Therefore, Aristotle's analysis of the form of value had to remain incomplete from the perspective of capitalism "because Greek society was founded on the labour of slaves, hence had as its natural basis the inequality of men and their labour-powers" (152). In contrast, value produces surplus-value "only in a society where the commodity-form is the universal form of the product of labour," whereby "the dominant social relation is the relation between men as possessors of commodities" and "the concept of human equality" has "already acquired the permanence of a fixed popular opinion" (152).

The emergence of capitalism presupposes a concomitant transubstantiation of labor-power and value, not unlike the parallel transmutation of energy that, at the same time, revolutionized scientific thought and produced the very machines that the capitalist mode of production would require. Jacques Lacan's rhetoric characteristically reflects the historical weaving of the two processes:

> Not that energy hasn't always been there. Except that people who had slaves didn't realise that one could establish equations for the price of their food and what they did in their *latifundia*. There are no examples of energy calculations in the use of slaves. There is not the hint of an equation as to their output. Cato never did it. It took machines for us to realise they had to be fed. And more—they had to be looked after. But why? Because they tend to wear out. Slaves do as well, but one doesn't think about it, one thinks that it is natural for them to get old and croak.[4]

Herein resides the entire *raison-d'être* of capitalist biopolitics: it is not natural for the proletariat to "get old and croak." In capitalism, the body's capacity of labor-power must be maximized. This is why Marx writes that the "worker's [...] productive activity," his labor-power, "is his vitality itself."[5] To maximize this vitality, therefore, biopolitics must first of all know what labor-power is.

Marx defines labor-power as "the use-value which the worker has to offer to the capitalist, [and] which," crucially, "is not materialized in a product, does not exist apart from him at all, thus exists not really, but only in potentiality."[6] In Paolo Virno's poignant paraphrase, labor-power designates not "labor services actually executed," but "the generic ability to work."[7] As such, "[l]abor-power incarnates (literally) a fundamental category of philosophical thought: specifically, the potential," that is, "that which is *not* current, that which is *not* present" (82). Nevertheless, potentiality "becomes, with capitalism, an exceptionally important commodity," so that "instead of remaining an abstract concept, [it] takes on a pragmatic, empirical, socioeconomic dimension" (82). For capitalism, biopolitics "is merely an effect [...] or [...] one articulation of that primary fact—both historical and philosophical—which consists of the commerce of potential as potential" (83-84). As Virno argues, "where something which exists only as *possibility* is sold, this something is not separable from the *living person* of the seller"; the "living body of the worker," in contrast, "is the substratum of that labor-power which, in itself, has no independent existence" (82). The body and life understood as "pure and simple *bios*, acquires a specific importance in as much as it is the tabernacle [...] of mere potential" (82), and it is "[f]or this reason, and this reason alone, [that] it is legitimate to talk about 'bio-politics'" in capitalism (83).

Foucault is therefore correct when, at the outset, he argues that capitalist biopolitics concerns, "the species body." However, what is at stake is not "the body imbued with the mechanics of life and serving as the basis of the biological processes: propagation, births and mortality, the level of health, life expectancy and longevity."[8] Rather, the body as the object of biopolitics is *potentiality*, insofar as the latter obtains within capitalism an *empirical, socioeconomic dimension* in the form of *labor-power.*

Possibly the first systematic account of the capitalist transubstantiation of the body is offered by Jean-Paul Sartre in *Being and Nothingness*, a work whose impact remains to this date invaluable: [T]he body [...] is [...] the point of view [*le point de vue*] on which I can no longer take a point of view. This is why at the top of that hill which I call a "good viewpoint," I take a point of view at the very instant when I look at [*regard*] the valley, and this *point of view* on *the point of view* is my body.[9] This is why "I can not take a point of view on my body without a reference to infinity" (433-434). Crucially, this infinity is introduced not because of what Sartre calls the "infinite possibilities of orienting the world," the infinite gazes from which the world could be perceived, but because of the self-referentiality between the gaze [*regard*] which is my body and the world in which my body is (419). It is the infinity that emerges by dint of the fact that the body as "a point of view supposes a double relation: a relation with the things *on which the body is* a point of view and a relation with the observer *for whom the body is* a point of view" (433). In other words, the body involves infinity because "my being-in-the-world, by the sole fact that it *realizes* a world, causes itself to be indicated to itself as a being-in-the-midst-of-the-world by the world which it realizes" (419). In realizing the world that realizes my body, my body—as a being-in-the-midst-of-the-world—is both the cause and the effect of the world; the body is an effect that is itself the cause of its own cause. As such, the body, which is nothing other than the gaze, is self-referential. The infinity in question is the temporality of this self-referentiality of the body.

Turning now to the earliest representation of the secular capitalist transmutation of philosophical thought, we can understand that the body or the gaze, which is sheer potentiality—the power of actualizing itself—is what Baruch Spinoza calls "substance." In "Nature," Spinoza writes, "there is only one substance," which is "the cause of itself," so that substance is "God, *or* Nature," as "*the immanent, not the transitive, cause of all things*," that is, as precisely the effect that is the cause of its own cause.[10] Accordingly, we can give to the temporality of the self-referentiality of the body its proper name: not "infinity" but "eternity," since the "eternal nature" of substance, which is "necessary and not [...] contingent," exists "under [the] species of eternity [*sub specie aeternitatis*]."[11] The necessarily self-referential potentiality, or power of self-actualization, that we call the body or the gaze, exists under the species of eternity. Inversely put, this is the secular transmutation of eternity, which since the inception of capital and secular thought designates the temporality of self-referentiality.

There is a kind of knowledge in which human thought can "perceive things under a certain species of eternity" and "conceive[...] the Body's essence under a species of eternity."[12] Human beings, however, would be incapable of functioning without their ability to operate outside the sphere of both eternity and self-referentiality in that quite more familiar territory where everything appears as a multitude of distinct objects in time. As Spinoza writes, in their everyday mode, human beings employ, depending on the clarity of their distinctions, two other kinds of knowledge, "imagination" and "reason."[13]

Lacan tells us, additionally, that "in order to constitute itself" as a consciousness that operates on the basis of imagination and reason, "the subject [...] has separated itself off" from the "gaze"—i.e., from the self-referentiality of the body that pertains to eternity.[14] Inevitably, this separation entails a "lack" which, albeit constitutive (without it the subject could not constitute itself as a conscious being), does not prevent the subject from seeking ways to fill it. Just as, although it "is no longer anything for" the infant that can feed itself without breastfeeding, the "object of weaning may come to function [...] as privation," the act of weaning from eternity may likewise generate its own search for surrogates.[15] The separation of the subject from the self-referential gaze leaves behind it a yearning for eternity.[16]It is precisely on this level that biopolitics intervenes. To say that *bios* is the potentiality of the body or the gaze is tantamount to saying that *the object of biopolitics is the subject's relation to eternity.*

To be sure, a veritable restitution of this primal gaze would result in the radical de-constitution of the subject; therefore, the biopolitical machinery resolutely shuns eternity and aims instead at proxies that provide only a controlled and safe illusion of eternity. But in order to unravel its mechanisms, we must delve into the capitalist transmutations of time. We must first examine what modes of temporality organize imagination and reason in secular capitalist modernity, and then how these can possibly succeed in providing substitute illusions that fulfill our yearning for eternity.[17]

CAPITAL TIMES

In the *Grundrisse*, Marx distinguishes "production time" from "circulation time." Production time is a finite diachrony, the linear time from the beginning to the end of the production of a specific product. In this realm of production, products exist in their material specificity and cannot be arbitrarily substituted by any other use-value—the means and material of an automobile factory can produce only cars. Labor itself enters production time as a specific use-value, that is, as a unique, specialized, non-exchangeable activity, which is bound to specific materials and takes place within a finite span of time. The moment the product—and with it, the labor, in the form of "objectified" or "*congealed labour-time*" within the product—enters circulation it becomes an exchange-value, that is, something that can be exchanged for anything else, regardless of its specific inherent physical qualities which, as a matter of fact, no longer exist.[18] For at the moment the commodity abandons the realm of production and enters circulation, it dies, as it were, as a physical object of utility and is resurrected as an immaterial, and hence immortal, value within circulation time. "*Circulation time* is [...] the time it takes [capital] to perform its motion as capital," that is, as exchange-value or abstract symbol with no inherent material qualities.[19] As Marx stresses, "[n]ot an atom of matter enters into the objectivity of commodities as values; in this [they are] the direct opposite of the coarsely sensuous objectivity of commodities as physical objects."[20] Matter exists only in production time, which is the exclusive realm in which commodities and laborers are subject to physical decay and mortality. Thus, while production time is marked by "*continuity*," circulation time "is the *interruption* of continuity contained in the character of capital as circulating," and whose tendency is "*circulation without circulation time*," that is, simultaneity or synchronicity, a mode of time in which the instant and infinity coincide.[21] Ultimately, it is only catachrestically that circulation can be said to involve "time," for it is a flat slice of space in which infinity springs out of the instant *in the same instance* that sucks it back into it, without any passage of time.

Here we see the capitalist transfiguration of two cardinal categories throughout history, time and infinity. On the one hand, there is the minor transformation in which the repetition of circular time no longer corresponds to the recurrence of seasons, but rather is expressed as the recurrence of finite spans of production, both of which can repeat themselves infinitely. This means, as it has at least since Aristotle, that only the species (be it the bovine or the laborers') continues to exist infinitely, whereas each particular specimen of the species (each ox or laborer) has a finite life. On the other hand, however, infinity now makes a second reappearance, not in the heavens but in the mundane realm of the market, as the temporality of exchange-values. This means that not only the species but the specimen itself is immortal—as long as it hovers in that vacuum of circulation time, in which both the instant and matter are turned into their opposites, infinity and immaterial abstraction, as in a Moebius band. Living as a value in the flat slice of circulation overcompensates for the loss of a threatening eternity by offering the much more tempting shelter of immortality.

There is only one last temporal transfiguration that is required in order for the immortality of circulation to be experienced by beings who, notwithstanding their permeative identification with the synchronic collapse of instant and infinity—facilitated equally by value and the signifier—nevertheless do experience themselves as living in linear time.

Here biopolitics faces the same puzzle that Marx encountered when, having distinguished between production and circulation time, he also had to note that "if the striving of capital in one direction is *circulation without circulation time*, it strives in the other direction to give *circulation time value*, the value of *production time*."[22] The tension that troubles Marx is that the accumulation of surplus-value cannot occur either in the finite diachrony of production time or in the synchronic infinity of circulation, nor even in the combination of the two taken together. For, in experience, it takes a *passage of time* for the total sum of value available in a given flat slice of synchronic circulation to increase. Similarly, the subject cannot have access to the illusion of immortality by simply bringing together its mortal existence as use-value and its immortality as exchange-value. Both surplus-value and the illusion of immortality require that a sort of valve, as it were, open up which would release infinity and let it flow out of the realm of circulation into linear time, allowing that which takes place in linear time to endure infinitely. Such an infinite duration would have to be distinguished from the diachronic temporality of production and physical bodies that, capitalism or no, always have an expiration date. Rather, infinite duration is the linear yet perforated time of the perpetual succession of synchronic discs of circulation required for surplus-value to accrue and, since this is its nature, to continue to do so. It is precisely this valve that surplus-value forces open, thereby, as Éric Alliez puts it, "opening up the duration of the durable" to infinity.[23] Thus we arrive at the last transformation of time brought about by the advent of capital—through which the primordial nature of the durable to remain, however long-lasting and resilient it may be, always confined within its durance—was transmogrified into the limitless duration of the undead. In its ever-ascending or descending (for economic crises are necessary too) spiral, the time of infinite duration unfolds by leaps, perpetually taking us from one synchronic disc of circulation to the next, *ad infinitum*.

This infinite duration is the temporality of repetition with ever more "same difference," the straight-line spiral that is the monstrous twin of that "straight-line labyrinth," of which Gilles Deleuze, following Borges, speaks.[24] The latter is time at the end of "the story of time," a time that, having "broken the circle" of both "the well centred natural or physical" seasons and of the recurrence of the synchronic discs, has "unrolled [...] itself and assumed the ultimate shape of the labyrinth," to become the time of the "eternal return" that, ever since Freud, we know as the "death instinct"—the "repetition by excess which leaves intact nothing" of the given conditions and "causes only" the "new, complete novelty," the "yet-to-come to return."[25] The infinite duration of surplus-value is as much the zombie-like masquerade of the death drive as the illusory disguise of eternity.

As we have seen, it was through exchange-value that capital landed infinity on earth in the form of circulation time. And, simultaneously, through surplus-value, capital released infinity to flow out of circulation, into the realm of duration, thereby inevitably splitting linear time into two lines: the finite and the infinite. The first is our familiar realm of diachrony which, as we have seen, is inhabited with physical mortal bodies. The second, by contrast, being a duration infested by infinity, is populated by infinitely durable bodies—undead ethereal bodies, which, not unlike surplus-value, consist of not an atom of matter, yet, not unlike matter, exist in linear time, but also in infinity.

The biopolitical cultivation of the illusion of immortality therefore involves the constitution of gazes and labor-power in ways that foster the subject's identification with infinitely durable value, that is, with something that both emerges through synchrony and endures in linear time infinitely.

SURPLUS-ENJOYMENT

Herein lies the importance of surplus-enjoyment, the most conspicuously evident object of biopolitics. For, like surplus-value, in the image of which Lacan notoriously fashioned it, surplus-enjoyment presupposes both the synchrony of exchange-value and the metastasis of infinity onto linear time.

Although Aristotle was not able to grasp all the intricacies of value, and synchrony eluded him entirely, he nevertheless discerned fully the effects of the colonization of linear time by infinity on human enjoyment. He was led to such oracular insights by observing nothing more than the limited practice in his time of *chrematistics* (χρηματιστικη), that is, trade for the purpose of "money-making" or acquiring profit or interest (*tokos*, which Marx adopts in his analysis of capitalism in its literal translation as "offspring"). Unlike *ekonomia* (οικονομια) or "household-management," which is a natural practice "carried on far enough to satisfy the needs of the parties," *chrematistics* is not part of "nature" because it is concerned with "how the greatest profits might be made out of the exchanges."[26] And one of the reasons why it is not part of nature is the fact that, unlike "household-management…[that] does have a limit," in *chrematistics*, "there is no limit to the end" money-making "has in view," so that it opens up the sequence of individual exchanges (miniature circulation discs) unto infinity.[27]

This, in turn, has immediate repercussions on people's enjoyment: "desire for life being unlimited" under any circumstances, *ekonomia* or *chrematistics*, people seek to satisfy life in the former case by satisfying the needs of life, whereas in the latter case, "they desire also an unlimited amount of what enables it [life] to go on." For, Aristotle continues, "where enjoyment consists in excess, men look for that skill which produces the excess that is enjoyed."[29] The unlimited practice of *chrematistics* eliminates the possibility of enjoyment by rendering it also unlimited: an enjoyment not in any thing but in excess, a surplus-enjoyment. Conversely, Lacan argues, if "on a certain day" there were no other form of enjoyment available but surplus-enjoyment, then it would become "calculable, [it] could be counted, [and] totalized," and that would be the day "where what is called accumulation of capital begins."[29] It would also be the day on which "the impotence of conjoining surplus-enjoyment [*plus-de-jouir*] with the master's truth"—part of which, notoriously, is to have conquered death—"is all of a sudden emptied," so that just like "[s]urplus-value adjoins itself to [*s'adjoint au*] capital," surplus-enjoyment adjoins itself to the master's immortality: "not a problem, they are homogenous, we are in the field of values."[30]

It is, therefore, with good reason that surplus-enjoyment is increasingly shifting toward the center of psychoanalytically informed analyses of capitalism. Grasping its biopolitical function as a mediator of immortality is however indispensable for the analysis of capitalism to advance. As Yannis Stavrakakis, among others, has emphatically argued, it is time to shift the emphasis in the analysis of the mechanisms of capitalism from the latter's production of so-called "false needs" and desires to the "administration" of desires and enjoyment.[31] Working in this direction, Todd McGowan has accurately observed that, in consumer society, "[t]he moment of acquiring the object represents the end, not the beginning, of our enjoyment."[32] For, as Ceren Özselçuk and Yahya Madra poignantly comment, "consumption as a means of enjoyment is bound to fail," but "this dissatisfaction is not a reason to abandon shopping."[33] Their explanation for this apparent paradox is that, "As long as the subjects of capitalism continue to believe that an ultimate enjoyment is possible, capitalism will continue to feed off of the very disappointment that the act of consumption produces[,] and shopping will go on ceaselessly."[34] Yet, McGowan's own thesis seems to imply that shopping can go on ceaselessly only as long as subjects do *not* believe that an ultimate enjoyment is possible. Shopping continues not because an ultimate enjoyment is possible but because it *must* continue for enjoyment, and life, to be limitless. As surplus-enjoyment enables infinity to conquer life, shopping, albeit central, is just one among the many biopolitical mechanisms—in this case, a frustration-machine—through which the illusion of immortality can be sustained.

Recapitulating, whether we say that *the object of biopolitics is bios, the body, the gaze, or surplus-enjoyment,* the important point is that what is meant is not "the administration of bodies and the calculated management of life," but *the administration and management of the subject's relation to mortality and immortality*, as a compensation for the loss of eternity.[35]

INFORMATIZED CAPITALISM AND BIORACISM

To avoid the impression that biopolitics is all about frustration, I would like to conclude by drawing our attention to another mechanism of the biopolitical administration of im/mortality that seems to me to obtain exponential centrality in late global capitalism. Just over a decade ago, Michael Hardt and Antonio Negri argued that in today's informatized capitalism (which is dominated by "the computerization of production" and its "immaterial labor") "the heterogeneity of concrete labor [say, tailoring versus weaving; Marx's favorite examples] has tended to be reduced [...]. [Both labors] involve exactly the same concrete practices—that is, manipulation of symbols and information [...]. Through the computerization of production, then, labor tends toward the position of abstract labor."[36] Evidently, based on the above line of thought, one could object to Hardt and Negri's argument that labor-power, whether it uses weaving machines, needles, book printers or computers, is sheer "potentiality" and, in this sense, "abstract," and that it has been so not since the shift to informatized capitalism but since the inception of capitalism. Yet, there is a grain of truth in Hardt and

Negri's observation, namely, there has indeed been a shift through the computerization of production; not, however, a shift from material to "immaterial" or from actual to potential labor. This shift, rather, is one in which the first shift introduced by capitalism, which transplanted the abstract concept of potentiality into the empirical socioeconomic field, now *metastasizes beyond labor itself to infest both the raw material of the means of production and the objects produced*, all of which are now forms of language or affects.[37] While in the past, the material and the products of the means of production were indeed material and, as such, subject to the linear time of physical decay—production time—now they are colonized by abstract symbols, "language and communication," and hence are imbued by their temporality: synchrony or circulation time.[38] To make this historical shift clear I turn to Marx's "general formula for capital," according to which "the circulation M—C—M′ [money—commodity—money] presents itself in abridged form, in its final result and without any intermediary stage [...] as M—M′, i.e., money which is worth more money."[39] The shift in question, then, means that if in the past "C"—the material object of production time—were eliminated from the formula only insofar as it was repressed or fetishistically disavowed, now it is actually eliminated.

Or is there anything in our informatized capitalism that still sustains production time? Hardt and Negri distinguish "three types" of informatized labor: (1) "industrial production," which too "has been informationalized"; (2) the "labor of analytical and symbolic tasks"; and (3) the "production and manipulation of affect."[40] The final two dominate the mode of production in advanced capitalist countries, while the first, "industrial production[,] has declined in the dominant countries [and] has been effectively exported to subordinate countries, from the Unites States and Japan, for example, to Mexico and Malaysia." This difference, Hardt and Negri continue, "should not lead us back to an understanding of the contemporary global economic situation in terms of linear stages of development," which would assume, for instance, that "an auto factory built by Ford in Brazil in the 1990s might be comparable to a Ford factory in Detroit in the 1930s." For, unlike the latter, the factory in Brazil today is "based on the most advanced and most productive computer and informational technologies available."[41] However true this may be, the geopolitical difference between our two contemporaneous worlds remains incommensurable, and this not only because undoubtedly there is much more shopping going on in the "dominant countries." Industrial production continues, however informationalized its methods may be, to produce *material* products, unlike analytical, symbolic, or affect production. And this means that in the "subordinate countries," the materiality of the products provides their inhabitants with access to production time and, hence, mortality. By contrast, in the advanced capitalist countries, in which the dominant mode of production involves not only abstract labor and raw materials, *but also abstract products*, circulation time becomes the dominant, increasingly exclusive, mode of temporality, reassuring ever-increasing parts of this population of their immortality. If this is so, what the dominant countries are exporting, along with industrial production, is mortality itself.

Needless to say, this geo-biopolitical map of the world can appear only to a gaze that has been biopolitically administered in order to see circulation time as the incubator of immortality—something which, as this line of argument indicates, is possible only in the "dominant countries." It is the map as drawn in and by the imaginary of these "countries," perpetuating in its own specific mode of late, informatized, capitalism the old and sharp discrepancy between the maps of the "dominant" and those of the "subordinate." And though maps are imaginary on both sides of the divide, the divide itself is real—which is why it cannot really be described but only circumscribed by often extremely reductionist and even caricature-like terms, such as "dominant" and "subordinate," and, for that matter, "immortal" and "mortal." But this increase in reduction and incongruous hyperbole is only the index of the intensification of the divide, and that culmination of conflict that we call war has always been carried out in the name of burlesque superlatives.

In one of their characteristically optimistic moments, Hardt and Negri conclude that because of its "cooperative interactivity through linguistic, communicational, and affective networks [...] immaterial labor [...] seems to provide the potential for a kind of spontaneous and elementary communism."[42] I wish they were right...but this will not be my conclusion. Mine will pass through a critical observation made by Foucault in 1976, namely, that: "racism [...] is in fact inscribed in the workings of all [...] modern States" (i.e., all biopolitical states). Foucault also added that the racism in question is "not a truly ethnic racism, but racism of the evolutionist kind, biological racism." He still had in mind the protection of biological life, "the idea that the essential function of society or the State, or whatever it is that must replace the State, is to take control of life, to explore and reduce biological accidents and possibilities."[43] I think we are way beyond that point. As I have argued, the level on which biopolitics operates is not biology but the body as potentiality and self-referentiality. This means that, whatever other tasks it may perform in the process—possibly including many that sustain biological life, at least of some people—its agenda is not to administer biological life and mortality, but rather an imaginary division between mortality and immortality. Accordingly, the racism in question is certainly not "truly ethnic" but also not "biological"; it is properly biopolitical—a bioracism in which the *ad hoc* biorace of the immortals launches war against mortality. For some years now it is being called the "war against terrorism"; soon it may bear a new name. Whatever its label, in a bioracial conflict the ever-reconstitutable assemblage of bio-immortals will continue to assault, with escalating arbitrariness and impunity, members of the ever-shifting group of bio-mortals. For the latter, whoever they happen to be, will increasingly be considered, as has been the case with all racism, not as humans. Perhaps they will not even be considered animals, as less and less rights apply to them, human or otherwise.

Notes

1. The quotations in this paragraph are from the editors' call for papers that was sent to the contributors of the 2011 issue of *Umbr(a).*
2. Giorgio Agamben, *Homo Sacer: Sovereign Power and Bare Life*, trans. Daniel Heller-Roazen (Stanford: Stanford University Press, 1998), 35.
3. Aristotle, *The Politics*, trans. T. A. Sinclair, revised by Trevor J. Saunders (London: Penguin Books, 1992), 82; 1257a5.
4. Karl Marx, *Capital: A Critique of Political Economy, Vol. 1.*, trans. Ben Fowkes (London: Penguin Books, 1990), 151; citing throughout Aristotle's *Nicomachean Ethics*, Bk. V, Ch. 5. Subsequent references will appear parenthetically within the text.
5. Jacques Lacan, *Book II: The Ego in Freud's Theory and in the Technique of Psychoanalysis, 1954–1955*, ed. Jacques-Alain Miller, trans. Sylvana Tomaselli (New York: W. W. Norton, 1991), 75.
6. Marx, *Grundrisse: Foundations of the Critique of Political Economy (Rough Draft)*, trans. Martin Nicolaus (London: Penguin Books & *New Left Review*, 1993), 267.
7. Ibid.
8. Paolo Virno, *A Grammar of the Multitude: For an Analysis of Contemporary Forms of Life*, trans. Isabella Bertoletti, James Cascaito, & Andrea Casson (New York: Semiotext(e), 2004), 82. Subsequent references will appear parenthetically within the text.
9. Michel Foucault. *The History of Sexuality. Volume 1: An Introduction*, trans. Robert Hurley (New York: Vintage Books, 1990), 139.
10. Jean-Paul Sartre, *Being and Nothingness: A Phenomenological Essay on Ontology*, trans. Hazel E. Barnes (New York: Washington Square Press, Pocket Books, 1956), 433; *L'être et le néant: Essai d'ontologie phénoménologique* (Paris: Gallimard, 1943), 369. Subsequent references will appear parenthetically within the text.
11. Baruch Spinoza, *The Collected Works of Spinoza*, ed. and trans. Edwin Curley (Princeton: Princeton University Press, 1985), 420, 412, 544, and 428; *Ethics*, part I, prop. 14, cor. 1 and prop. 7, dem., part. IV, preface, and part I, prop. 18.
12. Ibid., 481; part II, prop. 44, cor. 2, dem.
13. Ibid., 481 and 609; part II, prop. 44, cor. 2, and part V, prop. 29. It is, however, as Spinoza maintains, "[f]rom this kind of knowledge," under the species of eternity, that "there arises the greatest satisfaction of Mind there can be […] Joy […]." (Ibid., 611; part. V, prop. 32, dem). As I argue elsewhere, it is this modality of "knowledge" that defines human beings in their ethical dimension. See Kordela, "Spinoza: A Thought beyond Dualisms, Creationist and Evolutionist Alike," in *Spinoza Now*, ed. Dimitris Vardoulakis (Minneapolis: University of Minnesota Press, 2011), 494-537.

14. Ibid., 478; part II, prop. 40, schol. 2.
15. Lacan, *The Seminar of Jacques Lacan, Book XI: The Four Fundamental Concepts of Psychoanalysis*, ed. Jacques-Alain Miller, trans. Alan Sheridan (New York: W. W. Norton & Company, 1981), 103.
16. Ibid., 104.
17. As is entailed in my connection to Spinoza's Joy, derived from knowledge under the species of eternity, and (Lacanian) ethics, it is this yearning that instigates humans to act ethically.
18. In other words, and to conclude my brief subtextual references to the relevance of eternity to ethics, biopolitics is a mechanism of power that also usurps the ethical dimension in exchange for a surrogate of eternity.
19. Marx, *Capital*, 130.
20. Marx, *Grundrisse*, 659-660.
21. Marx, *Capital*, 138.
22. Marx, *Grundrisse*, 663 & 659.
23. Ibid., 659.
24. Éric Alliez. *Capital Times: Tales from the Conquest of Time*, foreword by Gilles Deleuze, trans. Georges Van Den Abbeele (Minneapolis: University of Minnesota Press, 1996), 7.
25. Gilles Deleuze. *Difference and Repetition*, trans. Paul Patton (New York: Columbia University Press, 1994), 111.
26. Ibid., 90-91, 111, & 115.
27. Aristotle. *The Politics*, 82-3; 1256b40.
28. Ibid., 84; 1257b25.
29. Ibid., 85; 1257b40.
30. Lacan, *The Seminar of Jacques Lacan, Book XVII: The Other Side of Psychoanalysis*, ed. Jacques-Alain Miller, trans. Russell Grigg (New York: W. W. Norton & Company, 2007), 177..
31. Ibid., 177-178, translation modified; Lacan, *Le Séminaire. Livre XVII: L'envers de la psychanalyse, 1969-1970*, ed. Jacques-Alain Miller (Paris: Seuil, 1991), 207.
32. Yannis Stavrakakis, "Re-activating the democratic revolution: The politics of transformation beyond reoccupation and conformism," *Parallax* 9:2 (2003): 56-71.
33. Todd McGowan, "Enjoying what we don't have: Psychoanalysis and the Logic of Accumulation," Paper presented at the conference Rethinking Marxism, Marxism and the World Stage, University of Massachusetts, Amherst, November, 2003.
34. Ceren Özselçuk and Yahya M. Madra, "Economy, Surplus, Politics: Some Questions on Slavoj Žižek's Political Economy Critique of Capitalism," in

Did Somebody Say Ideology? On Slavoj Žižek and Consequences, ed. Fabio Vighi & Heiko Feldner (Newcastle: Cambridge Scholarly Publishing, 2007) 82.

35. Ibid., 82.

36. Foucault, *The History of Sexuality, Volume 1: An Introduction*, 140.

37. Michael Hardt and Antonio Negri, *Empire* (Cambridge: Harvard University Press, 2000), 292.

38. Ibid., 293.

39. Ibid., 404.

40. Marx, *Capital*, 257.

41. Hardt and Negri, *Empire*, 293.

42. Ibid., 287.

43. Ibid., 294.

44. Foucault, "*Society Must Be Defended": Lectures at the Collège de France, 1975-76*, trans. David Macey (New York: Picador, 2003), 260-262.

Notes on Contributors

Joan Copjec is SUNY and UB Distinguished Professor at the University at Buffalo (SUNY), where she is also Director of the Center for the Study of Psychoanalysis and Culture. Author of *Read My Desire; Imagine There's No Woman*; and the forthcoming *Cloud: Between Paris and Tehran*, she was also an editor of *October* and of the Verso book series S.

Tim Dean is Professor of English and Comparative Literature at the University at Buffalo (SUNY). The author of *Beyond Sexuality* (2000); *Unlimited Intimacy: Reflections on the Subculture of Barebacking* (2009); and *What Is Psychoanalytic Thinking?* (forthcoming); he is a coeditor of *Homosexuality and Psychoanalysis* (2001); *A Time for the Humanities* (2008); and *Porn Archives* (forthcoming from Duke University Press).

Mladen Dolar is Professor of Social Philosophy at the University of Ljubljana and author of *The Bone in the Spirit: A Lacanian Reading of Hegel's Phenomenology of Spirit*, published in German, English and Slovene; *A Voice and Nothing More* (2006); and, with Slavoj Žižek, *Opera's Second Death* (2002).

Sam Gillespie was an American philosopher and activist. He was a founding member of the *Umbr(a)* collective. His *The Mathematics of Novelty: Badiou's Minimalist Metaphysics* was published by re.press in 2008.

Russell Grigg teaches philosophy and psychoanalytic studies at the Geelong campus of Deakin University. He is also a practicing psychoanalyst in Melbourne, Australia. He has been closely involved in the translation of Lacan into English, having translated Lacan's seminars *The Psychoses* and *The Other Side of Psychoanalysis* and having collaborated on the first complete translation of Lacan's *Ecrits*.

Dominiek Hoens teaches philosophy and psychology of art at Artevelde University College (Ghent) and Erasmus University College (Brussels). Publications include edited collections on catastrophe, Christianity, and Alain Badiou, and contributions to journals and books on Lacanian psychoanalysis and its adjacent domains. His recent work addresses Lacan's reading of Pascal's wager and is included a special issue on "The Object of Psychoanalysis" in *Continental Philosophy Review,* 46 (2013).

Sigi Jöttkandt teaches in the English Department at the University of New South Wales. She is author of *Acting Beautifully: Henry James and the Ethical Aesthetic* (2005); *First Love: A Phenomenology of the One* (2010); and coeditor (with Dominiek Hoens and Gert Buelens) of *The Catastrophic Imperative: Subjectivity, Time and Memory in Contemporary Thought* (2009). A former co-founding member of the *Umbr(a)* collective, she and Dominiek Hoens coedit the psychoanalytic journal of ideology critique, *S* (www.lineofbeauty.org).

A. Kiarina Kordela is Professor of German Studies and Director of the Critical Theory Program at Macalester College, and Honorary Adjunct Professor at the University of Western Sydney, Australia. She is the author of *$urplus: Spinoza, Lacan* (2007) and *Being, Time, Bios* (2013), and is co-editor, with Dimitris Vardoulakis, of *Freedom and Confinement in Modernity: Kafka's Cages* (2011). She has published on a wide range of topics in several collections and journals such as *Angelaki*, *Cultural Critique*, *Differences*, *Parallax*, *Political Theory*, *Radical Musicology*, *Rethinking Marxism*, and *Umbr(a)*, as well as in Japanese and Turkish translations. (URL: kiarinakordela.wordpress.com).

Juliet Flower MacCannell writes on literature, art, philosophy and psychoanalysis. She is author of over 90 articles and of several books including, *The Hysteric's Guide to the Future Female Subject* (2000); *The Regime of the Brother: After the Patriarchy* (1991); and *Figuring Lacan: Criticism & the Cultural Unconscious* (1986). She is Professor Emerita of Comparative Literature and English at UC Irvine, and current co-chair of the California Psychoanalytic Circle. She is co-editor, with Dean MacCannell of *(a): the journal of culture and the unconscious.* She also works as an artist, participating in some 19 group shows over the past 14 years.

Catherine Malabou is a Professor in the Philosophy Department at the Centre for Research in Modern European Philosophy (CRMEP) at Kingston University. She is author of numerous books on philosophy, psychoanalysis and neuroscience, including most recently *Sois mon corps* (with Judith Butler) (2010); *La Grande Exclusion, l'urgence sociale, thérapie et symptômes* (2009); *Changing Difference,* (2011); *The Ontology of the Accident: An Essay on Destructive Plasticity* (forthcoming); *The New Wounded: From Neurosis to Brain Damage* (2012); *Plasticity at the Dusk of Writing: Dialectic, Destruction, Deconstruction* (2004).

Steven Miller is Assistant Professor of English at the University at Buffalo (SUNY), where he teaches in the Center for the Study of Psychoanalysis and Culture. He is currently completing a book entitled *Hyperbolic Thinking: Essays* *on Literature, War, and the Death Drive.* He is the translator of Catherine Malabou's *The New Wounded: From Neurosis to Brain Damage* (2012) and, with Jason Smith, *Hegel: The Restlessness of the Negative* by Jean-Luc Nancy (2002).

Petar Ramadanovic teaches at the University of New Hampshire. He is the author of *Forgetting/Futures: On Meaning, Trauma and Identity* (2001) and a coeditor of *Topologies of Trauma: Essays on the Limit of Knowledge and Memory* (2002). His current project focuses on revisionist readings of poststructuralism.

Jelica Šumič is a researcher at the Institute of Philosophy of the Scientific Research Center of the Slovenian Academy of Sciences and Arts, and she also teaches at the University of Nova Gorica. She has written extensively on the relations between legal systems, ethics and politics. Her books (in Slovene) include *The Real in Performative,* co-authored with Rado Riha (1988); *Law and Judgement* (1993); *Authority and Argumentation* (1995); *Totemic Masks of Democracy* (1996); *Singularity in Psychoanalysis, Singularity of Psychoanalysis,* co-authored with Michel Deguy (1998); and *The Mutation of Ethics* (2002).

Charles Shepherdson is the author of *Vital Signs: Nature, Culture, Psychoanalysis* (2000); *Lacan and the Limits of Language* (2008); *The Epoch of the Body* (forthcoming),;and *The Ethics of Female Love*; a collection of essays translated into Serbo-Croatian for a special issue of the journal *Zenske Studije* (Women's Studies). His work has been translated into French, Portuguese, Korean, Chinese, and Serbo-Croatian. He is currently Director of the interdisciplinary Liberal Studies MA Program at SUNY Albany.

Colette Soler is a psychoanalyst practicing in Paris, who completed her early training in philosophy at the École Normale Supérieure. She was a member of the Ecole Freudienne de Paris, and has been a member of the the Ecole de Psychanalyse des Forums du Champ Lacanien since 1999. Her most recent books are *Lacan: The Unconscious Reinvented* (2013) and *What Lacan Said About Women* (2006).

Slavoj Žižek, Hegelian philosopher, Lacanian psychoanalyst, Communist social theorist. Researcher at the International Center for Humanities, Birkbeck School of Law, University of London. His latest publication is *Less Than Nothing. Hegel And The Shadow Of Dialectical Materialism* (2012).

Alenka Zupančič is a research advisor at the Institute of Philosophy of the Slovenian Academy of Sciences and Arts and Professor at the European Graduate School. She has written extensively on psychoanalysis and philosophy. She is the author of numerous articles and several books, including *Ethics of the Real: Kant and Lacan* (2000); *The Shortest Shadow: Nietzsche's Philosophy of the Two* (2003); *The Odd One In: on Comedy* (2008); *Why Psychoanalysis: Three Interventions* (forthcoming).

www.ingramcontent.com/pod-product-compliance
Lightning Source LLC
LaVergne TN
LVHW100256210926
848480LV00003B/935

* 9 7 8 0 9 8 7 2 6 8 2 4 2 *